The Badax Tigers

The Badax Tigers

*FROM SHILOH TO THE SURRENDER WITH THE 18TH
WISCONSIN VOLUNTEERS*

EDITED BY
THOMAS P. NANZIG

ROWMAN & LITTLEFIELD PUBLISHERS, INC.
Lanham • Boulder • New York • Toronto • Plymouth, UK

ROWMAN & LITTLEFIELD PUBLISHERS, INC.

Published in the United States of America
by Rowman & Littlefield Publishers, Inc.
A wholly owned subsidiary of The Rowman & Littlefield Publishing Group, Inc.
4501 Forbes Boulevard, Suite 200, Lanham, Maryland 20706
www.rowmanlittlefield.com

Estover Road
Plymouth PL6 7PY
United Kingdom

British Library Cataloguing in Publication Information Available

The hardback edition of this book was previously cataloged by the Library of Congress as
follows:

The Badax Tigers : from Shiloh to the surrender with the 18th Wisconsin Volunteers/
edited by Thomas P. Nanzig.
    p.cm.
    Includes bibliographical references and index.
    1. United States. Army. Wisconsin Infantry Regiment, 18th (1861–1865) 2. Davis,
Thomas Jefferson, b. 1832—Correspondence. 3. Soldiers—Wisconsin—
Correspondence. 4. United States—History—Civil War, 1861–1865—Personal
narratives. 5. Wisconsin—History—Civil War, 1861–1865—Personal narratives. 6.
United States—History—Civil War, 1861–1865—Regimental histories. 7.
Wisconsin—History—Civil War, 1861–1865—Regimental histories. I. Nanzig,
Thomas P.

E537.5 18th .B33 2002
973.7'475—dc21   2001041939

ISBN-10 : 0-7425-2084-6 (cloth : alk. paper)
ISBN-13 : 978-0-7425-2084-4 (cloth : alk. paper)
ISBN-10 : 0-7425-6019-8 (pbk : alk. paper)
ISBN-13 : 978-0-7425-6019-2

Printed in the United States of America

♾™ The paper used in this publication meets the minimum requirements of American
National Standard for Information Sciences—Permanence of Paper for Printed Library
Materials, ANSI/NISO Z39.48-1992.

To Rose and Reinard,
for sharing with me a love of history
and for allowing me the opportunity to share with you what I learned.

A WAR SONG FOR THE BADAX TIGERS

Oh, Tigers ! Arouse you—
Up, up from your lair,
With claws well distended,
and bristling your hair,
With red mouths wide open,
And tongues hot with wrath—
Go forth to the battle,
Go tread the war-path.

The battle is thundering
By river and hill—
But the foe, in dismay,
Will cower and be still,
When the roar of the Tigers
Is heard from the North,
And the soldiers of Freedom
March mightily forth.

The doom of the South
May be read in the night,
As your eyes in their wrath
Burn with glory and light;
And your growls–like an earthquake,
Or the roars of the sea–
Shall strike traitors dumb
And set captives free!

The Stars and The Stripes
Shall beam on your way,
As you go in your might
To seize on your prey;

And the Eagle shall scream
From the war clouds so dun,
When the smoke of the battle
Shall veil the bright sun !

Then Tigers ! arouse you,—
Up, up ! from your lair;
Go forth in your valor—
Bid Treason despair;
Then return from the field,
With wreaths on each head
Or sleep, like true soldiers,
On war's gory bed !
[NW Times, Jan. 1, 1862, p. 2]

Contents

Preface

I met T. J. Davis for the first time in an East Lansing, Michigan, basement in January 1973. An American Studies class at Michigan State University taught by Victor M. Howard had as its focus aspects of American culture during the Civil War period. As such, Howard required each student in the class to read, transcribe, and analyze a soldier's diary, journal, or letters. The documents assigned to us were part of the collection in the Michigan State University Archives, at that time located in the lower level of the University Library.

Howard's assignment of the somewhat larger Thomas Jefferson Davis collection required two students to work as a team because of the amount of work to be completed during our brief ten-week academic term. I was fortunate to have registered for Howard's class with a good friend and residence hall neighbor, David H. Arnold, who agreed to work on the Davis letters with me.

Dave volunteered to transcribe the several hundred pages of the Davis letters on his typewriter and I agreed to conduct the footnote and essay research. Nonetheless, at the end of the term we were only able to show a completed 476-page transcript. I had neither finished annotating the letters nor had we completed the obligatory essay. With Howard's encouragement and approval, our one-term project grew into a second term of independent study during which time we were able to complete our assignment to Howard's and our mutual satisfaction.

In the earliest stages of our study of the letters, Dave and I were graciously received and supported in our efforts by Mrs. Ellen A. Amman of Haslett, Michigan, a granddaughter of T. J. Davis and the donor of the Davis letters to the Michigan State University Archives. Mrs. Amman was kind enough to share her genealogy files with us and to secure from another family member a copy of the early-war photograph of Davis in his frock coat and Hardee hat.

Upon completion of the American Studies project in June 1973 until January 1996, the Davis transcript that Dave Arnold had typed and the research that I had completed lay in a box among my growing library of Civil War books. T. J. Davis was never entirely forgotten but visions of transferring nearly five hundred pages of typed transcripts once again, this time onto a word processor, all but extinguished my hopes of seeing the letters in print. Casual conversations over tea with Fred Moncrieff, a work colleague, writer, and raconteur, convinced me that I should somehow resurrect the project. At the suggestion of our good friends, Deb Masten and John Mansfield, and with constant encouragement and able assistance from my wife, Barbara, the typed transcripts of the Davis letters were transferred using scanning technology. The result was an almost perfect translation of the 1973 transcript into a computer-readable format.

My efforts to edit and annotate the Davis letters were nearly completed in October 1996, when an opportunity to attend an archival conference in Madison, Wisconsin, changed and expanded the scope of this effort. I used the Madison conference as an opportunity to visit Viroqua, Wisconsin, to see where T. J. Davis had joined the "Badax Tigers." Through the hospitality and intercession of June Zalewski, a member of the Vernon County Historical Society, I spent two productive days in the research room of the Vernon County Museum in Viroqua. It was during this visit that I "discovered" the published letters of Ransom J. Chase and other articles from the Civil War-era Viroqua newspapers and realized the possibilities of combining them with the Davis letters.

In addition to the people already mentioned, my thanks also go to John Kaminski of Madison House Publishers, Inc., who recognized the value of this "common soldier" study and encouraged refinements that have resulted in a more complete presentation of the documentary material and Rowman & Littlefield editorial staff members Martin Hayward, Mary Carpenter, Terry Fischer, and Lynn Gemmell; Mrs. Marjorie Bruce, Knoxville, Iowa; Larry and Sylvia Amman, Hanahan, South Carolina; Mrs. Betty Hall Payne, Anaheim, California, for their assistance in obtaining additional Davis family information and photographs; Fred Honhart and the staff of the Michigan State University Archives, East Lansing, Michigan; the staff of the National Archives and Record Administration, Washington, D.C.; the State Historical Society of Wisconsin, Madison, Wisconsin; Michael Winey, U.S. Army Military History Institute, Carlisle, Pennsylvania; Craig Wright, Minnesota Historical Society, St. Paul, Minnesota; Sioux City, Iowa, Public Library; Seattle, Washington, Public Library; Oshkosh, Wisconsin, Public Library; Jillah Biza (librarian) and Lance Burghardt (photographer), St. Joseph Mercy Hospital, Ann Arbor, Michigan; Dennis Ringle, Newport , Michigan, for his sagacity and caution regarding overzealous editing; Max and Brit Nanzig, Eden Prairie, Minnesota, and Rob Nanzig and Kim Mercatante,

Grand Haven, Michigan, for valuable photographic and bibliographic assistance; Pam Newhouse, Ann Arbor, Michigan, and Darrell Smoker, Strasburg, Pennsylvania, for their timely archival aid; Lisa Roberson, Shiloh National Military Park, Tennessee; Terrence J. Winschel, Vicksburg National Military Park, Mississippi; Lynn Wolfe, Wisconsin Veterans' Museum, Madison, Wisconsin; and Lynn Dolezel, Postmaster, Viroqua, Wisconsin.

EDITORIAL NOTES

All letters, newspaper articles, and soldier correspondence published from newspapers have been included in their entirety.

Minor corrections have been made in capitalizations and paragraph lengths. Capitalizations appear to have been irregularly determined in many of the Davis letters as well as in newspaper stories of the day. Lengthy paragraphs have been edited by creating multiple paragraphs wherever a distinct division of thoughts or concepts occur.

The spelling of Badax varies from source to source and is as often seen as Bad Ax, Bad Axe, and less frequently as Badaxe. The editor has chosen to use the variant, Badax, used in the two Viroqua newspapers of the 1860s.

TIGERS COURAGE

Much in sorrow, oft in woe
Badax Tigers onwerd go;
Fight the fight, and, worn with strife,
Steeps with blood oppressions life.

Onwerd, Tigers, onwerd go;
Join the war, and face the foe;
Faint not; much doth yet remain,
Dreary is the long campaign.

Shrink not, Tigers; Will ye yield?
Will ye quit the battlefield?
Fight till all the conflicts o'er,
Nor your foes shall rally more.

But when loud the trumpit blown,
Speaks old Jeffe overthrown,
Layne your Captain shall bestow
Crowns to grace the Tigers brow
One of the Tigers, D.K.
[NW Times, Jan. 1, 1862, p. 2]

Introduction

The "Badax Tigers" were as common a company in as common a regiment as may be found in the annals of the Civil War. They marched, camped, and fought their way through nearly four years of service with their fair share of battle honors and few blemishes to mar their record. They rallied at Shiloh, stood firm at Corinth, laid siege to Vicksburg, rescued Chattanooga, and saved Allatoona. They did what was expected of them and, on occasion, a little bit more. They supported Lincoln's reelection, voted for the prosecution of the war to the end, and they reenlisted enough men to "veteranize." However, as a result of their reenlistment and subsequent furlough, the "Tigers" missed participating in the storied "March to the Sea."

In short, the "Tigers" represented the backbone of the Federal volunteer army from 1861 to 1865. Neither heroes nor cowards, they did the best they could as volunteer soldiers, they helped to save the Union, then they dissolved back into their communities to resume private lives.

On 10 January 1862, more than one hundred "Badax Tigers" departed from Viroqua, Wisconsin, to be mustered into the service of the United States Army. The boys of Company C, 18th Wisconsin Volunteer Infantry, were destined for military service in the western theater of war that ranged from Tennessee and Mississippi to Georgia and the Carolinas.

The "Tigers" were not unlike thousands of local units raised to form regiments throughout the Old Northwest during the Civil War. They were a rural company; farmers, mostly, and lumbermen, merchants, teachers, and students. They gathered in Viroqua, the seat of Badax County, in the autumn of 1861 when it had become evident from the course of the war that the preservation of the Union was in jeopardy. They had little notion of what military service would demand of them but they were willing, in some cases anxious, to test themselves in the great War of the Rebellion. In the words of one volunteer, "There is a great desire to see the elephant, and if we cannot see the animal itself, to see some of its tracks."

1

What the "Badax Tigers" found was that many of their number would see little, if any, combat. They fell early and often to the well-documented diseases that plagued Civil War armies throughout the conflict. Dysentery, typhoid fever, influenza, smallpox and a dozen other maladies seldom seen in 20th-century America killed men who had led healthy, hearty lives until exposed to the unsanitary camps and harsh conditions of the Civil War. Those who survived disease were often so incapicitated as to be of no use to the country for further military service. They were mustered out and sent home. Still others were broken by months spent in primitive prison conditions after being captured at the Battle of Shiloh.

Those "Tigers" who were fit enough to march and fight soon learned that a Civil War army did far more marching than fighting. Whether they were tramping from Pittsburg Landing to Corinth, Holly Springs to Oxford, or Huntsville to Chattanooga, the boys of the 18th Wisconsin wore out their share of army brogans chasing Confederates and guarding supply lines. Shots fired in anger were far less frequent than shots fired at cattle and hogs who strayed too near hungry soldiers out on the picket line.

But for the Wisconsin boys who did see combat, they learned all too quickly that Mars, the god of war, has a strange way of choosing times and places for his battles. The "Tigers" and their 18th Wisconsin comrades at Pittsburgh Landing awoke on the morning of 6 April 1862, to find the battle of Shiloh a disaster in the making. Dozens were killed or wounded in the first minutes of fighting and hundreds were captured in the shallow, sunken lane known a the "Hornet's Nest." Those who survived the day unscathed physically had to deal with the ignominy of defeat and flight from their own camp and first battlefield. Later fights proved that the "Tigers" were made of sterner stuff than they felt they had showed at Shiloh but the chances of battle carried risks and several "Tigers" paid the ultimate price.

When the original "Tigers" returned to Viroqua at the close of the war, they numbered only fourteen men. Of the ninety recruits who had been mustered into service in January 1862, fully 86 percent had died of disease in camp or prison, fallen dead or wounded in battle, retired for reasons of disability, transferred to other units, or deserted. Simply stated, Company C was worn to the nub. When the boys returned to the streets of Viroqua in the early summer of 1865, there is no evidence of any crowds or parades as there had been on their departure. A six-line notice in a newspaper served as the benediction from their community.

This documentary history traces the "Badax Tigers" through the Civil War by using three types of primary sources: soldiers' letters to their families, newspaper articles, and soldiers' letters written and intended for publication in local newspapers.

The central focus of the work is the collection of 158 letters written by a confirmed private in Company C, Thomas Jefferson Davis. His letters were never intended for any kind of publication. In fact, in an early communication to his young wife, Lucinda, Davis advised her, "Don't make things too public that I write about the boys." Davis knew that his frank correspondence with his wife might, at some time, contain embarassing or compromising information about his comrades and fellow citizens. For this reason alone, Davis' letters form a solid core of common soldier documentation around which to build this company history. T. J. Davis was not writing to impress the home folks, to boost Northern morale, or to uphold a political agenda. He was sharing with his wife what he saw and heard and felt as he participated in the greatest single event of his life.

Thomas Jefferson Davis was born in Bethel, Clermont County, Ohio, on 21 July 1832, the fifth of eleven children of John Fleming and Nancy (Van Osdol) Davis. The Davis family moved west in 1836 where they settled a homestead in the Pike County, Illinois, farmland between the Mississippi and Illinois Rivers. The family stayed in Pike County for several years before moving across the Mississippi River to Madison County, Missouri.

After a short stay in Missouri, they moved back to Illinois, this time to Greene County. Although there is no family history to indicate the type of schooling Davis received in his youth, his spelling, vocabulary, penmanship, and expressions about learning indicate an early and continued regard for education.

Davis married Esther Delilah Ingersoll in Warren County, Illinois, in April 1854. The newlyweds bought forty acres of Illinois farmland and built a cabin in which to start a family. Two children were born to T. J. and Delilah; daughter, Malisa, died three months after her March 1855 birth, and son Charles M. (Charlie) was born in June 1856. Delilah contracted typhoid fever and died in March, 1857.

Leaving Charlie with relatives in Warren County, Davis moved to Springville, Badax County, Wisconsin, in 1858. There he met Lucinda Mary Spaulding but Davis stayed only a short time before heading west. From the frontier had come reports of gold strikes in Colorado that started a rush for the Pike's Peak country. Davis left Wisconsin for Colorado but traveled only as far as St. Joseph, Missouri, where he stayed for a year before returning to Illinois. Selling his forty acres and cabin in March 1860, T. J. Davis moved back to Springville, Wisconsin, where he married Lucinda Spaulding on 6 October 1861.

Davis enlisted as a private in Company C, "Badax Tigers," 18th Wisconsin Volunteer Infantry on 20 November 1861. He enjoyed good health through nearly four years of military service, seldom reporting for sick call, and participating in the battles of Shiloh, Iuka, Corinth, Jackson, Champion's Hill, and the sieges of Corinth and Vicksburg.

In November 1863, Davis volunteered to serve in the Pioneer Corps, 15th Army Corps, Army of the Tennessee. With the pioneers, he worked on military construction projects such as fortifications and bridges and was exempted from the daily picket and fatigue duties required of infantry regiments.

Davis reenlisted as a Veteran Volunteer on 1 January 1864 and remained with the Pioneer Corps until granted a furlough in November, 1864, with other Veteran Volunteers of the 18th Wisconsin Infantry. He returned with his unit to service at New Bern, North Carolina, on 10 February 1865. In April he once again joined the Pioneer Corps and served in that capacity until the surrender of Confederate forces at Durham, North Carolina, on 26 April 1865. With the 18th Wisconsin, Davis participated in the Grand Review at Washington, D.C., on 24 May 1865. After the Grand Review the 18th Wisconsin was sent by rail and steamboat to Kentucky to await discharge.

In all, Davis wrote 152 letters to his wife, Lucinda, and six to his sister and brother-in-law, Elizabeth and George W. Ditto. Most were written with pen and ink while a few were penciled when the regiment was on the march. Although Davis used patriotic stationary in some of his early correspondence and complimentary Sanitary Commission stationary in 1865, most of his letters were composed on plain paper that he purchased as he could find it. With but few exceptions, the letters survived the passage of time in excellent condition.

That these letters document a typical "western" volunteer of the period only scratches the surface. T. J. Davis wrote remarkably literate and revealing letters though there is little evidence of his having received much formal education. His use of capitalizations was eccentric yet his spelling, grammar, and syntax were consistent and are easily read today. In one letter of advice to his wife, Davis shares what was, perhaps, a reflection of his own frontier education experience:

> A few minutes time well-employed at home in study is worth a whole day idled away at school. . . . You can improve yourself much by selecting well-written pieces from books and writing them off. At the same time pay particular attention to the meaning of each word and how it is spelled. By frequently writing this way you will get it impressed on your memory. . . . I am ignorant and unlearned myself and I know enough of ignorance to understand the value of education and sound judgement.

In addition to his views on education, Davis' letters reveal much about this Wisconsin yeoman farmer. He was patriotic but not of the flag-waving type. He claimed, "I never pretended to be a very brave man. I actuated to go to war by a principal for my country's good."

Based on his letters and army documents he suffered only one injury during the war. Davis bruised his hip in a fall from atop a shed and he appears to have been a soldier who fulfilled his military obligations at every turn. Whether in training, on picket, on the march, or in line of battle, T. J. Davis was always present and discharged his duties to the best of his ability. He practiced good hygiene, bathed as often as conditions permitted, realized the shortcomings of the army diet of coffee, hardtack, and salted meat, drank little whiskey, and practiced an exercise regime when not actively campaigning. During the spring of 1862, when thousands of Federal soldiers fell ill from camp diseases, Davis was one of only thirteen men in his company to remain consistently on duty. Compared to the average Billy Yank, T. J. Davis was the picture of good health.

To say that he was as healthy in his assessment of the war effort, however, would be untrue. Davis' morale rose and fell with the Federal armies' successes and failures. At particularly frustrating moments, Davis was capable of cursing the upper circle of Federal war authorities, the army paymaster, officers as a class, all politicians from North and South, and Federal generals who let victory slip through their fingers. He was particularly hard on the "Southern chivalry" who he felt had caused the war and equally damning of the politicians who had done nothing to prevent the coming of war.

Davis was a man of morals and principles. On at least several occasions, he offered his views on the infidelity of husbands and wives separated by the war. Yet, he did not appear to be a religious man. Through the entire collection of Davis' correspondence, he never referred to "God," he only once calls on "Providence" to see him through the war safely, and in his only mention of chaplains or church services, Davis offered this weak, almost humorous, comment:

> I went to church last night and heard the chaplain of the 63rd Illinois make a sermon. I got tired, however, and went to camp before the sermon was concluded. I hope that those who offered prayers did it with the right spirit and pure motives.

Not uncommon to the time, T. J. Davis viewed African-Americans with a mixture of pity and ill will. He did not approve of slavery yet had no desire to see freed slaves being sent north. It is interesting to note, however, the particular lack of reaction in a Davis missive of April 1863 regarding the recruitment of United States Colored Troops in Louisiana and Mississippi. Had Davis felt strongly enough about the topic, it may be assumed that he would have expressed his disapproval of the employment of African-Americans as volunteer soldiers.

Davis was a pragmatic man who, in his own words, intended to "look more after No. One as that is every man's business." Throughout his military service, he frequently found ways to improve his situation. As circumstances arose, Davis sold newspapers, pens, homemade beer, and loaned money at interest to his more profligate comrades. His willingness to become first a cook and bugler, then a laborer in the Pioneer Corps reflected Davis' military opportunisim. The following passage typifies his maturing view of his army experience:

> I would much rather be here than in the regiment for I have more natural exercise in the daytime and less exposure at night. . . . It is quite fashionable for men to do the best they can for themselves in the army and I mean to do so myself the rest of my time. . . .

Davis' sixteen months of correspondence as a member of General William T. Sherman's Pioneer Corps constitutes an interest area unto itself. Long ignored as an important component of Sherman's success in the Atlanta campaign, the March to the Sea, and the Carolinas campaign, one author has noted "these were the pioneers who played a significant if unheralded part in winning Atlanta for William T. Sherman and the Union."[1] Comparable to combat engineers of World War II, the pioneers bridged rivers, constructed fortifications, and cleared roads for Sherman's armies. Davis' letters offer a glimpse into the life of the pioneers who could be expected to both build and protect, fight and destroy.

The correspondence of T. J. Davis is more, however, than just campground-and-battlefield reflections. Davis' letters reveal the Civil War-era family man through a variety of sometimes touching, sometimes frank paragraphs to his wife. Education, finances, neighbors, and family are put firmly into their respective places in T. J.'s half of what must have been an interesting exchange of correspondence between the older, worldly-wise husband and the young wife left behind in frontier Wisconsin. The letters reveal the more personal thoughts of a husband who is far from home. Davis' reaction to learning of Lucinda's pregnancy, his advice to her about her health and welfare, the subsequent birth of his daughter, Silva May, all offer us brief but intimate glimpses of another portion of the fabric that made up the 19th-century family.

In Badax County, "The North Western Times" and the "Viroqua Expositor" were the newspapers of record during the Civil War. "The North Western Times" was founded in June 1856 and continued to serve the citizens of Viroqua until November 1955, when, as "The Vernon County Censor," it finally ceased publication. The editor of "The Times" during 1861–1865 period was Joseph A. Somerby.

The "Viroqua Expositor" was founded in August 1858 and published its last issue on 9 May 1863. Through the two years of the Civil War during which the "Expositor" published, George A. Wolfe edited that newspaper.

---

1. Shiman, Philip, "Sherman's Pioneers in the Campaign for Atlanta," *The Campaign for Atlanta & Sherman's March to the Sea, volume II*, Savas, T. P., and Woodbury, D. A. (eds.), 1994, p. 251.

Both newspapers were openly supportive of the war effort, the "Expositor" being an avowed Republican publication and the "The North Western Times" publisher taking an independent stand with Republican leanings as seen in this March 1863 column:

> In politics, the Times will be independently Republican, sustaining the Administration in its Emancipation policy; at the same time urging the necessity of a more energetic and fearless prosecution of the War calling for a more Napolean-like system that shall be rapid in execution, following the enemy to destroy them after they are defeated with the force that is ready to follow, asking the President to take the matter in his own hands and supercede all but go-ahead generals.

In total, the "Viroqua Expositor" published six articles about the "Tigers," two of which were letters from soldier-correspondent Ransom J. Chase. "The North Western Times" featured more extensive coverage of the "Tigers'" experiences and published fourteen letters from Chase between January 1862 and March 1863. An additional, unpublished letter from Chase to his sister is also included in this history. "The Times" also featured recruiting notices, patriotic poems, coverage of war rallies, and lists of recruits throughout the autumn months of 1861.

Chase's missives offered, in his own words,

> a series of jottings concerning the location, welfare, and adventures of the "Badax Tigers." Anything, however trivial, connected with them, must be of interest to the loved ones left behind, and hence, if matters of little moment fill largely this communication, the uninterested critic must remember that they are written more particularly for the personal friends and relatives of the company.

His letters are clearly written, richly detailed, and sufficiently sanitized so as not to embarrass or offend the families of those comrades whose behavior did not always meet homefront standards. Chase described the "Tigers'" departure from Viroqua, their journey to Sparta, Wisconsin, and thence to their camp of instruction in Milwaukee. He detailed the rations, equipment, and living arrangements provided for the men, and the minimal training they received due to the harsh weather conditions in Wisconsin during the winter of 1862. He shared the news of a raucous celebration when the citizens of Milwaukee learned of the General Ulysses S. Grant's capture of Fort Donelson as well as the rumors that spread through army camps of the period.

Ransom Jay Chase's roots were in the Sugar River Valley country of western New Hampshire. Born in the village of Unity on 23 November 1840, Ransom was one of several children of Jacob and Sarah (Marshall) Chase. In 1847 the Chase family moved fifty miles southeast to Nashua,

New Hampshire, where they remained for ten years and where young Ransom was sent to school at the Nashua Literary Institute. Although the Literary Institute was a respected academy of learning, Chase later credited most of his early education to private study at home. In 1857 the Chases moved again, this time making a thousand-mile trek to the Old Northwest to settle a farm in Sterling Township, Badax County, Wisconsin. Young Chase taught school during winters and worked on the family farm during the growing season. According to an 1891 biographical sketch, however, at the outbreak of the Civil War, Chase had evidently resigned his teaching position and was engaged in reading law in Viroqua, the seat of Badax County.

Ransom Chase enlisted as a private in the "Badax Tigers" on 18 December 1861. Promoted to corporal while at the Milwaukee camp of instruction in January, he moved south with his regiment in the spring of 1862. Within a week he witnessed and survived the near destruction of the 18th Wisconsin during the first day of the battle of Pittsburg Landing (Shiloh), Tennessee, 6 April 1862. Chase helped to reorganize the regiment after Shiloh, participated in the siege of Corinth, Mississippi, in May 1862, and was promoted to sergeant following that campaign. Notice of Chase's leadership qualities by his commanding officers led to the offer of a commission in a newly recruited Wisconsin regiment during the summer of 1862. Offered a similar promotion within the 18th Wisconsin, Chase opted to stay with his comrades and was commissioned a 2nd lieutenant on 18 August 1862.

Chase marched with the 18th Wisconsin to Iuka, Mississippi, on 19 September 1862, where the "Tigers" skirmished with Confederate rear guard units who were retreating from a pitched battle fought earlier in the day. Two weeks later at Corinth, Mississippi, he was temporarily detached from Company C and placed in command of Company I, 18th Wisconsin. Chase's men were engaged in a fighting retreat back to the defenses of Corinth on 3 October 1862, losing two killed and five wounded of the twenty-one men present for duty. In the pursuit of retreating Confederate forces after the Federal victory at Corinth on 4 October 1862, Chase commanded his own Company C as well as Company I.

During this six-month period, Chase's letters documented the marches, bivouacs, battles, and campaigns from Shiloh in April 1862 to the defense of Corinth, Mississippi, in October 1862. His eyewitness descriptions of Shiloh were particularly moving as Chase's were among the first detailed accounts of the great western battle to reach his hometown newspapers.

As well, his description of the approach and investment of Corinth in May 1862 was nicely paced to allow the home folks to understand how deliberate were Major General Henry W. Halleck's tactics. Forward movement of the 18th Wisconsin was limited to an average of four miles with each advance. Entrenchments were dug in front of the Federal campsites every evening to prevent the kind of surprise attack they had suffered at Shiloh. Chase described several campsites and expressed the frustration that the common soldiers felt toward their own generals when it was discovered that the Confederate army had quietly slipped away from Corinth.

Summer maneuvers gave Chase opportunities to see southern farms and villages, and to meet southern civilians and slaves. Interestingly, as Chase and his Federal comrades moved into rural Mississippi and Tennessee, small numbers of Unionists came out of hiding and greeted their liberators with open arms and offers of food and forage. As for slaves, Chase related the case of one "contraband" who had allegedly been thrown off the plantation by his master. Chase's recreation of the slave's dialect in a speech to the 18th Wisconsin Infantry must have appeared both comic and exotic to the citizens of Viroqua.

Chase's last two campaign letters document the parts played by the "Badax Tigers" and the 18th Wisconsin Infantry in the battles at Iuka and Corinth, Mississippi. Although the 18th was not involved in the hardest fighting at either battle, Chase clearly documents the "small picture" view of the common soldier. The 18th Wisconsin was one of many units that were marched and counter-marched, placed in line of battle, ordered to fall back, then pushed forward again with little idea of the tactical situation into which they were being maneuvered. In all this marching, the "Tigers" narrowly missed an opportunity to capture part of Confederate General Sterling Price's force in a roundabout march at Iuka, then escaped capture by the same narrow margin two weeks later outside Corinth.

Ransom J. Chase's field correspondence ended when he fell ill in November 1862. He was sent to a field hospital in Corinth, incapacitated by fever and chronic diarrhea. His condition failed to improve and he was subsequently moved to a hospital at La Grange, Tennessee, then to Memphis, where he was issued a surgeon's certificate of disability.

He resigned his lieutenant's commission on 23 January 1863, sending his last letter to "The North Western Times" in March 1863 from his parents' residence in Sterling Township, Wisconsin, southwest of Viroqua. His closing correspondence detailed the status of the "Tigers" at the time of his departure from the south.

After recuperating at his parents' farm in Wisconsin, Ransom J. Chase resumed his study of law in Madison. He was admitted to the state bar in November 1863. On 3 September 1864, he reenlisted with a captain's commission in Company B, 42nd Wisconsin Volunteer Infantry, a company recruited primarily in Richland County. The regiment was sent to Cairo, Illinois, from which place Company B was sent to Springfield, Illinois, to serve as provost guard. Ransom Chase's primary duty through the spring of 1865 was to serve as judge advocate for courts martial.

By virtue of their position in Springfield, Chase and his men were drawn into President Abraham Lincoln's funeral activities. As officer of a provost guard detachment, Chase was charged with keeping the peace in Springfield from the arrival of the funeral train until the President's remains were interred at Oakwood Cemetery on 4 May 1865. With the war coming to a close and thousands of volunteer troops being mustered out of service, Chase spent his last weeks of army life on court-martial duty before he was discharged and returned to civilian life.

It should be noted that throughout the parallel correspondence conducted by Ransom J. Chase and Thomas J. Davis, there was not a single significant mention of the other man throughout their respective letters. Chase's roster report published in the "The North Western Times" is the single exception in that he included Davis' name among the active "Tigers." That the two men could have been members of the same small company and that they were probably in daily contact with one another for nearly a year and neither so much as acknowledged the other's existence in their letters is curious. It may be that they had so little in common that they seldom crossed paths in camp or battle. One can only imagine Davis as an "old shoe" who had no desire for promotion, wished only to serve and survive, and who confided only in his closest friends and messmates. Chase, on the other hand, appears to have been the quintessential "young man on the rise," supportive of his unit's interests, cooperative with regimental officers, willing to share his experiences with the homefolk in his news articles, and anxious to make something of himself while serving his country in the great adventure that was the War of the Rebellion.

CHAPTER ONE

They Had About
Become Bare-Assed Tigers

The 18th Wisconsin Volunteer Infantry Regiment was recruited and mustered into service as the fantasy of a three-month Civil War finally evaporated in the North. The defeats of Federal forces at Manassas and Ball's Bluff, Virginia, and at Wilson's Creek, Missouri, during the summer and autumn of 1861 convinced Federal authorities that additional time and troops were required to put down the rebellion in the South.

Recruiting activities throughout the state were initiated by eager community leaders who were often promised captaincies in the growing volunteer army if they could raise companies of eighty to one hundred men. Farmers, woodsmen, merchants, and rivermen flocked to the colors as the companies of Eighteenth began to take shape. Unlike urban regiments that were often recruited from one city or county, the citizen soldiers who filled the rosters the 18th Wisconsin came from counties across the state. They marched into recruiting stations from the pineries of the upper Wisconsin River in the north, the farm country on the Illinois border to the south, from villages along the shores of Lake Winnebago to the east, and along the Mississippi River region in the west.

They were generally fit men and capable of the physical exertions that were expected in the field. A camp correspondent boasted of the size and weight of the Eighteenth's recruits: "Capt. Compton's company from Grand [Wisconsin] Rapids average one hundred and sixty-six pounds to the man. There are but few small men in the 18th and most of them are used to hard fare and camp life, and are aching for a fight with the Secesh." The editor of Viroqua's "North Western Times" observed of the hometown "Tigers" that "several of the men weigh 180 to 200 lbs. averdapoise. Many of them are more than six feet high, and take them all together, they are a solid and determined sett."

In the Badax County seat of Viroqua, Newton M. Layne, a twenty-two-year-old lawyer, initiated his recruiting efforts early in November 1861, and within a month had met the required quota. Layne and his men voted to take as their nom de guerre, "The Badax Tigers."

In all, the ten companies that made up the 18th Wisconsin were:

Company and County	Nickname	Captain
A Fon du lac County	"Tacheydah Union Rifles"	James P. Millard
B Green County	"Eagle Light infantry"	Charles H. Jackson
C Badax (Vernon) County	"Badax Tigers"	Newton M. Layne
D Monroe County	"North Western Rangers"	George A. Fisk
E Marathon/Portage Counties	"Portage County Infantry"	William Bremmer
F Winnebago County	"Oshkosh Rangers"	Joseph W. Roberts
G Wood County	"Alban Pinery Rangers"	John H. Compton
H Green Lake/ Washara Counties	"Green Lake Rifles"	David H. Saxton
I Columbia County	"Lewis Rangers"	William A. Coleman
K counties from across the state	no company nickname	William J. Kershaw

The 18th Wisconsin's regimental officers and staff as appointed by Governor Louis P. Harvey were:

Colonel James S. Alban
Lieutenant Colonel Samuel W. Beall
Major Josiah W. Crain
Adjutant Gilbert L. Park
Quartermaster Jeremiah D. Rodgers
Surgeon George F. Huntington
Assistant Surgeons Erastus J. Buck, Larkin G. Mead
Chaplain Reverend James Delaney

The "Tigers" were directed to meet their recruit comrades in Milwaukee in January 1862. The first week in camp was set aside for physical examinations and the swearing into Federal service of the volunteers. Men who failed to meet fitness standards and those who decided against enlistment were sent home. Uniforms and accoutrements were distributed as they arrived in Milwaukee, although the unit's imported Belgian rifles were not available until the first of March. Frigid winter temperatures kept the men huddled in downtown buildings until new barracks were completed at Camp Trowbridge. Throughout the training period the cold, snow, and mud made battalion drill impossible. Officers did what they could to give the men a modicum of instruction. According to one camp visitor, "The quarters allotted to each company are sufficiently large to drill all the men in the manual of arms without their being exposed to the storms of the season."

Chaffing at their weather-related inactivity, a few of the "Tigers" turned to liquor as an outlet for boredom. However, the entire regiment had an opportunity to display patriotic emotion when news arrived in Milwaukee on Monday, 17 February, of General U.S. Grant's recent conquests of Forts Henry and Donelson. A spontaneous celebration and march throughout Milwaukee boosted the spirits of the untested recruits. Subsequent rumors of the regiment's assignment to the far southwestern territory of New Mexico proved wildly inaccurate but orders for the Eighteenth to embark for the seat of war finally arrived in mid-March.

Unique to this chapter are the number of newspaper articles that described the war-related activities of rural Wisconsin. The "North Western Times" and "Viroqua Expositor" followed the recruiting and war-related activities of the Badax County populace with sympathetic interest. Two poems dedicated to the hometown "Tigers," a humorous report of the company's first casualty in Viroqua, and the callous inquiry of a recruit's wife are particularly interesting items that were featured in the weeklies.

The soldier letters in this chapter follow the general pattern of early war correspondence. They describe the "Tigers'" journey to camp of instruction, enlistment into Federal service, uniforms and equipment, and, of course, food and quarters. Ransom Chase's letters, were intended for immediate publication in the Viroqua newspapers. They are filled with descriptive and patriotic passages and, if not entirely candid, furnish an entertaining record of "Tiger" activities. T. J. Davis' letters, though not as lengthy or informative as Chase's missives, show the confidential correspondence of the new recruit. Of particular interest, in addition to Davis' camp news, is his admonition to his young wife, Lucinda, to not "make things too public that I write about the boys."

Recruiting

Lieutenant Jerome S. Tinker has been recruiting here for about a week for the 12th Regiment. The Bad Ax and Richland Riflemen, to which company he belongs, are all well.

Captains Thomas Fretwell and Newton M. Layne and Lieutenant Ankeny are desirous of enlisting men for the present holy war for freedom. We hope all who can will go with them, go with some of the cavalry or infantry companies now enlisting in La Crosse or Sparta. We should like to see two or three companies more go from this county; but if you feel like serving your country in this war, go in some company soon. [NW Times, Nov. 13, 1861, p. 2]

[Untitled Item]

A most energetic movement is now on foot to raise a new company of volunteers. Men of indomitable perseverance are active at the work. A liberal fund has been already donated by the citizens to get music, etc. The members of the County Board now in session here have formed themselves into a committee to give assistance in their respective towns. Anyone who wishes to volunteer can go into quarters in this place immediately. [NW Times, Nov. 13, 1861, p. 3]

The New Volunteer Company

is progressing finely. They have already between thirty and forty men and will undoubtedly go into quarters next week in this village. Notwithstanding the large number of men in companies and parts of companies that have gone to the war from this county, this company will be filled in thirty days from its first start.

Now is the time to enlist. The Badax County Board, who have just adjourned, have passed an order to pay to all children of volunteers under twelve years of age one dollar per month. This added to the one hundred dollars bounty and thirteen dollars per month from the United States and five dollars a month from the State to the wife of each volunteer makes the pay of the Union soldier ample, whether he has a family or not. Come and join this new Badax County Company, now, that this war may be brought to a speedy and successful close.

The late successes of our arms at Hatteras, Bellmont, Pikeville, Port Royal, and Beaufort, S.C. should nerve every arm to strike home to the vitals of Secession.[1] [NW Times, Nov. 20, 1861, p. 3]

Commissioned

N.M. Layne, Esq., of Viroqua, has received a commission as Captain to raise a company of infantry and has already arrived at the number of 40, which looks very much like meeting with success. He spares no trouble or expense in getting his company full. He has already visited several parts of the county with martial music and banner and will as expeditiously as possible visit all other parts of the county in a similar manner. We sincerely hope that Mr. Layne will succeed in getting up a company that will not only represent Badax county but one that will reflect credit upon the inhabitants remaining here. We love to see our boys animated with the right spirit and energy; but we here enter our protest against them going out of our county and representing other counties as has been the case the number of nearly one hundred men. [Expositor, Nov. 23, 1861, p. 2]

---

1. The Federal victories included Major General B. F. Butler's invasion of the North Carolina coast in August 1861, Brigadier General U. S. Grant's drawn engagement at Belmont, Missouri, on 7 November 1861, a skirmish near Pikeville (Ivy Mountain), on 9 November 1861, the surrender of Port Royal, South Carolina, to Flag Officer S. F. DuPont on 7 November 1861, and the occupation of nearby Beaufort, South Carolina, two days later.

The Badax Tigers

This company has now 83 members. Several of the men weigh 180 to 200 lbs. averdapoise. Many of them are more than six feet high, and take them all together, they are a solid and determined sett. We hope that the patriotic citizens of Badax county will see to it that the company is made full to 101 men by next Monday when all who are not already boarding at the expense of the State in this place, will come in to quarters as they may be called on to leave for Madison any day after Monday next. Nine cheers for the Badax Tigers. [NW Times, Dec. 5, 1861, p. 3]

[Untitled Item]

The election of officers of the Badax Tigers took place at the Court House on Monday, which resulted as follows:—N. N. Payne, Captain; C. W. Pitcher, 1st Lietenant; John Goode, 2nd Lieutenant; Samuel Swan, Orderly Sergeant; Wm. N. Carter, 2nd Sergeant; R. S. McMichael, 3rd do.; John S. Dixon, 4th do.; A. A. Burnett, 5th do.; H. L. Baker, Tenor Drummer; Jos. Brightman, Base do.; John M. Stokes, Fifer. Henry C. Johnson, Clerk. [NW Times, Dec. 11, 1861, p. 3]

Muster Roll of the Badax Tigers

[Following a roster of citizens who had enrolled in the company was this statement]: About a dozen or more would be accepted if they should offer themselves. An opportunity like this, of enlisting in a home company which is accepted and almost full to the maximum, will not again be offered in this county and we advise those who desire to serve their country to stir their stumps and walk up to the captain's office and be sworn in. The company is composed of the muscle and sinew of the county and we doubt whether a hundred stouter and healthier men would be raised anywhere. [NW Times, Dec. 14, 1861, p. 2]

[Untitled Item]

Last Sunday evening as a squad of soldiers from Lynxville arrived at the North Star to go into quarters, they were cheered by their fellow soldiers, the horses became frightened, and a sudden dash threw the whole party violently to the ground by which Mr. Wm. W. Dikeman had his arm broken. Dr. Tinker was procured immediately and made the necessary reparation. Mr. Dikeman bore the painful operation with all the coolness of an old soldier! [NW Times, Dec. 14, 1861]

War Meeting

The Tigers held another war meeting at the Court House on Monday evening. We could not attend, but from those who did, we learn that everything went off cheeringly. Patriotic speeches were made by several gentlemen. Capt. Layne and Lieut. Pitcher, discoursed Dixie to a charm. The company will leave for Madison in a few days. We suggest that our Glee Club give the boys a parting token of friendship before their departure. Some of the boys have voices, in the music line, as clear and shrill as the clarion notes of the reveille bugle at early dawn, and that is saying some, we think. [NW Times, Dec. 18, 1861, p. 3]

The Badax Tigers

This company, of which we have spoken heretofore, will go into Camp Randall next week. The company is composed of the best metal and greatest physical ability of the population of the country. Among the number comprising this company, there are several men of wealth—some whose means are not on the unfavorable side of $10,000—men who leave prosperous avocations and lucrative stations to endure the hardships of a soldier's life.

We doubt very much if there has been called into service from this—and assuredly from no other state—a superior company than the Badax Tigers. And more than this—the little county of Badax, with a population of 11,000, after having sent about half a regiment of soldiers (and has credit for only about 200,) has, by the activity of Capt. N. M. Layne and Lieuts. Pitcher and Goode, succeeded in the shortest space of time imaginable in raising this company of soldiers, which is second to no one yet has gone from the Northwest. We will wager our interest in—this office, that there is not a county north,—and of course not south—of Mason and Sli—,Dixon's line, with a population no greater than Badax, that has succeeded in raising as good a company of soldiers, in as short a space of time, for the suppression of the rebellion, after having sent the number she has. Who will or dare accept the challenge.

The success thus attained is attributable, principally to the energy of the three commissioned officers, who patriotism, zeal and clear sense of duty prompted them to act. While we regret to part with such citizens, as compose this company, we are proud to be represented by what we will be known as the banner company of the Eighteenth. (*Expositor*, Dec. 21, 1861, p. 2)

The Tigers

Capt. Layne's Company to leave for Camp Holton[2] at Milwaukee today.

We must say a word or two in reference to this Company. From its first conception to its present number, Capt. N.M. Layne and his Lieutenants—Chas. W.

---

2. Camp Holten was one of Milwaukee's camps of instruction, two miles north of Milwaukee on the shore of Lake Michigan. The camp was named for Edward D. Holton, a well-known Milwaukee businessman and co-founder of the Republican Party in Wisconsin. The camp was occupied as a tent site in the winter of 1861–1862 by the 9th Wisconsin Infantry, a German unit, who called it Camp Siegel after the German-American leader, Franz Sigel. By February 1862, barracks were built for the 18th Wisconsin to occupy and the name changed again to Camp Trowbridge for Captain Joseph M. Trowbridge a Regular Army mustering officer. [National Cyclopedia of American Biography, vol. 2, New York, James T. White & Company, 1895, p. 238–239; Scott, Robert N. (ed.) The War of the Rebellion: A Compilation of the Official Records of the Union and Confederate Armies. Washington, D.C., General Printing Office, 1880–1902, hereinafter cited as OR, Series 2, volume, p.]

Pitcher and John Goode, have been untiring in their endeavors to raise a company of volunteers which the state might look upon with an honorable pride. In this they have been very successful. Time and money have been spent without stint and no such idea as fail has been for a moment entertained by them. T.C. Ankeny, Esq., who received a lieutenant's commission from Gov. Randall to organize this company, has also rendered valuable services in bringing about this result. He has not worked for temporary laudation nor for office; personal advancement has not been his aim; patriotism fills too large a place in his heart. He has joined the rank and file with a will that, if he has a promotion tendered him, it shall be for services rendered in camp or on the battle-field. This [is] a right spirit. Badax and Crawford Counties need not fear for the reputations of their sons.

A meeting was called at the Methodist church on Monday evening when it was expected that Rev. Mr. Nuzum would favor the Company with a farewell address but in this they were disappointed. Nevertheless, as it was understood that an Indian war spear was to be presented to the Tigers before their departure, the present opportunity was embraced for so doing.

The spear was given by Mr. H. Ferguson, of Victory, and the presentation was made by Mr. Wm. H. Purdy, who accompanied it with some interesting remarks. The spear was found on the battle-field at Badax after the Black Hawk war and has since been preserved by Mr. Ferguson. The blade of the weapon is of iron, some eight inches long, of a triangular shape and perforated with two holes at the heel to carry the scalps taken. It is a gift which the company will highly prize, either in camp or in battle.

After the presentation, Elder Hord offered some appropriate remarks giving the Company some useful advice. Capt. Layne, and others, entertained the meting a short time with interest.

The choir discoursed some fine music. The ladies and Mr. Connelly were in excellent tune. Mr. Connelly informed the meeting that if they did sing, they "would do it up brown." We were favorably inclined that way. [NW Times, Jan. 7, 1862, p. 2]

They Have Gone!

Yes, yesterday morning, with a cold bleak nor'easter facing the Badax Tigers, they mounted in vehicles and wended their way to Sparta, where, we presume they boarded the cars for Milwaukee this evening. One hundred and sixteen better looking, better behaved, stronger physical or more patriotic and enthusiastic soldiers has not left any county in the State of Wisconsin. [Expositor, Jan. 11, 1862, p. 2]

The Tigers

Last Friday morning the Company of Capt. Layne took its departure for Milwaukee. The morning was very severe but, notwithstanding that, the boys seemed anxious to test the breeze and face the storm.

Quite early in the morning some fifty women—wives, sweet-hearts, and children—thronged the North Star [Hotel] to bid a farewell to those they loved; and, with some of them, a farewell forever.

We were here and there among the assembled crowd and frequently witnessed scenes—scenes sad, but endearing—that portrayed the generous and noble feelings of mature manhood, in parting with the partners with whom they travelled through the sunshine and the shade of life's rough road. Witnessed the meeting and the parting of loving hearts throbbing with youthful vigor and ardent attachments; young men, impetuous in their desire to wipe out the accursed stain put upon our national banner by the hand of treason, and young female hearts swell with patriotic pride to see those whom they love so dearly, and so well, eager to

"Strike for their Alters and their Fires!
God! and their native land,"

Eager to share in a Patriot's fame, in life, or a Patriot's name in death. But at the last word—the last kiss welled up sacred tears as ever sprung from the breast of manhood. Many an eye, we noticed, was the harbinger of a tear.

When the cavalcade was under full march, it presented an imposing sight. Only one item occurred within our observation which marred the interest of the scene. A woman said she did not care much about her husband going, for she "know'd he'd be killed," but she was anxious to know about the pension she would receive in such an event.

On their journey, one of the Tigers was badly frozen in both feet before reaching Hazen's Stand. He was well taken care of by his comrades. The company arrived at Sparta at half past 2 o'clock and quartered at the Ida House. [NW Times, Jan. 15, 1862, p. 3]

Intelligence from the Boys
for the North Western Times

Milwaukee, Jan. 15
Mr. Editor,

In accordance with our arrangement, I herewith submit the first of a series of jottings concerning the location, welfare, and adventures of the "Badax Tigers." Anything, however trivia, connected with them, must be of interest to the loved ones left behind, and hence, if matters of little moment fill largely this communication, the uninterested critic must remember that they are written more particularly for the personal friends and relatives of the company.

The morning we left Viroqua was, as you know, intensely cold, in fact, presenting a contrast far from favorable with the morning preceding. Some of the boys, knowing that "discretion was the better part of valor," retired under cover of our quilts which the good people of Viroqua and vicinity had kindly loaned, while others, not being so well provided, were obliged to run a greater part of the distance to keep up the circulation of blood.

"It is a long lane that has nary a turn," and it is a long road that has no end. In short, we arrived at Sparta between three and four o'clock, and was escorted to our quarters— the large hall attached to the Ida House—by the North Western Rangers who had turned out to meet us. And here allow me to state that, notwithstanding the "rumors of war" which had been afloat in regard to the manner the Rangers would receive us, no reception could have been more cordial and earnest. Our boys had scarcely got warmed before the Rangers came over in large numbers and after some of their men had sung a number of songs, Private Noyes, of the Rangers, welcomed us in a patriotic speech and was responded to by Private Chase in behalf of the Tigers. "Hurrah for the Tigers!" and "Hurrah for the Rangers!" attested alike the soundness of our lungs and the general good feeling existing.

In the evening they furnished us with excellent music and more formally renewed their protestations of friendship through Lieut. Wilson, who delivered a good and patriotic speech. Capt. Layne appropriately responded. Singing and dancing ended the festivities of the evening and I think nothing can scarcely occur which will tend to mar our friendship thus strongly begun.

We expected to leave the next morning at 3 o'clock, and hence not much provision for sleeping had been made. Some lay down upon the benches and floor but the majority were too noisy to admit of sleep, and the sleepy ones soon gave it up as a bad job.

"Hurrah for the cars!" were given with a will as we marched down to the depot—a mile from town; but three groans were given for them with as much emphasis when we found that for some reason, the extra cars had not come and that we must march back to quarters. It afterward appeared that the engine had broken down, which rendered it impossible to come to time.

Saturday in town. "Mighty dull spot," said many; thus showing that a person may be lonesome, though surrounded by strangers. Some, however, amused themselves by reading newspapers, others by playing cards, and some few sought it by getting gloriously drunk. The second night was spent more comfortably, the noisy ones being rather sleepy, and all found better accommodations—the Rangers furnishing everything possible that could induce to comfort.

Sunday afternoon we were once more marched down to the depot and this time not in vain. We arrived at Milwaukee soon after daylight and were marched to our temporary quarters, about which I will write you in my next.

To illustrate the propensity that the boys have for fun and practical jokes, I have a mind to tell you of one which happened, notwithstanding the weather, on the way to Sparta. One of the Tigers jumped out of the team at Leon, six miles from Sparta, and hailing a man with a team, wished to know if he desired to sell his horses? Yes, the man would sell his horses, provided they could agree upon the price. After a little bantering, they were both well suited. The gentleman was [to] drive his team to Sparta the next morning and deliver them up for a price stated at which place he was to receive his money.

Morning came and so did the man, true to his agreement, out with a rather lengthened countenance. He had evidently got sick of his sale and though he said he would stand by the agreement to buy off, Tiger was not as hard as his name might indicate, and told him to treat the boys standing near to half-dollar's worth of apples and it would be all right. The man considered these remarkable easy terms and immediately complied with. Hurrah for the Tigers!—The boys are all well. Yours,—C.[3] [NW Times, Jan. 22, 1862, p. 2]

Milwaukee, Wisconsin, January 20th, 1862

Dear Wife,

After so long a time I sit down to write you a few lines to let you know that I am in tolerable good health. We arrived here one week ago this morning we had a verry cold trip being out all night Sunday night on a slow train and it was so cold that the cars could not be kept comfortable though I believe there was no person frozen. A few of the boys to[ok] cold and was sick a few days after we got here, though they are all straight on their pins again except, that is, one day old man Burnett was quite sick for two or three days from a hard cold. But he was kindly cared for and received medical attention in time so that he soon got able to leave his bed so that he is rating around with the rest of the boys.

Both of our lieutenants that we started with are now out of office. Charlie Pitcher resigned and John Goode could not pass muster. And tell Mrs. Burnett that I have the honor of introducing to her at a distance our second lieutenant, Mr A.A. Burnett, as the choice of the company by the influence of his particular friends. The decision was made last night, John Graham for first and A.A. Burnett for 2nd lieutenant and Col. Albin has sent to Madison today for their commissions.

We was sworn into the United States Service yesterday. The boys generally, I believe, are in very good spirits. All of the companies of the 18th Regiment is in the city except one. But we have not gone into camp yet as the barricks are not filed out for us yet. Our company is boarding at the Central Hotel and perhaps we will remain here for a week or ten days yet.

I got a letter from [brother] Jabe day before yesterday. He said they was all well and that he had got his pay and sent most all of it home.

I was out to Camp Washburn on Saturday 2 miles west of the city.[4] I was in Capt. Bishop's quarters and saw Bill Struthers & Hugh Thompson and

---

3. Ranson J. Chase usually signed his correspondence "C." though at least one letter that appears to have been written in his style is signed "Tiger."
4. Formerly the Milwaukee Fairgrounds, Camp Washburn was named for Colonel Cadwallader C. Washburn, a Wisconsin congressman who raised the 2nd Wisconsin Cavalry Regiment at the camp. [Wisconsin, Annual Report of the Adjutant General: 1861, Madison, Atwood & Rublee, State Printer, 1912, hereinafter cited as Wisconsin, p. 80]

several other boys that I was acquainted with that I did not know was in the company.

We have not got our uniforms yet. We are informed by our colonel that we will get them tomorrow. Then perhaps I will get my dogry type taken.[5] I believe I will not write any more at present so be a good girl at school and don't get licked. I will write more peticulars next time. It is getting so dark that I can't see the lines so good-bye.

Direct Thomas J Davis Milwaukee, Wisconsin
In care of Capt. Layne

Tuesday, January 21st/62

I inclose Jabe's letter in yours and also one to Mrs. Burnett from Allen

T. J Davis

Six of our company that was rejected starts for home this morning. There was 8 in our company that could not pass muster. I went to the office last night to mail this letter but I got there just as the office and I could get no stamps. I had 6 or 7 bushels of wheat I left in the mill and I told Lamech Graham to sell it and give the money to you. Write soon.

T. J Davis

Milwaukee, January 28th, 1862

Dear Wife,

I again seat myself to drop you another line. I have been looking for two or three days for a letter from you but have not read any yet. We are still boarding at the Central Hotel and I don't know how long we will remain here. Perhaps it will be 2 or 3 weeks before we get into camp. We are all tolerable well at this time. Some few of the boys have bad colds. We have had some quite cold weather since we have been here with about a foot of snow. Yesterday it stormed all day, both raining and sleeting and snowing and it is drizzling of rain today.

We received our clothes yesterday; all but our shirts. We will perhaps get them in a few days. Since the boys got their new clothes they don't hardly know each other. But some of the boys did not get their clothes any to soon for instead of Badax Tigers they had about become (Bare-assed) Tigers not having brought many clothes with them nor left many at home.

---

5. Daguerreotypes were photographs made on silver-coated, light-sensitive metal plates. Invented in 1839 by Louis Daguerre, a French photographer, they were also called tin-types.

The boys generally keep pretty steady for the reason that they have not mutch money to spree and carouse on. Walt Odell was first under guard the other morning for imbibing too much sod-corn whiskey on a company treat, having misrepresented things and doubled the dose two or three times. His punishment was not severe but enough to give him the hint in case of future offences. Ham Cummings got good gloriously and limber drunk last night for the first time since he left home. He will be pretty strictly watched. Don't make things too public that I write about the boys.

We have just one hundred and one men now in our company and considered the best company out of the nine that is here. Arch Morrison got released and went home several days ago. He was tickeled almost to death when he found that he could go home for a sicker child never recovered and I think it will be a long time before he will take another contract.

I think it is very probable that we will not get away from here until March or April. I will get quite tired of staying here so long but we must wait the motions of government. I think I will get a furlough and come home once before we leave here. Milwaukee is quite a large city, mutch larger than I expected to find with many large, well-built buildings some of which are six stories high.[6]

Write as soon as you get this and tell me how you are getting along and all the rest of the news. I believe I have nothing else to write this time so good-bye.

Thos. J. Davis

Milwaukee, Wisconsin January 30th/62

Dear Wife,

I wrote a letter to you 2 days ago but as some of the boys are going home today on a furlough I thought I would send along a few lines to let you know that we are all well. I could have got a chance to go home today but I thought that I would not be the first to get homesick. Burnett and myself will be apt to go home on a furlough in about 2 weeks if nothing happens more than I know of at present. Ben Greenman, Levi Allen, Henry Clery & Robert McMichael is all going on a furlough today.

Burnett received his commission last night of 2nd lieutenant of the Badax Tigers. You and Mrs. Burnett try and enjoy yourselves as well as you can and don't be uneasy about us nor get the blues yourselves.

---

6. According to the 1860 Federal census, Milwaukee had a population of 45,246. [Andriot, John L., Population Abstract of the United States, vol. 1, tables. McLean, Va., Andriot Associates, 1993]

The weather is quite cold today but it is clear and nice overhead. We have good sleighing here now and I saw a man improving it last night by riding in a small sleigh drawn by two large Newfoundland dogs.

I have not received any letter from you yet but I am looking everyday for one. I believe I have nothing more to write this morning so good-bye for this time.

T. J. Davis

From the Eighteenth Regiment
Written for the Times

Milwaukee, January 31st, 1862

Mr. Editor, I believe it was Webster who, upon his death, had awaking from a lethargic sleep said, "I still live." Your correspondent, resuming his pen, takes another opportunity of saying that the Tigers "still live," and just now, while he is writing, are quite busy with the frivolities of life—some talking, joking, laughing, and playing cards; others, like your humble servant, redeeming sundry promises to keep the folks posted at home. All good natured and apparently contented.

We have not yet been assigned permanent quarters but still occupy the rooms in which we were first placed. Not expecting to remain in them long, bunks have not been made for sleeping and we are obliged, therefore, to "pile in" on the floor. This is not so uncomfortable as one might think as we have straw to "harden the floor with," as some of the boys say.

The first night of our arrival, we were marching up [the] street to receive a blanket each as a loan, ours not having then arrived. They found them to be miserable things, torn and dirty, that the German Regiment had used. They did not do us much good, but we got along 'till last Monday, two weeks after arriving here— when we not only received another blanket of somewhat better material, but each the following articles of clothing, viz.: one great coat, one coat, one pair of pants, two pair of drawers, two pair of stockings, and one cap with oil-cloth cover. This sudden exodus of necessaries was, I need not say, hailed by the boys with pleasure. Such a trying on, inspection and putting off, to be again re-tried, you never did see. That coat was too large and this would be just right if it did not pinch under the arms. That pair of pants was too short for the large fellows and too large around for the short one. But at last all were fitted. Even the fat man of the company became proud and gave vent to his excessive delight at the new rig.

Though not at all of the best quality yet, taken as a whole, our outfit is of substantial character. The overcoats and caps, especially please the boys. The new blankets are heavy but of very inferior quality. We are to be furnished with another soon, I understand. The shirts have not yet arrived.

The Sunday after our arrival we were mustered into the United State[s] service. I regret to state that quite a number of those who were loud-mouthed in professions of patriotism in Badax, did not come up to the scratch. They took pains not to be present on the occasion. They had either obtained leave of absence at Viroqua promising to meet us here or had come on and obtained leave to be absent on "important business." The result was they did not wish to go as the company was full, or they had received some intelligence of a startling character which rendered it necessary to go home.

As you are doubtless aware, ere this, there has been a change of our commissioned officers. Lieut. Pitcher having resigned and Lieut. Goode not passing medical examination. The immediate cause of the resignation of Lieut. Pitcher was the circulation of a petition to that effect among the men; discovering which, he assured them that he would resign when he received his pay, and it was not further circulated. Upon reflection, it appears that he concluded to resign at once. His place is filled by John Graham, formerly of Lynxville. As a man, I doubt whether Lieut. Pitcher has an enemy in the company; but he was considered by the boys as a man possessing insufficient military tact and spirit, for the position that he occupied. Mr. A. A. Burnett, of Springville, was chosen Second Lieut. Mr. Calvin Morley was appointed Fifth Sergeant to supply vacancy caused by the promotion of Sergeant Burnett.

I will not attempt to disguise the fact that some regret is expressed by the married men of the company that their families are unable to receive the $5 per month from the State, as it becomes due, and that they did not receive their State pay at the time of mustering into the service of the United States, both of which they expected at the time of enlistment. The noble hearted fellows care nothing for themselves. They are willing to endure, uncomplainingly, personal inconveniences; but it touches them in a vulnerable point to know that loved ones at home are suffering—debarred from the necessaries of life on account of the non-arrival of expected remittances. Many have left families dependent on their daily labor, absolutely destitute—consoling themselves with the assurances that the State money and their pay would place them beyond the reach of want and the humiliation of asking charity. They do not blame the officers of the company for this, being convinced that they, too, were deceived.

They are sworn into the United States services, and cannot hasten to the relief of their families.

The question is, what is to be done?—It appears to your correspondent that there should be only one answer, viz: that the families of the men who have left their homes to battle for the protection of all, should be supplied with every possible comfort by the liberality of those who remain at home and receive the benefit of his toil. Sympathy and pity and the dictates of common humanity cannot require less than this.

Who of the loyal citizens of Badax County is not willing, yea, desirous, of doing this much? If there is one, let him express himself, that he may receive the contempt he so justly deserves. Let the finger of scorn be pointed at him as a traitor to the government.

Much can be done. Let our County Commissioners immediately make an appropriation to all the families whose head has thus enlisted, and issue the orders immediately without waiting to raise by tax, This plan, of course, would be open to the objection that there would be a shave upon the orders; but this would be trifling in comparison with the benefit conferred.

Some plan should be adopted. A petition directed to the County Commissioners and the County Poor Commissioners, setting forth the facts and praying for relief, signed by all the married men in the company, was sent a few days since. Perhaps the publication of it may be advisable. Every community should see it so that no evil comes to those left thus destitute.

I have written about this matter thus lengthily, knowing that of all subjects, it interests most, the soldier, and should interest most the friends at home. The boys are well, with the exception of colds. Yours, &c. C. [NW Times, Feb. 5, 1862, p. 2]

From the Eighteenth Regiment
written for the Times.

Camp Trowbridge, Milwaukee
February 18, 1862

Mr. Editor: In common with the rest of the soldiers I am so much excited at the glorious news from Donelson that it is with great difficulty and much self control that I gather sufficient ideas to form a decent correspondence.[7]

Hurrah for the brave soldiers who won the battle! Such news, coming at such a time, was indeed cheering. May it prove but one of a series of engagements and victories until the flag of our Union waves once more in peace over every state in our once happy Union. All honor to Illinois and her brave soldiers who have thus quickened the blood of the nation. The papers state that everywhere the people are wild with joy, which is manifested by processions, public dinners, the booming of cannon, and the paraphernalia attendant upon occasions of great public rejoicing.

Here in Milwaukee, there was considerable of everything that could demonstrate the joy of the people. Soon after dinner, Lieut. Col. Beall popped like a bomb into the encampment and gave, with considerable vehemence, the order: Form Battalion. Such a thing was never done before. Every thing was hurry skurry. Each officer ran one way and that was for his company. The men were formed in two ranks as fast as the speculation as to the meaning of the order would permit and the consequent confusion upon the circulation of the story that we were called upon to repulse the troops about to be landed from a British fleet, then about to effect an entrance into the harbor.

"We haven't any arms," said one. "They will be furnished us in the city," said another. "They won't land, but will shell the city from [the] lake," said another wise one. "How in the d—l did they get there?" said a fourth. "Yes, that's the question," was reiterated by a dozen voices. "It's all bosh." "Mighty good joke." "How mighty stupid we were," said all the duped ones.

---

7. Forts Henry and Donelson were captured by forces under Federal General Ulysses S. Grant on 6 February and 16 February 1862, respectively. [Long, E. B., The Civil War Day By Day, An Almanac, 1861–1865. Garden City, NY, Doubleday & Company, Inc., 1971, p. 167, 171–172]

But the reason at last leaked out and, of course, the news was received with delight. Fort Donelson was taken. We formed the battalion and did it quite creditable for the first time, marched down to the city and formed part of a procession composed of Colonel Washburne's Cavalry, the Eighteenth regiment, a small squad of the Nineteenth, and a large number of citizens. After marching through all the principle streets, we were addressed from the balcony of the Newhall House by Judge McArthur and Col. Sanders of the 19th, and remarched to camp. Thus ended with us the day.

You have doubtless noticed that I have referred to marching "down to the city," and, of course, must have inferred what is true, that we have gone into our permanent encampment. We came February 13th and gladly exchanged the uncomfortable quarters for the new ones at Camp Trowbridge, as the old encampment at Camp Sigel is now called. We like our food better than at the Central House and our bunks are arranged on a good plan and are very comfortable. Distant about three miles from the heart of the city, the attention of the boys is less diverted by the frivolities inseparably associated with such as place as Milwaukee, and all are pleased that they are now out of the way of temptation. There are at present only five companies in camp, quarters having not yet been prepared for the remaining companies.

Since my last, we have been supplied with those very necessary articles with which we were not supplied at the time of writing my last: six shirts, We are now fully clothed with the fatigue.

Since my last, five of our boys have been in the hospital, sick with the measles. They are now, however, all recovering; some of them have already rejoined us in camp. Our orderly, Mr. Swan, is at present an inmate of the hospital, but will, we all trust, be able to join us again in a few days. He is very popular with the men and makes a good orderly.

Capt. Layne is at present on a furlough, but is expected back in a few days. A great many of the boys have been back on leave, the greater part having, however, only twelve days furlough. This, deducting the time traveling, makes their time short, indeed.

There is nothing more of importance at present connected with the Tigers, only that it is reported that orders arrived yesterday for our regiment to repair within the next twenty days to St. Louis. There is some little doubt as to its truth, but it is, I think, true. Col. Sanders stated it as a fact in his speech yesterday. It is generally credited, the only fears expressed being that there may be some mistake about it and the 18th not included in the order. The boys are full of pluck and wish an opportunity to show the material they are made of before the war is finished.

It is reported by some of the boys recently returned from Badax that Caleb Ellis, Esq., offers 120 acres of good prairie land to the person from Badax county who kills Jeff Davis. I wish to say to him that the boys appreciate the patriotism that prompted the offer and, while kindly thanking him for its expression, would say that no reward of a pecuniary nature can increase their desire to do their whole duty. He may rest assured that the boys will endeavor to merit the approval of their friends at home. Enough for now. Yours truly, C. [NW Times, Feb. 26, 1862, p. 2]

[Untitled item]

Camp Trowbridge, Milwaukee,
February 23, 1862
In consideration of the death of Sergeant Samuel Swan, of the Badax Tigers, which took place on the evening of the 22nd inst., his fellow soldiers of the aforesaid Company assembled to bestow that mark of respect to his memory which was justly due a man who was so much respected by his comrades in arms.

The meeting was called to order by Sgt. Wm. N. Carter and Capt. N. N. Layne chosen chairman. After a brief recital by the chairman, of the many virtues of the deceased, and recalling to remembrance the many acts of kindness of which all could bear witness, a motion was made that a committee of three be appointed to give formal expression of grief of the company. The committee consisted of Capt. N. M. Layne, Corporals R. J. Chase and J. H. Brightman.

The committee submitted the following resolutions which were unanimously adopted:

Whereas Samuel Swan, our fellow soldier and the Orderly Sergeant of our Company, departed this life on the 22nd day of February, 1862, at Camp Trowbridge, near Milwaukee, Wisconsin, the members of the Badax Tigers do resolve as follows:

1st. That in the death of our fellow soldier Sergeant Swan, our country has lost a brave and valiant soldier, an ardent patriot, and a valuable citizen; our Company an efficient and faithful officer, and we, his fellow soldiers, and open-hearted and sympathizing friend.

2nd. That Sergeant Swan, in performing his duties as an officer in our company, and in his intercourse with us, had won the respect and love of his fellow officers and soldiers; that during the time he was with us, he did much to forward the discipline and good feeling of the company, by his patient and pleasant demeanor toward his men, and his faithfulness and promptness in rendering assistance to the officers, his experience as a soldier being invaluable service to all; that we extend to the wife and relatives of our departed friend, the condolence of soldiers and would remind that that it is "appointed unto man once to die" and that our beloved comrade and their dear relative having performed well his allotted task upon earth, departed this life while being engaged in the most honorable of all duties—defending the constitution of his country. May this prove a balm to wounded feelings and serve to reconcile them to the dispensation of Providence.

3rd. That a copy of the proceedings of this meeting may be sent to the widow of the deceased and also the publishers of the country papers of Badax county,

The meeting them adjourned sine die N. M. Layne, Chmn. Ransom J. Chase, Secy. [NW Times, March 5, 1862, p.2]

Headquarters Eighteenth Regiment, Wisconsin Volunteers
Camp Trowbridge, Milwaukee, March 5th, 1862

Dear Wife,

Today is Wednesday and I have been away from home nearly a week. I thought I would write you a few lines so that you would get them by Friday's mail. We got here last Saturday at noon all safe and sound and found the boys all well. We have have had quite a snow storm since we came back. It snowed all day on Sunday and the wind blew very hard Monday and Tuesday and snowed some at the same time. But today is quite mild and pleasant.

We have received our arms and are drilling with them both in company and battallion drill.[8] We have no orders to leave yet and don't know when we will. Bill Frazier visited our camp and staid all night with us. He is on his way to Ohio.

I received two letters from Illinois since I come back. I will send you one of them in this. No more. I must go out to drill.

T. J. Davis

[On the reverse side of this letter was a note from Allen A. Burnett to Burnett's wife.]

Milwaukee, March 5, 1862

Dear Wife, I had a safe journey although it was pretty cold. I found everything in order at Camp Trowbridge. Our company is Company C. So you can send for your state pay, two months only. You must look for a letter soon. Excuse these few lines for the present. Kiss the children for me. Good-by, I am officer of the gard today.

Allen A. Burnett

From the Eighteenth Regiment
Written for the Times

Camp Trowbridge, Milwaukee
March 12, 1862

Mr. Editor: Since my last the Badax Tigers have lost one of their number by death. It is always sad to chronicle the death of a comrade in arms but it is doubly so when the departed man was a man beloved by all. Orderly Sergeant Swan died on the evening of the 22nd of February after a short, though severe, illness of inflammation of the lungs. On Saturday night one week preceding his

---

8. The 18th Wisconsin was equipped with what they called "Belgian muskets," a term used to describe a variety of imported European arms early in the Civil War.

decease, he became suddenly ill and the next day the bad symptoms increasing, he was removed to the city and placed under the care of a hospital surgeon. He grew worse and it was evident his attack was one of no mild type. It soon became apparent that he could not long survive. His constitution, naturally consumptive, was poorly calculated to withstand the attacks which are inevitably made upon the health of a soldier. Poor fellow! Little did your correspondent think when chronicling in this communication his illness, and expressing a hope for his speedy recovery, that his remains would soon moulder back to Mother Earth.

Though not living long enough to serve his country upon the battlefield, yet his enlistment in the army testified to his readiness to do his whole duty. As a soldier, he was ever at his post and in the performance of his duties united faithfulness with perseverance and a just regard for the feelings of his men with that authority which he was obliged to exercise. So foreign to his nature were superciliousness and arrogance that, during all his connection with us, not one of those prone to fault-finding could point to an instance derogatory to his character a kind and considerate man. As a man and friend, none knew him but to admire and respect.

His remains were sent home by the boys—to a home made desolate and sad by the stern decree of death. May his family and friends, while mourning at his loss, consider and find consolation in the truism that "none can die so nobly as in the service of his country." He performed well his part in life and if good actions can claim special merit, he will enjoy naught but felicity through all eternity. Peace to his ashes.

At present, the sanitary condition of the company and regiment is reported good. None of the Tigers are very sick though a few are afflicted with colds. They are in good spirits and all apparently like camp life.

In regard to our leaving soon for the war, there are conflicting rumors. The order referred to in my last did not, it appears, include our regiment. We have, by turns, been ordered to St. Louis, Cairo, Chicago, and home again—all proving to be so much at variance with the truth of the matter that all agitation is finally settling down into a determination to cooly await coming events.

The boys were much pleased a few days since with the reception of a large sugar coated cake from Badax, the evidence of the thoughtfulness and kindness of Mrs. S.C. Lincoln, of Viroqua. It really does the boys good to receive such sure evidence that they are not forgotten at home. In this instance, they gave three cheers for the fair donor and by a unanimous vote returned thanks to her for her generosity. May every act of her life be productive of as much happiness as this simple testimonial of her sympathy and friendship for the Tigers.The circumstances attending its reception, as well as the present itself, will be long held, the fair giver may rest assured, in grateful remembrance.

While speaking of favors received from friends, it is not innappropriate to mention the fact that the boys receive frequent packages of papers from Hon. N. S. Cate, Senator from our district. The interest that he manifests for the welfare of the soldiers as shown by his numerous favors will long be remembered by them. Let me assure him no warmer or truer friends than the volunteers from

Badax. They will remember in the future who was the real friend of the common soldier.

Allow me to caution your readers against believing any of the startling stories which some of the boys, lately returned, state to be in circulation at home. It is quite curious how anything marvelous as that the Sparta company and ours had a pitched fight resulting in the death of five or six Tigers could have gained enough vitality in traveling so short a distance to entitle it to credence. Yet, such a story was in extensive circulation and, what is more wonderful than the story itself, believed in some portions of the county. Some unknown persons, also, manufacture stories derogatory to the morality of some of the boys and they obtain, it appears, ready hearers and believers. Nothing is entitled to belief unless it comes authoritatively through the Times or from the company over the signature of the writer.

I had almost forgotten to state that we have been furnished nearly two weeks with the Belgian rifle and the accompanying accouterments. For the few days immediately succeeding their advent, there might be heard "shoulder arms," etc. from morning till night; but, like all other things, time and frequent use have stripped them of whatever peculiar novelty they might have possessed. The boys are well pleased with them and you may rest assured that they will be used effectually whenever an opportunity occurs. Yours truly, C.

P.S. Since writing the above, we have been out on dress parade at which time the Colonel stated that he had it from high authority that our regiment would leave in ten days for secesh. He therefore ordered the captains to write to the men on furlough to repair within that time to camp. There, Mr. Editor, you have it as cheap as we. It may be so, and then again it moughtn't. C. [NW Times, Mar. 19, 1862, p. 2]

Camp Trowbridge, Wis.
March 16th, 1862

Dear Expositor:

After so long a time and much delay, for which I beg pardon, I will endeavor to fulfill the promise to keep you posted in regard to the Tigers.

Our history from our departure from Viroqua to a late date is, perhaps, already known to you and your readers, and I will not occupy space in relating old stories. I will confine myself to a brief description of our present home life and manner of living, believing that if I should enter into details it would not be without interest to those who have not had an opportunity of seeing volunteer life in Wisconsin.

Camp Trowbridge, formerly known as Camp Holton or Sigel, but now by its present name in honor to Capt. Trowbridge, the United States disbursing and mustering officer for this State, is situated just outside and north of the city of Milwaukee on the shore of Lake Michigan. The site is beautiful, high and dry, with a fine view of the city and the lake, and in the summer season would be very pleasant, but at this season the wind has an unfettered fling at us from all directions and particularly from the lake. The Ninth Regiment must have suffered much from the cold winds the past winter, in their tents.

Comfortable barracks were erected for our reception consisting of ten large rooms, one for a company, covered by a succession of roofs joined together at the eaves, with gutters to bear the water off, attached. To each room is a kitchen, with two large cook stoves and a sufficiency of cooking utensils. All the rooms are furnished with bunks for sleeping, two stoves, and all tables, benches, shelves, and other furniture that taste and convenience dictate, limited only by a want of variety of material. But with plenty of pine lumber, nails and tools, articles of furniture may be formed in many of the companies that remind one of home—such as fancy chairs, stools, writing desks, &c. If our quarters are always, while we are soldiers, as good as now, no complaint can be justly made. And while the outside is well cared for the inside is not neglected; we have plenty to eat.

As many of your readers may not know how much our allowance is, I will give in detail the rations that are furnished. Each man draws per day ¾ pound of pork or bacon or one and ¼ pound of fresh or salt beef; 22 ounces of bread or flour, and to each company 8 quarts of beans, in lieu thereof ten lbs. of rice.; one pound of potatoes to each man at least three times per week; ten pounds of coffee or tea per company; fifteen pounds of sugar ; four quarts of vinegar; one pound of sperm candles; four pounds of salt; and one quart of salt. With these liberal rations, good cooks, and other little luxuries that may be bought cheaply, we manage to live to our satisfaction.

By vote of the company, three men who had "seen service" were selected as cooks, with extra pay. We have regular hours for meals as well as for retiring to bed and rising, fixed by an order from the Colonel. A few evenings ago, the Colonel visited the quarters of the several companies and announced the stirring news that he had received orders to leave for St. Louis on the 27th inst.which caused tumultuous cheering and rejoicing. There is a great desire to see the elephant, and if we cannot see the animal itself, to see some of its tracks.[9]

The regiment now numbers nearly one thousand and is ready to march, (or at least as near ready as it will be if kept here a month and a half longer,) for we will not be able to drill to any advantage, the rain and mud preventing much tramping out doors.

The great question now is, shall we get our pay before going. We are encouraged to believe that we shall and I hope it may be so. The Second Cavalry (Washburne's Regiment.) leaves next Saturday without pay. It numbers considerably over eleven hundred men and is a fine body of men. It is not right to send men away to the seat of war without first paying them so they can, while near, send money home to their families, when the pay is due and nothing but inexcusable tardiness prevents it. The men leave their homes and cannot return to

---

9. "To see the elephant" was 19th century slang for any big event, in this case, combat. The origin of the phrase dates to at least the 1849 gold rush and probably refers to the rare event of the country folk seeing the wild animals of any traveling circus. [Dickson, Paul W., War Slang. New York, NY, Pocket Books, 1994, p. 9.]

them at pleasure, and not knowing how soon they may be permitted, they feel much solicitude for the helpless ones they have left. Brave and stout-hearted men who are willing to go anywhere and dare any risk in the defense of their country feel their ardor dampened when they think that there is a probability that their families are in need. If any portion of our people is patriotic and feel an undying attachment for the old flag, it is that portion which is now in the field as Union volunteers, not merely because the act of volunteering presupposes much devotion to the cause of the Union, but more from the fact that a soldier's life makes him enthusiastic and devoted in the cause he espouses; and the moral force of this feeling will long subserve the cause of Liberty when they have lain down their arms. I am sure no man who has offered himself for the defense of the Constitution in the present struggle for preservation, nor any of his children for at least a few generations will ever rise to overthrow it.

Let no man, then, say that his neighbor volunteered for any other reason than the true one and, from that groundless suspicion, neglect in any degree his duty toward the soldier's family. Let the wives write their husbands in the army that A and B were very kind and will not let them need for the necessaries of life. The Tigers regard C. Hunt, Esq., of the town of Clinton, as a moral man for his activity in seeing that no soldier's family in his town wants for anything. It were better if every prominent man in the county would follow his example in their several localities.

News has just been received here of the capture of New Madrid.[10] How the good cause speeds on! The sun of rebellion is fast setting, it is hoped never to rise again while we hold a place among the nations.

I will write punctually after we get orders to move and something new occurs occasionally. It is thought that when we leave St. Louis, we will be for the Western Frontier in the direction of New Mexico, but of course it is just conjecture.[11] I don't care where, so we go. Yours &c., TIGER [Expositor, March, 1862] [no other date or page number on clipping]

Headquarters, 18th Regiment Wisconsin Volunteers
Camp Trowbridge, Milwaukee, March 17, 1862

Dear Wife,

I received your letter last Friday evening and was glad to hear from you and to hear that you was well but sorry to hear that you had been afflicted with a bad cold.

---

10. Federal General John Pope's forces captured New Madrid, Missouri, along the Mississippi River on 14 March 1862. [Long, E. B., The Civil War Day By Day, an Almanac, 1861–1865; p. 184–185.]

11. A campaign near Santa Fe, New Mexico Territory, that culminated in a Confederate tactical victory but a strategic defeat at Glorieta Pass during March 1862 may have led to the belief that Wisconsin troops were to be sent as reinforcements. [Long, p. 189–190.]

I have been reasonably well since I came back. Untill a few days since I have had quite a bad cold and today I feel quite unwell. But I think by taking good care of myself I will soon get rid of it. You must be careful and not expose yourself to colds. Burnett is going to start home today so I will send this by him. I shall not come home this time for it is too expensive for the short time that I would be allowed to stay. We have orders to leave for St. Louis on the 27th of this month.

I wrote to you that I had received some letters from Illinois and would send you one, but I forgot it when I done up the letter. I have received two more since I wrote to you. I got one from brother Isaac at Leavenworth and one from my sister in Illinois. I will try to send them to you this time; two from my sister and one from brother Ike and one from David Ingersoll. Brother William is in St. Louis. Perhaps I may have a chance to see him when I get there.

You must be a good girl and try and do yourself all the good you can. Go to school all you can learn your grammar well. Study dictionary, practice writing, and using good and propper language. Practice originality by studying and writing compositions of your own. Learn to write pieces well and correctly, even on subjects of little importance. Write large letters to me. If you do not have verry much news to write originate something from your own. Resource composing something on some good subject that must interest you and try to take pride in your own merits.

E. Forsyth returned here this morning. He is not verry rugged yet but he says that he is improving fast. I supose it is unnecessary to write about the doings of our regiment as Burnett will tell all the peticulars.

I sent that letter from Jabe but have not received any answer from him.

There was two of my cousins in the Battle of Fort Henry and Fort Donaldson. They were from Illinois and and quite number of friends and acquaintences.

I believe I shall not write any more this time so good-bye for this time. Write soon. Tell me if you tried to get any money from the county.

Thomas J. Davis

[Untitled item]

Lieut. Burnett leaves this morning for Milwaukee with about a dozen and a half recruits for the Tigers. The occasion for needing more men was made by transferring men from the Tigers to another company in order to make that company full enough to organize the regiment. The 18th regiment, to which the Tigers belong, is soon to go to St. Louis.

To prove excellence of the Tigers, it is only necessary to say that they hold the place of honor in the regiment, that is they are Co. C., the color regiment. [NW Times, March 26, 1862; p. 3]

CHAPTER TWO

Events of No Ordinary Character

With little drill and no opportunity for target practice, the "Tigers" and their comrades in the Eighteenth were dispatched by rail to St. Louis on 30 March 1862. From St. Louis they were marched aboard a riverboat and sent downriver to Cairo, Illinois, then up the Ohio River to Paducah, Kentucky. Swinging out of the Ohio River, the riverboat churned up the Tennessee River toward General Ulysses S. Grant's Army of the Tennessee. Since the men had been supplied with ammunition early upon embarkation, they spent part of the trip firing at logs and water fowl.

The regiment disembarked at Pittsburgh Landing on 5 April and was immediately marched four miles inland to a division campsite with troops under the command of General Benjamin M. Prentiss. Short of rations and with only a portion of their ammunition, tents, and baggage, the Eighteenth was sent to bed exhausted, disoriented, and hungry.

The history of the Battle of Pittsburgh Landing, or Shiloh, has been recorded in volumes. The part played by the 18th Wisconsin at Pittsburgh Landing was but a small portion of the two-day affair and was over almost before the battle was an hour old. Placed at the extreme left front of Grant's forward line the Eighteenth was awakened at dawn on 6 April 1862 by the intermittent fire of Federal skirmishers meeting a Confederate army under the command of General Albert S. Johnston. The Confederates were arranged in attacking waves three corps in depth and were determined to roll over every Federal unit in their path.

As the weary Badgers turned out of their blankets that Sunday morning, a Confederate brigade under General Adley H. Gladden moved directly toward their encampment. The Federal brigade to which the 18th Wisconsin was assigned had just enough time to form a line of battle. They moved several hundred yards south across an open area known

35

as Spain's field and aligned under the cover of bordering woods. The Confederate attack struck moments later but was staggered by the fire of the Federal line. Inexplicably, Prentiss then ordered his men to retreat across Spain's field to reform nearer their camps. The Confederates were again severely punished as they tried to cross Spain's field in pursuit of Prentiss' men. Two Federal batteries tore into the Confederate lines with canister blasts and forced the Southerners to retreat. A second attack was formed in the woods and the Confederate line pressed forward, reinforced by General James R. Chalmers' brigade.

As Prentiss' nervous and inexperienced regiments began to show signs of breaking, he ordered a new line formed farther back at the campsites. Presenting a perfect silhouette against their white tents, the 18th Wisconsin awaited for the next attack.

Waiting in line of battle, the Badgers noted that the 15th Michigan had arrived on the field to support them. The Michiganians occupied the extreme left of the Union line. But in their haste to rush forward to help, the Michigan unit, also recently arrived at Pittsburg Landing, had neglected to draw ammunition. Aligned in perfect formation with empty rifles and fixed bayonets, the 15th Michigan suffered several dozen casualties before withdrawing to safety in the rear. The 18th Wisconsin was left open to attack on its left flank.

Chalmers' Confederates took advantage of the situation and swung around the Federal left through a concealing ravine. Gladden's Southerners massed in front of the Eighteenth and pressed attacks beyond the Federal right flank. According to one witness, "There the [18th] regiment stood in the open field as if on dress parade with its tents for a background, exposed to a merciless fire from the brow of the ravine in front, and also from both flanks. . . . If the regiment had been drawn up for the special purpose of giving the enemy all the natural advantages the field presented, and placing our troops in the most dangerous and exposed position, the plan could not have been better carried out."

Under pressure from Chalmers on the left and Gladden in front, the Eighteenth retreated through its camp leaving dozens of dead and wounded comrades behind. A brief stand was made on a slight rise behind the campsite but several hundred men continued to flee until they had reached the bluffs overlooking Pittsburg Landing. There, mixed with thousands of panic-stricken boys from other disorganized units, many of the Badgers spent the remainder of the day hiding from the horrors that had chased them from their bunks and breakfast fires. Reflecting on that portion of the battle some time later, a member of the regiment who stayed, fought, and was captured wrote, "What became of our men, we never knew, but thought that the fight in the morning had been too much for them, and [they] had gone to the river to cool off, as we have never seen them since."

The officers and men who stayed on the 18th Wisconsin firing line eventually retreated to a sunken road that became known as the "Hornet's Nest." Settling into this naturally entrenched position Prentiss' men, along with other Federal troops, held off several disjointed assaults over a seven-hour period before finally surrendering. Among the 2,300 prisoners captured by the Confederates at the "Hornet's Nest" were 200 officers and men of the 18th Wisconsin.

Grant's Army of the Tennessee had been reinforced by General Don Carlos Buell's 20,000-man Army of the Ohio during the night and early morning hours of 6–7 April. The combined Federal forces attacked the Confederate army on 7 April, driving the Southerners from the field and forcing them to retreat to Corinth, Mississippi. The few officers of the 18th Wisconsin who were not either killed, wounded, or captured gathered a battalion of 250 men and supported a battery of artillery during the second day's fight. The Eighteenth returned to its campsite that afternoon and by evening counted nearly 500 men available for duty.

A review of the casualties among the Eighteenth showed 41 men killed or mortally wounded, including Colonel Alban and Major Crane, 93 men wounded, including Lieutenant Colonel Beall and Adjutant Edward Coleman, and 200 prisoners of war. The 18th Wisconsin suffered 334 men lost of approximately 950 present on 6 April 1862. More significantly, the regiment lost most of its leaders. Nearly every captain was either killed, wounded, or captured. Seven first lieutenants were either wounded or captured. According to one wounded soldier-correspondent, "Our regiment will never be sent into the field again— they are cut to pieces, wounded, taken prisoners, and gone, no one knows where." In sum, the 18th Wisconsin was a regiment without leadership following Shiloh.

With their first combat behind them, the survivors faced a different sort of enemy, disease. During the weeks immediately following the battle, dozens of men suffered from camp maladies. Symptoms included fevers, diarrhea, and general debility. Polluted water, poor cooking, and generally unsanitary conditions aggravated by the unfamiliar warmth of a southern spring thinned the ranks of the already depleted Eighteenth by half. As one "Tiger" correspondent stated a week after the battle, "Our company was then 81 strong besides the officers. Now we have not more than half that number. This morning we have but seven reported for duty." This war was not at all the gallant warfare about which the men had read. It was dirty and it was deadly.

Among the letters in this chapter are several that described the battle of Shiloh. Ransom Chase's letter written to his brother on 12 April 1862 shines as an example of battlefield journalism. Chase gave a succinct introduction explaining the regiment's arrival at Pittsburg Landing, then immediately narrated the morning attack on his camp. His summary of the battle, only five days after the fact, was as accurate as could be expected from a soldier with a limited view of the engagement. Of great importance, too, are the casualty reports. Chase told his readers what he knew and, almost as significantly, what he did not know.

In contrast to Chase's journalistic prose, T. J. Davis' letters were somewhat less formal. He touched on the news he had received in letters from relatives, friends, neighbors, as well as the rumors and tales that have been passed around the camp. Although Davis could not have known much about the condition of the prisoners from Company C who were captured in the fight at the "Hornet's Nest," his reassuring tone was testimony to the regard the men showed toward their comrades and their families.

From the Expositor
Letter From Pittsburg Landing

The following letter was received here last Friday by young Mr. Chase, which is from his brother in the Tiger Company. The letter explains itself and therefore comment is unnecessary:

Pittsburg Landing, April 12

Brother Lucius:—I wrote at Saint Louis stating our probable destination. We arrived here on the afternoon of the 5th and marched four miles to an encampment and pitched our tents in the evening. Early next morning, before breakfast, we were formed to repulse the enemy, who had come down on us with force. We, being upon the extreme left and at the point of attack could not and did not withstand them long. Our General did not expect an attack. There was no force within a mile to support us and, of course, we were obliged to retreat. Many of our boys in the regiment were shot in the first attack.

The battle lasted two days. The first day they drove us until near night and we were almost whipped, and were it not for the reinforcement of Buell's men, would have been severely beaten. That night the men came across the river, as many as could, and with the morning light the fight again began.

It was a terrible fight. The hardest fought battle that America has ever had. Thousands upon thousands are killed and wounded. They were defeated the second day. Our regiment was not in this last engagement, they being all cut up and dispersed the day before. The Colonel was carried from the field mortally wounded and has since died. The Lieut. Col. cannot recover. The Major was found shot in twelve places, dead. The Acting Adjutant is mortally wounded.—Captain Layne is either killed or taken prisoner. The Captains of our regiment are nearly all gone—some are dead and have been buried, others are missing.

Of our company, two are known to be dead, their bodies found—Mr. Saxton, and Mr. Kittle of Lynxville. The wounded are B.F. Rantz, Samuel Sager, Wm. Dikeman, J.J. Swain, Samuel Fish, P. Singer, and John Kirkpatrick. These are known to be wounded and five others are known to be, but we cannot find them. The wounded were taken off the field as they fell and carried three or four miles to the Landing, shipped down the river nine miles to Savannah. There are 33 missing of whom we know nothing, making our Company small. I do not think our regiment, in consideration of our great loss, will be in another engagement soon, we being completely disorganized. I think we will be sent to guard prisoners.

I am now acting Orderly. Fretwell, Dixon, Brightman, Samuel McMichael, and several others we know nothing of.

I am writing under difficulties, having borrowed this sheet of paper, our things being taken by the rebels as we left them in camp. From your brother, Ransom J. Chase. [NW Times, Apr. 23, 1862, p. 2]

From the Eighteenth Regiment

Pittsburg Landing, Tenn.
April 14, 1862

Mr. Editor, Events of no ordinary character, both to the Badax soldiers and their friends at home, have occurred since my last made its unobtrusive appearance to your readers. Then, we were peacefully encamped at Camp Trowbridge looking forward to our probable destination with feelings of buoyancy and indulging in speculation whether we should ever see a battle. Then we were looking forward to a hasty campaign and in imagination, saw it speedily and the 18th march back with its numbers scarcely diminished. Yes, we looked beyond that and felt again the friendly grasp of loved friends.

Now, we are encamped "away down in Dixie" upon the hardest fought battlefield that America can produce. Now, instead of looking forward to expectations of pleasure and speculating as to future events, we are looking back, looking wistfully, looking mournfully at the events that have been crowded into the past two weeks, But I must not anticipate.

We left Camp Trowbridge Sunday, March 30, our immediate point of destination, St. Louis. I have no space here to expatiate on the small incidents

of the trip, other things more important to your readers claiming my attention.[1] At. St. Louis we embarked on the steamboat "John Warner" and arrived here Saturday afternoon. We marched through a large number of encampments and finally arrived at night about four miles from the Landing
and pitched our tents in the evening in a small open field on the extreme left
of our army. The men had been put through in a rather rough way on the trip,
lived poor, had no place to sleep, and went supperless to bed the first night
we landed on the soil of Tennessee. The next morning, April 6, we were
called upon while our hunger yet remained unsatisfied, to form line of battle to withstand the attack of the rebels, then unexpectedly coming down
upon us in force. The battalion was formed and was hurriedly assigned a position a few rods in front of our encampment in the timber. We had scarcely
formed the new alignment when the order was given to fall back. This was
necessary to prevent our being flanked by the enemy who was now pouring
volley after volley on the regiment next on our right. We formed upon the
open space between our tents and the advancing enemy and there awaited
further orders. Before us was heavy timber. Under this protection, the enemy fired with comparative safety while we could only now and then catch
a glimpse of their uniforms through the timber and shrubbery. Here, as I
shall state more particularly hereafter, a number of Company C were
wounded. It was demonstrated very soon what ought to have been apparent
to our commanders, that it was worse than folly to attempt to withstand the
enemy at this point.

At the commencement of the firing upon our regiment, the men of some of
the companies, a little startled, rather left the alignment and fell back about a rod.
Company C, however, stood firm. It never wavered until commanded to retreat
and then a few upon the right of the company still stood, determined to have a
few more shots at the now visible enemy. Here was a great mistake of our gen-

---

1. Although no itinerary of the trip from Milwaukee to Pittsburg Landing has
surfaced from a Company C source, the diary of Levi Minkler, Company F, 18th
Wisconsin, yields a concise summary of the journey. All spelling is as noted in a
typescript of the diary : "Left Millwaukee Sunday, 30th of March at 12 o'clock. Arrived at Chicao, 4 p.m., left at 8 p.m. Passed a broken down corn crib in Illinois
containing 15,000 bushels. Arrived at Williamstown Monday night about 6 p.m.
Slept in cars that night, got out in the morning. Remained on the bank of the river
till in the afternoon. Crossed over to St. Louis, shiped aboard the boat steamer
"Warner" for we did not know where. Laid on deck that night. Did not leave the
deck untill Wenesday, about noon the 2th. The wind blowing a gale, took 2 or 3
hours to get headed down stream. Landed at Cairo for coal in the morning of the
3rd. Took on board 30 of the 14th Regiment left behind sick. Landed at Paduca
4 o'clock the 3th. Paraded the streets. Saw lots of guns that was taken at Fort
Donolson. Took more soldiers aboard and started up the Tennessee River. Passed
Fort Henry in the morning of the 4th. Saw a dead man floating in the river. Passed
Suvanah [on] the 5th, 6 a.m. Arrived at Pittsburg [Landing] 10 a.m. Landed in the
afternoon." [Minkler, Levi. Diary, March 30–May 27, 1862 (typescript). Shiloh National Military Park Archives.]

erals, if I may be allowed to say it. To resist the whole rebel army with three or four new volunteer regiments were formed in an open field with neither artillery or infantry within a mile to support them and behind whom they could not reform. It could scarcely be denominated an oversight. It was bad generalship.

New troops made a fresh stand three quarters of a mile from our first one and more troops being hurried forward, the field from that point was disputed inch by inch. The battle raged hotly all day. There is no use disputing the fact that at five o'clock we were the same as whipped. A last grand stand was made at the Landing between three or four miles from the point of attack. I have no doubt but Gen. Grant would have surrendered did he not expect momentarily Gen. Buell and his troops. Just at the critical moment, he arrived and rode along our lines cheered by the soldiery. As fast as the steamboats could transport his men across the Tennessee, they came to our assistance. Probably three thousand arrived in season to participate in the engagement that night.

While the rebels were cannonading our last position, the gunboats did terrible execution with their shells.[2] The rebel prisoners state that it was terrific. The say that one shell chanced to pass some distance on their line of battle killing a number and then exploding. They declare that it must have killed at least sixty men. They also state that they certainly would have taken our last position had it not been for the destructive fire of these boats.

Be this as it may, a better fate awaited us. By morning enough of the reinforcements had crossed to recommence the contest under different auspices. It did commence and we drove them back foot by foot, retaking our lost batteries, regaining our former ground , and finally, very near sundown, totally routing them, our cavalry pursuing.

Thus ended the battle at Pittsburg Landing. I can form no estimate of the number killed and wounded of our forces. It probably equaled theirs the first day , but on the second, our loss bore no comparison with theirs.[3] It was truly a pitiful sight to witness the havoc, misery, and woe that the battle field exhibited the day following the fight. Here lay a man just breathing his last shot through the breast; another by his side so mangled that the mother who bore him would fail to recognize him with all her maternal instinct. Here might be seen, aye, and heard, the wounded sufferer begging for a little water: "Just a little, a very little. Don't go away. Give me a little water, do." Here, too, lay the slain whose spirits had been hushed amidst the strife and din of battle into that unknown land where even the soldier fighting for his country finds rest.

No language can describe a battle field and its attendant miseries—it is inadequate. The participation in the strife is trifling. It is the after scene that teaches the frailty of all things human, the extent of human suffering and the cost of "glorious war." Many a one in a far off quiet home will wait long and

---

2. The gunboats U.S.S. Lexington and Tyler helped stabilize Grant's defense line on the night of April 6.

3. Casualties for all troops engaged were 13,000 of 62,000 Federals and 10,700 of 40,000 Confederates. [Long, p. 195–196]

anxiously for the one whom fate has denied the blessed privilege of a return; but many a shout will rend the air at the success of our arms and many tears of joy be shed, all mindful that shouts of agony and tears of anguish were the purchase price of victory.

Our regiment suffered badly. After the first retreat, part of them collected together and prepared again for the conflict, They were again led into action in heavy timber west of an open field and here did some of the hardest fighting. It was at this place that the Colonel was mortally wounded and taken from the field. But the whole line at last retreated and with them the 18th. It is now almost worthless in point of efficiency. The battle played sad havoc with them.[4]

Our company is badly used. We found two of our men dead upon the field—Mr. N.W. Saxton and Mr. Wm. Kittle. The former was wounded in the abdomen at the first stand we made and was helped some distance but was obliged to be left with another of our wounded boys, Philip Singer, in a tent. Monday night, after the enemy had retreated, Singer was brought down to the landing on a litter and stated that they were well treated by the rebels, furnished with water, etc., that Mr. Saxton expired that morning in the tent in which he was placed.

Mr. William Kittle was found dead after the battle at the roots of a large oak, shot through the breast. The wounded, so far as we know, are the following, all injured in the first fight:

Philip Singer, badly wounded in the knee;
Laughlin Quinn, shot in the foot;
Benj. F. Rantz, shot through both thighs;
John Kirkpatrick, shot through the right shoulder;
Wm. Dikeman, shot through the left arm;
Samuel Sager, wounded in the ankle;
J.J. Swain, shot in the left shoulder;
Samuel Fish, shot in the left leg.

The last named person was too badly wounded to be got off the field and fell into the hands of the rebels. He was carried, he states, into the tent where we found him by a rebel lieutenant and kindly administered to, given whiskey, etc. He is now under the special charge of the company and no pains is spared to the end that he may speedily recover. These we know were wounded and taken off the field.

Here, however, a complete, truthful statement of the place and circumstances could not be made unless I added that the number might be much larger and we be entirely ignorant of their whereabouts. Thousands of wounded were taken aboard the boats. Soldiers not wounded were prohibited the entering in search of comrades. Many of them were sent down the river to Savannah. It was utterly impossible, also, to find the dead. The battlefield extended over miles—

---

4. Casualties in the 18th Wisconsin from the Battle of Shiloh were 41 killed, 93 wounded, and 174 missing. [Martin, p.66]

all, with the exception of a few small cultivated fields, heavy timber. Among the thousands of slain thus situated, it would be chance that could direct the eye to any particular person. I trust that the list above given includes all the wounded.

I come now to the missing. Of these we know nothing; but we infer that many of them have been taken prisoners. They are as follows:

Capt.	N.M. Layne	Privates,	Janes
Sergeant	Fretwell	do	Loucks
do	Dickson	do	Metcalf
Corporal	Brightman	do	Merrill
do	Hickok	do	McClelland
do	McMichael	do	Mills
Privates	Campbell	do	Powell
do	W. Cleary	do	Ross
do	J. Gander	do	Taylor
do	Gray	do	Tooker

These we know nothing definite of. There is a story afloat that Capt. Layne was killed and circumstances are adduced tending that way. It is your correspondent's opinion that he is a prisoner. Indeed, the Tigers have suffered badly.

Let me say to those who are friends and relatives of the persons named as missing, that they should not consider it inevitable that they will not return. This war ought not, and probably will not last long; and if prisoners—as we indulge the hope in preference to a worse fate—they will soon return to their homes.

A great many stories relative to the cruelty of the rebels to our men, I am happy to state, are untrue. Many of our wounded bear testimony to their kindness and sympathy. The fact is, there are in both armies those who regard little the feelings of the unfortunate. But to attribute to a whole army that which only a few who are naturally bad, practice, would be unjust, either to friend or foe.

I have in this extended communication attempted to give an accurate outline of the Company and the events in which it acted a conspicuous part. I have not attempted to excite the anxiety of friends, but rather to allay their suspense by giving the truth plainly and without equivocation. The boys that remain are troubled as all troops are, when they first come here, with diarrhoea. Few are now strong enough for duty but their health will improve, we are informed, after they have been here a while.

I had almost forgotten to mention the loss of our regimental officers. Colonel Alban died Tuesday morning of his wound received on Sunday. Lieut. Col. Beall is considered mortally wounded. Maj. Crain was found shot in twelve places. Acting Adjutant Coleman reported mortally wounded.

Of the captains, six are missing. Some are known to be dead, others are known to be dead or prisoners. As a regiment, we appear to be almost disorganized. There has been no little speculation relative to our disposition, some thinking we shall be detailed to guard prisoners, others that we shall go on with the army and others yet, thinking we will be sent home. The last is stated to the wish of the Colonel before he died.

The boys are bound to do their duty in any event, and that cheerfully. Some of them request me to mention that such and such a one is all right and safe. All those not specially enumerated to the contrary in this communication may be considered uninjured.

I am writing this sitting upon the ground and surrounded by such circumstances as renders it impossible to strive for accuracy in expression and, hence, your readers must consider the substance, not the form, of giving it utterance.

I shall write and keep you posted at the next favorable opportunity.

I am yours etc.,C.

P.S. All letters directed to us should be as follows: "St. Louis, 18th Reg. Wis. Vol., Company C." They will be forwarded to us wherever we may be. [NW Times, Apr. 30, 1862, p. 3]

Sunday March 14th, 1862.[5]

[I] do not wish you to feel uneasy about me for I feel in hopes through the kindness of Providence that I should get through and get home again.

Burnett happened to be in the fight, as he said, down at the river and did not have time to get to camp 'til after the fight commenced. And then he did not know where to find us for our army was fighting all over the woods for five or six miles around and when you get this you will know that I was not killed or else I could not write. Nor I did not happen to get touched though several of our boys got bullitt holes shot in their clothes.

I would have wrote to you before but everything has been in such confusion that that I did not know hardly what to write. There is a great many soldiers. The most folks I ever saw together before from all parts of the United States.

I received a letter from brother Isaac today he was still at Leavenworth and was well.

After you read this letter you may [let] one of the Viroqua papers have the other two leaves to publish but keep this o[ne]; that is, if they will return these again.

I have no letter paper so I am writing this on the cover of a book that I found after the battle and I have no pen and ink so I have to write with a

---

5. This appears to be the third page of a three-page letter. The first two pages are missing. According to T. J. Davis' instructions to his wife midway in the page, it appears that Lucinda Davis may have loaned the first two pages to a local newspaper. Also, the erroneous date at the top of the page, Sunday, March 14th, 1862, is probably the end of a sentence from the previous page. In any case, March 14 was a Friday.

pencil. It has been very wet since we came to here. It has rained over half the time. The leaves are getting green, the peach trees are in full bloom, and the wild flowers are aplenty in the woods. Write as soon as you get this. Direct St. Louis, Mo., 18th Regiment Wisconsin Volunteers, Company C, and it will come on through wherever the regiment is stationed at. If I had room I would send you some flowers but my letter is too large so good-bye for this time.

Thomas J. Davis

Letter from Pittsburg Landing

The following letter, from Mr. MORLEY to his wife, was received last Tuesday evening, and as it contains something interesting to the relatives and friends of the Tigers, we have been permitted to publish it. The letter is one day later than the one from Mr. CHASE which we published last week, and it will be seen that as yet the writer knows nothing of Capt. LAYNE, THOS. FRETWELL or SAMUEL MCMICHAEL who are well known throughout the county, and who were members of the Tiger Company. The letter is dated:

Headquarters 18th Regiment
Pittsburg Landing, Tenn., April 13, 1862

Dear Wife and Children,

One week ago to-day, I dropped you a line from here. At that time our company was in good health and spirits, but one short week has produced a sad change. Our company was then 81 strong besides the officers. Now we have not more than half that number. This morning we have but seven reported for duty. There are a few waiting on the wounded and the balance are unwell. I believe there are about 36 missing. I presume some are taken prisoners. Some wounded and taken in at other camps and died, and many living insensible. It will never be known what became of them. Some of the wounded laid on the field from Sunday morning until Tuesday, in the rain. Some of our company who were wounded in the first of the battle have not been found. We only found two of the Tigers dead. Benj. F. Rantz and Samuel Fish are severely wounded—others badly but not dangerously. Capt. Layne, Mr. Fretwell, Samuel McMichael, Peter Campbell and enough to make the aggregate about 36, are missing. The wounded are generously taken on the boats. Those who die during the night are brought on shore and laid on the bank in rows. The carts for carrying the dead are constantly running and hundreds and thousands will thus be disposed of and their friends never know what became of them. Hundreds would recover if they had proper treatment and care. A bandage and cold water is all they get.

I suppose you get accounts of the battle, and I will not attempt a description of it. It is an awful sight to see the ground covered with dead and dying—mangled in all shapes—some with an arm off, some with severed heads and others with both legs cut off ! In one place I saw five rebels killed with a cannon ball. I saw many of them with broken limbs, left to linger a few days in pain and died for want of medical aid. Our heavy Belgian balls smash the bones so that amputation is the only remedy. We have a large army here, and lost a great many men, but the rebels left dead on the field about five to one of ours.

A word about myself. I am not very well but keep about. The day is beautiful and we appreciate it, for the past week we have had rain every day. From the night before the battle until last Friday night we slept in the mud and rain without any shelter whatever. It appears now about like our June month in Wisconsin. Everything is in full bloom and one tree in particular is completely covered with large white blossoms. There are also some splendid climbing-roses growing spontaneously, but not yet in bloom. This is a great country for fruit, and if it was not for slavery would be a delightful country to live in. I have not had an opportunity of getting a "contraband" yet.[6] I have not seen the first one since we landed. They have all fled to the back country. Tell the little ones to be good children. Good bye.

Calvin Morley

P.S. I write this on the battle field sitting on a tree that was cut off by a cannon ball and a lime-stone for a writing desk. C.M. [NW Times, no date on clipping]

Returned Soldiers

. . . Mr. Corey had his eyes badly burned with powder by one of his companions discharging his gun close to them in the battle of Pittsburg. He brings the sad news that George Williams has died of disease; that J.H. Brightman was wounded through the mouth, losing several teeth and that he and several wounded prisoners have been exchanged for wounded rebels.[7]

Capt. Layne and most of the missing men of the Tigers are prisoners and perhaps all the missing are prisoners.

Henry Baker and an Illinois soldier took a rebel Captain prisoner at the late battle of Pittsburg and hold a certificate to that effect.

Of the Volunteer Companies that have left this county, only the Tigers, of the 18th, have had an opportunity to distinguish themselves, and their opportunity at Pittsburg was under discouraging circumstances. But notwithstanding lack of drill and familiarity with their profession, their behavior would have honored

---

6. "Contraband" was short for "contraband of war," a euphemism for slaves. The origin of the term is credited to Major General Benjamin F. Butler in 1861. (Long, p. 78)

7. Prisoner paroles and exchanges were common during the first two years of the war. Prisoners were most often exchanged rank for rank but a table of values was also developed so that one officer could be exchanged for multiples of privates. [Faust, Patricia L. (ed.), Historical Times Illustrated Encyclopedia of the Civil War. New York, Harper & Row, Publishers, 1986, p. 603–604]

old soldiers. Neither old Badax nor young Vernon need be ashamed of their soldiers who have been tried under fire so far; the honored dead are few and we hope that the number may not increase.

On furlough—Mr. L. B. Noyes, Hospital Steward of the Eighteenth Wisconsin Regiment, left Pittsburg Landing on the 19th ult. on board the hospital boat D.A. January, bound for Keokuk, Iowa, and arrived at that city on the 23rd; remained there three days, and then started for home, arriving here last Wednesday morning. He is out on furlough, having a severe attack of rheumatism, which has disabled him for service at present. He gives us some stirring accounts of the great battle, and thinks our loss was—killed 2,300; wounded 6,000; taken prisoners 3,000. He will probable furnish us with some incidents of the battle for our next issue. Mr. Noyes was formerly one of the editors of this paper. [Expositor, no date on clipping]

Pittsburgh Landing Tennessee, April 22nd, 1862

Dear Wife,

I received your letter last week and was glad to hear from you again and to hear that you was well. I am in tolerable good health at this time. I have nearly got over my cold which troubled me for sometime. I would have answered your letter before this but I just started a letter to you a few days before I received yours.

We are still here at Pittsburg Landing and I don't know how long we will remain here. Perhaps some time as our regiment has been pretty badly cut up. I think we will be held back for a reserve for sometime as we was put in in the advance in this fight. We may not be taken into another fight at all if our forces get them licked out soon. Uncle Sam has a verry large force stationed here.

I have not heard anything from Jabez since I come here only I seen a member of the 3rd Wisconsin Battery who said that they left Foster's Battery[8] at Louisville and that they was going to Lexington, Kentucky, to exchange for larger guns. He said that Foster was going get 20 pounder guns.

You wrote sometime ago to know where you should live while Mrs Burnett went to Illinois. Perhaps you could suit yourself better than I could tell you. So you get a good place. You said you hoped I would not feel bad about what you wrote to me. I do not feel bad about it if you can take good care of yourself. I think that we will all get home before cold weather comes again.

You wrote for me to keep up good spirits. You need not get uneasy about about me getting discouraged for I thought of all this before hand. I will not allow myself to think of getting homesick. I hope you may still

---

8. Foster's Battery was named for Captain Jacob T. Foster. It was also known as the 1st Wisconsin Battery or the La Crosse Battery. [Wisconsin, 1863, p.411–412]

continue to forebear with my absence and please don't tease me to come home which I don't believe you will.

There was a letter come here yesterday for Sam McMichael. Burnett and I opened it. It was from Julia. We thought if there was anything special or valuable in it we would send it back. She wrote as though she was about discouraged and wished for Sam at home again. I really felt sorry for her. You and Mrs. Burnett must talk incouraging to her. Sam is a prisoner-of-war in the hands of the Rebels. I hope she will not trouble herself too mutch about it. I think he will be well-used and will be exchanged back for some of their men that is in our hands as soon as our officers can arrange the matter.

Julia Mc wrote you had a hard snowstorm the 7th & 8th of April with a foot of snow. I have not seen any snow or frost since I left St. Louis.

I shall try to write to you every week and I would like for you to do the same.

I found quite a number of old acquaintence in several of the Illinois regiments that are here.

You said Mary wanted me to write what kind of soldier Ike made. He come through the battle all right and said he knew that he killed one Sesesh that tried to make a charge on him.

Direct your letters to St. Louis as you did before and they will come all right. No more this time so good-bye. Write soon.

Thos. J. Davis

Pittsburg Landing Tennessee, seven miles out, April 28th, 1862

I sit down to write you a few more lines to let you know that I still live and in tolerable good health. Hoping this may find you well. I have been looking several days for a letter from you but have not received an answer to any letter that I have written to you from here This is the 3rd letter that I have wrote to you from here but I think that I will get one in a few days.

Robert McMichael, Orderly Sergeant Carter, John White, Bas Munyon, Ike Newell and several others arrived here night before last. They got through all safe. Robert brought several letters for the boys but he did not have any for me. I hope you have got the letters that I have wrote to you since the battle as I supose you would be somewhat uneasy until you heard.

Walt Odell received a letter from Jabe today. It was dated April 6. He was then at Lexington, Kentucky. He said that they would start for Cumberland Gap, Tennessee, in a few days. He said he was well. He did not say that he had received any letter from me. Several of the boys have just got letters today, the first that any of them have received in answer to letters they have written since the battle. Some had become uneasy for fear that our letters had not been sent out.

We have moved our camp out out seven miles from the landing towards Corinth.[9] We are in the 6th Division and will be in the reserve in case of an attack instead of the advance as we were before.[10] There is all kinds of gas and gammon talked through the camp. It makes a sensible man sick to listen to the different reports that is afloat every day. Some think that the Rebels will soon attack us again and some think that they will soon evacuate Corinth and leave and it is hard to tell what will happen as soldiers and company officers know little of what is transpiring in our camp. If the Rebels do not attack us soon, from the movement of our army we will soon attack them for there is bound to be a big fight or a fast foot race here before many days. Buell is trying to get Beauregard's[11] army surrounded. If he succeeds in doing it there will be a pretty hard fight or else no fight at all. But Beauregard is an old fox and understands sharp tricks as well as the best of our generals. But if we could succeed in spiking the Sesesh army at Corinth it would tell a bad tale on Rebeldom. I would give all the boots I have and throw in my old hat if the thing could be did.

Several of our company are sick at this time. One of our men from Kickapoo by the name of Starbuck died last night. He was not very healthy when he enlisted. E. Forsyth has been quite sick but is getting better. He feels very bad over the death of his child. Several of our sick taken away today to some hospital. Burdette Fletcher was one of them. He has not been able for duty since he had the measles.

I believe all the rest of the Badax boys are tolerable well. Burnett sent his trunk home today or started it. I don't know whether it will ever get through or not. I sent my fiddle and three blankets and some clothes in it though I believe he sent it to Illinois so that Mrs. Burnett would see to it when she went down there. Robert McMichael said that you was going to stay with his wife a while. I supose he meant when Mrs. Burnett had gone. Tell Mrs. Burnett there is a prospect of a rite smart chance of peaches down here in Tennesy this season.

---

9. Corinth, Mississippi, population 1,500, was the junction of two important southern railroads, the Memphis & Charleston Railroad and the Mobile & Ohio Railroad. [Andriot]

10. The 18th Wisconsin was assigned to the 2nd Brigade (Col. John M. Oliver), 6th Division, (Brigadier General Thomas J. McKean). [OR-I-10-2-154]

11. General Pierre G. T. Beauregard assumed command of the Confederate Army of Tennessee upon the death of General Albert Sidney Johnston at the Battle of Shiloh. Under Beauregard's command, the Confederates retreated from Shiloh to Corinth. [Davis, William C. (ed.), The Confederate General, vol. 1., Harrisburg, Pa., National Historical Society, 1991, p.88]

We just received this evening a report that New Orleans had been taken by the Union forces.[12]

My paper is about out and I must stop for this time so be a good girl until I see you. Good-bye, write often.

Thos. J. Davis good bye, Sis

Pittsburg Landing, Tennessee Tuesday, May 6th, 1862

Dear Brother & Sister

I received a letter from you yesterday by the politeness of Mr. Pickett of the 30th Illinois which found me in tolerable good health and I was very glad to hear that you was all well. You said you had wrote a letter about 2 weeks before and directed it to Saint Louis. I received it a few days after after the battle. Letters directed to Saint Louis or by way of Cairo to Pittsburg Landing, either one, will come through all right.

I have written two letters to you since I have been here. I found Captain Winters' son in the 61st Illinois who informed me that brother Will had got well and had been back to Illinois on a furlough and that he had again rejoined his regiment and was in the Battle of Pea Ridge in Arkansas and that he was not hurt in the battle all of which I wrote to you in my second letter from here.[13]

The 30th Illinois is here. They have been here about ten days. I visited their camp last Friday. I seen Jim Ditto, Jim Wells, Henry Pendegraph, & Will Curry. They were all well and were quite surprised to see me. I also seen Orla Ritchison and Capt Shea of Aledo. I saw Perry Gibson at a distance but he was in the ranks going out on picket and I did not have a chance to speak to him.

I found quite a number of my neighbor boys from Warren County in the 17th Illinois. Among them was Merrill Landon, Delilah's cousin. He got shot on the belt plate with a partly spent ball, doubling the plate wrong-side out. Had it not been for the heavy leather belt under it, the ball would have drove the plate into his bowells. As it was, it bruised him quite severely so that he has not been put on duty since. Jim & Frank Burnett have both gone home on furlough and neither of them had got back the last time I was at their camp.

We are now camped at a little Sesesh village called Monterey, 12 miles out from Pittsburg [Landing] and 10 miles from Corinth. This place is intirely evacuated by its inhabitants. Last week we run five Rebel regiments

---

12. New Orleans, Louisiana, was taken by Union naval forces under Admiral David Farragut on 25 April 1862. [Long, p.203–204]

13. The Battle of Pea Ridge, Arkansas, took place on 7–8 March 1862 and was a Union victory. [Long, p.179–180]

out of this place in such a hurry that they left their tents, provisions, and several wagons behind them [and] bursting open the the most of their barels of beef and pork and throwing the meat on the ground before leaving it.[14] Some parts of our army in advancing in diferant parts have a little squabble with Sesesh nearly every day.

We are now within about six miles of the Rebels' fortifications and our army are still slowly advancing on them. Our regiment has moved up four times since the battle. I think that it will not be but a few day until we will have another heavy battle here at Corinth unless they evacuate it, which I think they will not be likely to do for they have a verry heavy force there and have no hopes of whiping us any easier any other place. This is a very heavy timbered country and is a slow place to get a large army through. I think our generals are figuring hard to surround and bag the whole pile of them.

You must excuse this hard looking paper for I have to carry my paper in my knapsack and it gets rumpled and dirty so that I can hardly write on it. Sometimes it is hard to get any paper here and convenients for writing. You may judge when a man has to sit on the ground and use his knapsack for stand.

I have not read but one letter from Isaac since [I've] been here. I am looking for a letter from him every day.

Tell Uncle Henry Redman I will bring him a live Sesesh if I can tame one. I will bring it in a hickory withe cage,[15] though they [are] quite wild here and they shoot very careless right at a man's face as quick as any other place.

My sheet is out and I must quit.

Thomas J. Davis

The 18th At Pittsburg

The ridiculous story that the Tigers, or any portion of the 18th regiment ran away at the battle of Pittsburg, is now fully exploded. The whole particulars of the battle having been received, it appears that the 18th were formed in line of battle but a few moments before the rebels were upon them, and undrilled as they were, and as inexperienced were men and officers, they stood their ground like old heroes, and that the "Tigers" were the last to fall back, when they were ordered to do so, and that Capt. Layne had to recall such

---

14. According to war records, the action was a 29 April 1862 skirmish in which the 2nd Iowa Cavalry cleared Monterey of stragglers. Federal reports identified the five Confederate regiments as the 4th, 13th, 17th, 20th, and 25th Louisiana Infantry Regiments. [OR-I-10-1-p.799]

15. A woven, wicker basket.

men as Thomas Fretwell, J.H. Brightman, Samuel McMichael, Ransom J. Chase and others who had not heeded the order to fall back in the first place. The brave men of the "Tigers" and of the 18th generally, as well as all our Wisconsin boys, have won imperishable honors on the bloody field of Pittsburg, or Shiloh, as it is called by the rebel General Beauregard. [NW Times, May 7, 1862, p. 2]

CHAPTER THREE

We Live As Woodchucks

In the wake of Shiloh, Governor Louis P. Harvey of Wisconsin visited the 18th Wisconsin at their camp. He offered his thanks and condolences to the survivors and, before departing, Harvey made an appointment that met with mixed reaction. Instead of promoting Lieutenant Colonel Samuel W. Beall to replace the slain Colonel Alban, Harvey reached outside the ranks of the 18th Wisconsin and tapped a more experienced officer to reorganize the regiment. Gabriel Bouck was promoted from a captaincy in the 2nd Wisconsin Infantry to assume the colonelcy of the Eighteenth. At the same time, Captain William P. Lyon of the 8th Wisconsin was promoted to major. While the new officers were in transit to the Army of the Tennessee, Captain Charles H. Jackson, Company B, commanded the unit. When Colonel Bouck arrived on May 12, the regiment numbered only 250 men fit for duty.

The "Badax Tigers" participated in the occupation of the Corinth, Mississippi, after Confederates evacuated the city on 30 May 1862. The health of the company reached a low point in late June when it was reported that only thirteen men of an original strength of over one hundred remained fit for duty. With time and rest, however, many of the "Tigers" recovered and joined their comrades in camp. They performed picket and guard duty through mid-July, which carried the additional benefit of giving the entire regiment time to practice and perfect battalion drill.

The 18th Wisconsin was sent to garrison Bolivar, Tennessee, on 21 July where they remained until 16 August. Returning to Corinth, the Badgers performed more general guard duty. On 17 September the regiment was part of a move from Corinth toward Iuka, Mississippi, to reinforce General William S. Rosecrans' division. Rosecrans faced a strong Confederate force under General Sterling Price. Federal tacticians hoped to trap Price by a quick, coordinated movement of two Federal divisions. On 19 September, the brigade that included the 18th Wisconsin made a circuitous march to the east side of Iuka to cut off the Southern force. Although the Eighteenth was involved in a minor skirmish with Southern cavalry pickets, the march was in vain, as Price had evacuated Iuka before the trap was able to be sprung.

The letters and reports from the "Tigers" during this period of the war contain more variety than in later correspondence. From Ransom Chase came lengthy reports of the advance upon Corinth as well as colorful descriptions of camp life, the routines of the soldiers in the field, and the inconclusive battle at Iuka. There were, of course, sympathetic comments about those "Tigers" who were still held in Southern prisons, as well as status reports about those who had fallen ill, and notices about men who had died of disease. Although he was not a critic of the army or the war effort, Chase took the Federal generals to task for their lack of military intelligence and initiative and lambasted the medical staff in Federal field hospitals. T. J. Davis adds to these views of common soldier life with a number of letters describing picket duty, field rations, and the ubiquitous sutlers, or merchants, who followed Civil War armies with goods to sell at inflated prices.

Both Davis and Chase were fascinated by the town and country scenes of the Corinth district and, whether on the march or camped in town, they took time to make note of the inhabitants, residences, crops, and regional vegetation. Chase, who received a promotion from the ranks to a lieutenancy during this period, is at his best describing an elderly Union sympathizer in one letter and, in another letter, narrating the circumstances of a runaway slave seeking protection in the camp of the 18th Wisconsin. Finally, both correspondents were eager to bring their Confederate foes to battle after the near disaster of Shiloh. The Confederate evacuation of Corinth settled nothing as far as the common Billy Yanks were concerned. They ached to test their martial skills in pitched battle and the reports from Chase and Davis after the Iuka fight only confirm the renewed confidence the men had in themselves and in their cause.

While Chase continued to entertain newspaper readers with his columns, Davis' frequent letters to his wife, Lucinda, carried reports of his good health, news about his comrades, and mention of neighbors in nearby regiments. There are frequent passages regarding family finances and, in one missive, Davis reassured Lucinda of her safety from the Indian depredations that were taking place in southwestern Minnesota. The Davis letters are not without occasional flashes of temper, though, as, in one letter, he denounced "a lot of wide-mouthed patriots" who had come down hard on a convalescent soldier in Viroqua. For the most part, however, Davis' letters show a calm, thoughtful man willing to do his part in putting down the rebellion but intent, as Davis tells, Lucinda, "to take it as easy as an old shoe until Uncle Sam gets through with me."

Appointment of Capt. Bouck[1]

The News expresses the opinion that Gov. Harvey, in appointing Capt. Bouck to the Colonelcy of the Eighteenth Regiment, did manifest injustice to Lt. Col. Beall of the same regiment, who, in accordance with the custom of promotion, was entitled to the place; and additionally entitled to it from the pluck and courage exhibited at the battle of Shiloh, in which he was wounded.

Our opinion in this matter is that the appointment of Capt. Bouck, whether made by the late Gov. Harvey[2] or Gov. Salomon, is justice to the State, the regiment and the service, and therefore can properly be considered injustice to no one. We have not a word of disparagement of Lt. Col. Beall's pluck and bravery. On the contrary, we believe in it to the fullest extent, but it is no disparagement of him—because in the circumstances it could not well be otherwise—to say that he is not proficient in what the Eighteenth Regiment now most needs and has needed, and that is a commander versed in military movements and of experience in military matters. When the greatest battle of modern days is pending and the fate of the nation is trembling in the balance, it is no time to sacrifice essentials to custom or compliment. Did Lieut. Col. Beall hold to us the dearest relation of any object on earth, we nevertheless should say that in this matter, the Governor acted well and wisely, and such, we have not a shadow of a doubt, is the universal conviction. We know Captain Bouck tolerably well and have seen him with his regiment and are satisfied in qualification, a better selection for the command of the Eighteenth regiment could not have been made.

The state authorities deserve and will have the thanks of the deeply interested people for the scrutiny which sought him, an the disregard of red tape that appointed him to the place.—Sentinel. [NW Times, May 7, 1862, p. 2]

---

1. Gabriel Bouck (1828–1904), descendant of a Dutch-New York family and the son of a former governor of the Empire State, had migrated to Wisconsin after finishing at the head of his Union College class in 1847. He completed his law studies in Milwaukee in 1849, then moved to Oshkosh where he founded a successful legal practice. He became active in Democratic politics and served a two-year term as Wisconsin's Attorney General, then was elected to a legislative seat in Madison. At the outbreak of the war, Bouck raised a company of infantry, The Oshkosh Volunteers, and was elected captain for his efforts. Designated as Company E, 2nd Wisconsin Infantry, the unit saw combat at the battle of First Manassas in July 1861. Under General John Gibbon, a strict Regular Army officer, Bouck had gained valuable instruction in drill and battlefield tactics after the bitter Manassas defeat. Although Bouck considered refusing the colonelcy of the 18th Wisconsin, Major Edward Bragg of the 6th Wisconsin said, "Bouck, don't be an infernal fool! Accept the commission. The war isn't over by a great deal and we'll both go home with stars on our shoulders." ["Oshkosh Northwestern" no date.]

2. Governor Harvey accidently drowned in the Tennessee River when he slipped while stepping from one army hospital boat to another on 19 April 1862. [Faust, p.348]

Pittsburg Landing May 8th, 1862

Dear Wife,

I again take my pen to write you a few lines. Received your letter yesterday morning dated April 28th which found me well and I was very glad to hear that you was in good health. You don't know how glad I was to receive a letter from you for that was the first one that I have received in answer to any letter I have wrote to you since I have been here. I have wrote four letters to you before this before this one since the battle.

We are now about 12 miles from Pittsburg Landing and about 8 miles from Corinth. We have been moving up slowly for nearly 2 weeks. We have moved five times so we are now within five or six miles from the enemies fortifications. We have two lines of breastworks thrown up this side of the enemies works.

You wanted to know if I had any money and that you would send me some if I was out. I am mutch obliged to you for your offer but I shall not need it. I have $2.50 left yet and we are mustered for pay again and I suppose we will get paid off again in a few days.[3] Then I shall have nearly fifty dollars, more than I shall need here.

I will tell you all the news about the boys that that I know of: Henry Clery is taken prisoner, said to be wounded in the arm. Will Clery is not hurt. We heard from our prisoners yesterday morning. They are in Memphis all well.[4] Captain Layne is there. They will perhaps be exchanged back before a great while. Alvin Caulkins, Walt and Ike Odell are all safe. Burdette Fletcher has been sent to the hospital. He has not been able for duty since he had the measels in Milwaukee. I think he will be discharged. E. Forsyth has been quite sick for some time but is gaining slowly. Robert McMichael is not able for duty yet on account of his eyes though they still gaining.

This ink is so thick that I can hardly write with it and I have to sit on the ground and write of my knees. I am mutch obliged to you for sending this paper and stamp though I have managed to get stamps and paper enough so far. The first letter I wrote you I was out of paper and used some leaves out of a book that I picked up. You wanted to know if I lost my clothes and things. The Sesesh got my overcoat, knapsack, haversack, canteen,

---

3. Pay for a Union private at the start of the war was $13 per month but was raised in 1864 to $16 per month exclusive of enlistment bonuses. Soldiers were to be paid every two months. [Boatner, Mark M. III, The Civil War Dictionary. New York, Vintage Books, 1991, p.624–625]
4. Memphis was held by Confederate troops until 6 June 1862. [Long, p.222–223]

and my quilt and blanket. But after the battle I made it all good again for there was all kinds of equipag left scattered on the battlefield.

I got a letter from my Sister in Illinois a few days ago. They was all well. She wanted me to let her know where to write to you. I wrote her your directions. I supose if she writes to you that you will answer it. When you write to her direct to Elisabeth Ditto, Keithsburg, Mercer County, Illinois.

I have found several of my old acquaintances in the army from Illinois together with two of my cousins.

Mr. Burnett is not very tough yet. His two cousins, Jim & Frank, are at home on a furlough. I dont know whether they are coming back or not. They are both in the 30th Illinois, the regiment here.

If you was only here a week and see the soldiers in every direction you would think there was no men left in the North at all. We are expecting everyday to have another fight with the Rebels. I hope we will clean them out and get back further north before the hot months come.

Perhaps if I was at home I might joke you a little about that furlough but I do not feel bad about it, only I would like to be at home with you.[5] I hope I shall be before fall. You must take care of yourself the best you can and take times easy. So good-bye for this time.

Thos. J. Davis

Near Corinth, Mississippi, May 22nd, 1862

Dear Wife,

I again endeavor to write you a few lines to let you know that I am still in the land of the living and injoying usual health and I hope this may find you well. I have not received but one letter from you in answer to letters that I have wrote to you since I have been here. That one was dated April 28th. I have wrote to you nearly every week since I have been here. I want you to write often whether you get any letters from me or not. Robert McMichael got a letter from his wife night before last and Alvin Caulkins got one from his folks and so did Walt Odell, but I didn't.

May 24th, 1862

I started this letter two days ago but I had to stop writing to go out on picket and did not get back until last night. We are within about three miles of Corinth. Our forces are building breastworks on the outside of the Rebels works. I think our generals are trying [to] run breastworks clear around Corinth and cut off all their railroads and then starve them

---

5. Davis is referring to the news of his wife's pregnancy, evidently the result of his furlough visit in February 1862.

out or make them attack us in our own fortifications. I [think] that we may manage to trap the whole caboodle of the[m] here without having to follow them any further north before the weather gets too hot.

There is a great number of the northern soldiers getting sick now.[6] Several of our company are in the hospital now. Walt and Ike Odell are both sick but not dangerous. Neither of them in hospital. Forsyth is not well yet. Levi Allen is in the hospital. So is Jim Williams and John Kingston. William Hunter died day before yesterday. I think that Burnett will go home before long. He has not been able for duty mutch of the time since we have been here.

We have not got paid off yet but I think we will be in a few days. If I get my money I will send the most of it home with Burnett if he goes and my watch, also. I don't want you to get uneasy about me getting sick for I intend to take as good care of myself as I can. Alvin Caulkins stands it first rate better than most of the men.

A fellow from 8th Wisconsin Regiment was over here yesterday.[7] He said Seal's son-in-law, Henry Allen, received a flesh wound in the side a few days ago in skirmish with the Rebel pickets. The wound is not dangerous. He said that the rest of the Badax boys in the 8th was all well. I have not had a chance to visit them yet.

We have not heard anything from our boys that was taken prisoners. Only we heard that they were all in Memphis where I supose they still remain under the guardianship of Rebeldom.

The vegitation here now looks like midsummer in the north. Peaches and apples are now about half grown and the orchards are well-loaded with them. If we only had such orchards in Illinois and Wisconsin then fruit would be cheap.

Ed Crandall got a letter from Cal Hagerman a few days ago. He wrote to all the Badax boys. He said that he heard that we was in the fight at Pittsburg Landing. He wanted the boys to write to him and tell him all about the fight.

I don't know as you can read this. I have a poor pen and I have to sit on the ground and write on my knee. Nothing more this time but be a good girl.

Thomas J. Davis

Please to write often.

---

6. In the hot, wet weeks following the Battle of Shiloh, thousands of Federal troops gathering near Pittsburg Landing suffered from dysentery. [OR, I-10-1-672]

7. The 8th Wisconsin Infantry was most notable for its mascot, "Old Abe," a young bald eagle carried in camp and battle on a special pole and tether by members of the regiment. [Faust, p.543–544]

[Untitled Item]

A private letter from Capt. Layne received last week confirms our prediction that he is a prisoner of war. He also states that Thos. Fretwell is with him a prisoner, likewise. The receipt of this letter brightened the countenances of his many friends, who feared he was dead. The letter states that 140 of the 18th are prisoners with him. At the time the letter was written (April 9) he was in Memphis but was about to be removed further South. They are all doubtless in Tuscaloosa, Alabama, at this time. [NW Times, May 28, 1862, p. 2]

Capt. N. M. Layne

Those who have fathers, sons, husbands, or brothers in the 18th regiment Wisconsin Volunteers, as well as all other people of this vicinity, are pleased to know that a letter was received here from Capt. N.M. Layne bearing date "May 27, 1862" written at Selma, Alabama, a small town about 50 or 60 miles west of Montgomery, the capital of that rebellious state where he and some 60 others are guarded in a tavern. He has not heard from the privates for seven weeks and he also states that Capt. Fisk is with him and are both well. He has sent a letter to Montgomery to the privates for them to bring with them when they should be paroled, but it has not yet arrived. He says all the privates were well when he last heard from them. He writes to his folks not to write anything *contraband* in their answer to this letter or that it will not reach him, this comes of course from the fact that the letters are overhauled and the contraband matter confiscated. Gen. Prentiss was with him.

This letter was brought to Washington by the delegation spoken of in the account taken from some paper and handed to us by Mr. Layne. This shows conclusively that the assertion made in the Captain's first letter written at Memphis that he was not captured until the evening was correct and corroborates the account that Gen. Prentiss did not surrender in the morning, but fought well until in the evening. We infer that Sergt. Thomas Fretwell is at Talledega, Alabama but know not. [Expositor, no date on clipping]

May 30th, 1862

Dear Wife,

I once more sit down to write you a few lines to let you know that I still live and enjoy tolerable good health and I hope this may find you well. We are camped within three miles of Corinth and have been here about two weeks, the longest time that we have been in one place since we came from Milwaukee. We have been slowly moving upon the Rebels for several weeks and fighting between theirs and our pickets has been going on every day for three or four weeks. There was considerable fighting yesterday and day before with both artillery and infantry. Yesterday the

Rebels begun to evacuate Corinth and this morning they blew up their magizines and all left the place. Our troops now occupy Corinth and the Union flag is floating over the place. The Rebels succeeded in getting away with the most of their property. They burned all the best buildings in town together with quite a quantity of artillery and and supply wagons, being determined to leave nothing that the Yankee can make use of or distroy. I wrote to you that we expected a big fight or a big fizzle. So they have fizzled out as I was afraid they would and compel us to follow them up. I am not mutch of a military man but it seems to me that if our generals had done their best they might [have] traped the Rebels here and not let them get away.

I have not been over to Corinth since the Sesesh left but there is boys coming in from there every few minutes. I think I will go over there tomorrow and see what kind of a nest the Rebels had over there. I don't know what our next move will be, whether we will chase the Rebels up or or take us back further north for the summer. This is getting to be a hard place for water. The spring rains are about over and the ground is fast drying up and all the water we get now we have to dig holes in ravines and it is poor and scarce at that. The inhabitants say this is a hard country to get water in dry weather.

I cannot promise you when I can come home. I will come when I can but I intend to take it as easy as an old shoe until Uncle Sam gets through with me.

I received a letter a few days ago from brother Isaac who is in the First Kansas Cavalry. He wrote that he was in the hospital in Leavenworth City awaiting his discharge on account of his lame leg which was crippled with the white swelling.

I also got a letter at the same time from sister Elisabeth from Illinois. She wrote they was all well.

About two weeks ago I got a letter from David and Nancy Ingersoll. They said they was all well and that little Charlie was well and was going to school. They got the five dollars that I sent to Charlie.

Walt Odell is in the hospittal. He is quite sick but he is getting better. We have 9 men in the hospittal out of our company besides quite a number that has been sent home. Forsyth is in the hospittal yet.

I received a letter from you dated April 28th and I have not received any letter from you since. I have anxiously been looking for a letter from you for three weeks, but in vain. I began to think that something was the matter with the mail or that you was sick. If you are sick get somebody to write for you. I have wrote to you regularly ever since I have been here. I wish you to write.

Allen Burnett has resigned on account of his health and will go home as soon as we get paid off.

News has just come into camp that part of General Pope's division have returned from chasing the Rebels bringing in seven thousand Sesesh prisoners.[8] It takes the last stamp I have to put on this letter. They don't keep any stamps at the post office here and we can't buy them. If I can't get any I will have to send them without stamps and let you pay the postage there.

T. J. Davis

Camp Near Corinth, Mississippi, June 2nd, 1862

Dear Wife,

I take great pleasure in sitting down to write to you again. I wrote a letter to you day before yesterday telling you that I had not received any letter from you so long that I was uneasy about you for fear that you was sick but night before last I received two letters from you which was truly welcom and I was very glad to hear that you was well. One of the letters was written the 18th & 19th of May, the other one the 11th which Mrs. Burnett mailed in Illinois. She wrote that she had arrived safe to her folks and that she found them all well. I thought I would write you this letter for fear you would be uneasy about me when you got the last one I wrote thinking perhaps that your letters did not get here.

We have signed our payroll today. The officers say [we] will be paid off tomorrow. The pay master and his body guard is here now.

Burnett will probably start home in a few days. He will stop in Illinois and go home with his wife. I will probably send you some money by him and my watch and I will send you them notes that I have on Baker, Whitney & Johnson least I should loose them.

The Rebels left Corinth on double quick badly panic-stricken and scared half to death. The Yankees had too many big guns for them. Corinth is quite a nice little place about half as large as LaCrosse.[9] The inhabitants have all left the place except for two families. They burned several buildings together with the depo and quite a quantity of provisions. Generals Pope, Buell, and Mitchel[10] are in hot pursuit of the Rebels. They

---

8. General John Pope commanded the Federal Army of the Mississippi that constituted one wing of General Henry W. Halleck's advance on Corinth. While Corinth was being occupied on 30 May 1862, Pope's troops pursued retreating Confederates to Booneville, Mississippi, where the 2nd Iowa Cavalry captured and paroled 2,700 Confederates and burned a supply depot and twenty-six-car supply train. [OR-I-10-pt.1, p.861–864]

9. La Crosse, Wisconsin, had a population of 3,860 in 1860. [Andriot]

10. General Ormsby M. Mitchel commanded the 3rd Division in the Army of the Ohio under General Buell. [Boatner, p.557]

have overtaken part of them and taken some prisoners, but I don't know how many. I have seen several squads of them brought in. Our division has not been called out to pursue the Rebels yet. We had orders today to prepare ourselves for a long march but whether we are going on south or not I cannot tell. I am inclined to think that is the calculation.

This is the 2nd day of June and the weather is getting some warmer but it is not so hot here as I thought it would be though this is a great fruit country. Peaches are nearly grown and will be ripe by the first of July. Plums and cherries are ripe and wheatfields begin to look yellow and will be ripe in a few days.

You say Mrs. Cleary is nearly crazy about Henry. He is taken prisoner and is at Memphis with the other prisoners that was taken and he will be compelled to stay there untill we lick the Rebels or they are exchanged for their prisoners in our hands. She might just as well keep cool about it as to go crazy. His life is perhaps just as safe as if he was in our army.

This paper is so greasy the ink will hardly stick to it . I dont know as you can read it. If you can't let me know and I will write you another one.

We have not had mutch rain here for two or three week. It has been trying to rain today but it can't rain so easy as it could a month ago.

Walt Odell is getting a little better but he is quite sick yet. Ike Odell is slowly getting well again. I hear that E. Forsyth is getting better. He is at the hospital about ten miles back. Levi Allen was sent away in a boat a week ago to some hospital. He may get sent home. Alvin Caulkins is as fat as a bear, John Kingston was in the hospital a couple of weeks but he has got about well and has come back to the regiment again. Bill Downie is in the hospital with a sprained ankle.

I am tired writing on this greasy paper so I will close for this time. Write soon. Direct your letters as you did before. Be a good girl and take care of yourself and don't get the blues. Tell Mrs Mc. that Robert is well and makes quite a good soger. So nothing else to add this time.

                                                      Thos. J. Davis

I will have to send this without a stamp as I cannot buy any here. There is none to be had.

                              For the Times
                    from the Eighteenth Regiment

Camp before Corinth
June 2, 1862

Mr. Editor: Amid the various shiftings of encampments, the duties of soldiers in the presence of the enemy, the engrossing excitement attendant upon picket and fatigue duty, and the unimportant, exciting rumors with which the camp is visited, I have been derelict of doing that justice to the Times which it deserves.

That I might chronicle the taking of the rebel army at Corinth in my next, was my earnest and a part cause of my long delay, but as the bird has flown and we have the mortification of surveying our gigantic operations, the splendid lines of breastworks constructed for our safety, and well made roads and bridges for the advance of our batteries, and have to come finally to the mortifying conclusion that Beauregard has out-generaled us again, I despair of having the pleasure of announcing a decisive victory for a long time.

Since the battle, the melancholy results of which, as concerns the Tigers, were stated in my last, our regiment has made seven regular advances, the last one, May 17th, bringing us to our present encampment, three miles from Corinth.

At our first camp were left a number of the boys quite sick, under the care of our fellow soldier, Hiram Moody, who has proven to be an excellent nurse, where they remained a number of days, when they were sent down the river to some place or places unknown. No, I erred: They were not all sent: William Starbuck will never be nursed in an Army Hospital. Our comrade lies buried upon the battlefield of Pittsburg Landing near the line of battle which he, in common with his comrades, helped so manfully to maintain on the eventful morning of the 6th of April. His was not the lot to die amid the storm of leaden hail, the roar of cannon, the rattle of musketry, and the explosion of bursting shells, nor to expire of honorable wounds received on the battle field. Such a death we are led to believe a glorious consummation of a patriot soldier's life, one if not to be desired, certainly not to be lamented. But to waste away by disease in the citadel and death at the door, away from the care of dear relatives or warm friends, is to a soldier a gloomy closing up forever of the ledger of life and a sad breaking of the golden chain of existence. His case was not considered dangerous when the regiment marched away; yet, so sudden did his illness change and end fatally that three days after, the 27th of April, he breathed his last. The immediate cause of death was typhoid fever.

The day following his decease, the remaining sick were transferred to hospital steamers and sent down the river. Among the number was Lawrence H. Page, one of the best of our company, physically as well as in every other respect; but who, weakened with the diarrhoea incident to the climate, was one of those unfortunates attacked with typhoid fever, which taken in connection with a long standing of the former disease, generally proves, in this climate, fatal. We received officially from the surgeon in charge a statement of his decease which occurred aboard hospital steamer "Imperial", May 4th, which was the first intimation we had of his death. Quiet and unassuming in manner, never officious or proud, he was respected no less for those qualities than for those which make up the mortal wreath with which every honest man is crowned, and of which our friend had undisputed and just possession.

Following this came the death of Samuel Fish, one wounded comrade mentioned in my last letter who was sent away on the boat, has also gone to explore the unknown coast upon whose waters the martyr sails but will not return. This has all occurred since leaving Viroqua.

First came Sergeant Swan, then Norris W. Saxton and W. Kittle whose lives are given in defense of the constitution upon Pittsburg's bloody field; then Starbuck, Page, and Fish in quick succession, all good men and true. While musing over the circumstances of their death, we feel that we can say in spirit, as well as repeat the words of the poet:

"Soldier rest! Thy warfare o'er,
Sleep the sleep that knows not breaking;
Dream of battle fields no more,
Days of danger, nights of waking."

While at the second encampment where we stopped ten days, nothing of interest occurred except the marching of our Division ten miles one afternoon through swamps and over hills in the futile attempt to capture a regiment or two of Secesh who were encamped in a ravine, but who, while we were waiting a mile distant for morning, left, and we, much chagrined and exhausted, were marched back to camp after our profitable explorations.

At the next advance, three more of the Tigers were left sick at the Division Hospital which had been established half a mile from our camp.

Advance third took us four miles further and left us in a very pleasant location, which, as usually happens when we have such a one, we left after a short stay of three days. Here we once formed the battalion in the expectation of hurrying forward to support our forces engaged a few miles ahead in driving the enemy's lines and who, judging from the cannonading, were having a warm time of it. But the enemy retreated and we ordered to be dismissed. Five or six more Tigers were left behind at this place quite sick and sent back to the Division Hospital.

Advance fourth lodged us in a thick growth of young timber, in a marshy sort of a place, made worse by heavy rains, four miles further towards Corinth and a half mile from Monterey, a village of three or four log houses, to which we were exceedingly glad to say farewell in the short space of three days, and taking up the line of march to rest in a more comfortable place two and a half miles further on.

This was advance fifth. Before us were breastworks, the extent of which we could not determine, made in a strong and almost impregnable manner, by the sharpening of poles and imbedding them with point outward in the dirt, and timber composing the main portion of the works. They could never be taken at a charge bayonets.

Our new Colonel joined us here on the 10th of May and though his personal appearance struck us as anything but favorable, yet a better knowledge of the man convinced the boys that a better selection could not have been made. Well drilled, he exacts strict discipline while on duty but is mindful also that the commissioned officers attend to their business and do justice to the men, a matter that has been too much overlooked heretofore. He is popular and appreciated as a good tactician.

At advance sixth, we marched three miles and encamped, as we thought, for the last time before the expected battle. Anticipating, as we did, that the engagement would take place in a few days, the whole regiment went out on picket once while here, but did not have any brush with the enemy.

Advance seventh brought us here, or rather what was left of us, as at every advance some of our number were sent to the Division Hospital by the surgeon.

Since May 17, we have been in camp or on fatigue and picket duty, waiting for the great fight to commence—the fight which was to effectually crush Secession in the Southwest and reestablish the authority of the National Government—the fight which was to eclipse by its brilliant success all other victories achieved during the war, and cheer alike patriots at home and in the army.

It was delayed when delay seemed, unless some great reinforcement was expected, not only impolitic but detrimental to our success. We had established a complete continuous line of breastworks, on an average 3.5 miles from Corinth, in the shape of a horse shoe, and an inside straight line cutting of the bow of the figure. We were well established , and in case of an attack and repulse would be secure from pursuit and could arrange for another attack at leisure.

We went on picket on the 28th and were placed in the advance where we could see the fellows dressed in butternut and might, were it not an infringement of our orders not to fire unless fired upon, have picked off some quite easily. We saw one fellow climb a tree, the better to inspect our position.

There was brisk firing and some cannonading immediately on our right during the afternoon and quite hard fighting within half a mile on our left, and we expected that the 18th was certainly engaged for the next ball as a number of regiments were at one time deployed in plain sight in an open field immediately in front; but they marched off and we remained unmolested. The next morning the firing continued but more feebly and we returned to camp receiving orders to sleep while we could and be ready at a moments warning to march; but there was a cessation during the latter part of the day and at night everything was quiet.

Early the next morning several dull, heavy rumbling reports in the direction of Corinth indicated that something unusual was being enacted at that place and much to our surprise, and I may say much to our disappointment, the report came soon that the enemy had evacuated the place and the strange sound was the report caused by the blowing up of their magazines, which were confirmed by subsequent news.

So we are again behind, owing to a lack of information of the movements of the enemy, who, it appears, had been evacuating the place for four days and their attack was only to cover their retreat and make a semblance of strength.

There is a fault somewhere and it cannot and ought not to be concealed. Army movements do not seem to indicate that our generals have any knowledge of the numbers, disposition, and intentions of the enemy, while they are kept posted of our every movement and have an accurate knowledge of the number of our forces and the number and size of our batteries through the medium of spies who assume our uniforms—sometimes a private's but generally officers'—and pass our lines at pleasure. One of these was taken prisoner while at Camp No. 2 by Melvin Brayman, of De Soto, a member of Company K, formerly of the Tigers, whose suspicion was excited by being questioned as to the name, number of men, etc., of the regiment, the number of the brigade and division, and on following him, saw him take notes when he thought himself unobserved. He proved, as his notes showed, to have commenced at the river and passing through the whole of Pope's army, obtained the number composing each regiment, their position, and all useful information desirable.

Some of the boys were at Corinth the day following the evacuation and they report that in size it is three times as large as Viroqua, containing quite a number of fine blocks; they say also that some of the best were burned and that large piles of equipage of all kinds and fire arms, wagons, provisions were promiscuously piles and burned. Those in the rear appear to have been panic stricken and left very much in a hurry. The boys brought back a number of little trinkets to keep as mementos of their visit, which though not of much value, will be prized for the curiosity which they will attract at home.

Pope and Buell are in pursuit of the enemy, but whatever success they may have will be trifling in comparison to that which might have crowned our arms had an attack been made before a total evacuation.

Conjectures are rife as to the destination of our regiment. Previous to the evacuation and while in expectation of a general engagement, it was said to have come from high officers that the 18th would be sent after the battle to some point north to guard prisoners or to recruit in health and numbers, and the boys are very naturally on the que vive for indications that may settle the general curiosity; but if anything is known to the Colonel it is strictly kept from the men. The inclination of the boys may be stated to be towards some northern point, as the regiment does certainly require some addition to its numbers and be in a better sanitary condition to fit it for much further effective duty. Reduced in disease and loss in battle more than any other regiment in the same length of time in the whole service, and numbering less than two hundred men fit and reported for duty, it would seem that some other disposition should be made of the remaining, some of whom are also very weak, besides inflicting the fatigue of long marches of which we, as yet, have had little to do. Time will show.

Many of our company, we are advised by late letters, have arrived at home, being sent by the proper medical authority, either to stay permanently or on a sick furlough, and others we hear are on their way. Allow me to say to the citizens that they merit a warm reception and should receive the sympathy which unfortunate men in the service of their country have a moral right to demand of those whose property and interest they left the comfort of home to protect. Let no one take upon himself to criticize the action of the Medical Department in this respect and by saying that such a one "looks pretty well" insinuate that he has no business there. Why has he no business there? Because he was more patriotic than you and became sick through exposure? Out upon such a sentiment, yet, Mr. Editor, it exists—it has insulted those who have been home previously on sick furloughs and is exhibited the most by those who prate the loudest of their patriotism and show it by staying closely at home. I assure you that society is all wrong in this respect and should receive that condemnation requisite to inaugurate a more humane feeling. If anyone is heard saying that the sickness with which one of our men suffers is shammed, let him be confronted with the demand for his own immediate enlistment or the closing up of his libelous throat. Let such a man's patriotism be impeached rather than a lisp be heard derogatory to the conduct of a man who has shown himself the possessor of it by the act of his enlistment. May those I have mentioned receive as good treatment and recover their health as speedily as the remaining Tigers most earnestly wish.

I am finishing this communication by the light of a candle fastened in a bayonet seated at the roots of an oak in front of our encampment and, as you may conjecture, am surrounded by quite a variety of sights and sounds. The bands have just played retreat. More than fifty bands have been playing; from those near by where every tune could be discerned to the distant ones hardly audible, all was music—each, in itself harmonious, yet as a whole discordant. Immediately in front is the band of the 15th Michigan, which, each day, has not failed to discourse the sweetest of music, just ceased playing "The Marsallaise Hymn". But though the music has ceased, the noise has not. Horses are neighing, mules braying, dogs barking, guards crying, "Halt, who goes there"—men in one of the tents near by are singing some piece of sacred music—from another sounds forth a new ditty ("Dixie" is not heard here now)—and a hearty laugh compliments the abilities of a story teller in another, and I know that others by and by are about to shuffle off this mortal coil and be at rest. A strange but common medley and a most solemn commentary upon human life.

Such a scene is presented only at this time of evening when the soldier is about retiring for the night; but it is one which once seen will never be forgotten. Every tent present now a cheerful illumination, but in a few minutes "Taps" will be beat and the scene be changed as by enchantment—light will become darkness—an uproar, quiet, and the stillness of the wilderness will brood over the encampment. Such a scene naturally inspires—but "Taps" is being beaten and with the blowing out of my candle, I must reluctantly close this communication and remain, Truly Yours, C. [NW Times, June 25, 1862, p. 2]

[Untitled Item]

[Our townsman Merrill, who has been in painful anxiety about his son who was reported "missing" from the 18th Reg't at the battle of Shiloh , was quite naturally much releaved and gratified by the reception of the following letter. A soldier like John is worth his weight in gold to the government. After all he has endured, he very quietly "would like to give them another try."]

Nashville, Tenn., June 5, '62

Dear Folks, At last I have a chance to write and let you know that I am in the land of the living and am still able to move around slowly; but I look more like a shadow that anything else.

Our regiment was in the battle of Shiloh on the 6th of April and your humble servant was taken prisoner after about ten hours of the hardest fighting there has been done in the present war.

We stopped at Pittsburg Landing on Saturday and marched out to our camping ground, about three miles, and got there near sun down; did not get our tents pitched that night; I was out on picket duty all night; got into camp about daylight and laid down to sleep when the order came to "fall in with guns and cartrage boxes!" and the regiment has scarcely time to get into line when the firing commenced on our right with all the fury imaginable, and the enemy kept flanking to the left, and we were soon engaged with the butternut coats bearing the secesh flag. The reg't on our right gave way and rebs flanked us on the left, and poured in a most destructive fire on two sides, when we saw it would be foolish to stay until we were all killed, and were ordered to retreat. We retreated about a half a mile and about 200 of us rallied and reformed in line and again went into the thickest of the fight where the bullets came like hail. The secesh charged on us three times with fresh troops, but we drove them back with great slaughter; we held them in check until about five o'clock when we were surrounded on all sides and compelled to lay down our arms and surrender as prisoners of war.

They marched us off about five miles that night and we lay in an old cornfield without blankets or shelter in the mud and rained at that. They gave us one cracker to eat and marched us to Corinth about twenty miles through the mud, then put us aboard some cattle cars where the mud was about two inches thick, fifty-five in a car at that. We went to Memphis and to Jackson, Miss., down to Mobile, Ala., from there to our prison at Tuscaloosa where we received all the barbarous treatment that you could think of, besides lots you never dreamed of.

But enough of this. I am out of their hellish clutches now and I don't believe they will get me as a prisoner again. I have not been sick a day since I have been in the service. There has been lots of sickness among the prisoners; many have died, but I have been lucky and I begin to think I am a tough cuss!

I don't know what they are going to do with us; some say we are going to be discharged. We took the parole to save our lives as it looks hard to see men die for the want of something to eat. It looks tough to see men shot in battle but harder yet to see them pine away and die by inches.

I have not heard a word from any one of "yees" since I left.

We don't know how long we shall stay here or where we shall go; but I have got so used to being jagged around that I don't mind it much. When we stop and find out what is going to be done with us, I will write and let you know all about it. We have heard all sorts of stories about our reg't on the battlefield; lots of our boys ran after we were ordered to fall back; they left for the river and left us to fight all day against overwhelming odds.

I don't think of much to write; just write to let you know that the secesh didn't scare me very bad; would like to give them one more try. J.B. Merrill. [Expositor, no date on clipping]

Near Corinth, Mississippi, June 8th, 1862

Dear Wife

I again take pen in hand to write to you once more I am as well as usual and I hope this will find you in good health. I received your letter last night dated May 25th & 26th and was very glad to hear from you again and to hear that you was well.

We have moved about five miles since I last wrote to you. We are about one and a half miles south of Corinth on the Jackson Road. I don't know how long we will remain here. We may stay near Corinth 2 months and again may not stay a week. Corinth is quite a pleasant looking village but the most of the houses are built in old-fashioned style. The town is nearly entirely deserted by its inhabitants and the buildings are used for hospital purposes by our forces. The Rebels destroyed quite a quantity of their commissary supplies and supply wagons and several buildings before leaving Corinth. Rebel tents and camp kettles and barrels of beef and beans were broken open and scattered over the ground in large quantities. I suppose they left here in somewhat of a hurry and did not have transportation to carry all their traps away.

There is two railroads here, the Memphis and Charleston and the Mobile & Columbus. They cross each other here at Corinth. A little over a week ago we could distinctly hear the cars hooting as they were running under the control and for the use of the Rebel army.[11] But now we have possession of the road and have captured some cars which our forces are running on the roads. I do not know how far each way the roads are in order to run. The whistling of the cars seems to have a different sound since they are under the control of Yankee interprise.

Sutlers[12] and huxters carry on quite a business here in the army and at an enormous profit. I will give you a list of the prices of some of the articles that are sold here: soda crackers, 23 cents per lb; cheese, 30 cents; butter, 30 cents; eggs, 30 cents per dozen; lemons & oranges, 15 cents each;

---

11. During the Corinth evacuation, Confederates ran locomotives in and out of the city sounding their whistles in order to deceive the Federals as to their intentions. [Ambrose, Stephen E., Halleck, Lincoln's Chief of Staff. Baton Rouge, Louisiana State University Press, 1990, p.52–53]

12. Sutlers were merchants who were allowed to accompany troops in order to sell food, drink, and articles not supplied by the government. The Articles of War prescribed that items be sold "at a reasonable price." [Boatner, p.822]

pickles, 1.00 per bottle—worth 25 cents retail in LaCrosse—though I am happy to say that I do not have occasion to pattonise these swindling institutions to mutch extent.

Walter is back behind in the hospital quite sick. I have not seen him for four days. Ike has not got well, yet. He has been quite puny for several weeks. I will send the letter to Walt as soon as I have a chance perhaps today. I think the boys stand this climate now better than they did a month ago. But there is considerable sickness in the army now. A great many are too careless about taking care of their health. I could be sick enough to go to the hospital in a week if I should try but I take care of my health. I am temperate both in eating and drinking, especially drinking, from the fact that whiskey is worth a dollar and a half per quart done up in bottles and I am sorry to say that large numbers buy it at that price. But I never seen so many men together where so few get drunk.

Alvin Caulkins & Bill Cleary both got a letter last night. Robert McMichael got a letter from his duck, also. Alvin is still tough and rugged, Bill Cleary has got the yellow jaunders though he is not much sick . Ed. Crandall has been on the sick list for about a week but he is able for duty again now.

The paper and stamp you sent came verry acceptable as I am out of stamps and can't get any for love or money.

I am going to write write a half sheet to Mary Caulkins you can hand it to her.

T. J. Davis

For the Times
from the Eighteenth Regiment

Camp Beyond Corinth, Miss.
June 14, 1862

Mr. Editor: Such long intervals have occurred between my letters that my communications have almost necessarily been constituted of the mere outline of the most important changes, advances, and events transpiring in and about our company while the more minute matters and not the less interesting have passed by unnoticed.

I propose to make this one a medley of the little and the great, the interesting and some that may not prove so.

The question is often asked, "How do you soldiers pass away the time?" No answer can be given to this question which will apply at all times as our duties are dependent upon our situation. But while in camp, a certain routine of duty is observed. Our new Colonel is very particular that each specified duty is performed at its alloted hour. The first thing that awakes the slumber of the soldier is the beating of the "Reveille," at five in the morning during which he must be out and in the ranks and ready to answer to his name when the drums have ceased. Then comes the raising up of the tents to air, the shaking and hanging out of the blankets, the sweeping out of the tents and streets, and washing up for breakfast, which is at six. I might interpolate here that we have two men detailed from the company for the purpose of cooking.

At seven the Surgeon's Call is beaten, at which time all those who are unwell and wish to be excused from duty during the day must be marched up by the first sergeant to the surgeon's tent for examination and prescription. Of course, many are ordered to duty who are not really able and some excused who ought not to be,—all depending upon the will or caprice of the surgeon, from whose decision there can be no variance unless a special application is made to the Colonel and he sees fit to grant it.

Dr. Huntington, the "Chief Cook and Bottle Washer" of the Medical Department is not appreciated by the men as one suited to the post.

First Assistant Surgeon, Dr. Buck and Hospital Steward Mr. Alexander are men who labor assiduously for what they conceive the best for the health of the Regiment.

It is sad to witness the patients, some of whom have possessed iron constitutions, come tottering up and lay down on the ground awaiting their turn, and when it comes, rise with difficulty and narrate their complaints and their feelings. Some have one disease and some another, but nine-tenths of all can be traced to that parent of ill health here, indigestion. The water and lack of variety of food have something to do in causing this but the chief cause is, I think, the use of what is called "hard bread." They made some sick at first who are now accustomed to them while others cannot even now take them into the stomach without nausea. Dr. Buck assured your correspondent that nearly all the cases which have come under his treatment were attributed to this cause. Diarrhoea, cholic, and fevers are the fruits

Guard Mounting takes place at eight at which time the men detailed for guard duty relieve those who went on the day previous. This is not uninteresting to a casual observer. The call for "Company Drill" is beaten at nine o'clock and each company must appear on parade and drill one hour. Dinner only intervenes between drill and the forming of the battalion, at five p.m., for Battalion Drill which occupies two hours. Dress Parade immediately follows.

Supper is usually dispatched before drill but it frequently happens that the call finds the men about, engaging in that quite necessary occupation, when, of course, the claims of nature have to succumb to the command of the Colonel. But little time remains till the beating of Retreat, when everybody is expected to go to bed. Fifteen minutes later, Taps say that lights must be out and quiet reign supreme. These are the certain duties and their order while in camp; but besides these, we have every Sabbath morning our inspection, much garrison duty to perform at every change of encampment, picket duty to do, and before the evacuation, fatigue duty. Our rifles, also, must be kept bright and our accoutrements in order. These and some others occupy one's time and leaves him little time for idle musing. He is expected, also, to write home very often and to friends.

There is one feature of our camp life that, among others, would do your readers good to witness. It is the eagerness and deep concern manifested by the boys when the mail arrives. It is first taken to the chaplain's tent for distribution to the first sergeant of each company, who in turn distribute to their men. Near the chaplain's tent the boys gather as soon as word is passed around that the mail has arrived, all eager to see "if there is much mail." Then you may hear someone say, perhaps, "Company F takes it all" in such a disappointed tone that, should your reader, Mr. Editor, hear it, I am sure that Company C would be pleased with the reception of more letters. Then to crowd around the orderly when the letters are being called and hear the satisfied, yes—triumphant tone with which they say "here" and receive their latter. The mail is always a welcome visitor and never did a child express more concern at the prospect of receiving a toy from an absent parent than do the boys at the contents of the mailbag for the Eighteenth.

Here let me say to the friends of the Tigers, generally, that cheerful and frequent writing is the best way to testify to their remembrance. (You cannot write too often.)

Our encampment is in a beautiful grove of timber nearly two miles southwest of Corinth through which place we marched June 6th, and is surrounded with a number of fine plantations, now mostly in the possession of the returned inhabitants. The country becomes better as we advance. It occurred to the boys that such a poor soil as bordered upon the Tennessee was not worth contending for; but exclamations are now frequently heard, "give me a farm here and let cold Wisconsin be to those who like it." The peculiar pride of habitation is fast going away before a more genial clime and it can scarcely be wondered at as we now see large apples and peaches, ripe blackberries, and all kinds of plumbs in abundance. I saw a new potato yesterday as large as my fist. All vegetation is proportionably mature. The soil is excellent, much unlike that near the Landing. I must say that the people do not make a proper use of all these facilities of successful agriculture. But notwithstanding, they plow with a small shovel corn plough and one horse, they make money, have good and tasty residences; in short, in spite of their negligence and ignorance of any system of farming, they are prosperous—something which the soil and climate give in spite of their opposition. But the tasteful array of shrubbery and the general neatness about their residences would furnish a model for Northern imitation.

As we advance the country is more beautiful. I confess to having a very poor estimate of Southern enterprise, when viewing the few scattering log houses near the Landing; that estimate has undergone some change since, but even now it is far below the common in the North. I may be compelled, as we advance, to write more favorably yet. On the march we saw men harvesting wheat, and for the moment, thought the Fourth of July had been and gone two weeks before. It is not very stout, as they never sow, the inhabitants tell us, more than one-half bushel of seed to the acre. Such farming!

Before I close this communication, I must refer to a subject which forget-fulness alone has previously prevented, viz; the sending of articles to the sick in the army. It has been and is now considered a meritorious act to send deli-cacies through the Sanitary Commission to the invalids. I speak the unanimous sentiments of the Eighteenth when I say—"send nothing!" The sick soldier does not get it. Of all that was stated in the Wisconsin papers to have been left for the regiment, I have yet to learn of the distribution of any to the sick. What is done with it? It is difficult to state where all of it goes; but some that passes into the hands of the surgeons and hospital attaches never pass anywhere else but down their throats. Fine shirts and other things that minister to the outward comfort may be sent; but preserves, wines, and delicacies are more than thrown away, as they serve to please the palates of those who steal from the sick soldiers.

Our company retains the number of men mentioned in my last. Two have gone to the hospital and one, Azariah Brown, of Viroqua, has been discharged. Three here returned quite well from the Division Hospital viz: William Downie, Robert Graham, and John Kingston. Brown was the first man in Company C discharged by the certificate of the surgeon of the regiment on account of ill-ness.

We remain in complete ignorance of passing events and of our destination. I will make you advised of any change in our location. Truly yours, C. [NW Times, July 9, 1862, p. 1]

Corinth Mississippi, June 15th 1862

Dear Wife,

I again sit down to endeavor to write you a few lines to let you know that I am well and I hope this may find you the same. I received a letter from you night before last. I was glad to hear that you was well. I did not expect a letter quite so soon. Your letters begin to come regularly for the last three weeks. Before that I did not get a letter from you for over three weeks.

We are still camped at the same place we was when I wrote you last. That is, about a mile-and-a-half-south of Corinth. This is the 3rd letter I have wrote to you since the evacuation of Corinth by the Rebels. We now hold peacable possession of Corinth and the Rebels have all cleared out. Some say that part of them have gone to Richmond, Virginia, and part to Jackson Mississippi. I think that we will be kept here in Mississippi this summer to guard the railroads even if we don't have any fighting to do, though it is hard for us to tell what we will be used for. We do not know half as mutch about the war here as the citizens do in Wisconsin. For the most we find out about the war we read in the papers after they are a week old with the exception of what happens in our own army.

The weather has been quite warm here for the past week. The weather has been verry dry here for three or four weeks and water is getting verry scarce. We have to dig wells for all the water we get. The small streams here have nearly all gone dry.

I was glad to hear that you had got your state money. We was paid off last week. Burnett is going to start home now in a day or two. I think I shall send forty dollars home with him. I think you had better deposit what money you have and what I send you in the county treasurer's office at Viroqua with James Lowne, with the exception of what you want to keep for present use and take a receipt of deposit for it in your own name so that you can draw on it as mutch as you want at any time. I would not loan money to any person as times are hard and even good persons are uncertain and it is uncertain when I may be at home and will want to use it. If we are prudent and saving we may have something to start with when I get back though I do not wish you to want for anything nesessary. This is merely a caution for I know that there are plenty persons who would tease you to borrow money if they knew you had it. You have been very prudent so far and never so mutch as asked me for a dollar which is verry common for women in general.

Monday, June 16th, 1862

Well, as you sent me two sheets of paper I supose you meant for me to write on both of them and send them back. That does not take me long after I commence.

Walter Odell is still sick in the hospital and I have not heard from him since he was taken there. Ike is getting better. Ike has spent about all of his money and he has not been paid a week yet. Several of our boys was sent away to St. Louis or some other place to a hospital last week. E. Forsyth and Jim Williams was among the number. Bill Downie has got well and has come back to the regiment again. Bill Cleary has got about well of the jaunders again so you can tell Mary that she need not be uneasy about him.

I received another letter from Illinois, the same time I received your last one. It [was] from David Ingersoll. She wrote that they was all well. He said that little Charlie was blowing the fife while he was writing.[13]

This is another hot day the sun beams down through these tents so hot in the middle of the day that we sit around under the shade of the trees where it is more cool.

---

13. Charles Davis was T. J. Davis' son by his first wife, the late Esther Delilah Ingersoll. Charlie lived in Warren County, Illinois, with Delilah's brother and sister-in-law, David and Nancy Ingersoll. [Davis family papers]

We go out on picket about every week. We was on picket a week ago yesterday and I expect we will go out again in a day or two. The way we do on pickett, several regiments go out at a time and three men are put on a post or generally at a tree some thirty paces apart. One man on a post stands sentinal at a time. They relieve each other every two hours. Each man stands two hours and off four. When we start out we take one days rations in our haversacks consisting of ham and bread or hard crackers whichever we may have at the time. We tie up some ground coffee and put in our haversacks. When we want to eat our grub we build up a fire and take our tin cups and boil some water and make coffee and broil our ham. So we live as woodchucks and when we want to go to sleep, if it is raining or damp weather we bend down a bush and stretch our rubber blankets over it and thus have a waterproof tent.

This forenoon John Greenman and Henry Allen of Springville come over to our camp from the 8th Regiment. Hank got wounded on the 9th of May but the wound is about well now and he looks hearty.[14] John Greenman is also hearty. They say that the boys are generally in good health with the exception of Jim Berry of Springville. They say he has been unwell for sometime and that he has resigned and is going home soon. George Esler just landed here today from Milwaukee. He has been there in the hospital ever since we left. Then untill now he has been sick for a long time but he begins to look quite well again.

This is Monday afternoon and we are having quite a nice little shower of rain. But I am afraid we will not have enough of it. We should have a good rain for it has been sometime since we have had any rain before. I am getting pretty well climated to this country now. For the first month or more after I came here the climate did not verry well agree with me but now the boys say I am getting as fat as a bear and I know that I feel mutch better. I will tell you how I do to keep healthy. I am careful not to eat anything that does not agree with me and I don't drink mutch bad whiskey. I take my regular sleep and I exercise some every day by walking around if I don't have duty enough to exercise otherwise. I bathe or wash myself all over two or three times a week and keep my underclothes clean.[15]

Write soon. So good-bye, be a good girl till I see you.

T. J. Davis

14. The action on 9 May 1862 was an attack at Farmington, Mississippi, on units of Pope's Federal Army of the Mississippi by Ruggles' Division of the Army of Tennessee. [OR-I-10-pt.1-p.804, 808–810]

15. Davis' emphasis on hygiene and exercise was the exception to the rule. Many soldiers, Union and Confederate, knew little and cared less about personal hygiene and exercise habits. [Adams, George Worthington, Doctors in Blue. Baton Rouge, Louisiana State University Press, 1996, p.17–19]

Corinth, Mississippi, June 23rd, 1862

Dear Wife,

I again sit down to write you a few lines by way of answering your letter dated June 8th which I received last week. It found me well. I hope this will find you in good health. I received 4 other letters the same time. I received yours, two of them was from sister Elisabeth, and one was from brother Isaac. The other was from brother William. Isaac is still in the hospital in Leavenworth, Kansas. He wrote that he expected to get his discharge soon on account of his lame leg. [Brother] William is down here at Corinth or near it. I did not know he was here until I got his letter. He is about four miles from where we are camped. I got a pass from the colonel day before yesterday and went to see him. He is well and hearty. I had not seen him for nearly three years.

We are camped in the same place we was when I wrote you last. The weather is quite warm here in the daytime but the nights are cool and nice so that a person can sleep comfortable.

Elisabeth wrote that all of our folks in Illinois was well. She wrote to me sometime ago for me to tell you to write to her. I wrote back to her and told her to write to you first and I would insure you to answer her letters. She has not said anything about it in her letters lately.

Mr. Bixby has been sick for sometime and was sent away on a boat to some one of the general hospitals some two or three weeks ago. Elijah Forsyth was very sick when he was taken away from here to the general hospital. The doctors said he had a hard chance to recover. I have not heard from Walt Odell since I wrote to you before. What there is left of our company at the present are in good health. We have now 13 men in our company and they have all been reported well for three or four days. We have not made out a morning report without having more or less sick since I come back to Millwaukee from my furlough untill now. I hope the soldiers will remain healthy; those that are now well, at least. For I am tired of seeing walking ghosts in the army. Care and temperance in diet is verry esential for the health of the soldiers here.

Mr. Burnett started home last Friday morning. He will stop in Illinois and go up home with his wife. I sent that note with him that I have on Johnson, Baker, & Whitney. I also sent my carpet sack and my watch and forty dollars in money.

I am obliged for the paper and stamp you sent me though you need not send anymore paper for I can get plenty of that here now. There is all kinds of predictions afloat here in reference to the probable duration of the war. Some think that the war will be over in thirty days, some say peace will be declared in sixty days, and some think the war will continue three years.

My paper is out and I must close. So good-bye, Sis. Write soon.

T. J. Davis

Camp No, 9 Southern Confederacy
Corinth, Mississippi, June 26th, 1862

Dear Wife,

I received your letter last night dated June 15 was glad to hear that you was well. I am in very good health and I hope your health may continue as good as you say it has been this spring and summer. I have nothing of great importance to write to you this time. I started a letter to you four or five days ago. I could write considerable in this but the mail is going to start to the river in about an hour and I want to get this letter in the mail.

We are still in the same camp yet that I wrote you from last. The weather down here is becoming quite warm. You said when you wrote your letter that the weather was cold enough to snow. I would like to have such weather mixed up with the weather that we have here. It has not been verry warm here until a week or ten days since, though we do not have mutch work to do while it is so warm. It has not been so warm that we suffer from heat yet.

Mrs. McMichael writes to Robert that my letters are behind his in date in reaching you. I do not know the reason unless they have been overlaid in the mails by some means for I think I have been just as punctual in writing as he has. Robert is writing to his sweetheart as I write and we will mail them together and see how they will come out.

You wrote that you were afraid that we would be taken further down south this summer. I do not think that we will be taken any further south in the hot months. I am of the opinion that we will be kept here for sometime to come to do guard duty around Corinth. I am getting tough so that I can stand the hot weather quite well. you said you wanted me to send you a Sesesh for you to kill. I could dig you up plenty of dead Sesesh that would save you the trouble of killing.

I have not heard from Walt Odell yet since he was sent to the hospital. Ike is slowly getting better. Ed. Crandall is about well again as usual. Alvin Caulkins and Will Cleary are well.

I was out on picket guard last night. I was at the houses of quite a number of Sesesh but there was scarcely anybody to be found except women and children and negroes. Three-fourths of the men are off in the Rebel army and I supose a great many of them would be glad to come back to their families if they could get a chance to do so. I will write more about the Sesesh in my next letter as I have not time to do so now.

When you write after this direct your letters to Corinth, Mississippi; 18th Regiment Wisconsin Volunteers, Company C, and it will save being overhauled in the mails so mutch.

I will close for the present so good-bye.

Thos. J. Davis

Excuse bad writing for this was wrote in a hurry. Write often.

Camp No. 9 Corinth, Mississippi, July 5th, 1862

Dear Wife,

I received your letter today bearing date of June 22nd. It found me well and I hope this will find you in good health. I have not received any letters since I received the last one from you and from my folks.

The weather is quite warm here though not so warm as it was a week or ten days ago. It is so hot however that we do not think of drilling in the middle of the day. You say that you was visited with a heavy frost there. I wish we had part of it down here for I have not seen any frost since I left St. Louis. I do not like to freeze mutch but I believe I would rather bear considerable cold weather than to suffer so mutch heat.

This is the day after the fourth. I supose you Badax folks made a grand demonstration yesterday in celibrating the 4th. I suppose that you would like to know how we spent the 4th down here in Dixie. Well, I will tell you. At daylight there was a salute in each division which lasted for over an hour. Then again at 12 o'clock the batteries of each brigade was drawn out in lines of battle and a salute of 34 guns was fired from each battery of which we have a large number here. They are scattered over a large scope of country. The thundering peels of the canon sounded really romantic and was really exciting. It reminded us mutch of the celebration of the 6th & 7th of April last at Shiloh.

Ike Odell is getting better still, though he is not stout yet. I have not heard from Walt since he went to the hospital. Allan Swain went to the hospital the same time Walt did. We got a letter from him a few days ago. He was then in the hospital at Quincy, Illinois, but he did not say a word about Walt. As for me going to see him, he may be five hundred miles from here and I cannot get a pass to stay over night from camp. We have lost several of the boys of the Badax Tigers since we left Viroqua. I will give you a list of those that have died that I know of at present and the places where they di[ed].

Samuel Swan	of West Prairie	died at Milwaukee
A.W. Saxton	Badax Valley	Killed at Shiloh
William Kittle	Lynxville	Killed at Shiloh
L.H. Page	near Viroqua	St Louis
William Starbuck	Kickapoo	Pittsburg Ldg.
Charles Ames	West Prairie	New Burg, Ind.
Julius Morley	Viroqua	New Burg "
Samuel Fish	South Badax	New Burg "
Aaron Cooley	Desoto	died near home on return
William Hunter	Springville	Hospital near Shiloh
Joseph Hunter	Springville	Huntsville Ala
Joseph Gander	Kickapoo	Huntsville do
Orin Tooker	Lynxville	Huntsville do
George Williams	Springville	died on the way home

Joseph Hunter, Orin Tooker, and Joseph Gander was among the prisoners that was taken at Pittsburg. They had been released by the Rebels and was on there way back to be mustered out of the service. They was so mutch reduced with disease and starvation that they only reached our forces at Huntsville, Alabama, and there died. They was tended in their last illness by friends and was buried in the neat little cemetry at Huntsville. There may be others of the Tigers that have died that I know not of for they are scattered so much in different hospitals besides them that were taken prisoners. I think the prisoners will soon be sent home if they are not before this time. They were in Nashville some time ago. Burnett started home about ten days ago. I supose he is with his wife in Illinois before this time. He said that he should not stay but a few days in Illinois 'til he would start for home. It seemed to affect him as mutch or more to leave the company as it did on leaving home. My paper is played out and I must close this sheet.

Thos. J. Davis

For the Times
from The "Tigers"

Camp Near Corinth, July 7th, 1862
Mr. Editor:

The Eighteenth still remains encamped where my last communication left it. Things, too, remain generally very quiet, the only startling rumor or rumors being conflicting ones relative to the success and defeat of Gen. McClellan and the announcement that five miles from here a body of our forces had a sharp skirmish with a reconnoitering party of the enemy. Report says that the skirmish was a brisk one. We do not know the number of men engaged nor the result. We only know that very early next morning a battery and two regiments of cavalry from our division went out in haste and have not yet returned. There are, doubtless, many guerrilla bands on our immediate vicinity. It is generally believed here that something of a larger nature will be allotted us soon besides skirmishing with the enemy, as it would show too much neglect, the boys argue, for us to remain here the life-long summer without their paying us a visit of ceremony in the latest approved secesh style. I predict that should such a visit be made, a reception worth the visitors and occasion will be awaiting them.

The defenses in the rear of Corinth are going on. Breastworks are not being constructed but batteries are being placed, well protected, about one-half mile of each other, with timber cut away to give good range.

There is still a large force here of effective men, notwithstanding Buell's withdrawal of troops and the large decimation by sickness.

It again becomes, Mr. Editor, my melancholy duty to announce formally the death of a number of Tigers. A letter was received by one of the company a few days since from Patrick Mooney, in hospital at Newburg, Indiana, stating that Julius Morley and Charles Ames had departed this life at that place—date of decease not given.

We also see it stated in the papers that Joseph Gander, Orrin Tooker, and Joseph Hunter—all prisoners—were dead. Time of death not stated.

We have also received from Vernon County an account of the death of Aaron Cooley, our drummer, at a neighbor's residence, having arrived nearly home. Today, too, we followed the remains of William Thompson to their final resting place. He died yesterday afternoon. He had been an inmate of the division hospital a long time and was one of those thought fitted to return to the regiment when it was discontinued. Some others of Company C were sent North. He came to us about three weeks ago and his appearance indicated that only the bracing air of Wisconsin could revive sinking nature. An application was immediately made and the papers sent to headquarters for his discharge. They have not yet returned. Poor fellow! A higher power was not so tardy in releasing him and sending him home as Gen. Halleck.

Fourteen men who left Viroqua with us are now reported deceased. Of these, Charles Ames, George Williams, and Joseph Hunter afterward entered other companies. Mr. Nash, of West Prairie, a private in the 17th Wis., died here in camp a short time since.

A rumor prevails here that Government has made a fresh call for three hundred thousand more men. Incredible as it may seem to your readers, I believe that number absolutely requisite to bring this war to a speedy termination. None can doubt the policy of closing soon this struggle. The financial and industrial, no less the moral and religious world, demand that energetic measures, supported by the adequate force, should be immediately carried into effect.

How did you spend the Fourth? We see by the Times that Hon. Carson Graham was to deliver the oration in Viroqua.

Here a suspension of drill, duty, and dress parade was the only formal observance—if it be called an observance at all—of the day. An impromptu assembling of the companies before the Colonel's tent, by the first sergeants, took place in the evening. The Colonel was absent, but in the meanwhile, Lt. Col. Beall, in response to a call, made a pithy speech for which he received the cheers of those present. Col. Bouck soon arrived and made us an eloquent address, which though short, was well received. The boys conjectured more than once that day on the probability of their "celebrating the Fourth" next time in Vernon County. They are in good spirits.

By the way, Mr. Editor, did you ever see a contraband? I don't mean one of your civilized Northern specimens but a real, live, Gen. Butler sort of one, fresh from Secesh. Of course you have not. We have just that sort of a one in the regiment. He attempted to pass into our lines and was brought by the Officer-of-the-Guard to the Colonel to account for himself. He is a comical young fellow about eighteen, and according to his own story, which subsequent accounts verified, belonged to a plantation about a mile directly in front of our encampment, and passed frequently by our boys going to bathe. In answer to a stern command to account for himself, he said: "Berry well, Massa, I'se dar chile dat b'long to dar man in der white house; but I'se specs I b'long to dis chile now, yah! yah! Case Massa, he fotch me out to dar gate and say, 'You am a bad nigger;

you am be more troubl' as am worf; you concite dar udder nigs to rebel and all dem ar tings; now lebe dese diggins an' go to h—l.' Yah! yah! An' so I'se come ober to dar Eighteenth, yah! yah!"

Good for that contraband! The Colonel is thought to be satisfied that he was only obeying his master's commands, as he was allowed to remain and is now employed by some of the officers. But it is a rich note on our regiment. We have two others, also, in our regiment employed as cooks.

Lieut. A.A. Burnett's resignation was accepted June 16th and he soon after started home—ill health causing him to take the step.

The Tigers have now the least number on the sick list of any company in the regiment, having now about 33 men, only two excused from duty on account of sickness. Both are cases of swelled limbs.

Truly Yours, C.

P.S. Since writing the above, the sad intelligence has arrived of the death of Elijah Forsyth, at U.S. Hospital, Keokuk, Iowa, June 28. Also of John Stokes, at Jefferson Barracks, Mo. He died May 21st. Deceased was a young man and one of the first sent to the hospitals. C. [NW Times, July 23, 1862, p. 2]

Corinth, Mississippi, July 9th, 1862

Dear Wife,

I again sit down upon the ground to write you a line in answer to your letter dated June 29th which I received day before yesterday. It found me well as usual & I hope this would find you in good health. I would have written sooner but we went out on picket guard yesterday and returned today at noon and this is my first oppertunity, though I have no strange news to write more than common.

If I had known that Mrs. Burnett would not have herd from her man of- tener I would have written to her myself though if he has had luck he is where she is before this time and perhaps they are on their road home.

We are having verry warm weather here again for the last few days with no appearance of frost in the least but I think we will have rain soon for we need it badly.

You wanted to know if I done my own washing and cooking & who I sleep with.

As for cooking, we have a man paid for cooking for the company.[16] But any little extras that we forage out among the Sesesh such as potatoes,

16. Although Davis does not specifically say so, the paid man who did the cooking for Company C may well have been a runaway slave. According to Civil War historian Bell I. Wiley, "Sometimes members of a mess engaged the service of a Negro, obtainable . . . at nominal compensation, to relieve them of the drudgery of cooking." [Wiley, Bell I., The Life of Billy Yank. Garden City, N.Y., Doubleday & Company, Inc., 1971, p. 244]

apples, roasting ears and pheasants each individual cooks his part thereof and is satified.

We have some nice times out on picket for there we have a chance to talk with the inhabitants, some of whom do not hardly know what to think of the Yankees. Some of them think that the Yankees want to free the niggers, some think that the Yankees want to rob them of all their cotton. One woman who had two brothers and a husband in the Sesesh army verry earnestly asked me if we had railroads up north like they have down here. The majority of the folks around here seem to wish their friends out of the Sesesh army for they begin to think their is some danger even in fighting Yankees.

I do my own washing, though I do not wash as fancy perhaps as some of the Wisconsin ladies would do. Though I boil them every time I wash to keep them free from lice which infest the camps of all the regiments that I have been in yet.

As for bedfellows, I have slept with several of the boys since I left Milwaukee but with no niggers. At present I sleep with John Kingston when he is not on guard and when he is I sleep with Ben Greenman.

You wanted me to write where Ben was. He is here and well and all right. You wanted to know how Ike Odell spent so mutch money. As for what he bought, I could not tell you though I supose he is like some of the other green boys [and] thinks he must buy everything enticing that he sees. Things are so [expensive] here that it does not take long to spend twenty-five or thirty dollars and not get mutch for it at that.

We lost another one of our men. He died last Sunday. His name was William Thompson. He lived over near the Kickapoo [River]. I have not learned anything of the whereabouts of Walt Odell yet. Edw. Crandall is not verry well. He has not been real stout for sometime though I hope he will soon recruit again. The rest of the Tigers were in tolerable good spirits.

I believe I have nothing more of interest to write this time so good-bye for this week.

Thos. J. Davis

Tishomingo County, Corinth, Mississippi, July 11th, 1862

I commenced writing this letter two days ago but having so mutch other duty to attend to I did not finish it. A soldier's rest is uncertain & he knows not what minute he may be called upon to perform some duty. So he has to take time as he can catch it. Sometimes he may not have much to do for three or four days then again he may be kept nearly busy for that length of time.

We had quite a heavy nice rain yesterday and last night and the air is somewhat cooler today.

Whitney wrote to Will Cleary that Dick Powell was going to move back to Ohio, bag and baggage, oxen and all. If he does move back he is getting fooler and fooler everyday. I thought he meant to go out west and get him another farm what was a farm.

There is considerable excitement here at present about McClellan's army at Richmond that have been having considerable fighting there lately with considerable loss on both sides. I hope McClellan will scoop the Rebels out clean & smooth.

I think Burnett will be at home by the time you get this. If he does tell him to be sure to write to me. There was a letter came here directed to Burnett since he left. I opened and read it. It was from Mr. Lowrie of Viroqua though nothing in it of importance.

Our company got a letter from John Dickson the other day. He and ten others of the Tiger prisoners were at Cairo. Henry Cleary was with them. They don't know whether they will be set free or be kept in the service to guard prisoners.[17] They say they have seen some verry tough times and I should rather think they had. Sam McMicheal, Gould Hickok, Joseph Brightman, and Captain Layne are yet held prisoners. They held all the officers even down to corporal. John Dickson was a sergeant but he took off his stripes or otherwise deceived them in refference to his position; hence his getting away.

Tell Mary Caulkins I will write her a long letter one of these times when I have time (after I hear from her again) explaining things in general as far as I do such business. So no more this.

T. J. Davis

Corinth, Mississippi, July 18th, 1862

Dear Wife

I sit down once more to write you a line to let you know that I am in tolerable good health. Trusting this may find you as well. I have not received any letter from you this week. If I had known I should not get one before this I would have written several days ago though I am anxiously looking for a letter from you everyday when the mail comes in.

There has nothing unusual happened since I last wrote you. The weather continues quite warm. We had a verry heavy rain here night before last and

---

17. Early in the war it was customary to discharge or furlough paroled prisoners-of-war. In the second year of the war, paroled prisoners from western Federal regiments were sent to a parole camp at Benton Barracks, St. Louis, Missouri, for approved, non-combat duty. Thus the confusion among the paroled men of the 18th Wisconsin. [Lord, Francis A., They Fought for the Union, Westport, Conn., Greenwood Press, 1981, p.319]

yesterday the first good rain we have had for over a month. But still it does not seem to cool the air scarcely any.

There is rather more sickness in the regiment now then there was two weeks ago. Alvin Caulkins has not been very well for several days. The first time he has [been] sick since he has been here though nothing serious, I hope, ailing him now.

Bill Downie got a letter from his father today. He said Burnett and his woman got home. Ed Crandall got one today from Sarah. She said that Burnett had not got home yet. Downie's letter was dated July 10th and Sarah's July 9th. Sarah being away from home, I suppose she did not know he had got home. Tell Burnett to be sure and write to me. Ed Crandall is getting quite smart again and so is Ike Odell. I have not yet heard anything from Walter yet. I think he must be in Quincy, Illinois, in the general hospital if he is not dead. I believe the rest of the Badax boys are as well as usual those that are here.

I received a letter from [brother] Jabez this week. It was dated July 1st. He said that he was at Cumberland Gap, Tennessee, and expected soon to march on to Knoxville where there was plenty of Rebels. He did not say they had been in any fight yet, though they had chased the Rebels away from Wilson's Gap.[18] They run without fighting. He said he was well. He said he had just got a letter from you and Mary.

I got another letter this week from brother Isaac at Leavenworth, Kansas. He had not got his discharge yet though he was expecting it soon. He said he was well as usual. His letter was dated July 4th. He said they was firing salutes with their large siege guns while he was waiting though nothing extraordinary transpiring.

I do not hear anything from Levi Allen lately.

I understand that the folks had a good time at Newton on the 4th. I am really glad to hear of good interest the citizens take in the wellfare of our country and the esteem with which they hold the sacred rights bequeathed to them by their revolutionary fathers.

There was a letter came here for Burnett since he went away. It was from James Lowrie. I opened and read it. There was nothing of peticular interest in it or I would have sent it to him. I wrote back, however, to Mr. Lowrie in behalf of Mr. Burnett though I expect Burnett was at home before the letter got there.

I have no special news to write this time. Our cavalry is scouting through the country all the while and are picking up a few loose Sesesh that are straying around and once in a while they have a squabble with

---

18. One month earlier, 18 June 1862, General George W. Morgan had led a Federal division in occupying strategic Cumberland Gap near the Kentucky–Virginia–Tennessee border. Fifteen miles southwest is Wilson's Gap, Tennessee, a minor mountain pass connecting with the larger Rogers Gap. [Long, p. 228]

some of the Sesesh cavalry and loose a few of our men. But such is war. Some folks think that the Rebels will collect in force again and try to retake Corinth. But I don't think they will try soon.

Thos J. Davis

Corinth, July 19th, 1862

I received a letter from you this morning dated from 4th to 8th of July. Calvin Morley brought it. He started from Viroqua a week ago last Thursday. He looks well and hearty again though he looked more like a dead man when he left here than a being of life. He brought us the news of the death of Elijah Forsythe. He died at Keokuk, Iowa, on the 21st of June.

Morley said that he saw Burnett the day before he left Viroqua. You wrote that you heard that there was folks around Springville that was ready to tar and feather him (Burnett) when he got home. I would like to have the power to draft a lot of wide-mouthed patriots that I could pick out in the vicinity of Springville and Viroqua. You generally see those that are the loudest in denouncing others as cowards are the stick-the-closest-to-home themselves. Those patriotic folks still have a fine chance yet to display their valor as Wisconsin is called on to furnish several thousand more men. Burnett was sick all the time he was here and I do not believe he ever would have got well as long as he would have remained here. Burnett would not have went home if he thought he would get well here. He really disliked to go as it was.

You wanted to know if I meant for you to live at Burnetts' again. That is the calculation I had if you perfered staying there. I would rather you would stay there than anyplace else up there. Burnett says you can stay there as long as you wish. Tell Mrs. Burnett that I appreciate her well wishes but I hope I may not, while in the army, need any personal asistance from friends at home. Though it is a cheering consolation for one to know that he has friends in time of need. There was a letter came here today for Burnett. It speaks for itself and so I will not write any of the details.

News came into camp yesterday that one company of the 17th Wisconsin who was detailed to work out on the railroad toward Memphis had been captured and taken prisoners by the Sesh. The report was that the Rebels had torn up a portion of the track and awaited the approach of the train carrying the company above mentioned and the cars run off the track killing six and the remainder fell in the hands of the Rebels. Such is the yarn but I don't believe it until I am better satisfied of the fact.[19]

---

19. Company A, 17th Wisconsin, was stationed about fifteen miles north of Corinth guarding the Mobile & Ohio Railroad from July until early October 1862. There is no indication in war records or regimental histories that the incident ever occurred. [Wisconsin, 1863, p. 344–345]

I received the money that I loaned in Milwaukee to Mr. Cox. He paid me when we was paid off here. I do not wish you to work hard. Give yourself propper exercise to keep up a healthy circulation of the blood but do not fatigue yourself unnessarly.

Ben Greenman got a letter from his wife today. Ben is well. Alvin Caulkins has not had a letter from home for three weeks. He thinks the old folks are getting too careless about writing to him.

I would been glad if I could have seen David Ingersoll & Green Sallee for they are good boys. How did David like the country? Not verry well, I guess.

You say you want long letters from me. I would like long letters from you and I will write all I think nesesary. My paper is out and I must close so good-bye.

T. J. Davis

INDUCEMENTS TO ENLIST

We conceive it scarcely possible that the present war can last a year longer and the chances are that it will be terminated in six months. Persons hesitating about enlisting will bear this in mind. The government bounty of money and land, and all other bounties, apply whether the war is long or short. Those who enlist now will have all the bounties provided by the State and Government, and in all probability, will be back to their homes and business in six months. Very certain it is that a prompt response to the call of the President will make short work of the rebel force and the rebellion. A state bounty of $50, Government bounty of $100 and the pay at $13 per month will, in six months, put $228 in cash in the pocket of every man who enlists, besides his board and clothing. Thirty-eight dollars a month and found is good wages.—Sentinel. [NW Times; July 30, 1862, p. 4]

Camp Near Bolivar, Tennessee
Army Corps of Tennessee, August 1st, 1862

Dear Sister,

I have received a letter from you quite a long time since and though I have not written directly to you since, yet you know my letters home are to all. I cannot with all my correspondence write two letters to the same house containing in substance the same matter. This is intended, of course, for all.

You will perceive by reference to the date that we are once more in Tennessee and by reference to the map you will find our present location (you should not be without a war map). We left last Monday, July 28th, our old encampment near Corinth and occupied nearly 3½ days on the march here

making the distance of about 70 miles; which is pretty good time, carrying ones own provisions, his accouterments, canteen, etc, etc. Five regiments and two batteries of our division was the force that came. They expected a fight here last Sunday and hence the sending reinforcements.
There must be now about 12 thousand men encamped about this place.
The march was somewhat forced and some rather gave out but all stood
it much better than I anticipated. There was considerable confiscation
done along the route. The apples that are now getting ripe, peaches nearly
so. Chickens, geese, pigs, and green corn especially were assaulted with
sweeps; in fact, there were even (missing) "confiscated."

We travelled through a [missing] country; but it was nearly all the way
a fine one. The South is all one field of corn literally speaking. We saw but
one field of cotton on the route, the land being all put in with corn and
beans.

There was some expectation of a fight on the route by a large body of
rebel cavalry known to have been recently in this section. The last night
we camped on the route was beside a large corn field, probably of 20
acres. It was completely stripped. We lived on it that night and next morning. Corn looks well here. It is quite good. Large ears and just right for
roasting.

The rebels suddenly left here Monday and nothing is known of them..
It is reported that we shall leave here in three days for Memphis which is
65 miles from here. There appears to be no need for staying here now.

We are encamped about a mile north of Bolivar passing through the
place on the march. It is a very fine place, three times as large as Corinth
and very beautiful—containing nice residences, surrounded by splendid
shade trees and all kinds of ornamental shrubbery. There were plenty of
spectators as we came through, but everything was quiet, not a word of
secession nor a cheer for the Union. The people were nicely dressed.

The last night on the route lots of "contrabands" came into camp desirous of taking "friends [French] leave" of their masters. Our regiment
took a number—probably a dozen. The other regiments did likewise. So
we have now niggers to forage for us on a march and help the cook in
camp. When I come home I shall try and bring a young boy home with
me just as a curiosity and to act as waiter to Father and Mother. There is
a bright little fellow now in Co. D of Sparta who is going to act as a waiter
to Lieut. Sloggy of that company who would make a good one.

I am sorry to be obliged to write that Henry's health is not good. He has
been unwell for two weeks or more and has some doubts about the propriety of coming on the march and could not have arrived here were he
not carried part of the way in the ambulance and his accouterments the
whole distance. As it was he stood it better than I anticipated. He has
grown poor and weak. I do trust that he will soon recover. Henry and I

have hitherto stood it very well, that is, I mean, without having any long or serious illness and when compared with others and I trust that the future will prove as auspicious as the past through all of this. I have sometimes, I must confess, had my doubts. A person in the service is subject to so many changes both in the duty he has to perform and the food and cooking of it, that more chances exist for his becoming finally debilitated than in the North or even in this climate with a different occupation.

We are in a fine country now. Of this and our march you will read more in my contemplated communication for the "Times." I shall write tomorrow to that paper. We shall not stay here long, probably but a few days, when we shall again march somewhere. I cannot write much more, but must now close. I rest as heretofore. I will follow the regiment.

Write often and all the news. I have written frequently home. I shall write frequently to some of you. I will expect you all to answer frequently. I must close now. My health is good. I remain,

Your Brother, Ransom J. Chase.

P.S. Give my love to Lindley and request him to write to me. Also to all who inquire. I should have liked to have heard C. B. Whitman's oration and been present on the occasion. R. J. Chase August 4th——As usual until I further advise you to the contrary. I am just going on a foraging expidition and will only say that we will stop here sometime. RJC

Bolivar, Tennessee, August 1st, 1862

I received your letter three days ago bearing date of July 20 & 21st which was thankfully received and I was glad to hear that you was well. I am in as good health as usual. I would have answered your letter before this if I could but we was on a march when I received it and I had no chance until now.

We left Corinth last Monday morning and arrived here at Bolivar yesterday, Thursday, being four days on the road. The distance is 60 miles and quite a crooked road. You can see by looking on the map the rout we come. We started north from Corinth and marched about 18 miles. We then turned west and crossed the railroad leading from Corinth to Columbus. We kept on in a northwest direction for about four miles from the railroad. We then elbowed around to the southwest and crossed the Memphis & Charleston Railroad at a town called Chewalla. We then turned west again keeping on the south side of the railroad for about (20) miles. We again turned north and recrossed the M. & C.R.R. at a town called Pocahontas. We then traveled in a northwest direction until we arived at Bolivar.

We come through some rough and romantic country with quite a variety of timber that does not grow in the north, among them are chestnut, beech, sasafras, sweet gum, dogwood, persimmon, poplar, cypress, rock oak, and also what they call live oak. We also come through some nice looking country with, now and then, a large cotton plantation, though the most of them are planted to corn this year calculated for the supply of the Sesesh army, though some cotton is raised. One hundred acres is the most that I saw on one plantation. The most of the inhabitants were seldom visible. Some forty or fifty Negros, both women & children, come to our division at diferant places on the road and wanted to go with us. The wenches and children were driven back but some fifteen or twenty men were permitted to follow us away. Some would come away laughing in good spirits and some would look solemn as though they regretted to leave friends behind and was in doubt as to the prospect of getting their freedom.

The implements for farming here is far inferior in improvement to those used in the North. Some of the plows used are patterns of fifty years ago and would be considered curiosities of the dark ages in some of the northern museums. I have not seen but one reaper and one threshing machine since I have been in the south and the threshing machine was a small, two-horse, endless-chainpower concern; a poor looking trap. The cotton presses and cotton gins are odd looking machines to a person that never saw them before. They are run by horsepower.

Our forces here have about three hundred Negros at work on breastworks fortifying this place.

I have not said anything about Bolivar yet. Bolivar is a verry pretty place, full as large as Corinth with rather better buildings, the most of them brick. There is some splendid residences here. The grounds are tastefully laid out and well ornamented with shade trees & shrubry. This place is not so mutch deserted by its inhabitants as Corinth. As they found that the Yankees would not molest them in their traitorous habitations.

Apples and peaches are now fairly getting ripe and roasting ears are in good condition for use and, notwithstanding, the strict orders to the contrary, the soldiers would fall out of the ranks and confiscate all the corn, apples, and peaches they wanted as we was on the march. Many chicken roosts were also left desolate, the poultry being pressed into the U.S. service as the boys would say they would not take the oath. They considered that a "fowl" stomach on the march was no peticular disadvantage to the system.

You wanted to know what kind of bed that I have to sleep on. When we was at Corinth I had a bunk fixed up from the ground by driving down forks and laying two poles on them and then fasten corn sacks to the poles for the bottom, then put my blankets on that. But when we are marching or stay but a short time in a place, we sleep on the ground. The boys have got used to it so they stand it verry well. I could not sleep on a feather bed now if I had one untill I got used to it again.

You wrote that Dick Powell wanted you to pay him some money that I owed him. I don't know that I owe him a cent. He never hinted to me that I owed him anything and more then that, I never promised to send him any money. It was nothing less than an attempt to swindle on his part. I don't owe anyone in the county and I dont want you pay any attention to any such demands. If I owed Dick why did he not write to me about it?

August 2nd/62

I do not know how long we will remain here. There is some talk of us being sent on to Memphis in a few days. There is quite a large Rebel force off south of us thirty or forty miles and it is thought that they intend coming through this way and attack this place. We may however stay here sometime and perhaps have a squabble with Sesesh.

Robert McMichael has been unwell for several days but he is better again. The rest the boys are as well as usual. The weather is not so warm as it has been and I hope we will not have so mutch weather as we have had this season. I will send you a leaf from the cotton plant and also a flower of the plant. The flower on its first appearance are white but a few days before then drop off they turn red.

We have not been paid off since Burnett left. Our payroll has been made out and signed nearly a month. We have three months pay due us the first of this month. I don't know when we will get our pay. We may not get it until in September and then draw four months pay. It is time that you had ought to have some more money from the state. The returns have been sent to Madison long ago.

Tell Burnett if he don't write to me I will nearly kill him if I ever get back [to] Springville again. Direct your letters to Corinth as you did before. They will follow us up. Nothing more this time so good-bye. Write soon

Thos. J. Davis

Bolivar, Tennessee, August 12, 1862

Dear Wife,

I sit down to write you a few lines to inform you that I am well and hope this may find you the same. I have not received any letter from you since two weeks ago today. So I thought I would write anyhow. I would have written sooner but I kept looking for a letter from you. But none came yet. Though I shall look for one every day until I get it.

We are still here in Bolivar and I think it is probable the we will remain here all summer. I would mutch rather stay here than at Corinth for we have good water here and at Corinth it was very poor and scarce at that. There is nothing of importance transpiring here at present, though when we was ordered here they thought that this place would soon be attacked by the Rebels. But I have not heard of any Sesesh forces of any size near here though there is a band of girillas prowling around here but are careful to keep their distance.

I received a letter from brother Isaac last week. He is still in Leavenworth. He said that he was in tolerable good health. He has not got his discharge yet. He's now detailed on extra duty in the hospital and gets extra pay.

I got a letter the other day from James Lowrie of Viroqua dated July 30th. He said that Jim Berry and Jerry Rusk was trying to raise a company for the 25th [Infantry Regiment] but say that recruiting goes slow and will go so until after harvest.[20] I guess so, too.

I also received a letter two or three days ago from David and Nancy Ingersoll dated July 24th. David Ingersoll and Green Sallee had got home from Wisconsin. David said that the folks was all well. He said that he had bought a drum for Charlie and while he was writing he said Charlie was trying to play the fife and drum at the same time. He said that Charlie and Grand Ma said they would give all the old shoes they had if they could get to see me. David said he was going to write to you before that I would send you the letter that I got from Susan but I forgot to put it in. I will send it in this if I don't forget it again.

Will Cleary got a letter today from Henry Cleary and Old Lorry Stevenson. They are still at Benton Baricks, St Louis. Henry is awful homesick. He is afraid that his wife's heart will break and cave in if he don't get home soon. But he is still afraid that he will be exchanged and sent back to the regiment again.

I found one of my cousins the other day in the 61st Illinois Volunteers. I had not saw him for three years. He was verry glad to see me and so was I to see him.

I believe all of the boys here are tolerable well. We left four of our company back in the hospital at Corinth: Old David Arnott, our fifer, J.M. Stokes, John Pennell, and Ed Crandall. Stokes and Pennell was quite sick but Crandall and Arnott was not considered dangerous.

Write soon

Thomas J. Davis

We was paid off last week. I would send twenty dollars home but it is not verry safe sending money in the mail.

I will write more next time.

T. J. Davis

---

20. Jeremiah M. Rusk was a leading citizen of Viroqua. He raised and served in the 25th Wisconsin Infantry. After the war, Rusk was elected to Congress, served two terms as governor of Wisconsin, and was the first U.S. Secretary of Agriculture. [Boatner, 713]

From the "Tigers"

Camp at Bolivar, Tennessee
August 15, 1862

Mr. Editor:

The most that is worthy of recording in the TIMES from the Tigers is the re-moval of their camp near Corinth, Miss., to the town of Bolivar, Tennessee.

Orders were received in the evening of July 27th that our brigade should at daybreak, commence the march for this place. Maps were put into immediate ser-vice and the question, "Where is Bolivar?" occupied the "attention of the house." It was found at length, snugly ensconced on the connecting railroad running from Jackson, Tennessee, through Grand Junction to New Orleans, between the first two places, and the fact finally determined that it was distant about 70 miles.

Of course, every one in the camp knew all the map taught and more, too, in five minutes and some even had, as if a sudden light had illumined their mem-ories, it's whole history at tongue's end and quite interesting details were given, if not without a few inconsistencies, certainly with every advantage which ap-parent honesty and veracity could clothe them. We were informed that "reveil-lie" would be beaten at 2 o'clock and that tents must be struck, folded, all nec-essary property packed, loaded, and we ready to start at daybreak; consequently, we took "time by the forelock," by packing our "little all," per-sonal effects in our knapsacks before retiring. The Colonel is prompt, but doubtless some, while rubbing their eyes, unjustly complained that they "had scarcely gone to sleep." But they were soon all merriment and jollity; things were fixed in double-quick, the battalion formed and our brigade, with another and a battery, precisely at daybreak started en route for Bolivar.

No intimation was given of the reason for our hurried departure but we soon judged that something important depended upon our arrival , or that our horse-back generals were very desirous of giving the sun's rays an opportunity of penetrating a tent duly shaded, before it could discommode their precious per-sons. The sun, seldom so discourteous as to refuse to smile seemed uncom-monly anxious that day to assure us of its uncommon friendship, refusing to leave us for a single moment. Its melting sympathy was certainly felt and duly acknowledged with a frequent doffing of caps with soldiers' usual politeness. But though a few of our regiment were obliged to fall out, they overtook us af-ter we camped in the evening.

Twelve miles from Corinth, thro' which place we repassed, we went through the dingy, low village of Chewalla, deriving its importance from being a rail-road station. We were informed before entering that the small pox was preva-lent and cautioned not to straggle, which piece of information, subsequently confirmed, was the only item I could gather. One regiment, on duty, constituted the force here. The place of encampment the first night was a low piece of land, about twenty miles from Corinth.

Delayed the next morning by the wagontrain having been hindered by some of the teams getting stalled and it being policy to keep it as near the main body as possible, we made up by our celerity, before night, the lost time. Pocahontas River was crossed during the day, a considerable stream where we rested long enough to give an opportunity, well improved, for the men to bathe; also went through the village of Middleton, entirely deserted by white population; a wench perched on a stump in a cornfield giving us the only welcome as she cried out," 'Urrah for dar Union,"—the color of which sentiment meeting the approval of the soldiers, they of course, laughingly responded. The succeeding night the encampment was in an open cornfield well adapted for that purposes.

The third day was a repetition of the second, with the exception of a re-freshing rain in the afternoon. At night we encamped in an uncultivated field. The location added a cornfield of twenty acres to the attractions presented by the previous night, which, being in that state, remarkably good for roasting, scarcely an ear was left. I might observe here that along the whole route , the boys considering that while our wise men (?) might wrangle about the theory of confiscation, it was the part of the soldier to practically test it expediency and judge of is merits by its results. Like so many unruly spirits, they would leap fences into orchards, cornfields, poultry yards, and even pigs were carried off in triumph.—Those orchards where the apples were ripe, or approximated to ripeness, were stripped of their fruit, while every cornfield by the roadside was ransacked and haversacks filled, for fear that we might not halt near the article. Confined by strict camp rules at Corinth and unable to obtain green food, the small effort made by officers to restrain was scarcely noticed.

One incident occurred, however, worthy of record. While at a halt during the rain, the men became acquainted with an old man living a short distance in the advance who came with a beaming countenance to say, "Welcome!" He stated that he was the only Union man for miles; that as a consequence of his love for the old flag, the guerrillas had taken away his cattle, hogs, horses, and even his life was so insecure that at night, he slept in the woods; "But," said the old man with tears in his eyes, but with the fires of youth rekindled, "I will talk." He cor-dially invited the soldiers to help themselves to his corn, which, indeed, was all he had left, saying that it would be a pleasure to assist men fighting for the Union. I am pleased to relate that with the exception of a few ears previously taken by the cavalry scouts, not an ear was taken and when we passed his house he was saluted with cordiality. Glorious old man!

During the third night a large number of Contrabands desirous of "taking French Leave" of their masters, came into camp and were duly installed as of-ficers' cooks or assistant cooks in companies, which employment I may here state, is not quite natural to them as they are mostly field hands.

We were told that it was now only ten miles to Bolivar and we started off in fine spirits, though, perhaps caused as much by the good supper and breakfast as any inspiring effect the announcement might produce. At the distance of a mile, we passed a large plantation, the wenches and little ones all out perched upon the fence near the house, gazing at what was to them a novel sight—the first army of Yankees passing through that section. They appeared to be in good humor, with one exception; a female about thirty-five years of age, who gazed eagerly at every one as they passed, with tears rolling down her cheeks and whose sobs could be heard by all. She said not a word. Perhaps the acquisition to our number included a husband at whose departure pent up nature could not fail to exhibit by outward demonstration the intensity of grief within! Perhaps her boy was with us, and she was looking with anxious eyes to extend a last farewell! But we passed on—and did not molest to satisfy our curiosity.

Suffice it to say that we arrived at Bolivar about eleven A.M. and did not fail while passing through to express our admiration of one of the most pleasant of villages, which, though not very large, exhibits a taste for the beautiful in its inhabitants. There are some stately residences and they, with houses of lowlier pretensions, are environed and shaded by numerous varieties of ornamental shrubbery and trees. It is indeed a village hid by an artificial forest. Everything was quiet. The spectators were "mum"—not a word for Jeff nor a cheer for the Union. Our brigade was stationed north-west of the town. Thus ended our march in three and a half days.

We have passed through, as a general thing, a fine country, and had seen many fine plantations, and could not fail to observe with what exactness had complied with the wish of the bogus Confederacy regarding the cultivation of corn and beans. During the whole trip, but one small field of cotton was passed; nothing but corn, corn, beans, beans! Destined for whom? Why, for Jeff, of course. The demand exists in no other quarter! Meantime our wise men (God save the mark) ponder, debate, and reason upon the justice of confiscating food for the army, for weeks together. An infusion into their counsels of a little more practical common sense might be of infinite value to the army and, consequently, to the country, as well as redound to their own honor and future fame.

I have referred to our sudden start and hurried journey; after our arrival we learned the reason. The force then here was threatened with an attack by a force of rebel cavalry and infantry encamped a short distance from town, and the necessity for its augmentation was too apparent to admit of necessary delay. The first night of our march they retreated to parts unknown. Our whole force here is variously estimated from ten to fourteen thousand men. Double lines of pickets completely environ the town and no person allowed to pass but by pass of Provost Marshal. By order of General McClernand,[21] all planters in the country are required to report and furnish three-fourths of all their male slaves to work on the fortifications being erected, under the penalty for refusal of being considered traitors and arrested, their slaves and personal property seized and used for benefit of the Government. The plan of fortifications is said to be extensive.

The removal to Bolivar, besides a change, gave us a healthier atmosphere, good spring water, better opportunity to obtain the little luxuries from the

---

21. John A. McClernand had represented President Lincoln's Illinois home district in Congress for ten years and was known and respected as a popular Illinois War Democrat for which he was commissioned a general early in the war. In March 1862, McClernand was promoted to major general, second in field rank in the Army of the Tennessee only to Ulysses S. Grant. [Faust, p.456–457]

planters and more agreeable duty to perform. Items which, of course, are duly appreciated.

August 4th we hurriedly formed the battalion and with the 15th Michigan Infantry and one howitzer marched westerly in pursuit of a supposed guerrilla band said to have cut off a number of teams out foraging, but at the distance of two miles, they were met loaded with corn returning—the sight of cavalry which proved to be our own having caused the report. We, however, went on to the distance of eight miles and halted at a plantation, the slaves of which were detailed to bring out water in pails for the accommodation of the men. While thus engaged, the report of fire arms in front called us to attention while almost instantaneously a cavalry captain and five men on scout dashed into our presence, saying that they were pursued by about forty of the rebel cavalry and that they had exchanged shots. The gunners unlimbered the howitzer, the Belgians were loaded, bayonets were fixed and all ready for the secesh, when behold! there came a party of our own cavalry, their horses foaming with the chase. What a shout! The whole affair was turned into ridicule and, amid laughter, we countermarched and returned to camp, arriving half after nine. Sixteen miles in one afternoon was not bad; but the boys are getting, or rather, are hearty and rugged, and none felt any bad effects.

As we approached town, a lady came out of quite a fine house and opening the gate, set down a basket of pies telling the men to accept them with her wishes for their success in the cause in which they were engaged and immediately retired but not until they saw through the deepening twilight that she was white and neatly dressed. The pies were disposed of and the lady cheered. This shows that the ladies of the South are not all secesh, as represented. May she be rewarded for her kindness.

Noah Garrett has returned recently from Wisconsin and Harvey D. Lindley from the hospital, quite recovered. We left four men at Corinth, sick, but we trust they will soon be able to rejoin us.

Excuse the fault of lengths and believe me, Yours truly, C.

P.S.—We received orders to march previous to the departure of the mail and, hence, here we are again in Corinth. We arrived yesterday. More next time. C.
[NW Times, Sept. 3, 1862, p. 2]

Camp Near Corinth, Mississippi, August 23rd, 1862

Dear Wife,

I received your letter to day dated August 11th and was glad to hear from you and to hear that you was well. I am as well as usual.

We have moved again since I wrote to you last. On the evening of the 15th we received orders with 2 days rations to leave Bolivar for Pocahontas, a little town on the Memphis & Charleston Railroad about 30 miles west of Corinth, in search of a band of guirrillas who were in that neighborhood burning cotton and pressing all citizens they could find into the

Rebel service that are able to bear arms. We started from Bolivar on the morning of the 16th and traveled south about 16 miles and camped.

The next morning we persued our march and come to a little town called Middleton on the Charleston and Memphis Railroad at this place. Some Rebel guirrillas had burned a quantity of cotton the evening before. A company of the 11th Illinois Cavalry was sent out in search of them but could not find them, then went on to Pocahontas 7 miles further east. We traveled several miles on the road that 180 Rebels traveled the day before. We stopped overnight at Pocahontas and, finding that the Rebels had gone south, we were ordered back to Corinth.

We are now camped about 3 miles southwest of Corinth on the line of forts that surround the town. It is hard to tell how long we will remain here. We may be kept here to help defend this place and then again we may be called out after Rebel guirrillas in less then a week.

When we left Bolivar the Rebels got news that five thousand of our troops had been withdrawn from the place and the next day Bolivar was attacked by a Rebel force from Grand Junction and they had quite a fight. I have not heard the peticulars of the fight yet but heard that our forces whipped them and took six hundred prisoners and that our side lost 30 men killed and 60 wounded but didn't say how many Sesesh was killed. The Sesesh sliped up on the wrong side that time. There was only our regiment and the 15th Michigan that left Bolivar and there was not five hundred men in both of them.[22]

I received a letter today from Sarah McLain. I will send it to you and it will save me the trouble of writing about it. I also received a letter from brother William and one from brother Isaac today. Brother Isaac is still at Leavenworth. He wrote that he was well. William is at a station on the Memphis and Charleston Railroad called Iuka Springs, 25 miles east of Corinth. I had not heard from him before since the 7th of July. He wrote that he was well. He said they had routed several band of Rebels and took some prisoners and had captured about 150 bales of cotton.

Mrs Burnett's letter don't get along yet nor Burnett's either. I sent you twenty dollars in a letter the day before we left Bolivar. I don't know whether it will go through or not. Direct your letters to Corinth as you did before. My papers is out and I must close. Good-bye,

Thos. J. Davis

---

22. An attack on Bolivar, Tennessee, on 17 August 1862 is not mentioned anywhere in the official records. However, a reference by Federal Colonel I. N. Haynie to a small party of about fifty Confederates, not well armed, is made in a 16 August alert to Federal troops near Bolivar. On 18 August, a followup message from Haynie at nearby Bethel, Tennessee, says he has seventeen Confederate prisoners and fourteen horses. It may be that Davis' story was an exaggeration of this smaller raid. [OR I-17-pt.2, p.175, 180]

[Written upside-down on the same page]: Don't pay any attention to Dick Powell or anybody else that dun you for money that I owe them. Tell them to wait untill I come home and I will settle with them. And if I owe them anything I will pay or if they will come to the war I will settle with them here. Tell John I will answer his letter the next time.

Camp Near Corinth, Mississippi, September 1st, 1862

Dear Wife,

I received your letter today dated August 23 & 24th and was glad to hear that you was well. I am as well as usual. Alvin Caulkins received a letter from home today the same date of yours.

The weather is quite warm yet but I am glad that the fall of the year is coming around again and ere long we may begin to expect a more cool and bracing atmosphere. I am getting tired of summer weather in this climate. I am glad that you received that money all safe. Quite a number of the Tigers sent their money by express before I sent that but they have not got any returns from it yet. But I hope they will not lose it for the soldiers earn all the money they get without loosing any.

You did not write whether Burnett gave you them notes or not that I sent to you that I had on Baker, Whitney, and Johnson. It is in two notes of fifty-nine dollars each making one-hundred-and-eighteen dollars with interest since a year ago last June. If he did not give them to you, you must try and get them before Burnett goes away. I think Burnett has acted quite indifferant towards me since he went back. Rather too mutch so to look well and you must make him "come down to Limerick" [behave properly] and get the money and watch and if Lowrie will not give you a receipt for it payable when called for in the same kind of money, just take it and keep it yourself and be careful not to loose or let it get stolen.

I am verry glad to think you are so prudent in saving money but I do not wish you to suffer for the want of it. I can assure you that I will not spend money extravigantly while I am in the army and I hope by being prudent we will be able to live more easily by and by. We will be paid off again sometime this month, perhaps in ten or fifteen days. As that money went through all right I will send you ten dollars more in this letter.

I got a letter from my brother, O.K. Davis. Today he lives in Green County, Illinois. He writes that his family is well. He has four girls and nary boy.

You must excuse a short letter. This is the third letter I have wrote today and am somewhat tired. Tell John I will try and answer it the next time.

I don't think that the Newton Band would interest me mutch as I am sick and tired of hearing the fife and drum when they are well-played. But let them rattle away if it amuses them.

Ed Crandall is still in the hospital here. He is able to walk around and has been all the while. He is rather convalesant. I think he will right up when the weather begins to get cool.

My paper is out and I must stop so good-bye. Take good care of yourself and be a good girl.

Thomas J. Davis

[Untitled Item]

A Deserved Promotion—We learn with pleasure that Ransom J. Chase, of the Tiger Company from this county, 18th Regiment, has been promoted to the 2nd Lieutenancy in his own company. This is an excellent appointment. Mr. Chase is a young man of superior talents, unquestioned courage, fine military figure, and we understand is very popular with his fellow soldiers. The interesting letters that we have published from the Tiger Company over the signature of "C" are from the pen of Mr. Chase. We wish him joy and success in his new position, as we know of no one more deserving of honor and reward. [NW Times, Sept. 10, 1862, p. 2]

Camp Near Corinth, Mississippi, September 13th, 1862

Dear Wife,

I once more sit down to write you a few lines to let you know that I am as well as usual and hope this may find you in good health. I have not received a letter from you for over a week so I thought I would write again. Robert McMichael has received two letters from his wife since I had one from you. He got one from his wife this morning dated August 31st. The last one I received from you was dated August 23rd & 24th which contained a letter from Hariet to me and a day or two after I received another letter from Susan Wilson dated September 1st. I answered both of them.

You wrote that you had received the money I sent you from Bolivar. So in my last letter I sent you ten dollars more but I don't know whether you will get that or not as they say that they open many letters at Cairo for investigation.[23] We have not been paid off yet but I supose we will be paid before a great while for our time is up for pay now.

---

23. It is clear that Davis is not referring to thievery but that he believed the Federal operatives were reviewing soldiers' mail at Cairo, Illinois. Few, if any, common soldier studies make reference to such mail censorship.

I received a letter the other day from sister Elisabeth. She wrote that they was all well. She said she meant to write to you. She said she intended to have written sometime ago but said she had so mutch writing to do that she had neglected you. I received another letter from brother Isaac yesterday. He is wardmaster at Leavenworth, Kansas, and wrote that he was well. I have not received any more letters from Jabez and I don't see see any account of their battery in the papers.

I hear that there is some fears intertained by some in Wisconsin that the Indians will get in there but I do not apprehend any danger for I think they will soon be checked.[24]

Three or four days ago we received orders to keep in readiness to march with three days cooked rations on hand and two days rations uncooked. Some thought that we would be sent up in Kentucky and some thought that our generals was expecting an attack on this place by the Rebels and wished us to be ready for a determined defense.[25] There is some troops leaving here and some coming in. There is some Sesesh around here but whether there is enough of them to risk an attack on this place or not I cannot tell. It will require quite a strong force to take it at this time. However, the Rebels are making a desperate struggle to whip out our old troops before our new ones can get into the field.[26]

Ed. Crandall is still in the hospital in town. I have not heard from him for several days. He was running around then. Ike Odell is still in the hospital gaining slowly. He is able to rat around town, also. Alvin Caulkins is well. He received a letter from home to day dated August 31st.

I have not received any letter from Burnett, yet, and have given up the idea of getting any. I shall not send word for him to write anymore. I have nothing verry interesting to write this time and you must excuse bad writing as I am quite nervous today and do not feel like writing. Your letters generally come quite regularly so I will not grumble. I think I shall get one from you tomorrow or next day.

---

24. A Sioux tribe uprising had begun near New Ulm, Minnesota, on 17 August 1862. The fighting, which never moved beyond the borders of Minnesota, ended on 23 September after total casualties of 450 to 600. On 26 December 1862, thirty-eight Sioux men were tried and hanged at Mankato, Minnesota. [Long, p.252]

25. General Braxton Bragg's and Major General E. Kirby Smith's Confederate armies had only recently marched north into Kentucky to threaten Louisville and Cincinnati. Smith's men were only fifty miles from Louisville on 12 September 1862. [Long, p. 265]

26. A call for 300,000 troops had been made by President Lincoln on 11 July 1862. By September some of those Federal troops would have been expected in the field as reinforcements. [Nevins, Allan, The War for the Union, vol. 2. New York, Charles Scribner's Sons, 1960, p.144]

Our soldiers here are anxiously waiting for the new troops to arrive from the North so that we can double teams on them and scoop out Mr. Sesesh. Some think that we will be obliged to evacuate and leave Corinth but I think our generals will try to hold unless approached by a verry heavy force of Rebels.

The weather continues quite warm in the daytime but the nights are quite cool. We are mutch in need of rain as we have not had any for several weeks.

Be a good girl and take care of yourself and write often. I remain yours as ever.

Thos. J Davis

Headquarters, 18th Regiment
Camp Near Corinth, September 23rd, 1862

Dear Wife,

I sit down to trouble you with another line to let you know that I am injoying reasonable health and hoping this may find you well. I received a letter from you today dated September 14th & 16th and mailed at LaCrosse the 19th. I have not received any letters from anybody since I wrote to you before. The longest period without receiving a letter from some one for three months. I expect to get several of them however, in a few days.

We have been on another march since I wrote to you before. We started here last Wednesday morning, the 17th, under orders for a place called Iuka, 25 miles east of Corinth on the Memphis and Charleston Railroad to scoop out the Rebels. General Price who had taken that place from a small force of Union troops that had been stationed there to guard the railroad.[27] We had a tough old march first day as it commenced raining early in the morning and continued so with a heavy wind until about 3 o'clock in the afternoon. We all got nicely wet and muddy. We camped at dark after marching upwards of 20 miles. After eating supper we wraped ourselves up in our blankets and laid down on the ground with our guns by our sides to take a night's rest. We rested verry well until about three o'clock in the morning when it begun to rain again. So we had to get up to keep from laying in the water. We stired up the fire and set around it with our rubber blankets over our heads until day light when the rain ceased. The weather was pleasant the rest of the trip.

---

27. General Sterling Price commanded the small Confederate Army of the West (14,000 men) in northern Mississippi. His intention in taking Iuka was to distract and prevent Union reinforcements from moving north against General Braxton Bragg's Confederate troops who were moving north into Kentucky. [Faust, p.386–387]

We traveled a verry crooked route being two days getting within 5 miles of Iuka. The 3rd day our regiment and and the 14th Wisconsin Regiment, our regiment in the advance, was detailed as skirmishers and sent around to the east side of Iuka to drive in the Rebel pickets. We took a circutous route and about 2 o'clock we came upon the Rebel cavalry pickets. They opened fire on us quite briskly. Our regiment advanced upon them returning the fire killing three of them, wounded two, and took five of them prisoners. They found that they were getting in rather too hot a place so the rest of them wheeled their horses and skedaddled for Iuka. We also captured six horses and several double-barrell shotguns and cavlry swords. After we got the pickets thoroughly routed and alarmed, we cut off through a ravine and circuled around back to our main army, getting back about 8 o'clock in the evening.

The next morning our whole army marched upon the place to make a general attack. The right wing under General Ord being in the advance, they marched upon the place without any resistance and found the Rebels leaving.[28] A force of our cavelry made a charge on their rear, killing and wounding several hundred of them before they could get out of the way. We also captured their amunition train and part of their provisions. The Rebels being all mounted men, the larger portion made their escape.

On finding the Rebels had left, our division was ordered back to Corinth while General Rosencrans with his division followed the Rebels.[29] We started from Iuka last Saturday, the 20th, about one o'clock and got back to our camp at Corinth on Sunday evening being out five days and traveled over a hundred miles. You may guess that we felt some like resting.

The most of the boys are well. Ben Greenman has been unwell for several days but is getting smart again. I saw Ed Crandall the other day. He begins to look quite well again. He has not come to the regiment yet. Ike Odell is also at the hospital yet.

I have never had any letter from Burnett's folks yet.

My paper is out and I must close. Keep in good spirits and take care of yourself. There is better times coming.

Thos J. Davis

---

28. General Edward O. C. Ord commanded an 8,000-man Federal force against Price's Confederates. Ord was told to approach Iuka from the northwest while a second Federal force of 9,000 under General William S. Rosecrans came up from the south. As Rosecrans' Federals closed on Iuka, Price attacked his force, then slipped away to the southeast on an unguarded road. Ord's men hardly participated in the Battle of Iuka. Casualties were 1,516 Confederates and 790 Federals. [Faust, p. 387]

29. General William S. Rosecrans actually commanded the Federal Army of the Mississippi during this period of campaigning in northern Mississippi. [Faust, p. 642–643]

[Upside down on the same page]: I forgot to say that none of our men got hurt in the skirmish with the Rebel pickets. One man, [Adam] Bower, had a hole shot through his coat sleeve and another one had a hole shot through the side of his coat.

Spell St. Paul, not Poll; whole the entire, not hole; going, not goin.

"From The "Tigers"

Camp near Corinth, Miss.
September 27, 1862

Mr. Editor: Away down in Dixie we are looking eagerly and anxiously for the assistance of the new levies now being raised in accordance with proclamation of the President, and hoping that their help may soon be made available to us. It is now time for the fall campaign to open in sober earnest, and time that we should be enabled to effectually act on the offensive. It cannot be hid that with our present force it is impossible to leave for any length of time the immediate vicinity of Corinth while the enemy threaten the less important places in this region and attack the towns in our rear to cut off our communications. In this they have heretofore been unsuccessful, but we are unable for the want of more men to follow up the repulses we give them and scatter or capture them.

The Eighteenth, since my last, has been doing for the most part, picket duty, the only interruption worthy of mention being our trip of five days after Gen. Price who had occupied Iuka. For a number of days preceding the expedition preparations were made for a general movement of some kind though, of course, its nature was strictly kept. Rations were constantly kept on hand and things in moving order. Finally, orders were orders were received on the 16th, that at daybreak our division would march. That was all we knew. We were to march.

Soon after we were fairly on the route, the rain descended; not, however, a rainbow-bespangled, sunshiny shower that imaginative writers so beautifully describe but a real old-fashioned soaking, driving rain such as we seldom witness in Wisconsin; in fact, it united perseverance to the many manly characteristics of the fast falling drops, for all day long rain, rain was the order of the day, mud its consequence, and we trudging along in both. Frequently some voice would cry out, "Who wouldn't be a soldier?" or perhaps utter some other poser of a question, which, under the circumstances, was fully as difficult to answer as the one named. Such, however, is the natural condition of men on a march and is seldom taken seriously in such a state as the deluge vouchsafed us that day, when congratulatory expressions are frequently made to the effect that it is a fine thing "to soldier" and that Dixie is, of all others, the choicest of places for the occupation. To be sure, a little irony may sometimes be detected in the modulation of the voice, enough to give hardness and strength to the expression—but that is only a slight distinction and you know that in war times, if drawn at all, they are not heeded.

All day we marched and did not halt till night had thrown her mantle over the sombre forest. The rain had meantime ceased. Our company ground assigned and fires built, we doffed our accoutrements and, ranging around the blazing pile which made the surrounding darkness appear more gloomy, dried our clothing and feet and made out of hard bread and pork—our accustomed food on march—the latter cooked on sticks, a hearty supper. Then in true soldier style did we wrap our blankets about us and lie down, some to sink into complete unconsciousness—some to roam again over the hillsides of nativity or to revisit the peaceful shades of home—some to engage in the strife and hear the roar and din of battle—while some few, perhaps, in a waking reverie, too tired for slumber, attempt by the exercise of feeble mind, linked as it is with matter, to outdistance time and break the barrier of space and determine the location and occupation of those whom he feels closely connected with himself—their thoughts, whether of him, and perhaps pleases himself with the supposition that at that moment a mutual concern pervades each mind. Be their situation of mind and body what it may, a renewal about midnight of the day's copiousness disturbed both—some, however, merely ascertaining the cause of the disturbance, turned over to court anew the favors of Morpheus, others to arise and shiver around the renewed fire. It rained; no mere sprinkle always welcomed to moisten the earth, but water, real water came down in such quantities as left no reasonable doubt but, "it rained." "It is a long lane that has nary a turn," and so was the maxim proven in this case. Morning came at last and with it came fair weather, breakfast, drying of clothes, and a renewal of the march.

During the preceding day we had traveled about twenty miles, tending in direction toward the south of Iuka. Whether the route was discovered to be impractical for artillery, of which we had considerable, or whether different orders arrived, we do not know, but we occupied nearly all the forenoon in traveling the backtrack in order to take another road more to the north. We were at night seven miles of Iuka. It was expected that an early advance and a simultaneous attack would be made the next day when all felt assured that Price, notwithstanding his skedaddling qualities, would be captured.

Morning came, dispatches were read to the soldiers announcing a decisive victory of McClellan in Maryland, which so excited their enthusiasm that cheer after cheer rang in response through the woods. Whether it was really the program to attack that day, I am ignorant, but if it was, the result proves that the plan must have been modified as regarding a general engagement.

Our brigade was assigned a special duty, to make a circuit of about twenty-five miles to the north and east of Iuka and falling upon the rear of the enemy to drive in his pickets, and lead him to infer that we were attacking in force from that quarter. Conducted by a citizen guide, who led us through fields, over hills, and across streams, sometimes by a mere footpath, this object was successfully achieved.

Coming upon the rebel pickets about 4 o'clock p.m., a sharp skirmish ensued between them and our skirmishers, thrown out in advance. The 18th being the advance regiment, was formed in line of battle in the brushy timber and marched forward. The pickets were driven in, three killed, four wounded, and five captured who were not hurt, and five horses taken. Fortunately, no one in the regiment was hurt. There is little doubt but the reports of the pickets had much to do in determining Price to back water and get out of difficulty.

After advancing quite a distance and finding the job done, we made a short detour and about ten at night, rejoined our division, which had advanced during the day. It was a long march but not a murmur was uttered by the men.

A little subsequent to our skirmish, the battle of Iuka was fought by Rosencrans. Of this we knew nothing at the time. The next morning came the general advance & it was found that the place that had known Price knew him no more forever.

He had left between two days. Nothing remained for us but to return to Corinth and resume our usual occupation of picketing, all of which was done, arriving at camp the 21st, having been gone five days, marching all the time after the rascal Price.

The boys are mostly well. But for the length of this article I would give a tabular statement of the condition of the Company, the number dead, their names, those absent sick, and also those who compose, at present, the effective men. My next will include this statement. Yours &c., C. [NW Times, Oct. 8, 1862, p. 2]

CHAPTER FOUR

The Sound Was Anything But Musical

Following the Iuka Campaign, the Federal troops marched back to Corinth, where they were placed on alert. Generals Sterling Price and Earl Van Dorn had combined their Confederate armies to mount an attack on Corinth.

On 1 October, Federal troops, including the 18th Wisconsin, marched to the northwest toward Chewalla, Tennessee, to wait and watch for the approaching Southern army. Confederate troops appeared the next morning and pushed the outnumbered Federals back toward Corinth. After dark on 2 October, the Eighteenth was detailed to guard Smith's Bridge over the Tuscumbia River and to burn it, if necessary. By mid-morning of 3 October, Colonel Bouck learned that the enemy had pushed down the main road to Corinth, bypassing Smith's Bridge, and was threatening to cut off the Eighteenth's route of retreat. Smith's Bridge was hastily set afire and the regiment returned by a side road to the safety of Federal lines.

After a few hours rest, the regiment was sent back to scout the approaching enemy force. The Confederates were found in numbers and skirmishing soon gave way to rolling volleys of rifle fire. Once again, the Eighteenth retreated to the safety of Corinth's inner defenses. There they supported Battery Phillips on the extreme left flank of the Union line.

The next day, 4 October, the Confederate army attacked and suffered appalling losses in a series of ill-coordinated and unsuccessful assaults against Battery Robinette. The "Tigers" watched from a distance as hand-to-hand fighting carried the day for their Federal comrades. That evening the Southern army slipped away from Corinth leaving their dead and wounded on the field of battle. A day after their withdrawal from the field, Federal troops under the command of William S. Rosecrans began their pursuit. The 18th Wisconsin joined in the cross-country chase but returned empty-handed after three days of fruitless backroad marches.

The "Tigers" left Corinth again on 2 November to join General U.S. Grant's first attempt to take Vicksburg, Mississippi. After weeks of preparation at Grand Junction, Tennessee, the Federal army moved south on 28 November. The column had marched as far as Oxford, Mississippi, when the campaign came to a sudden halt. Confederate cavalry had struck at Holly Springs, forty miles behind Grant's army, and had captured the town and burned the Federal army's huge supply base. The loss of the depot at Holly Springs ended the autumn campaign in northern Mississippi.

With Grant's first effort to take Vicksburg stymied, the 18th Wisconsin returned to Holly Springs, then to Moscow, Tennessee, to stand railroad guard duty. While encamped at Moscow, the line officers who had been captured at Shiloh finally returned to their respective companies.

With nearly a year of service behind him, Davis' letters began to display a more relaxed style. The routine of army life held few surprises for the veterans. Among his observations, he noted that the men were becoming tired of war, the army was behind in paying them, and men continued to sicken and die with little sympathy from army doctors. However, one letter does contain some happy news. Lucinda shared the news of the birth of their first child, a daughter. T. J.'s response was typical of a proud father, though tempered by a veiled reference to infant mortality of that era.

Descriptions of the unit's combat near Corinth were to be expected from the Davis and Chase letters but what were less common were the details offered by Davis of unsoldierly behavior during the pursuit of the Confederate army after Corinth. Davis described the "jayhawking" that was visited on the farms along the route of march, a technique that was becoming more practiced and accepted in the western theater of operations than in Virginia.

Davis' commentary in the fall of 1862 reflected the historic soldier vote in the off-year elections, the first time soldiers were able to vote in the field. He also noted celebrations of the Emancipation Proclamation by runaway slaves. Although his observations are tinted with the racial stereotyping that was typical of the 1860s, Davis neither blamed the slaves for the national crisis nor did he display the racism that was often exhibited by white Northerners and Southerners alike.

Finally, Davis expressed his doubts in the success of the Northern war effort and in the nation as a whole. It is at once a keen expression of bitterness, disappointment, disenchantment, and chagrin and at the same time it ends with a barely discernible prayer of hope. Davis had not lost heart entirely but it would require better planning by the generals and harder fighting by the men to turn the war in favor of the national government.

Headquarters 18th Regiment
Corinth, Mississippi, September 28th, 1862

Dear Wife,

I sit down to write you a few lines in answer to your letter which was received this morning bearing date of September 21st & 22nd and was very glad to hear from you and to hear that you was well. I am as well as usual.

The weather is getting considerable cooler and we are begining to get our fall rains. It is raining today though not verry hard. I like to see a reasonable portion come but when there comes a little too mutch it makes the muddiest roads here that I ever saw in my life.

We are still at Corinth doing picket duty. Since we came back from Iuka, I was on picket every other day for over a week. It is thought that the Rebels are fishing around to try and lick us away from Corinth, though I do not think they will undertake it unless they have a verry heavy force.

Ed Crandall and Ike Odell came back to the regiment yesterday. Ed look quite well but Ike looks quite delicate, yet, but is considered out of danger. Ben Greenman has had the rheumatism for several days though he is able to hobble around and he is now sitting and talking to the boys about running the old threshing machine. Many of the boys are getting tired of war and would rather run a threshing at home than to help thresh Rebels for Uncle Sam. But there is one consolation for there is many Rebels tired of threshing for Jeff Davis and if they could conveniently do so many of them would abandon the machine and quit the business.

One of our company is getting his discharge made out today. His name is Stokes from Kickapoo. He was fifer.

We had general inspection this morning. We have inspection of arms the last Sunday in every month to see that we have our guns and all our accoutrements; all in good order and that nothing is lost.

We have not had our pay yet but our payrolls was sent in a few days ago so I guess we will get our pay the fore part of next month. I am glad that you got another payment from the state. They should be more punctual in paying soldiers' wives than they have been. For some of them, I supose, need it verry much. I am glad that you have a good place to live and I am glad that you are so prudent in saving your money. But I do not wish you to deny yourself of anything nesessary for your comfort for the purposes of saving money. I know that many of the soldiers' wives spend more money than is really nesessary.

I supose that the boy you spoke of will be around in the course of a couple of months from now or somewhere thereabouts. You must try and take care of yourself the best you can. I would like to be with you this winter but under the circumstances I don't expect to do so but I hope you will get along without me until I shall get back home again. I am not homesick but a person does not know the comforts of home and friends until they are kept awhile from them.

I have not mutch news to write this time. I have not received but one letter since I wrote to you before. That was from brother Isaac. He is still at Leavenworth, wardmaster in the 7th ward in the general hospital. He wrote that he was well. I begin to look for a letter from Susan and Sarah. I wrote to Susan and Hariet before I went to Iuka though if Hariet has gone to Wisconsin, she may have started before the letter got there. If she comes, tell her I wrote to her and Susan together.

My paper is about out and I must quit for the present so good-bye for this time.

T. J. Davis

From the Eighteenth Regiment

Corinth, Miss. Sept. 30, 1862

[We have been handed the following letter addressed to E.R. CHASE, from a friend of his in the 18th Wisconsin regiment, formerly from this village, from which we extract the subjoined:]

Last Sunday Price's army made an attack on Rosencrans' division, stationed at Iuka about twenty-five miles southeast from here, driving them out of town and capturing a large amount of commissary stores which they stood greatly in need of. Rosencrans sent to Corinth for reinforcements and Monday a division was sent out and Tuesday our division (the 6th), commanded by General McArthur, started for Iuka. On Friday they had a brush with Price's army, retaking the stores captured by them on Sunday. One of our batteries, firing double canister, mowed down rebels by hundreds. Our men could hear the rebel officers give the command to "Close up the Ranks !" after each discharge of the guns. The rebels were armed with all sorts of weapons: old smooth-bore muskets, double-barrel shotguns, squirrel rifles, &c.

The 18th Wisconsin had a small share in the engagement; receiving a volley from the rebels, which did them no harm, and returning it, killing two rebels and taking four or five prisoners. The rebels fought well as long as they thought they had only Rosencrans to deal with but took "leg bail for security" as soon as they discovered that Rosencrans had been heavily reinforced.

The 6th division returned to its old camping ground on Sunday, having been gone five days, during a heavy rain, without tents. There is a prospect of a fight before long between our forces at Bolivar and the rebel army under Breckinridge and Van Dorn. The first Mississippi (white Federal) regiment is being organized at Iuka; its ranks are nearly full and no doubt will be of service.

All that the rebels have to eat nowadays is fresh beef and corn meal, without salt or molasses. They suffer greatly for want of salt. A sutler in Corinth brought on some two hundred barrels of salt intending that the secesh inhabitants would buy salt and haul it off to the rebel army. The Provost Marshall learning of this, prohibited the sale of salt except in small quantities.

The rebels prowl around our camp and occasionally cut off a stragler; three men belonging to the 18th have returned who were taken prisoners, one at a time in this manner. Wisconsin papers are very scarce here. I would like to see a copy of the Record. Truly, W.C. [William Cox] [Expositor, no date on clipping]

Camp Near Ripley, Mississippi, October 9th, 1862

Dear Wife,

I sit down to write you a few lines to let you know where I am. I received your letter yesterday dated September 26th but I have not time or paper to write mutch now.

We had a battle at Corinth on the 4th and we whiped the Rebels out and we are following them up. We are now near Ripley, Mississippi, and I expect we will go on to Holly Springs 25 miles farther and fight the Rebels there if they should make a stand.

Two of the Tigers was wounded at Corinth, Robert Graham and William Downie, both wounded in the shoulders, neither not dangerously. None of our company was killed. I will send this with Robert as I have no envelope here & tell Hariet I cannot write any to her this time.

I received a letter from Sarah Mclean the same time I did yours. She said the family was well and that Hariet had gone to Wisconsin.

I only write this to let you know that I was not hurt in the battle at Corinth. I shall write when I get around more of the peticulars. So do not be uneasy if you do not get letters very regular for sometime to come. But I wish you to write regularly. The mail carrier is going to start back to Corinth in a few minutes with the mail so I must [end this] letter for this time. Write soon. Direct to Corinth as before.

Thos J Davis

P.S. Will Cleary, Ed Crandall, Ike Odell, and Alvin Caulkins is all right so far.

Headquarters 18th Regiment
Camp Near Corinth, October 13th/62

Dear Wife,

Again I sit down to write you a few lines to inform you of my whereabouts and to let you know that I am in tolerable good health at present. I wrote a few lines to you on the 9th while we was on the march but I did not have time or paper to write mutch of a letter.

I supose that you have heard in the papers sometime ago about the battle at Corinth on the 4th of this month or rather the 3rd & 4th. Well, I will tell you something about it. On the 1st day of October our regiment was ordered out to a little town called Charualla [Chewalla], ten miles west of Corinth on the railroad, for the purpose of guarding some bridges to prevent a surprise by the Rebels as we was looking for an attack on Corinth by them.

On the 3rd day our advance guards consisting of our regiment, the 14th & 17th Wisconsin, and the 15th Michigan was driven in by the whole Rebel force, our forces making an occasional stand and firing a few volleys into them and again retreat. About 2 o'clock our regiment had retreated into our camp. They got a hasty dinner and again went out to battle. By this time a considerable force of our men was coming out from Corinth to help check the advance of the Rebels. Our regiment was this time sent out to find the position of the Rebels but we was informed by General McArthur that there was a division of our men between us and the Rebels.[1] I do not know whether McArthur was mistaken or whether he told us so to keep us from being afraid. So we marched up within fifty yards of the Rebels, (it being in thick woods), before our men saw them, and that was with a heavy volley of musketry in the midst of our ranks which was instantly returned by our men and then laid down flat on the ground and loaded and fired as fast as they could for about ten minutes when, being overpowered [by] largely superior numbers, we had to fall back which was done quite rapidly for about two hundred yards.

It was in this fight that William Downie and Robert Graham was wounded. Downie was shot in the left shoulder and Graham in the right, neither of them considered dangerous. They will both start north tomorrow. They will, perhaps, go home.

The next day, the 4th, we was not immediately in the engagement. Our division was detailed to support two forts. We lay down on our faces and seen part of the performance but the forts that we suported kept the Rebels back without our assistance. But balls whistled quite rapidly over our heads. The sound was anything but musical though none of us was hurt. It was at the forts on our right or northwest part of town that the Rebels made the most desperate charge. Though desperate it was, but they were repulsed at every attempt with heavy loss. We was in sight of one of our forts that the Rebels charged upon three times and took it each time. But our in-

---

1. General John McArthur had only just returned from another assignment and commanded a brigade in the 6th Division of the Army of the Tennessee at the Battle of Corinth. [Welcher, Frank J., The Union Army: 1861–1865, Organization and Operations, vol. II: The Western Theater, Bloomington, Ind., Indiana University Press, 1993, p. 555]

fantry each time in turn rallied and took it back at the point of the bayonet so they did not have time to spike any of our cannon.[2]

I do not have any idea how many was killed and wounded on either side. The Rebels was laying dead thick over the ground where they charged upon our forts. Our gunners loaded the guns with double charges of grape and canister which fairly mowed them down at short range. The opinion is that the Sesesh lost five men to our one.[3]

I did not have a chance to pass over mutch of the battlefield after the fight as we started after the retreating Rebels. The next morning before daylight we followed the Rebels for three days. We picked up quite a number of stragglers and captured part of their trains and artillery. By the time we got to Ripley, 45 miles distant, we had them so scattered that it was useless to follow them further.

Thos J. Davis

"From the "Tigers"

Camp at Corinth, Miss.
October 14, 1862

Mr. Editor: The glorious story of the repulse of the rebels in their attack on Corinth is known to you, and doubtless, justly applauded as an evidence of the invincibility of the Western Army as well as adding new lustre to the Union Army in general. It only remains for me to rejoice with you at the result and perform a duty of briefly narrating the portion that our regiment had in contributing to it.

Near noon, Oct. 1st, we received orders to strike tents and change our encampment to the right of our position one and a half miles and near the Chewalla Road. These orders were obeyed so far as removing was concerned, but before opportunity was given to encamp, our brigade was ordered to proceed immediately to Chewalla to meet an unknown force of the enemy then advancing towards the village and which had caused a small detachment of our forces to flee the place and burn it. We arrived just [at] night and lay down quietly upon our arms in a small open field and close to the edge of the timber. A few scouts thrown out discovered such facts in regard to the enemy and his position to cause Col. Oliver, acting brigadier, to quietly withdraw us

2. Davis' position was supporting Battery Phillips. He is probably referring to particularly vicious fighting that engulfed Battery Powell first and then Battery Robinette, Federal artillery positions that were strongly supported by Union infantry brigades. [Welcher, pt. 2, p.556–557]

3. Casualties at the battle of Corinth amounted to 2,520 out of 23,000 Federals and 4,233 out of 22,000 Confederates. [Long, p. 275]

nearly a mile to a small ridge where we slept on our arms the remainder of the night.

Early the next morning a brisk skirmish ensued between a company of the 15th Michigan, which was on picket duty, and the advance scouts of the enemy and the company [was] compelled to fall back. We were, meantime, in line of battle and the two field pieces, in company with us, placed in a position all ready to receive the enemy when our pickets should have fallen back far enough to bring them in range. Our pickets came in but were not followed. A long silence ensued. It was at length discovered that the rebels were making a circuit to get into our retreat and cut off our retreat. This demonstrated two things; that the enemy must be in considerable force, else they would not have attempted the movement; secondly, that it was their intention to attack Corinth and considered their force sufficient, else it would have been entering into a locality from which retreat would have been almost impossible for a small force. In this view of the matter, amply confirmed afterward, it was rendered necessary to retire to save ourselves from complete capture, which was accordingly done and a new position taken four miles nearer Corinth. Thus, we changed one position for another till night, when our regiment was ordered to the left one mile to guard a bridge across the Tuscumbia.

With us the night of the 2nd was without special interest. But in the morning the Colonel received orders to get into camp the most feasible way, as the enemy had possession of the Chewalla road and was rapidly getting in our rear. We were hurried by a bye-road almost on a double quick into our line of defenses. We must have been just in time as soon afterwards the enemy appeared in that direction. A short time to rest and obtain rations was given us, when we again fell into ranks and marched to the right where a sharp firing had occasionally occurred during the morning. We here joined the rest of the Sixth Division. Meantime, the enemy had advanced and entered the line of our fortifications at the Chewalla road. One of our brigades had made a charge upon them in the timber some half mile from us and driven them but were, in turn, compelled to retire before a superior force. To support this brigade, the 18th was ordered down the hill to the right of it into action.

At the foot of the hill and while crossing the railroad, Brigadier General McArthur told the Colonel that we had a line of battle in front of us and that we were to assist it. We marched forward in line of battle. Everything was quiet.—The firing to the left and front where the supposed brigade was had ceased some minutes before.—It was heavy timber—we could not see positions, but we had confidence in what had been told us. All at once a number of bullets whistled over our heads, fired only a few rods in front of us. It was thought a mistake by all—it was believed that our own men must be firing to the rear upon us. We were ordered to lay down. It was scarcely done when from a solid line of battle, at pistol distance, a whole volley from the rebels was fired into us. They must have been lying down and witnessing our advance. Our men replied gallantly. The Belgian rifles, in this short action, by their good behavior endeared themselves to the men. There was no brigade for us to support; it had retired some minutes before and the 18th alone was confronting the line of the enemy which had in the meantime advanced. The air may be said to have been "alive with bullets." Few would have escaped uninjured had not the order to lay down been given. As it was, the enemy fired low. All who were wounded were hit while down. At so short a distance, one line or the other must soon give way—in this instance, both retreated; the enemy, I think, first, for the firing from their ranks entirely ceased before many of us left.

It was error that we were there and worse than folly to charge alone an advancing line, which is, of necessity, always strong, with no supporting forces near. Our regiment only number 124 men in ranks,—of the remaining, 50 were on picket away on the left where they had been two days unrelieved, and "K" Company was entirely absent with the 15th Michigan.

Our loss is about 30 killed, wounded, and missing. Company "C" had two wounded, and had fourteen men only in action—Wm. Downie in left shoulder and Robt. E. Graham in right shoulder. They were both sent North today and doing well. Your correspondent was assigned to the command of "I" Company, the Captain being unwell. It numbered twenty-one men and suffered more than any other company as two were killed and five wounded.

Soon after, the whole division was marched into town and assigned position; It was now dark and we lay down to rest. You have read of the rebels throwing shells into town early in the morning; they passed a little to our left, we being then and until nine o'clock at the identical spot where the rebels charged into the place. An apprehension that the enemy contemplated an attack upon our left caused our division to be transferred there, where we remained all day inactive, not being attacked.

I have not space to write, neither would you have patience to read any statement concerning the glorious termination of the contest. It has been written and read till, with the North, it is already a well learned story. I shall only remind you of a prediction in a former article that "should the rebels come they would get a reception worthy the visitors and the occasion," a prediction which has been amply fulfilled.

At midnight we started in pursuit and followed close till the 9th and saw many evidences of the precipitate nature of their retreat. They threw away baggage, wagons, ammunition, and guns to expedite their flight, but we captured many prisoners. But it was all nonsense following Price. Who ever heard of his being caught? His well known running propensities were, in this case, needed and put into full requisition. We returned to Corinth, arriving in the evening of the 11th.

Our company is getting very small. A number are being discharged for disability and some sent North to hospitals—of the last, Sergt. Morley, Sebastian Baltz, and Benjamin Greenman may be mentioned. The tabular statement of our condition as a Company promised in my last, I reserve for my next in consideration of the extreme length of this. Believe me,

Yours truly, C. [NW Times, Oct. 29, 1862, p. 2]

Headquarters, 18th Regiment Wisconsin Volunteers
Camp Near Corinth, Mississippi October 15th, 1862

Dear Brother & Sister [G. W. and E. Ditto],

I once more sit down to write you a line to let you know that I am in tolerable good health and hope this will find you all well. I received your letter a few days ago bearing date of September 29th and was verry glad to hear from you all once more. I would have answered it before now [but] I have had no chanse to write untill now. We have been marching or fighting or laying in line of battle or laying on our arms day and night from the first of this month to t[he] twelfth so you can judge whether I ha[ve had] time to write mutch or not.

I suppos[e you] have heard that we had a fight at Corinth before this time. It was fought on the 3rd & 4th of this month and we whiped the Rebels a little the nicest they have ever been cleaned out yet, though it took some hard fighting to do it. We had to fight the combined forces of the Rebels Price, Villipigue,[4] and Van Dorn.[5] They greatly outnumbered the forces that we had here. The fighting commenced on the 3rd about six miles west of town. Our brigade commenced the fight with the enemy as they was out there guarding against a surprise as we was looking for them. We would take a position and when the enemy's advance came up we would fire into them and hold them in check until the main Rebel force come up and then we would retreat back towards town and take another position. We kept on in that way until about the middle of the afternoon [w]hen we had retreated back within about [?] miles of Corinth where two divisions of [our] forces was drawn up in line of battle when a general fight ensued lasting untill night. Being largely outnumbered we had to give way to them in the open woods but hotly contesting every inch of ground at night all of our forces was drawn inside of our forts.

After night the Rebels got a position within half a mile of town and built a fort and at daylight in the morning they commenced shelling the town from their new fort. But they did not have time to do mutch damage before our our siege gun fort got range on them and silenced their fort and run them from their guns and we captured their pieces. Skirmishing was kept up untill about 10 o'clock when the Rebels made two charges on the town, one on the north and the other on the northwest side, both at the same time which lasted about 4 hours. Our batteries and infantry re-

---

4. General John B. Villepigue commanded a brigade of Confederate infantry at the battle of Corinth. [Davis, William C. (ed.), The Confederate General, vol. 6., Harrisburg, Pa., National Historical Society, 1991, p. 84]

5. General Earl Van Dorn commanded the Confederate Army of West Tennessee and Price's Confederate Army of the West at the battle of Corinth. Soon after the battle he was transferred to a Confederate cavalry command. [Davis, pt.6, p. 75]

pulsing every charge that the Rebels made and after they got terribally mown down and cut up.

The Rebels ceased firing and commenced a retreat about 2 o'clock leaving the field literally strewn with their dead and wounded. We followed them the next morning before daylight. We threw out skirmishers through the woods and picked up quite a number of their straglers and about noon on Sunday we run the main Rebel force into General Hurlbert's Division on the Hatchie River, being on his road from Bolivar to Corinth. Hurlbert had a hard fight with them whiping their whole force with six thousand men and taking eleven pieces of artillery.[6] We kept on after them until we took all their artillery but one piece and the most of their trains and amunition. By the time we got to Ripley, a distance of 45 miles, we had them so mutch scattered that it was useless to follow them further. So we gave up the chase and came back to Corinth again.

Our regiment was in the fight the first day but we was on the reserve the 2nd and was not immediately in the engagement. Our regiment lost about forty men killed, wounded, and missing. Our company had two wounded, none killed or missing. Our regiment now musters about one hundred fighting men.

I had letters from Isaac and Mother Ingersoll's folks and my wife lately. They all wrote they were well. I have so many letters to answer or I would write you more this time. So I must close for the present. Write soon, direct as before.

Thos. J Davis

October 16th, 1862

Well, I thought I would write a few more lines as I did not write mutch of a letter before. We started back to Corinth the next day after I wrote to you, being the 10th and arrived here the 12th, and I have not had time until now to write and I have several letters to answer now; one to my brother at Leavenworth, one to my sister Elisabeth, one to Sarah McLain, and one to David Ingersoll's mother and sister. I got a letter from them a few days ago. The folks was well, little Charlie well and going to school. David had gone to war or was in camp at Peoria. They said they had received a letter from you and was going to answer it. They said they would like verry much to see you. Sister Elisabeth wrote that she received a letter from brother William. He was taken prisoner in middle Tennessee and

---

6. General Stephen A. Hurlbut commanded the 4th Division of the District of Jackson, Tennessee, in the battle of Corinth. During the pursuit of Van Dorn's army, Hurlbut took command of E.O.C. Ord's troops when Ord was wounded in a fight at the Hatchie River. [Boatner, p.420; Welcher, pt.2, p.557–558]

was released on parole. He was at Nashville when he wrote. I have not had a letter from him in over two months. I have not received any letter from Jabez yet.

We just heard last night night that there had been a heavy battle in Kentucky between the forces of General Buell and the Rebel General Bragg and that Buell had whiped the Rebels badly and taken all their artillery and many prisoners.[7] We have not heard the peticulars of it so I don't put much confidence in the report until I hear more about it.

Our men had quite a time jayhawking on our last march and I thought some of them was rather too hard hard on the Sesesh.[8] We found many of the houses deserted by their owners with their furniture left in the houses and chickens, geese, sheep, hogs, cattle, mules, and horses left on the place. All of which was eaten up and destroyed in many cases. One morning our boys stoped at a house to get some water and a woman come out and threw some lime and soap in the well. The boys kept on drawing water. She finally got an axe and cut the well rope and let the bucket to the bottom. The man that belonged to the house had shot at one of our men that morning so the boys thought they were carrying the joke rather far. So they set the house on fire and burned it to the ground.

One of the 15th Michigan boys stopped at a good looking farm house and asked the woman of the house for some milk. She informed him that she had not a drop of milk in the house. He told her that he [could] see plenty of cows on the place and he knew that she had milk and said he (putting a bundle of straw under the corner of the house and pulling out a match) and [said], "If you dont give me some I will burn your house down."

Becoming scared she said, "For God's sake, don't burn my house and I will give you all the milk you want." Rather a novel way, I should think, to bring a woman to her milk.

In the late fight our regiment lost about forty men in killed, wounded, and prisoners. Three of the Tigers started north the day before yesterday morning. They were Calvin Morley and Sebastion Baltz of Viroqua and

---

7. The battle of Perryville was fought on 8 October 1862 and stopped Bragg's Confederate invasion of Kentucky. However, Federal General Don Carlos Buell's poor battlefield coordination (only nine of twenty-three Federal brigades were heavily engaged) cost his army the chance to achieve a significant victory against Bragg's Army of Tennessee. [Welcher, pt.2, p.638–639]

8. "Jayhawking" was a Civil War soldier slang term for raiding or stealing, particularly food items. In this letter, Davis also documents destruction of Southern property, which recalls comparisons with "bleeding Kansas" in the 1850s when anti-slavery Jayhawkers and pro-slavery Border Ruffians destroyed opposing farms and villages. [Dickson, p.178]

Ben Greenman. They have all been unwell for sometime. I think they will be sent home before long.

Hariet thinks I was too bad to scold her so I don't know what I have written that she takes as scolding. I have only answered her own propositions. I have not tried to get ahead of her, as she says, or out-blackgard her, either, for that is not my style of correspondence, though I supose I could hold my hand if I wished to engage in it. She did not write mutch for me to answer. Tell her to write again.

We have not received our pay yet. Write soon.

T. J. Davis

Camp Near Corinth, Mississippi,
October 20th, 1862

Dear Wife,

I received your letter day before yesterday dated October 5th. It found me as well as usual and I hope this may find you well. I was sorry to hear that your health was not so good as it has been. It is nothing more than natural that you may expect to experiance some illness. But you should be very careful of your health as I have cautioned you before. Mutch depends on the care you take of yourself and if people wish to laugh at you, let them laugh at you. Let them laugh if they have nothing else to do and it does them any good. Old folks should give good advice rather than repremand infirmities. You should never do wrong because other folks wish you to.

We have moved camp about a mile-and-a-half since I wrote you last. All is quiet about Corinth now. I do not know how long we will remain here. [The following was written upside down on the same page]

I will send you a piece of Sesesh ribon so you can tell them you have a ribbon from Rebeldom.

[now right side up]

War is uncertain. We may stay here a month or two and again we may be called out on a march in a few days.

Since writing the above I received another letter from you dated October 12th. I am glad to learn that your health is better. You seemed uneasy [about] the Corinth battle. I thought you would be. I wrote as soon as I could so you know before this that I was not killed. I have wrote you two letters since the battle or rather one and a piece.

The weather is quite pleasant here at the present though rather too warm in the middle of the day. The nights are quite cool we had a light frost last night; the first frost I have seen since I left St. Louis the first of April last.

I have just wrote a letter to Burnett. I thought perhaps he might have wrote to me and the letter never come though.

I forgot to tell you in my other letter that my brother William was taken prisoner in a battle in east Tennessee sometime ago. He was paroled and was at Nashville when I heard from him last. I do not know whether he was in the late battle in Kentucky or not. I think that the LaCrosse Battery is with General [G.W.] Morgan. I see from the papers that he has left Cumberland Gap in a northeasterly direction towards Portsmouth, Ohio. I think you will hear from them soon.

I was sorry to learn the Hariet was so unwell and hope her illness will not continue long and that her portables will soon regain their original runing order. I hope she will remain in Wisconsin until I get back.

I hope I shall get home by next April. I think this war will take a turn this winter. It is getting to be too large a thing to last a great while without disgrace both to the North and South. The South has a much larger force than the people in the North generally supose and are not so easily starved out as is so mutch talked of and the Rebels have the advantage of us in many respects. We have to open transportation and keep all railroads guarded and guard all forts and towns that we take from them while they can use the most of their forces for fighting. It is my honest conviction that this war will have to be compromised for I do not believe that it will be settled by fighting as the South is greatly indignant with the government and will not unconditionally submit to the Northern government so long as they can carry on a war which, in my opinion, they can do long enough to bankrupt this nation. I judge from the past what the future will bring.

As to your state pay you spoke of, the state treasury war fund will run out on the first of November but the state is bound for it when it gets the money, if it is not for ten years.

Write soon,

Jefferson T. Davis

Good-bye to Sis, L.M. Davis

Headquarters, 18th Regiment Wisconsin Volunteers
Camp Near Corinth, November 2nd, 1862

Dear Wife,

I received your letter this morning dated Oct 26th and was very glad to hear that you and the rest of the folks was well. I received a few lines from you three days ago dated Oct 16th, mailed at Hockley.

We are now under marching orders with our knapsacks and tents all packed and awaiting the orders to start. So I am stealing these few minutes to write to you. I do not know where we are going but we have six days rations to take with us. We may be gone a week or ten days and we may not be gone so long though you must not be uneasy if you do not get a letter as early as common from me.

Tell Mother and John that I was glad to receive their letter and I will write to them again when I get time. I have not time to write mutch news this morning so you must excuse a short letter this time. Also tell Hariet to write, too, and I will write more in my next. I have not received any letters from Sarah or Susan since I wrote to you before.

All the Badax boys are as well as usual. I have told Ike Odell to write to his folks so often that I have poor incouragement to tell him any more.

You cannot brag for having all the cold weather in Wisconsin for we had a snowstorm here the 25th of October with about an inch and a half of snow and several days of blustery cold weather. But it cleared up and we are having nice pleasant weather again with some appearance of rain today.

You must take extra care of your health and be a good girl. Perhaps there is better times coming. One year ago today I was cutting wood on the river and the weather was pleasant, mutch like it is here today.

We was mustered for pay again last Friday. We have not been paid yet. There is four months pay due us the last day of October. I don't know when we will get paid. They have been rather careless about paying the soldiers this fall but I think we will get it before a great while.

I must bring my letter to a close. Write soon, direct as before. So good-bye

T. J. Davis

I don't know whether you can read this or not after it gets cold.

Headquarters, 18th Regiment Wisconsin Volunteers
Camp Near Grand Junction, Tennessee, November 6th, 1862

Dear Wife,

I sit down this morning to pencil you a few lines to inform you that I am as well as usual and trust this may find you in good health.

We started from Corinth on the 2nd of this month, being 4 days ago, and arrived here at Grand Junction night before last a distance of forty miles. We are camped two miles south of the Junction at [a] nice clear, runing creek, something that is not very common in this country. We had quite a hard trip on account of so mutch dust, which in many places was shoetop deep and when the wind would blow we could not see but a few rods distance.

We held election on the 4th while on the road. Robert McMichael was one of the judges and I was one of the clerks.

We are concentrating our forces here from Corinth, Bolivar, and Jackson for the purpose of making an attack on Holly Springs 18 miles south of here where the Rebels are fortified. We are getting quite a large force here but I believe the Rebels will evacuate Holly Springs before we pitch onto them for I don't believe they will stand us a fight unless they have a heavy force and are well fortified.

Some of our men went out foraging yesterday and they brought in all the fresh beef & pork, and sweet potatoes that we could use and a considerable amount of chickens, turkeys, and honey and, in fact, many of our men will take anything they want that they can get hold of around the citizens' farm houses. This is a better farming country here than it is about Corinth but the products of the soil quickly vanish when the Yankees come along. When our brigade was marching as rear guard for our train every few rods we could see a hog skin or beef hide laying by the roadside that our troops ahead of us had killed.

We had quite a windstorm last night and it was quite cold but it did not rain but little. We need rain verry bad to settle the dust. I have not much news to write today. I wrote to you the day we left Corinth. I just write this to let you know where I am. There is some talk that our brigade will quarter this winter at Columbus, Kentucky. I hope they will. Perhaps they will keep us marching several weeks yet before we go into winter quarters. I am obliged to write this with a pencil and I don't know whether you can read it or not. I will close for the present. Write soon, direct as before.

From your most obedient servant,

Thos. J. Davis

Headquarters, 18th Regiment Wisconsin Volunteers
Camp Near Grand Junction, Tennessee, November 12th, 1862

Dear Wife,

I received a letter from you yesterday dated November 2nd. It found me as well as usual and I was glad to hear that you was well. We are still hear at Grand Junction and more of our forces coming in every day. I supose from the movements that our generals mean to make an attack on Holly Springs, which is 25 miles south of this place on the railroad to New Orleans, at which place the Rebels are concentrating their forces and making fortifications to defend the place. I think we will route them out of there before a great while but I don't think our generals will be so foolhardy as to charge upon their works as they did on ours at Corinth but will surround them and shell them out unless they smell a mice and leave before we get ready to commence on them. I said, "I supose from the movements of our army," for the movements is all that I can judge from for under-officers and privates are never informed of the intentions of our generals until after they are carried into execution. I don't think that we will have more than a month more of good fighting weather here this winter before we will go into winter quarters.

My health is better now than it has been for several months and the rest of the boys are in good health. Ike Odell was left at Corinth in the hospital. I hear that they are making out his discharge. Ed Crandall is growing like a weed and is getting fat as a china pig. We have plenty to eat now with the exception that we have to use hard crackers for bread since we come here but we have plenty of fresh beef & fresh pork and salt porks and bacon and most of the time all the sweet potatoes that we could use. We have tents to sleep in and clothes enough to keep us comfortable except in verry bad weather.

We had a nice shower of rain last night which the dusty roads mutch needed.

I received a letter from Sarah McLain the other day. She said she had just received a letter from you and Hariet. I saw a young man yesterday, Jo Graham, I used to be acquainted with in Illinois. He has been home on a visit. He left Illinois last week. He seen little Charlie. He said he was well. I received a letter from David Ingersoll's sister yesterday. I will send it to you.

You must excuse a short letter as I have a poor way of writing and I have several letters to answer now and I am cooking for the company and can't always get time to write when I wish. Direct your letters as before as they will come to the regiment if we are not at Corinth. You must not get so uneasy as you did before if you hear of another battle down here.

Thos. J Davis

Headquarters 18th Regiment Wisconsin Volunteers
Camp Near Grand Junction, Tennessee, November 23rd ,1862

Dear Lucinda,

I again sit down to write you a few lines to inform you that I am as well as usual and hope this may find you well. I received a letter from you last night dated November 9th conveying the intelligence that another Badger of the female persuasion had emigrated to Wisconsin.[9] But I had got the news nearly a week before in one of Robert McMichael's letters so you see it did not surprise me much, though I was glad to learn that you was doing well. You wished me to send a name for the gehal [gal]. I don't hardly know what to say about it for it seems like rather small business to engage

---

9 Davis' first child, Silvie May, a daughter, was born on 8 November 1862. [Davis family papers]

in, yet. I guess I had better wait a while and see if it will grow big enough to be worth sending a name to so far. It would scarcely understand its name yet awhile anyway.

Don't you think I make a regular spread eagle of myself with the idea of being called dad, when I get home and entertain imaginary ideas of being a man of a family. Tell it not to cry after me for I will be at home one of these days. Mrs. Smith says it was good-looking but did not wish to tell you so lest it would make you proud, I supose. That was a sly way she took to flatter me, though, I think I will get over it for I'm tough. Well, I supose that is enough about the baby for this time.

We are still here at Grand Junction, yet, and I don't have any idea how long we will remain here or how soon we will leave. We have a larger body of troops here. Enough I supose to lick any force of Rebels in this part of the Confederacy. There is so mutch said and talked of about the war that I almost dislike to write anything about it and I hope how soon we may have no war to be talked of. As to the honors of war, they have no charms for me farther than doing my duty for the good of my country. I almost think this war is a curse put upon the people for the wickedness of the nation. At least thousands are being punished by it. I have some hopes that the war may be settled this winter. I never allow myself to get the blues except the red, white, & blue and sometimes that runs to a low ebb.

We are having a pretty good time here. The weather is pleasant and appears healthy. We are beginning to have heavy frosts, cold nights. Ice will freeze on pudales at night about the thickness of window glass but it all melts again before noon.

The boys are generally in pretty good health. Ben Greenman is in the hospital at Jefferson Barricks ten miles below St Louis. I got a letter from him the other day. He said he was not getting any better. Jim Williams has been sent north since we left Corinth. I received a letter from brother William yesterday. He is in Benton Barricks, St Louis. He is a paroled prisoner. He was taken prisoner at the Battle of Perryville, Kentucky, on the 8th of October. He said he was well.

I wish you would send me a half-dollar's worth of letter stamps if you can get them here. [I get them] only as I happen on individuals [that] has had them sent to them. I have used a dollar's worth since I left Bolivar besides what you have sent me. I have over 60 old letters in my knapsack and have sent away and burnt up as many more since I have been down here. I will send some cotton just as I pulled it out of the pod. Give my respects to Hariet and Mrs. Smith and your mother's folks. Tell your mother and John I will try and answer their letter in my next

Yours as ever,

T. J. Davis

Camp At Abbeville, Mississippi, December 5th, 1862

Dear Wife,

I received a letter from you and Hariet dated November 18th and was glad to learn that the folks was well and that you was as well as could be expected. I am as well as usual at present and I believe all the Badax boys are well that are with us now. Ben Greenman is in the hospital at Jefferson Barricks.

We have been marching again since I last wrote to you. We started from Grand Junction on the 28th of November and arrived here 2 days ago. We come upon the Rebels 8 miles south of Holly Springs on Wolf River last Saturday; that is their advance guard. We routed them from there and drove them into their fortifications 8 miles further south on the Talla-hatchie River. They had heavy fortifications on the Tallahatchie but becoming afraid that we would surround them and get in their rear and cut off their supplies, on Monday they got up and skeddaddled and left their fortifications. They are retreating towards Jackson, Miss. I don't know whether they mean to make any stand between here and Jackson or not.

We are about 50 miles south of Grand Junction on the railroad. The Rebels burned both the railroad bridge and the state road bridge on the Tallahatchie. We will remain here for a few days untill we get the railroad repaired so we can bring up our supplies and then I supose we will march ahead if the road don't get too muddy.

We have had considerable rain for three or four days past. Last night we had a heavy rain which wound up this morning with a dash of snow but it was all gone again by noon. I supose you are having some cold weather now in Wisconsin but we see nothing hardly that tells us it is winter. But I expect we will have a good old muddy time this winter.

We have not been paid off yet. There is over five months pay due us now and many of the soldiers are anxious to get it as the state pay is stopped. There must be many soldiers families that need money though there are some families that would not save any money if they got a hundred dollars per month.

Hariet must not be so jealous as to herself in peticular. She writes as though she thought I had some great spite or grudge towards her and thinks I don't want to answer her letters. I thought my letters would do you and her both for Hariet has never written mutch anyway and I have considerable writting to do and a verry poor way to do it and not much time to write in.

I received a letter the other day from brother Isaac at Leavenworth. He said he had got well again he has taken to himself a rib after the fashion of Adam. He was married on the 20th of last month. He is still acting wardmaster in the hospital. I also got a letter from Elisabeth. She said the folks was all well. She did not say anything about writing to you any more she says she had to do all the writing for the family and there is considerable of it to do. So I supose she neglects it on that account.

I have not studdied up any name for that girl, yet. I am afraid that it is such a nice girl that I can't immagin a name pretty enough without the Bible dictionary. So I will let it grow a while longer.

My paper is out and so am I.

Yours as ever so good-bye.

T. Jefferson Davis

Camp at Abbeville Mississippi, December 9th, 1862

Dear Wife,

I received two letters from you to day one dated November 23rd and the other December 1st. I was glad to learn that you are doing well. I am as well as usual.

We are having fine weather here for winter: frosty nights & suny days except when it rains. We have not had any for four or five days but we may look for mutch rain and mud this winter.

I received a letter this morning from David Ingersoll's sisters, Belle & Ida. They say times is hard and lonely in Illinois. Belle said that little Charlie was well and going to school but says that her mother was unwell, has had spells and fears that she will not survive the winter. Belle said she had written to you at last.

We are still here at Abbeville. We will be likely to stay here untill we get the railroad repaired so that we can bring up supplies for the army and then we will move on towards Jackson, Miss.

You say that Mrs. Johnson and Baker are both talking of paying them notes. It does not make any difference to me which pays it so it is paid. But as you said, "Don't receive anything on them only U.S. paper or coin." I suppose that government paper is as easy to be got as any other good paper. The notes draws 7 percent interest from their date. If they pay it you must add up the interest and have it all paid together. The notes were given for $1,118.36 and on the 21st of next February interest and all will amount to about one hundred thirty three dollars and fifty cents ($133.50). The interest runs 'til it is paid and stops when it is paid. I know that times must be hard up there and goods high. All I have to say is to try and do the best you can and keep yourself comfortable and be consistantly economical and I hope we will come out all right when the war ends.

Our boys say that I get more letters than anyone in the company; when the mail comes in and the orderly comes out with but few letters. Some of the boys will hollow [holler] out, "No letter for me, I know. Only a letter or two for T. J. Davis !" Sometimes when the mail comes in before it is distributed some one will say, "T. J., go and get your letters."

I would say, "How do you know I have any?"

"Because the mail has come. For you always get one when there is any mail." I burned about 70 letters when I left Grand Junction because I could not carry them. I would like to have kept them all and taken them home with me if I could.

Alvin got a letter yesterday from his father they had got to their new home in Iowa and was all well and well satisfied.

I would like perhaps as well as any man for this war to end and disliked as mutch as any one to see it come but I do not mean to get the blues. I did not enlist with that intention. If I knew the war was settled and was to start home in three months I would feel more anxious about getting home than I do now.

I would like first rate if you would send me your likeness. I meant to have mine taken at Corinth but neglected it until we left there and now I can't get it taken at all.

You have been teasing me so mutch about naming the girl that don't hardly know what to say. I am not mutch of a hand to name babies but I will send you one and if it does not suit you, you can name it yourself or get somebody else to do it. The name I propose is Silva May. I send my respects to your mother's folks and Mrs. Smith & family. Direct to Cairo, Illinois, when you write.

My paper is out and I must close.

Yours as ever,

Thos J. Davis to Lucinda M. Davis

Holley Springs, Mississippi, December 24th/62

Dear Lucinda,

I once again sit down to write you a few lines to let you know that I am as well as usual. We are now at Holley Springs. We came here day before yesterday. We went down ten miles below Oxford about forty miles south of here and a force of the Rebels come around behind us and took this place last Saturday and burnt up all the government stores that was here and burnt the houses they were in and blew up our magizine and in the fray burnt considerable property belonging to citizens. They took about a thousand of our men here and paroled them. Old Man Moody was here and was paroled with the rest. The Rebels knew there was not many men here so they made a dash and paroled our men, burnt the supplies and tore up a portion of the railroad and left again the same day for fear they would get into a trap.[10]

The railroad is also obstructed up near Bolivar by Bragg's forces so we have had no mail for already a week. The Rebels captured two mails. The last letter I received from you was dated December 1st. I got it about two weeks ago. I think it is likely the Sesesh has spiked some of my letters. I have not had a chance to send out a letter since the foray untill this afternoon. I am on detale today husking corn in a mill here. So you see, we will get some corn dodger.[11] I have not mutch time to write today and the mail will start out in a few minutes.

We have not had any news in so long a time that don't know what is going on in Virginia or anyplace else. We have not been paid off yet. Perhaps we will get it when the war is over, if ever. This is the nicest winter weather I've ever seen. No snow and about enough rain to keep the roads from getting dusty and warm enough in the day time to go in our shirt sleeves.

You must excuse this short letter. I will write more in my next. We have a report that Richmond is taken but I don't believe it yet but hope it may be so.

Direct your letter to Cairo, Illinois, and they will follow the regiment. Write soon.

Don't mail anymore letters at Bergen if you can help it. Yours,

Thos. J. Davis

[Untitled Item]

Illness of Lieut. Chase—We regret to learn that Lieut. Chase of the Tiger Company is very low in hospital at La Grange, Tennessee, of chronic diarrhea. Lieut. C. was unable to move with his regiment when they left Corinth on a forward movement but remained in Hospital till the 27th ult. when he started to rejoin his company, but was unable to proceed further than La Grange. A change of climate is recommended by his physicians as being the only hope of preserving life. This is a sufficient excuse for not corresponding as usual. [NW Times, December 24, 1862, p. 2]

---

10. A Confederate cavalry force under General Earl Van Dorn successfully attacked General U.S. Grant's Holly Springs, Mississippi, supply depot on 20 December 1862. Damages were estimated at $1 million in lost supplies and 1,500 prisoners. The raid on Holly Springs disrupted Grant's approach on Vicksburg from northern Mississippi. [Long, 298–299]

11. A small cake of cornbread.

December 29th, 1862

Mr. Lincoln & Co.

I received a letter from you yesterday dated December 13th. The last one I received before this was dated December 1st. So I guess there is one lost that you have wrote. I am as well as usual and was glad to learn that you was well.

We are still here at Holley Springs but I don't know how long we shall remain here as things seem rather unsettled at this time.

I received a letter from Jabe yesterday. It was the same date of yours. He was at Memphis, Tennessee. He said that he was well. He said he was getting tired of the war and wanted it to close so he could go home again. He said he had just received a letter from home and that he heard that he had another niece in Wisconsin.

Christmas has come and past but I did not see anything that reminded me that it was Christmas except occasionally I would hear someone repeat the words "I wish you a Merry Christmas." I did not hear the jingling of sleigh bells or the merry laugh of the belles and beaus enjoying their Christmas sleigh ride, nor did I see the young bouyant hearts of the fun loving public as usual assemble at the dancing hall to shake the fantastic toe with the music of the violin though the Niggers had a jollification dance uptown at night in honor, I supose, of Massa Lincum'z Proclamation but I did not feel enough interested on that important occasion.[12]

We have verry nice weather for this time of year. It hardly seems as though it is winter though it makes it that mutch better for military business. We have not had mutch rain yet but we may soon begin to look for the rainy season and then we may look out for muddy roads and slow and hard traveling for the army.

We have just received orders to march at 2 o'clock this afternoon. So I will not have time to write as mutch as I intended to. The boys, I believe, are all in tolerable good health at this time. Ed Crandall got a letter yesterday which informed him that Sarah, one of the other girls, was sick with the dyptherea.

I dont know where we are going to march to but I think we are going to Grand Junction. When you write direct to Cairo, Illinois, and they will come straight to the regiment no matter where we are. I must close and go to packing my knapsack. Oh, I forgot, H.L. Johnson is here in the 12th Wisconsin Battery. No more this time but remain

Yours truly
Thos. J. Davis

---

12. The Emancipation Proclamation freed slaves in areas defined as "still in rebellion" and took effect on 1 January 1863. [Long, p.306]

P.S. I wish if you could, without mutch trouble, send me 50 cents worth of letter stamps.

T. J.D.

Moscow, Tennessee, January 7th, 1863

Dear Lucinda,

I received a letter from you last night dated December 21st. It found me as well as usual and I was glad to learn that you was well and in good spirits. Our mail communication has been cut off by the Rebels so that we have not had any mail from the north for over two weeks until last night. But when the mail come in I got five letters: one from you and one from Sarah McLain, one from sister Elisabeth, one from brother O.K. Davis, and one from brother Isaac.

You will see that we have moved again since I wrote to you before. We left Holley Springs a week ago last Monday afternoon and got here the next day. This is about 25 miles north from Holly Springs on the Charleston and Memphis Railroad, 12 miles west of Grand Junction and 33 miles east of Memphis. We have just got the railroad fixed up and two trains came in from Memphis yesterday. We was put on half rations when our provisions was burnd at Holly Springs on the 18th of last month and had strict orders not to jayhawk or forage any from the citizens; only when ordered by the quartermaster. Notwithstanding the the order, jay-hawking still went on and we generally had plenty to eat. We commenced drawing full rations yesterday. We have been been down about seventy miles south of here and the Rebels got in behind us so we was compelled to back out and come back to this railroad to keep our supplies from being cut off and await the result of the river forces which I hear has been fighting at Vicksburg.[13]

I don't think we will go south again before spring and by that time I hope the war will be settled. The Sesesh say that we shall not use this road from the Junction to Memphis but we have got it open now and we will try it a clatter anyway.

We just received a dispatch last night that Rosencrans and Bragg had a fight in middle Tennessee and that Bragg got severely whiped.[14] So mutch

---

13. General William T. Sherman commanded 32,000 troops in a 27–29 December 1862 assault on Vicksburg by way of Chickasaw Bluffs, Mississippi. After several unsuccessful attacks, Sherman withdrew his forces on 2 January 1863. [Long, p.301–302]

14. The battle of Stones River, Tennessee, took place from 30 December 1862–3 January 1863. General Braxton Bragg's Confederate attacks on General William S. Rosecrans' Federal positions were unsuccessful, although casualties on both sides were heavy, approximately 12,000 each. [Long, p. 302–307]

good for that. Our western forces can lick the Sesesh everytime but the ill success which our forces have had on the Potomac is not flattering and I fear that they will never take Richmond.[15]

I believe I wrote you a letter since Christmas. Perhaps you would like to know how I spent New Year's. Well, I will tell you. We had a New Year's Eve frolic and a watch meeting. The day before New Year's our company and company B was detaled to go about five miles west of town to guard a railroad bridge. In the afternoon some Negroes came to us at the bridge and told us that there was five hundred Rebel cavalry about four miles north of the bridge [and] that they intended to pitch on [and] capture us all that night, So we kept a sharp lookout and kept all the roads guarded coming to the bridge. At dark two companies of Ingineers that was working on the bridge and our two companies, making about 150 men in [all] , we all went to work and built a fort of cord wood near the bridge about a hundred feet square and about breast-high. We got it done about nine o'clock. We then felt pretty safe and kept near our guns and watched for the Rebels 'til morning. But they didn't happen to come and I wasn't anxious to see them come. But if they had we was well fixed to give them "Hail Columbia".

I am on guard today watching a railroad bridge half a mile from town on Wolfe River. I brought out my pen, ink and, paper and am setting on a rock and writing on my knee. Robert McMichael is by my side setting on his knapsack and writing on the head of an empty nail keg.

The whole number of the Tigers now present is 23. Two of them are new recruits leaving 21 of the old Tigers, officers and all. Two of them are teamsters, one lieutenant, and three sergeants which leaves 15 privates of the old Tigers for duty. We have had some some men lately returned from the hospital which makes our company larger than it was after the Battle of Corinth. Our company was reduced to nine privates. The boys are all in tolerable good health now.

Alvin Caulkins has received several letters from his folks since they went to Iowa. They were all well, I believe, the last he heard from them. Mary has written to Bill Cleary for two or three months though I am not certain. At least Will has not said anything to me about it. The last I heard from Ike Odell he was in the hospital at St. Louis and had not got his discharge yet. Ike has got badly run down and should have had a discharge last fall. But a man scarcely ever gets a discharge here for being sick unless he happens to be a favorite with the doctors. Many of them would rather make out a man's death warrant than his discharge for the doctors

---

15. The Federal Army of the Potomac had sustained another serious defeat at Fredericksburg, Virginia, on 13 December 1862. [Long, p. 295–296]

in the army will not discharge any more men than they can help, especially privates for fear of loosing their reputation as a successful physician
and gaining the ill favor of the commanding officers who wish to hold as
prominent a command as possible for self aggrandisement irrespective of
justice or humanity. They, themselves, at the same time, would not care a
cent for their country or raise a musket to save it only for big pay and
making themselves a great name.

Sister Elisabeth wrote that my stepfather was dead. He died the 20th of
November which I was verry sorry to hear for he was a good man and
was well respected in his community and was kind to my mother.

Old Abe is beginning to inforce his proclamation or his boys are en-
forcing it for him in this vicinity. We are sending out foraging parties and
bringing in all the Niggers in the country where our forces have the
power to do it. A large train of cars just now passed loaded with Negros
& cotton going to Memphis. I don't know what Massa Linkum is goyin'
to do wid 'em but I supose he will distribute them around and let them
work for their living. They say Massa Linkum is a mighty good man and
that him and all his soldiers will go to heaven. Many Negroes have been
patiently waiting for New Year's to come with great hope of being set free
and take their families with them.

I received a letter from Jabe before I wrote you last. He was then at
Memphis. I have not answered it yet. I will tomorrow.

I found five stamps in your letter for which I am much obliged. You
must not think because you are getting to be a woman of a family that you
are getting too old to learn. You should, when you have any leisure time,
turn your attention to your books and improve yourself especially in
grammar and in spelling. You spell tolerable well, though I find many
words spelled incorect and some language placed in bad form. I will give
you a specimen in a slip of paper so you can see how to avoid some of it.
My paper is out. Yours as ever

T. J. Davis

[All spelling on this page has been left as found in the original letter]

page one
January 8th, 1863

Propper language and propper form adds greatly to a persons personal
appearance and should be practiced in common conversation as well as
in writing. Therefore a person should know the exact meaning of every
word they write and the propper place for it. Children learn their their
first language from their parents. I have often heard parents talking silly,
improper language to their children and as the children learn from their
parents they will talk silly in return. Therefore, it is necessary to talk propper in the family circle.

I will show you a few words you are in the habit of writing and spelling; Often not ofton; whole the entire, not hole; going not goin, mother intends going to Springville not mother is agoing to Springville. "I told him you was going", not "I told him you was agoing". I don't write this for the sake of scolding you or finding fault with your writing it is only intended to induce you to try and improve yourself when you can. I am a bad schollar myself and need to be taught rather than be a teacher. But all that I know I informed myself and I am still trying to learn a little every day. A person can learn useful knowlege just as easy as they can simple nonsense if they have a disposition to try, though a little fun now and then is relished by the best of men.

I don't know as I am mutch interested in everybody's babies or care who has babies if they want them and can take care of them. Babies has been a common thing ever since the human family began. A man & wife should write and talk to each other as if they were only neighbors so far as unnecessary, imprudent, or unimportant language is concerned as too mutch familiarity becomes stale and disgusting.

Sister Elisabeth has been talking of writing to you so long that she has forgotten where to direct a letter to you and asked me if you still lived at Springville yet and said if I would give her your address, she would write to you.

We have not been paid yet. There is six months pay due us now but if we are paid soon we will only get four months pay. It is getting time we was paid and many of the soldiers does not like it verry well but I suppose they will get more when they are paid.

I see by the "Viroqua Times" that the county board has passed an act for the county to pay two dollars per month to the wife of each volunteer in the service of the United States and one dollar per month for each child of said volunteer under the age of twelve years to take affect on and after the first day of January. The wife is required to go before a justice of the peace and swear that she is the wife of a volunteer. So you can call on Mr. Lowery for three dollars per month for you and the little one. I supose you have got that name I sent before this time.

Tell John he must excuse me for not writing to him this time. This letter is too large.

We have had considerable rain lately. The weather is cool enough to be pleasant.

We heard that Captain Layne was in Memphis yesterday and will be here on this afternoon's train.

Well, I have written more this time than I meant when I commenced so I will close for the present. Please to write soon.

Yours as ever and always,

Thomas J. Davis

Memphis, Tennessee, January 15th, 1863

I again sit down to write you a few lines to let you know that I am enjoying reasonable good health. I have not received any letter from you since I wrote to you before, which was about a week ago. I have only received two letters from you dated since the first of December, though I have been looking for another one for several days. Robert McMichael has received a letter from his wife dated as late as December 31st. I have not received any letters since I wrote to you.

We left Moscow on the 10th, and arrived here the 13th Inst. Memphis is mutch the largest city I have seen in the South. It is well laid out and is a very pretty town and has been quite a business place and is about two-thirds as large as Milwaukee.[16]

I was in hopes of seeing some of the boys in Foster's Battery when I came here but the battery had gone down the river before we arrived here.

General Sherman made an attack on Vicksburg and had quite a heavy fight but was not strong enough to take it and was forced to fall back. I understand that he fell back with his forces to Napoleon, Arkansas, and that another attack will be made on Vicksburg as soon as forces enough can be concentrated to bear on it. The Rebels, they say, are very strongly fortified and will require hard fighting to take the place. I have not learned whether Foster's Battery was in the fight at Vicksburg or not.

We are having the roughest weather just now that we have had this winter. It commenced raining night and all day yesterday and last night it commenced snowing and it snowed all night last and all day today and now it is nearly night and it is snowing, yet. There is about a foot of snow on the ground now but the ground was wet and a great deal of is melted as it fell.

When we was ordered here we expected we would be sent down to Vicksburg but we received orders today to get read[y] to march out on the railroad about seven miles to do guard duty for a few days. I think we will then be marched back here and sent down the river.

We was partly paid off yesterday. That is, we got 26 dollars: two months pay. Some of the men are getting mutch dissatisfied about their pay and swear if they are not paid up better they will not do duty. I will send you ten dollars this time. I bought a watch that took part of my money and I owed the sutler a little and I want to keep a few dollars for tobacco and other necessaries.

Friday morning, January16th/63

It has stoped snowing but it is quite cold this morning but it cannot last more than two or three days.

---

16. Memphis, Tennessee, was a city of 22,623 in 1860. [Andriot]

This morning we received orders to get ready with seven days rations to go to Vicksburg. I don't know how soon we will go. This warfare is uncertain. We may have some warm fun down there and we may not fight any.

There was four thousand and eight hundred Rebel prisoners landed here today from below. They was a cold, ragged looking community. They was taken in Arkansas this evening.[17]

I was downtown today and got my likeness taken. I will send it to you. It is not verry good but perhaps it looks as well as I do. I had on the same coat that I had my likeness taken in last winter in Milwaukee.

I received a letter last night from Belle Ingersoll. She writes that Charlie was well but it was too muddy for him to go to school. Good-bye for this time,

T. J. Davis

Memphis, Tennessee, January 17th/1863

Dear Brother & Sister,

I again sit down to write you a few lines to let you know that I am in tolerable good health hoping this may find you all well. I received your letter about a week ago bearing date December 19th and was very glad to hear from you and to hear that you was all well.

We have been runing around considerable since I wrote to you before. The last time I wrote to you I believe I was in Abbeville. We left there and went on south to Oxford then Van Dorn got around behind us and took Holley Springs and burnt some of [the] government supplies and paroled five or six hundred of our men and left again. So we turned around and come back to Holly Springs and remained there about a week. We then come up to Moscow on the Memphis & Charleston Railroad and guarded the road about two weeks. We started from Moscow the tenth and got here the 13th of this month. We are now under marching orders for Vicksburg. I expect we will start tomorrow.

I saw Henry Pentagraph, Jim Wells, and Will Curry a few days ago. Hen said he had not had a letter from you for a long time. I give him the letter I got from you.

There was five thousand Rebel prisoners landed here last night from below. They were taken in Arkansas. I wish we had all the Rebels prisoners and was ready to start north with them.

---

17. After Sherman's repulse at Chickasaw Bluffs, General John A. McClernand immediately took command of the 30,000 Federal troops on the Mississippi River. He led them up the Arkansas River to lay siege to Confederate Fort Hindman at Arkansas Post on 9 January 1863. Fort Hindman's 4,800 troops surrendered to McClernand on 12 January 1863. [Long, p.310–311]

You said you wished me to give my opinion of the war. Well, I will tell you. It is decidedly the worst thing that ever happened to this country and goes to show what monarches of the old world has always claimed; that man is not capeable of self-government and does not appreciative his prosperity when he is doing well. I do not believe that the Union will ever be re-established as it was unless it is done by compromise and the day of compromise, I believe, is now passed. The time has been when when I believe an honorable compromise might have been affected, but of late the Rebels have been mutch encouraged by the actions of our own traitors in the North who would, if they could get into power, at once acknowlege the independence of the South. The South is mutch stronger than most people in the North are aware of and with the advantange they have of us, they cannot, in my opinion, be subjugated with twice their own numbers. When the war ends it will be done by a compromise or a recognition of the Southern Confederacy. If the first hundred men that advocated secession principals had been hung without trial, we now, no doubt, would be living in a peaceful and prosperous country. I used to feel proud of the name of an American but I fear that America has disgraced herself in the eyes of the whole civilized world, though I sincerely wish the war may terminate more favorable than my anticipations can hope to realise under the present circumstances.

I would like to write you a long letter this time but I have about a half dozen letters to answer today. So I have not time.

If you wish to write to the old lady Ingersoll's folks their address is Warren County, Illinois. I received a letter from them last night. They were all well except the old lady. She has been unwell all fall and winter.

I received a letter from Isaac and one from Will & O.K. the same time I got yours. They were all well.

We have just been having an old fashioned snowstorm. It is now about a foot deep and the weather is quite cold for this climate. You must excuse me for bad writing as I am in a hurry. Well my paper is out and I must close. Write soon. Direct as you did before. Give my respects to all.

Thos. J. Davis

To George & Elisabeth Ditto

CHAPTER FIVE

The Canal That
General Butler Commenced

The 18th Wisconsin broke camp at Moscow, Tennessee, on 10 January 1863 and marched to Memphis, where the regiment was directed aboard transports to begin a winter campaign along the Mississippi River. Steaming south to Young's Point, Louisiana, the regiment joined other units to work on a canal that was intended to shortcut the Mississippi River near the Confederate stronghold of Vicksburg. With batteries mounted along high bluffs, Vicksburg's location on a great horseshoe bend in the Mississippi had closed the river to all northern shipping since the outbreak of the war. A canal deep enough to allow Federal warships and transports to bypass the Confederate batteries was planned to render Vicksburg's position harmless. An effort by Federal General Benjamin F. Butler to cut a canal in 1862 had failed but the idea and advantages to be gained by such a detour of the mighty river were evident to Grant and his engineers.

Work on the canal by the Eighteenth began in the last week of January 1863 and continued until 8 February when the Badgers were transferred upriver to Lake Providence, Louisiana, to begin a second canal. Work on the Lake Providence canal ended on 17 March when engineers broke the levee between the Mississippi River and Lake Providence. The effort, however, failed to raise the lake level high enough to ship soldiers past Vicksburg and on 20 April the 18th Wisconsin was sent to Milliken's Bend, Louisiana, to await orders.

The letters from these first months of 1863 include the last correspondence from Ransom Chase. His ill health forced his resignation. Prior to his return home, though, Chase filed a complete report of the status of the "Badax Tigers," almost exactly a year after their arrival at training camp in Milwaukee. According to Chase, only about a quarter of the original 109 men remained fit for duty while another quarter of the men had died of wounds or disease. Of the remaining "Tigers," two dozen had received discharges for health reasons (at least one of whom was also included on the death rolls), and others had transferred, deserted, or been dismissed. More than a dozen "Tigers" were still either being held in Southern prison camps or were awaiting exchange in Federal parole camps.

T. J. Davis continued to correspond with his wife and family. Although he often filled his letters with newsy items and anecdotes about his fellow "Tigers," one missive to his sister contains a vitriolic condemnation the war, its lack of progress, and of "self-styled patriots" on the homefront, slaves in the south, and "swindlers, thieves, and traitors in office." Although Davis' spirits appear to have reached low ebb with this diatribe, within a week he was back to his old form predicting a vigorous prosecution of the war by the Federal high command. In addition, he described views of the Mississippi Valley countryside, Federal canal efforts, and an intriguing effort to recruit white officers for U.S. Colored Troops being raised in the south. Finally, Davis' irritation at having an express box filled with surplus army clothes stopped by the authorities serves as an amusing example of unchanging human nature.

On Board the Steamer "Maria Denning"
Memphis, Tennessee, January 20th, 1863

Dear Lucinda,

I received two letters from you last night and was very glad to hear from you. I had not had a letter from you for over two weeks. One of your letters was dated December 31st and the [other] January 11th. They found me as well as usual except that I am troubled with rheumatism. I was glad to hear that you and the little one was well and I hope you may remain so until I get home, if I am permitted to be lucky enough to do so.

I wrote you a letter few days ago and sent my likeness and ten dollars in it. We was paid two months wages about a week ago. There is over four months yet behind.

We are now onboard a boat lying at the wharf ready to start down the mouth of Arkansas River and then turn and go up White River. For the present we have been on the boat two days and it may be a day or two longer before we start. I hope we will soon get through for we are so mutch crowded that it makes it verry disagreeable. What do you think when I tell you there is three regiments of infantry, one battery of artillery with all their horses, and over fifty mules and the wagons belonging to them besides all our provisions and other freight on board of this boat? There is not room for all of us to ly down at once. We are stowed in like cattle in a car.

Calvin Hagerman is here. He come down from Cincinnati a few days ago. He was left back there sick. He is going down with our fleet to rejoin his company.

Foster's Battery is up White River in Arkansas. I may get to see Jabe. Cal is getting quite stout again. He seemed quite glad to run across some of the old Bager boys.

It has been raining considerable for two days. Frost and the snow has about all melted off but the air is raw and cold and the river is rising yet.

Ben Greenman is discharged. Ed Crandall is well and hearty. Alvin Caukins received a letter from Mary last night. She said the folks was well. She said she had just got a letter from you.

You need not send any more paper, only what there is writing on for I can manage to get what blank paper I want. I wrote on that ledger just for fun. I had other paper. You must excuse this writing for I am lying on my belly in a bunk and it is so dark that I can hardly see the lines. It is a poor place to write but I thought I would scratch you a few lines before I left here.

I heard that the 25th Wisconsin had passed here and gone south but I have heard since that it is a mistake and that they are in Madison, yet.

I hope this cursed war will end for it seems that the soldiers are suffering hardships, exposure, sickness, and death and but little good is accomplished by it and their services but little appreciated. And but little prospect in future of gaining mutch credit for what they have done.

Well, I must close for this time. You must not think I have the blues for I never get them. I will send you a specimen of Sesesh money. I will write again soon as we get in camp. Direct your letters as you did last. Good bye

Thos. J. Davis

Milligans Bend, Louisiana, January 25th 1863

Dear Lucinda,

I wrote a letter to you while we was on the boat at Memphis but the boat started before I could get it mailed so I will write a little more and put it in this letter. We arrived here yesterday evening. There was 13 steamboats in our fleet all loaded with soldiers and supplies. We just came off the boat today. We are opposite the mouth of the Yazoo River and about 7 or 8 miles above Vicksburg. We can hear occasional firing down the river yesterday and today between the Rebel forts and our gunboats but I don't think there will be mutch of a battle for some time to come if at all. Our forces are at work on the canal that General Butler commenced last spring and if we get that accomplished, we we can run down the river past Vicksburg and be out of range of her guns.[1]

Foster's Battery is here. I went to their camp yesterday. I saw Jabe and the other Badax boys. Jabe and Levi Nobles has been unwell for several days but their health is improving and will probably be all right in a few days. Foster's Battery has been in two battles since they come south, viz: at Vicksburg and at Arkansas Post up the Arkansas River. They lost one man killed at Vicksburg, the only man they have yet lost in battle though they done good execution at Arkansas Post.

This is a low, dismal looking [land] here along the river. The planters throw up large levys to prevent the water from inundating their plantations when the river raises. I will send you some flowers that bloom here in January. I picked them yesterday. I sent you some flowers and leaves last summer and some cotton seed but you did not say whether you got them or not. I must close. Good-bye,

Thos. J. Davis

Milligans Bend, Louisiana, February 1st, 1863

Dear Wife,

I once more sit down to write you a line to inform you that I am as well as usual and hope this may find you well. I have not received any letters from you since I left Memphis, though I have been looking for one for several days. The mail come in last night and I felt sure I would get a letter from you but when they was distributed T. Jefferson Richard D's name was not called. So I did not get any.

The weather has been quite pleasant for several days until last night and this morning we had quite a shower of rain which makes it quite muddy today.

Foster's Battery is camped about 2 miles below us, Robert McMichael and myself was down there yesterday and saw Jabe, Levi Noble, Chester Morley, and E. Caulkins. Jabe and Levi is getting stout again. The other boys was well.

We are still lying here. There has not been any fighting yet except small skirmishes between the scouts of each side and occasionally between our gunboats and the Rebel batteries below. We are waiting for reinforcements

---

1. The Mississippi River loops back and forth dozen of times above and below Vicksburg. General Benjamin F. Butler had planned to cut a canal across the narrow neck of land near Vicksburg called DeSoto Point, Louisiana, to expedite the passage of Federal ships past the threatening Confederate river batteries. The effort to bypass the Mississippi River at DeSoto Point did not succeed. [Bastian, David F., Grant's Canal. Shippensburg, Pa., Burd Street Press, 1995, p.6]

and to hear what Banks and Farrigut[2] is doing below. It was their failure to get here that caused the defeat of Sherman but the Rebels have a verry strong position here and will be a hard place to take unless we can surround them and starve them out. But perhaps it will require a long time to concentrate our forces so as to accomplish it.

Monday, February 2nd

Well, I didn't finish my letter yesterday so I will scratch you a few more lines. There was heavy artillery firing for about an hour and a half early this morning among the gunboats at the mouth and up the Yazoo River. I don't know what it was for but they say the Rebels have three rams up the Yazoo and they said they meant to run them down from there and drive away our gunboats. I think that is what they attempted this morning. But I guess they could not make the riffle and was compelled to run back as the firing has ceased and I don't hear anything more from them. They would have had a verry hot gauntlet to run to get through our blockade of gunboats which is in the mouth of the Yazoo River.[3]

The weather is pretty mutch clear today with a cool, raw wind not cold enough to freeze but colder than it has been for several days.

The river is still raising and part of our men is working everyday throwing up a levy to prevent the water from flooding our camp ground.

John Cready is here in the 14th Regiment in Company D. I see him every few days. He don't feel so patriotic as he did when he used to be riding around on the Badax trying to recruit. In fact, I find nearly all the soldiers in all regiments are getting sick and tired of soldiering but many of them are too gritty to grumble about it and takes it as easy as possible A declaration of peace would be hailed with a more hearty welcome by the soldiers than was the Year of Jubilee by the bondmen of Old Testament times. The fact is that many of the soldiers are discouraged— they have been jaded from pillow to post and compelled to carry their own provisions, bedding, and clothing besides guns and accoutrements. First chasing the Rebels then being chased by them, being in many cases

---

2. General Nathaniel P. Banks, with 12,000 soldiers and a portion of Admiral David G. Farragut's river fleet from New Orleans, planned to lay siege to Port Hudson, Louisiana. Banks spent most of February preparing his troops and the effort did not begin until early March 1863: [Cunningham, Edward, The Port Hudson Campaign. Baton Rouge, Louisisna State University Press, 1963, p.19]

3. The firing on 2 February 1862 may well have been the "U.S.S. Queen of the West," a river ram, running past the Confederate river batteries at Vicksburg. On her way past the city, the Federal ship set fire to the "C.S.S. City of Vicksburg," then continued south to the Red River on another assignment. [Long, p.318]

compelled to attack Rebels in far superior numbers and having the same ground to fight over a half a dozen or more times and no prospect ahead for anything better while the big men at Washington are quarreling, conniving, and wire-working to see who shall be chief commander and what commander shall be court-marshalled for whiping the Rebels, and who shall be next in turn entitled to a brigadier or major general's commission and arguing the question whether the Nigger is a black man or an African, and whether or not a private that dies in the service without leave is entitled to an honorable discharge and whether or not a private is allowed to speak to a general after having a written permit to do so signed by the colonel of his regiment after making the formal salute and throwing his neck out of joint making military jestures. Some of the boys go so far as to say that all the difference there is between a mule and a soldier is that a mule don't have to stand guard or go on extra duty for missing roll call.

There has been quite a quantity of Negros come into our army from the country. There was thirty come in a few days ago who said their masters had just got things fixed to run them off to Texas in a few days to keep the Yankees from getting them.

I will send a letter to John in this. I will also send you a ring that I made of a beef horn. I do not send it for its intrinsic value or beauty. I only send it for you to keep as a memento of the maker.

I also appen below a map of my own make to show you the position of our army and the Rebels. The canal is one-and-an-eighth miles in length and the bend in the river is ten miles. General Butler commenced digging the canal last summer but the water in the river fell so that he had to abandon the job. Our men are at work on it now but with what result I can only conjecture. By making this canal navigable we could have command of the river without taking Vicksburg.

Well, I must close. Write soon

T. J. Davis

[Below signature is the map of the canal and Vicksburg]

Millikens Bend, Louisiana, February 7th, 1863

Dear Wife,

I received a letter from you night before last dated January 18th. It found me as well as usual and I was glad to learn that you was well. We are still at camp where I wrote to you before. There is nothing of great importance transpiring here at present. I heard some canonading down at Vicksburg today and I heard that the cause of it is that two more of our gunboats run the blockade the day I wrote you last which makes five that have run through the fire of their blockading batteries.

We received the official report night before last of the death of William Downie. He died on the 25th of January in the hospital at Jefferson Barricks. The news took me rather by surprise as we thought his wounds not dangerous and suposed he was getting well.

Our officers say we will move from here in a couple of days. They say they think we are going back up into Arkansas and some think we are going to east Tennessee to reinforce General Rosencrans, the former I think the most probable.[4] They say the boats are laying here at the shore that is to carry us.

You said the last letter you had received from me was dated December 27th. I think you must be mistaken in the date. It was in my letter of the date of December 21st that I sent you the name of the girl and you spoke of it in your letter of the 28th. From the 27th of December to 18th of January would make it three weeks old.

I have not had any letters since I have been here except the one I received from you. I got a letter from Sarah McLain at Moscow and I have not answered it yet. I expect she thinks I am slow about writing but I must try and write to her soon.

I have not had a letter from Susan since last September. I wrote to her last so I will not write until she writes again. I have not mutch news of importance to write today so I will give you a short letter this time.

I will send you another ring in this letter that I made of black horn. I cut a shield and a diamond in it but the ring was rather small to cut the shield wide enough for the length. Perhaps you think that whittling rings is small business for soldiers. But some of the other boys was at it so I thought I must try my inginuity with the rest for I did not want them all to beat me.

Well, the mail is going out soon so I must close. You need not put yourself to the trouble to send me any money for if I get out I can borrow what I need. I have never been entirely out of money since I have been in the service though many of the boys are straped in less than two weeks after they are paid. I was lucky enough to get a dollar's worth of stamps at Memphis so you need not trouble yourself about them. So good-bye for this time. Write soon

Thos.J Davis

---

4. General William S. Rosecrans spent almost the entire winter and spring of 1863 refitting and strengthening his Federal forces at Murfreesboro, Tennessee, to the exasperation of the Lincoln administration. [Cozzens, Peter, This Terrible Sound, Urbana, Ill., University of Illinois Press, 1992, p.14–16]

Providence, Louisiana February 14th, 1863

Dear Lucinda,

I received a letter from you last night dated February lst and was glad to hear that you was well. I am as well as usual I was glad to hear that you had received my picture and the money I sent you. Perhaps it was the way I was shaved that caused you to think that I looked poor as I did when I come up from Illinois. And perhaps I looked too sober at the time which gave the picture a sad appearance. As for being sad I don't feel any more sad than I did when I was at home, although I do not enjoy myself so well. I do not give myself up to hysterics but live in hope of again enjoying a civil and peaceful life with my peaceful little family which I feel proud of and whose society would be more pleasure to me than any other of earth.

Today is Valentine's Day. One year ago today I arrived at home on my furlough from Milwaukee though there is a great contrast between the weather there and here. A year ago today the weather was verry cold with about two feet of snow but today the weather here is warm, wet, and muddy. The peach trees are in full bloom and we are having warm rains which has much the appearance of spring. I am in hopes, however, that I shall not have [to] remain in the south another summer for I would rather stand the cold winter weather of the north than the hot summer sun of Dixie's climate.

The talk is that we will be paid again soon but it is uncertain when for that was the talk before. There will be six months pay due us again the last of this month

We have moved again since I wrote you last. We left Milliken's Bend on the 8th and come up the river on boats to Providence, sixty miles above Vicksburg. There is only our division here, about 8000 men. We left Foster's Battery down at the Bend. I have not seen Jabe since I wrote to you before. This is a verry rich country here or has been. There is some large plantations here with two to three hundred Negros on a plantation.

You wrote something about getting a certificate of Mr. Keyes. You said you wrote something about in your letter of the week before but I have not yet got the letter. Of course, I did not mean to allow your mother to lose her land if we was able to save it for her. So if you have got the certificate, keep it and not allow it (the land) to be deeded away.

You wanted to know if I had clothes enough to keep me warm. I have all the clothes and blankets that I need and, in fact, more than I can conveniantly carry on a march. We also have plenty to eat, though, sometimes in no great variety.

I received a letter last week from brother Isaac. He has got his discharge and left Leavenworth with his wife and gone back to Illinois to live.

Perhaps you thought I was too hard on you in writing about those errors. I have no doubt that you are kept quite busy and have not mutch time to study. But people verry often become careless and neglect what they really know for that is the case with myself. I did not say anything against the quality of your writing. It was only the form and spelling. Neither did I wish to overtask you. But do as well as you can conveniently is all I desire for I know you have a head that is capable of learning. I must close for the present. Farewell,

Thomas J Davis

Providence Louisiana, February 17th, 1863

Dear Sister,

I received a letter from you last Saturday dated February lst. It found me as well as usual with the exception that of rheumatism which I have been troubled with for some time, though, I have not been laid up with them, yet. I was sorry to learn that you had suffered so much with your eyes though I was glad that they were getting better. I hope that this may find you all well. I received a letter from William yesterday dated January 27th. He was at O.K.'s. He had just come up from St. Louis. He said he had been exchanged and was going to start to his regiment the first day of February. If you wish to write to him, direct your letter to Nashville, Tennessee. He wrote that he and Okey's folks was well. Okey wrote that he intended to have gone up to Mercer County [Illinois] on a visit in the fore part of the winter but the weather was so bad that he could not get started so he gave it up.

I received a letter from Isaac last week and answered it the 12th. You said that Isaac and his wife had gone up to Frost's for a visit. I suppose he will go and see the old lady Ingersoll's folks before he comes back. I wrote to my frau a long time ago that you intended to write to her. She says she thinks you are long time in writing. I received a letter from her the same date of yours. She said that she and the baby was well and that the latter was growing finely.

We left Memphis on the 20th of January and arrived at Milliken's Bend near Vicksburg on the 23rd. Here I come across J.Y. Spaulding, my wife's brother. He is in the first Wisconsin Battery and was in the fight at Vicksburg and also at Arkansas Pass. He has been at Cumberland Gap all summer.

In your letter you give a description of some of the self-styld patriots that remain at home and do their part of the fighting with gass at a distance. I notice both in civil life and in the army that those that do the most spouting and blowing always do the least fighting and are the first to run when fighting comes. I never pretended to be a verry brave man. I actuated to go to war by a principal for my country's good; but that principal seems to have been overruled, ridden down, and lost in the dim distance. Thus far I have served my country honestly and faithfully so far as my power to do so was concerned. I have been in several fights and run some narrow risks, but I have become dissatisfied with the way this war is carried on. I now sometimes think If I get into another battle I will get out of it the quickest way I can, that is, if my legs serves me a good purpose. I do not however saddle the war on Lincoln and his Proclamation, as a great many of late do, for the war is older than the Proclamation. As far as the Proclamation is concerned, itself amounts to just nothing one way or the other toward stopping or prolonging the war for the Rebels was fighting us with all their available force; their strength and ambition could devise and probably dispised us just as bad before the Proclamation had not been issued. I do not approve of sending Negros north into the free states and I do not think there will be mutch of it done. I would almost give my existence to see every Nigger removed from the face of the American continent and the whole Southern Confederacy (that is their power) crushed to the earth, never more to rise and every northern office-seeking traitor piled on the ruins, there to moulder through eternal ages as a public example to future traitorous, rotton-hearted, office-seeking, political aspirants who may have brass enough to revive them again. I dispise the Northern traitors a hundred percent worse than I do those in the South. It grinds my spirit as a free American citizen (now military slave) to think that I, with thousands more, are enduring nearly every unconceivable hardship in fighting for our country while we have politicians at home and all through the North who are opposing all war measures [by] the Administration, all war appropriations, and everything else but the Southern traitors and their cause, thus weakening our strength at home and encouraging the Rebels south. Shall we throw down arms and ask traitors for peace on their own terms? Shall we humbly stack arms and ask Rebels for an armistice while the muzzles of their cannon is pointed full in our faces and defiantly tell us they abhor our authoridy? Should we ask for peace and go home with our fingers in our mouths and leave the traitors in triumph and disgrace the graves of a hundred thousand of our brave soldiers who have fallen in battle without having avenged their death? Shall all this be submitted to at the hands of the traitors? It is horrible to think of, yet I fear it will come to pass. Swindlers, thieves, and traitors in office have been gnawing at the vitals of the government ever since the war commenced. Many of them who would sell their birthright for a mess of potage or sell their best friends for a small office. And among the upper circles of military authority, they seem to have more disign in making big officers and killing privates than they have in putting down rebellion. All this to a great extent has discouraged and demoralized our army. The result is many are deserting and many more would hail a peace with great joy, no matter how dishonorable, so it would relieve them from the service and fatigue of a soldiers life. And many miserly citizens would have the war stoped, too, for fear they will have a few dollars of extra taxes to pay.[5] I believe, however, this war will be settled in the spring by acknowledging the Southern Confederacy and letting them go. There may be a row raised in the North and a division of the East and West attempted.[6] It is dificult now to determine how this war will end.

My paper is out and I must close;

Yours with brotherly love,

                                                                    Thos. J. Davis

[to G.W. and Elizabeth Ditto]

                                        Providence, Louisiana , February 23rd, 1863

Dear Wife,

I received a letter from you last night dated February 8th. It found me as well as usual and I was glad to hear that you was well and in good health.

The weather is clear warm and pleasant today. But there has been a great deal of rain here for the last three or four weeks.

We are still at Providence. Another division of our soldiers landed here today. They just come down from Memphis. They are commanded by General Logan.[7]

I received a letter from little John Graham last night. He said the 25th Regiment was still at Madison and was under marching orders for Cairo but did not know when they would start.

I also received a letter from Susan Wilson dated February 15th. She wrote that her folks was well. They are living in Bloomington but intended going back to Marshall in the spring. I will send you the letter.

---

5. The Civil War saw the introduction of the first income tax by the Federal government in August 1861. The tax was 3 percent on all income over $800. Additional taxes were enacted with a Federal internal revenue law in July 1862. [Faust, p. 380]

6. Talk of a split between the northeastern states and the Old Northwest was not new. Significant numbers of settlers called "Butternuts" lived in Ohio, Indiana, and Illinois but had strong southern roots. They had long differed with Yankee banks and settlers from New York and New England. This southern identity and hostility to the Northeast led some "Butternuts" to talk about a "Northwest Confederacy" that would reunite Northwest with South. However bizarre such a scheme appears in retrospect, it commanded much rhetorical support during the war. [McPherson, James M., Battle Cry of Freedom, The Civil War Era, New York, Oxford University Press, 1988, p.593]

7. General John A. Logan was a Democratic politician from southern Illinois with Mexican War military experience. [Faust, p. 443]

There is not mutch going on here yet in a military point of view but perhaps we will have something to do before a great while. Things seems to be getting into shape for some more hard fighting [with] the coming of spring. I think there will still be more troops brought into the field and the war be more vigorously prosicuted than ever. At least I hope they will drive it through as fast as possible and either whip the Rebels or get whiped and not have it on hand so long.

Providence, February 25th/ 63

Well, I commenced writing this letter day before yesterday but was detaled to go out on picket and did not have time to mail it.

This is in the afternoon. It is cloudy and there is heavy thundering in the west and I think it will rain before night. John Kingston got a letter last night from John Herron which stated that John Downie was dead and that Ben Greenman was not expected to live long and also that George Esler and Jim Williams had got home. Alvin Caulkins received a letter from his folks dated February 8th. The folks were all well. All the Badax boys that are left are in tolerable good health. John Graham wrote that Burnett was running the mill in Springville but did not say whether his wife was there or not.

We are having inspection today.

If Silva continues to grow as she has commenced, I am afraid I shall not know her when I get back. I would like to be there this evening to see you and the little one, but I guess I will be there after a while so I wait with patience 'til the time comes. Direct your letter to Cairo as before.

Yours truly for several days

Thos.J. Davis

Providence, Louisiana, March 2nd, 1863

Dear Lucinda,

I received a letter from you to day dated February 15th & 17th. I was sorry to learn that you and the baby was unwell but I hope this may find you both well again. I am as well as common. I wrote a letter to you several days ago and when I finished it I put it in my book until the shower ceased (as it was raining at the time) before I put it in the office and I forgot it and did not know but that it had gone until I found the letter in my book this morning. So, I thought I would write this little sheet and put it in the old letter.

I received a letter from Belle Ingersoll this morning dated February 15th. She wrote that little Charlie was well. David Ingersoll has got his discharge and gone back home. War business soon used him up. He was discharged on account of his broken arm which got too lame for use. Little Charlie says he wants me to play off sick and get discharged and come home and see him. It looks hard that Mr. Smith must get up from a sick bed and return to his regiment. If I thought my life was indangered by it, if I were he, I should not [have] started.

It is verry nice weather here to day clear warm and pleasent mutch like a May day in Wisconsin. It is so warm that it gives me the spring fever.

I have not heard from Jabe since I left Vicksburg.

I did not answer Sarah McLain's letter you spoke of until last week. She has perhaps got it by this time. I partly neglected it and partly had no time to write.

We mustered for pay again day before yesterday. Uncle Sam owes us six months pay again. But I don't know when we will get any of it.

I believe I have nothing new to write today. The boys, I believe, are all well. The mail will soon go out so I must close and try to get this one in the office.

Excuse haste and write soon yours as ever,

Thos. J. Davis

Letter From Lieut. Chase
For the North Western Times

Sterling, Vernon County, Wis
March 10, 1863

Mr. Editor: Protracted sickness and long absence in hospitals have, as you are aware, prevented me from giving you, from time to time, as formerly, sketches of the marches and daily incident of the Eighteenth. I can now simply state that at last advices, it was at Lake Providence, La., leaving to the many letters written by the men, the province of rehearsing those many marches experienced since Nov. 2d, when the regiment left Corinth. It was in the advance when Grant abandoned his project of piercing the center of Miss. On returning, it stopped a number of days at Moscow, Tenn., then at Memphis, and finally with the rest of the division, embarked for Vicksburg, leaving Memphis Jan. 21st. When it left the latter place, all of Co. "C." present were in the enjoyment of good health and was composed of the following persons:

Capt.	N.M. Layne	[Privates]
1st Lieut.	Wm. N. Carter	J.H. Singles
Sgt.	Wm. N. Carter, Jr.	T. J. Davis
"	R.S. McMichael	L. Davis
"	Wm. Cox	Wm. Delap
"	G. Hickok	N. Garret

Wagoners	T. J. Decker	F. Harris
	C. Coher	J. Kingston
	Wm. Dikeman	J. Metcalf
Privates	N. Bankes	I.C. Newell
"	L. Broderick	J. Pennell
"	Wm. Cleary	S. Pokeland
	Geo. Chadeayne	

Total 24

The deaths in the Company are as follows:

From battle—

Wm. Kittle,	killed at Shiloh, April 6th, 1862.
Norris W. Saxton	died of wounds, April 7th, at Shiloh.
Samuel Fish	died of wounds, April 20th, at Evansville, Indiana.
Augustus Singer	wounded at Shiloh—time and place of death unknown.
Wm. Downie	wounded at Corinth, died Jan. 25th, 1863, at St Louis.

From Disease:

Sergt. S. Swan,	Feb. 22d, '62, Milwaukee.
Sergt. T. Fretwell	July, 19th, '62, Macon, Ga.
Corp. S. McMichael	June 27th, '62, Macon, Ga.
Musician Aaron Cooley	Wheatland, Wis.

Privates	
Levi E. Allen	Aug. 19th, '62, Evansville, Ind.
Travis Day	June 28th, '62, Keokuk, Iowa.
Burdett Fletcher	Henderson, Kentucky.
Elijah Forsythe	Jan. 28th, '62, Keokuk, Iowa.
Joseph G. Gander	Huntsville, Ala.
John S. Gray	July 26, '62, Macon, Ga.
Jas. McClelland	Nov. 30th, '62, Dist. Columbia.
Julius C. Morley	Evansville, Ind.
W.W. Odell	May 29th '62, Monterey, Tenn.
L.H. Page	May 4th, '62, Steamer "Imperial".
John Stokes,	May 21st, '62, Jefferson Barracks.
W.P. Starbuck	Apr. 27th, '62, Camp at Shiloh.
Orrin Tooker	Huntsville, Ala.
Wm. Thompson	July 6th, '62, Camp near Corinth.

Died after transfer to Co. "K"
Joseph Hunter, Charles Ames, Geo. Williams, T. J. Finley

Total 27

The last four were transferred at Milwaukee and I have no means of ascertaining at present the time or place of their deaths. In consequence, also, of the neglect of the surgeons in charge of the hospitals, to send us official reports, I am unable in several instances to state the time and place of decease. With the facilities before me, as perfect a statement as possible is presented, but any further information desired, will be cheerfully given, in response to letters of inquiry.

The Discharged are:

For wounds—
Robt. E. Graham, John Kirkpatrick, Benj. F. Rantz, John J. Swain.

For disease—
Sergt. C. Morley   Sebastian Baltz
Corp. D.J. Spear   William Dailey
"   R.F. Corey   B. Greenman
"   Jos. Buckley   D. Mosholder

Musicians—
Jno. M. Stokes   B. Munyon
Aaron Cooley   S.C. Prince

Privates—
D.D. Bates   D. Rantz
L.B. Bugbee   H.V. Swain
A. Brown   A.L. Swain

Resigned on account of ill health:
2nd Lieut. A.A. Burnett,   2nd Lieut. R. J. Chase

Total discharged 24

Miscellaneous Losses
1st Lieut. J.H. Graham, dismissed; H. Johnson, deserted; Parley Whitney, enlisted in U.S.N.; H.L. Baker, Chief Musician of Regt.; Geo. W. Taylor, missing since April; H. Cummings, transferred to Co. "K"; J. Clear, ditto; M. Brayman, ditto; John Tippin, ditto.

Total 9

On detached duty:
C.B. Heust, C. Raymer, M.V. Day

Total 3

In hospitals:
S. Sager, A. Carwell, P. Mooney, B.F. Walls [Welles], W. Masterson, J. Williams

Total 6

Shiloh prisoners exchanged but not yet returned

Total 11

Evansville, Ind., prisoners not exchanged.   4
Holly Springs: ditto [prisoners not exchanged]   1

Total 16

We have received five new recruits since leaving the state, who are included in the above. Mr. Cooley's name appears both in the deaths and the discharges. He was discharged but died at a neighbor's almost in sight of home, which he so longed to reach. The length of this will, I trust, excuse the omission of the names of the paroled prisoners. It is quite probable that two of those mentioned as in hospitals may have swelled the list of the deceased. No report can be obtained from the surgeon, of Samuel Sager, who at last accounts was in South St. Hospital, St. Louis, in a critical condition. Adam Carwell, a boy who came to us last fall and who ought never to have left his mother, was fast pining away and "awaiting his discharge" in the Overton Hospital, Memphis, at the time your correspondent came away. The surgeon promised to especially attend to his welfare but unless his discharge came very soon, he has before this been an inmate of the "dead room" to receive the last earthly attentions.

Trusting that this communication may not be considered unimportant by the friends of Company "C", I remain,

Truly yours,   C. [NW Times, March 25, 1863, p. 1]

Lake Providence, Louisiana, March 14th, 1863

Dear Wife,

I take up my quill this evening to write you a few lines to let you know that I am as well as usual and hope this will find you well. I received a letter from you last night dated February 25th. I was sorry to learn that you was unwell with the rhematism but I hope they will not remain with you long. We all must suffer to a greater or less extent from disease and we must bear them with the best fortitude we can where they are unavoidable, though we should guard against them as far as possible.

The boys are all as well as usual. Alvin Caulkins is well. He received a letter from his folks last night dated February 23rd. His folks was all well. His father wrote that D. Caulkins was dissatisfied in Iowa and says he means to go back to Badax this spring though Orin says he likes the country first rate himself. He says timber is scarce, though it is not verry dere, yet. He says he would like to have some of his old Badax neighbors to come out there and settle. But says he would not advise anyone to come lest they should be dissatisfied with his judgement. He wants them first to come and look for themselves. Alvin is almost froze for a chance to go home so that he can go and help his father make a farm on the broad prairies of Iowa.

The weather here is quite warm and pleasant and spring has fairly opened. The trees begin to look quite green.

You wrote that you had found another tax certification on your mother's land and asked me if you should buy it. I do not mean to have your mother lose her land, but I would only buy enough certificates to keep the land from being deeded until I come back and I will see farther about it. It stands in hand to be as equinomical as we conveniently can so that if I ever get back we may have a little to start life with.

We received two months pay yesterday. I will send you ten dollars in this letter and if it goes through all right I will send you some more. I think some of sending my overcoat home by express before long. If I do, I will write to you about it. Then if I should get killed the coat might fit your next husband if you should be so lucky as Mrs. Allen for she has become a widow twice since I saw you.

I have not received any letters from any of my friends since I wrote to you before.

We are expecting to march soon but I do not know where and it matters but little to the soldier where he does go unless he could go home. There has been no fighting of any note here since I wrote before. I have no news of importance to write this time so take care of yourself the best you can. You wrote that Baker said he could not pay them notes this spring. I took the notes on so long a time that I do not think that I ought to wait long after they are due. I would, therefore, tell him or whoever pays them that I could not give any extension of time but have it paid over as soon as convenient. Write soon.

Thos J. Davis

[News Item]

Lieut. Chase of Co. C., 18th Reg. Wis. Volunteers resigned on account of ill health. He arrived at his father's on West Prairie, Feb. 20th. We learn that his health is improving. [NW Times, March 18, 1863, p. 2]

Lake Providence, Louisiana, March 20th, 1863

Dear Wife,

I sit down this afternoon to write you a few lines in order to inform you that I am as well as usual. I received a letter from you last night dated March 8 & 10th and I received another one from you this morning dated March 1st & 4th. I was verry glad to learn that you was gettin' better.

The weather is getting quite warm in the sun so that it is uncomfortable in the tents but there is a breeze stiring on the plantation so that it is comfortable out under the shade of the trees. I think it will be sometime before we will have mutch hot weather at a time.

I received a letter this morning from James Spaulding and one from Susan Wilson. Jim said that his folks was getting well. Susan said her folks was well and said that they would go back to Marshall in April. She said she had just received a letter from Hariet which stated she was about well again. Susan said that there had been a great deal of sickness in Illinois this winter. I also received a letter from Sister Elisabeth and Mahala. They said there was a great deal of sickness in their part of the state this winter. Elisabeth's man had been verry sick with the inflamation of the stomach and was not expected to live for a while but had got better again.

You wished me to write if I had plenty of clothes. I have all the clothes I want and more, too. I have a good pare of boots and can draw shoes whenever I wish them or any other clothes except when the quartermaster happens not to have them in hand. We have tents and have had them ever since we come south but they are now getting old and leaky. But we shall draw new ones in a few days. We have plenty to eat though in no great variety. We get but few vegetables.

Robert McMichael, Bill Cleary, Ed Crandall, John Kingston, and myself filled a box with clothes and expressed it to Mrs. McMichael, Viroqua, in care of old Mr. Newell. It will go by express to Sparta and will then be sent to Mr. Newell and then Mrs. McMichael will get it from Viroqua. My things, I believe, are all marked. I sent one overcoat with my name in the sleeve, one new uniform dress coat marked the same way, one pair new blue pants, my name on the waist band, and the lower end of the pockets placed one new pair drawers and one old pair, and two woolen shirts sewed together with a card on the collar with my name on it If the drawer and shirts are of any service to you or the baby, you can make use of them. We paid the express charges in advance to Sparta. It cost us five dollars. If the box comes through, you will help Mrs. McMichael pay whatever extra charges there may be on them from Sparta down. Will Cleary sends his overcoat in your care so you will keep it until he comes or sends for it. What extra charges, as I said before, there may be on the box you will pay about twice as mutch as Mrs. McMichael as I have the most in the box. I forgot to say that I sent a blanket. There is a card on it with my name on the card. Since I comenced writing our quartermaster has come up from the river with our new tents.

I was sorry that ring I sent you got broken. I will send you another one in this letter that I made of bone with a silver diamond fastened in with red wax with a heart on each side also filled with wax.

We was paid two months pay the 12th of this month. I sent you ten dollars in my last letter and if it gets through I will send some more. I do not expect we will get any more pay before May.

I have not seen or heard directly from Jabe since we left Vicksburg.

There has not been mutch fighting at Vicksburg since we left there except with heavy artillery. We can hear canonading from Vicksburg to this place verry plainly.

We have cut a channel from the [Mississippi] River into Lake Providence. We started the water into the lake three days ago and the lake has risen about ten feet and is still rising and the channel wearing larger. A large scope of country is now being overflowed and many citizens are being driven from their homes by the water. The water has driven us from where we first camped and we have moved back near the river. Perhaps in a few days we will be compelled to move on the other side of the River. The Sesesh around here begin to feel quite blue over the area of their land being put under water by the Yankees.[8]

I see that the citizens of all the Northern states are getting are getting fully as sick of the war as the soldiers are.[9] I am mutch better contented in the army now than I was last summer, though I am anxious to see the war close and peace once more return to our once peaceful, prosperous, and happy country and again enjoy our homes and friends and I look forward to that day as a day of great rejoicing with the American people and I hope to see that day.

Write soon. Good-bye. Yours as ever,

T. J. Davis

Lake Providence, Louisiana , April 1st, 1863

I endevor to write you a few lines to let you know that I am well and hope this may find you the same. I received a letter from you to day dated March15th. I had been looking for a letter from you for several days or I

---

8. The Lake Providence canal was the second canal project of the 1863 Vicksburg campaign. Under the command of General James B. McPherson, 17th Corps, the effort meant to divert the Mississippi River into Lake Providence and thence into Bayou Macon, the Tensas River, the Red River, and back into the Misssissippi River well below Vicksburg. (Steele, Matthew F., American Campaigns, Harrisburg, Pa., The Military Service Publishing Co., 1949, p.401.

9. By early 1863, Grant's loss at Holly Springs, Sherman's repulse at Chickasaw Bluffs, General Ambrose Burnside's defeat at Fredericksburg, Virginia, and Rosecrans' drawn battle at Stones River, Tennessee, left Northern homefront morale wavering. According to one historian,"The President had ample grounds for concern. The peace faction of the Democratic party grew stronger with each setback of Union armies." [McPherson, p.591]

would have wrote 3 or 4 days sooner. I received letter to day from brother Isaac and his wife and Ida Snyder & Belle Ingersoll, David Ingersoll's sisters. I will send you the letters. You complain that my letters do not come regular. I find that your letters do not come so regular here as they did when I was at Corinth and are more than as long again in getting here.

Old Mr. Moody got back to the regiment today. He looks quite well. Captain Layne come to us at Moscow, Tennessee, on the 10th of January. I think I wrote to you of his return before. He has been unwell for sometime but is getting better. The rest of the boys are all well. We have had less sickness in our company the past two months than we have had the same length of time since we have been south. I hope it may continue through the summer.

The weather is not so warm now as it was two weeks ago. We had a heavy wind and rainstorm on the night of the 29th. It injured several steamboats that were lying here, blowing off their chimneys and stoving in their wheelhouses and doing other damage. This is a verry nice clear cool pleasent day. I hope this spring will be as cool as last spring was though there was warmer weather in the summer than I wish to see again.

This is the first day of April, the day for all fools and the boys are making great sport over it by making April fools of each other in every conceivable way.

I sent you ten dollars to you a little over two weeks ago in a letter. I thought if it went through safe I would send you some more. I did not want to risk mutch at a time. There is five months pay due us now. There is talk that we will be paid again soon and that we will get four months pay the next payment. But I do not look for it until it comes around.

There is not mutch doing in the army here at present excepting making preparations to reduce Vicksburg but I do not think our generals will undertake to carry the place by storm. I would like to see the place leveled to the earth.

I got a letter from little John Graham the other day he wrote that he had been sick in the hospital a few days but was better. The 25th is at Columbus yet. I have not had a letter from Jabe since I left Vicksburg April 2nd.

I will close my letter. I have nothing more of importance to write today. I shall look for another letter from you next mail and I will write again. Direct your letters as usual and write the news. Yours always,

Thomas J. Davis

Headquarters,18th Regiment Wisconsin Volunteers, Company C
Lake Providence, Louisiana, April 10th, 1863

Dear Wife,

I received a letter from you three or four days ago dated March 25th and was glad to hear that you was well. I am as well as usual. The wether continues about the same as when I last wrote.

I received a letter from brother William the same time I received yours. He had got back to his regiment at Murfreesboro, Tennessee. He wrote that his family was well with the exception of colds. He made considerable appologies for not writing before.

We had a review day before yesterday. General Thomas, the Agutant General of the United States, was here and we had several speeches re: there is to be two nigger regiments raised here by his order and comissions given to white men from among the soldiers here for the nigger officers.[10] Robert McMichael and Isaac Newell handed in their names for subjects for commission but don't know yet whether either will be successful. As for myself I did not make an aplication for any office. There is plenty of niggers in this vicinity and I think that two regiments can be easily raised at this point. General Thomas says those Negros that will not make soldiers will be put on the evacuated plantations here and be allowed to cultivate them for their own support.

We drew four months pay day before yesterday. Robert, Ed Crandall, and myself is starting a package of money home to day by express. It is directed to Robert's wife. She will give you yours. I sent sixty dollars. You will pay your part of the express fees when you get the money. I will send you ten dollars more in this letter. I have not yet heard from the ten dollars I sent you the other payday, but I hope you received it.

The Badax boys are all well. We expect to have general muster today at ten o'clock and I have not time to write a long letter, though there is no important news since I last wrote. We are kept so busy drilling and guarding that I scarcely have time to answer all letters I receive. I will close this epistle hoping it may find you well. Write often as convenient and give me the news. Do the best you can and be a good girl. Nothing more this time so good-bye.

I Remain Yours as Ever

Thos. J. Davis

P.S. I send my last stamp on this letter and there is none here to be bought.

---

10. General Lorenzo Thomas was, indeed, active in recruiting white enlisted men and officers to lead United States Colored Regiments. Many officers and enlisted men initially criticized the effort but according to the soldier-historian of the 4th Minnesota Infantry a unit soon to be brigaded with the 18th Wisconsin," . . . the feelings of repugnance that had before been rife gave way, for the men would reason, 'Why should we not use them to suppress the rebellion when we have them in such great numbers? '" [Brown, Alonzo L., History of the Fourth Regiment of Minnesotta Volunteers During the Great Rebellion 1861–1865. St. Paul, Minn., The Pioneer Press Company, 1892, p. 180]

Lake Providence Louisiana, April 15th, 1863

Dear Wife,

I again sit down to write you a few lines in answer to your letter dated April 1st which I received two days ago and was glad to hear that you was well. I am as well as usual and the health of the company is reasonably good. Robert McMichael received a letter from home the same date of yours. His wife had received his money that he sent in March but you had not received the letter yet that I sent the ten dollars in on the 14th of March. But you had received the one next to it so I suppose you have it before now. In my last I wrote you that I had started you ten dollars more in a letter and sixty dollars per express. You will, perhaps, get the ten in the letter first as the money that I expressed did not leave here until yesterday. As I said before, the sixty dollars was directed to Mrs. McMichael and you will get it of her and pay your part of the express charges.

I wrote to you before that I sent some clothing home by express. I have heard since we started the box that it was stoped on the way and was not permitted to go through. This may be true and it may not, but I do not think the authorities had any right to stop it after the express company receipted for it but if it goes through you will get it and if it don't, it is gone up and that is all there is about it.

You wrote that Baker could not pay them notes until June. If he cannot easily get the money now and will pay it in June, I have no objections to wait. But when it is paid be sure and reckon up the interest. If I was in your place, I would not loan any money to anybody unless it would be for a verry charitable purpose to friends in want. For if I should come home and wish to use it, it would probably be more trouble to collect loned money than the interest would be worth and, perhaps, in some cases not get it at all. It is verry dificult to know who to trust, especially strangers.

I was sworn in for three years unless sooner discharged and not during the war though I do not think the war will last the three years out. There is no war news of importance to write to day. Some think there will be a fight at Vicksburg soon.

I find one or two words you use in your letters every time. You spell them wrong or incorrect. And also some bad form to get in the habit of writing. I have looked over your letter and marked the places. I will send them back so you can look over them.

I have nothing more of importance to write. Write soon and often and give the news.

I forgot, there is some talk that there will [be] 20 days furlough to five soldiers out of every hundred at a time. It will require about all of the three [years] before they can all get their furloughs in and more than that, it will take nearly 20 days to go home and return. I would be verry glad to get a furlough if I could remain at home any length of time. Verry respectfully yours as ever,

Thomas. J. Davis

Milliken's Bend, Louisiana, April 25th/63

Dear Wife,

I sit down this afternoon to answer your letter bearing date of April 5,6,& 8th which I received this morning and was verry glad to hear from you as I have not had a letter from you for nearly two weeks before. We moved from [Lake] Providence back to Milliken's Bend on the 20th and our mail was detained several days on that account. I shall look for another letter from you in a few days. I expected several letters today but I did not get any but yours.

The weather is getting quite warm again and the green foliage in the forest look like mid-summer in Wisconsin.

You said you had received ten dollars that I sent you in my letter of March 14th. I supose you have received the other ten that I sent you in a letter since last pay day and the sixty I sent with Robert by express before this time. I was glad that the last ring I sent you got through without being broken. When I get leisure perhaps I will make another one.

You say that Baker is selling his wheat and intends to pay them notes when he gets money enough together but says he cannot get government money. That, I must confess, is a singular idea to me for there is plenty of United States money in the country and it can be procured just as easy as any other good money. He can get it if he feels so disposed and if he will not pay you United States currancy or coin, though I do not expect coin for coin is hard to get now without a large premium, but if he will not pay you government notes, I do not wish you to receive a dollar from him. For the notes of these individual and company banks are very uncertain stuff to keep on on hand in these times of money fluctuation. Be sure and remember that the notes draw interest from their date until paid.

Several of our transport steamers have run the Rebel blockade at Vicksburg lately with good success having, I believe, only lost one or two boats out of 15 or 20 that went past.[11] A large number of our troops have gone

---

11. On the night of 16 April 1863, Rear Admiral David D. Porter ran twelve Federal warships south past the Vicksburg batteries, losing but one to Confederate fire. Six days later, Porter ran six transports and a dozen barges past the same batteries, losing seven of vessels in the effort. [Long, p. 338–339]

around by way of Richmond [Louisiana] to Carthage,[12] 25 miles below Vicksburg.

A report come here last night that our forces had captured the Rebel General Hindman and fifteen thousand Rebel troops near Carthage.[13] It is said they were coming down from Arkansas and was trying to cross the river to reinforce Vicksburg. I do not give it as the truth but it is believed by many.

I have not seen Jabe since we come down from Providence. I think the battery is 5 or 6 miles below here. You say that Jabe wrote that he would be at home by the middle of April on furlough. I think his prospects for furlough was rather vain delusion. I don't expect a furlough nor I don't think he will get one until the siege of Vicksburg is decided and probably not then. I would like verry much to go home on a visit if I could consistantly but I would rather the war was over before I went so I need not come back. I am better satisfied to stay in the army this summer than I was last, though I have not yet fallen in love with Dixie.

We have marching orders; we are going out to Richmond tomorrow. Our Colonel says our regiment will be stationed there as provost guard. Richmond is ten miles from here on the railroad from Vicksburg to Monroe [Louisiana].

With this letter I send you some of my machine poetry: "New Father Abraham", a burlesque on Copperheadism.[14] [not included in the letter] I have not time to write a verry lengthy letter today, though there is nothing of great importance to write. This leaves me as well as usual. Write soon direct as usual,

T. J. Davis

---

12. Davis' meant New Carthage, Louisiana, a town about twenty-five miles downriver from Vicksburg.

13. The rumor of General Thomas C. Hindman's capture was untrue.

14. The term "copperheads" was used to designate peace Democrats in the North, many who opposed the Republican Administration's war effort and favored a negotiated peace with the Confederacy. The term originated as an epithet as it likened Peace Democrats to poisonous snakes. Some Democrats eventually adopted the Liberty "copperhead" penny as a lapel pin in an effort to show their opposition to Republican "tyranny." [McPherson, p.494]

CHAPTER SIX

Closed Up Snugly
Around Vicksburg

On 26 April 1863, the 18th Wisconsin departed Milliken's Bend and marched for New Carthage, Louisiana. The regiment remained in New Carthage for two weeks of rest and recuperation, then departed on 9 May for transports to cross the Mississippi River to Grand Gulf, Mississippi. Marching to Raymond, Mississippi, from Grand Gulf, the Eighteenth joined Colonel John B. Sanborn's 1st Brigade—3rd Division—17th Corps on 12 May as the Federal 17th Corps prepared to move on the Mississippi state capital, Jackson.

The 18th Wisconsin was the new regiment in the brigade and they had only a day to adjust to their new circumstances and new comrades. The march resumed on 13 May with no Confederate resistance. On 14 May, however, the brigade came under artillery fire and sharpshooting as it neared the outskirts of Jackson. The 18th Wisconsin took its place in line as Sanborn's troops and another brigade marched forward to occupy a sheltering ravine. With division flanks secured, the two brigades were ordered forward on the run across a 400-yard ridge to another ravine. The move was made with few losses. After reforming his line, Sanborn gave the order to charge a Confederate battery: "The whole line with banners unfurled went forward at double-quick," reported Sanborn later, "and with more regularity than at an ordinary battalion drill . . . [The charge] made up a scene that can never be effaced from the mind of any who witnessed it, and can never be properly represented on paper."[1] The Confederate line, outnumbered and about to be overrun, dissolved and fled through the streets of Jackson. One of the brigade flags, that of the 59th Indiana, was hastily run up the flag pole atop the capitol building where it remained until Sanborn's unit left town the next day.

---

1. OR, vol. 24, pt. 1, p. 729.

In the charge at Jackson, the 18th Wisconsin, which had started the fight in reserve, lost two men killed and eighteen wounded, more than half of the brigade's total of thirty-two casualties.

The night of 14 May was spent supplying the men with three days rations of bacon, meal, and sugar, most of which was taken from the state penitentiary storehouses. On the 15th, other brigades engaged in the business of destroying Jackson's few wartime industries, railroad yards, and public buildings while the 18th Wisconsin marched with Sanborn's brigade westward down the road they had only a day earlier used to approach the city. The troops were headed toward Vicksburg.

A day's march found Sanborn's men at Edwards Station, the halfway point between Jackson and Vicksburg. Marching before daybreak on 16 May, the men of the 18th Wisconsin stood to the side of the road later in the morning to allow the passage of a group of officers. It was Grant and his staff on their way to the front of the column. Without slowing his brisk pace, Grant called out to Sanborn, "Colonel, we shall fight the battle for Vicksburg today. Come on with your brigade as rapidly as possible and have your men in condition to go into action when they reach the field."[2] Within the hour, the men could hear the thump of artillery fire ahead at Champion Hill. Colonel Sanborn sent two regiments of the brigade to support a battery in General John Logan's portion of the Federal line. A third regiment was assigned to hold a position on Logan's left flank. Sanborn, perhaps because the 18th Wisconsin was still an unfamiliar regiment, retained the Badgers as his reserve unit.

"The Eighteenth Wisconsin was moved from right to left and back two or three times by order of the general commanding [McPherson], as the attack was made more fiercely on either hand. The regiment moved with great promptness and held every position firmly until removed by orders," wrote Sanborn after the battle.

Greater Federal numbers finally defeated the Confederate force at Champion Hill and opened the road to Vicksburg. Sanborn's men resumed their march and camped several miles west of the battlefield on the night of 16 May. Losses among the 18th Wisconsin were light with but one killed and five wounded.

Other Federal troops marched ahead to clear Confederate defenders at the Big Black River crossing. Sanborn's men arrived at the Big Black at noon on 17 May and were assigned fatigue duty through the night building a floating cotton bale-and-board pontoon bridge. Sanborn's men broke camp on 18 May and had marched three miles toward Vicksburg when they were ordered to return to the Big Black River to guard wagon

---

2. Sanborn, John B., "The Crisis at Champion's Hill: The Decisive Battle of the Civil War," [St. Paul, Minn., 1903] p. 10.

trains at the crossing. Departing the Big Black again on 19 May, the brigade approached the Federal lines at Vicksburg on the 20th through scorching heat and choking dust. What the men did not know until they arrived at Vicksburg was that their delay at the Big Black had kept them from participating in a bloody but unsuccessful assault on the Confederate lines the day before.

Sanborn's men were placed in position near the center of the Federal lines facing Vicksburg and the men of the 18th Wisconsin were assigned skirmish duty on 21 May. Though skirmishing was a dangerous undertaking, the Badgers were once again touched by good fortune. It was learned on the night of the 21st that another assault was planned for the next morning. The rest of the brigade would be sent scrambling through obstacles and up steep hillsides against strong Confederate entrenchment's while the Eighteenth remained in rifle pits providing covering fire.

The Federal assault on 22 May was a massive effort but failed to break the Confederate line. Sanborn's three assault regiments were shifted away from their original position to another part of the line and sustained nearly 200 casualties; their heaviest losses of the campaign. Understandably, the 18th Wisconsin suffered far less as skirmishers and counted five killed and eleven wounded after the days actions sputtered to a halt. On 24 May the brigade was reunited and went into camp as the siege of Vicksburg began in earnest.

While Federal troops dug trenches and artillery positions around the besieged city, a nine-day expedition into the Mississippi countryside from 26 May to 4 June 1863 carried the Wisconsin boys away from Vicksburg in order to burn cotton mills, gins, and bridges behind the Federal lines. On their return from the expedition, the 18th Wisconsin spent hot, humid days and nights digging rifle pits, building entrenchments, skirmishing, and avoiding return sniper fire. The siege work was slow, dirty, and frustrating. But on 4 July 1863, Confederate General John Pemberton asked for terms of surrender, yielding Vicksburg to General Ulysses S. Grant.

The capitulation of Vicksburg's garrison ended forty-three days of heat, dust, and danger. The brigade in which the 18th Wisconsin had been serving since May was accorded a position of honor when they entered the captured city. Confederate soldiers were paroled within a week leaving Vicksburg entirely to Federal troops. The 18th Wisconsin moved inside the old Confederate lines and settled into a warm but comfortable routine of camp police and picket duties. According to Colonel Sanborn, "During the entire siege the health and morale of the command was excellent and none seemed to have a desponding thought or a doubt as to the successful result, and whether called upon to dig rifle-pits, throw up entrenchments, skirmish with the enemy or stand to arms . . . all was done with the greatest alacrity."

For a month the Badgers enjoyed the relative peace and quiet of camp life. On 3 August 1863, camp routine was given a start when it was announced that the Eighteenth's second-in-command, Lieutenant Colonel Samuel W. Beall, had resigned his commission and was returning to Wisconsin. Beall's duties were distributed among the remaining officers and the Eighteenth functioned without a lieutenant colonel for several months.

The transfer in May of the 18th Wisconsin to the Vicksburg side of the Mississippi River threw Davis and the "Tigers" into the most active campaigning they experienced during the war. Although his correspondence necessarily suffered in the two weeks during which he was on the march, he more than made up for the delay by detailing his travels as soon he had the time to write. Throughout the siege, Davis wrote not only of the danger but also of the boredom and heat, visits with enemy pickets, and of his ability to earn extra spending money when opportunities presented themselves.

On a more personal level, Davis wrote several heartfelt letters of encouragement to Lucinda during the war regarding her reading, writing, and general intellectual improvement. Sounding as much like a father as a husband in this chapter, he promoted not just the ideals of intellectual pursuits but of a refreshed and invigorated mind through useful and practical reading. Compared to the neighborhood gossips who waste their time in idle chatter, observed Davis, Lucinda would be much better served by reading and writing in her spare time. Regarding his infant daughter, Silva May, Davis also took time in his correspondence to school Lucinda in child rearing techniques. Whether or not she needed such tutoring as she raised her first child is hard to tell but clearly T. J. Davis reveled in his role, distant as he was, as the family patriarch.

Headquarters,18th Regiment Wisconsin Volunteers
Camp Near Carthage, Lousiana, Sunday, May 3rd, 1863

Dear Lucinda,

I endeavor to write you a few lines to let you know where I am. I am as well as usual. I have not received a letter from you since I last wrote.

We left Milliken's Bend on the 26th by land for this place. We come by way of Richmond, 16 miles west of Vicksburg. The distance from Milliken's Bend to this place is near (50) miles through a low flat country with occasional sloughs and bayous that we had to bridge. Although the country is low and wet, yet we passed many large and well-improved plantations. The Mississippi Valley is a much richer and wealthier country in the south than I had anticipated and it is the quaint essence of secessionism, many of the inhabitants of which are now reaping the reward which they so richly deserve by having their plantations devastated and their Negros taken from them.

We are about forty miles below Vicksburg by way of the river and twelve miles above Grand Gulf where the Rebels are fortified on a bluff with about 15,000 troops. We have a force of thirty or forty thousand troops in that vicinity and will probably drive the Rebels away from there before many days. There has been considerable fighting going on down there for several days and our forces have taken some prisoners but I have not heard the peticulars or if I did I would not believe them for there is so many diferant reports circulating through the camps.

We arrived here yesterday in advance of our division in charge of some siege guns. We will probably remain here untill our division comes up, which probably will be today or tomorrow.

We have not had a mail for nearly a week. Our mail has to be carried fifty miles by land and we will not be likely to get it verry regular while we are down here and if you do not get mail regular from me you must not be uneasy.

Foster's Battery came down here ahead of us. It is now down near Grand Gulf. I have not seen any of the boys.

The last mail, I received a letter from Susan and Hariet. I will send it to you. I must answer them today. I will send them my "Father Abraham's Song".

You would hardly believe how forward vegitation is here. Young corn is a foot high in many fields, peaches are larger than quails' eggs, blackberries are half grown, and roses and poppies are in full bloom.

You said you had bought a pair of eardrops. Of course, I do not object to that. I would [have] bought you a pair before I left if you would [have] said you would wear them.

I shall look for another letter from you as soon as the mail comes through—perhaps today.

You give the price of some things in your letters so I will give you the price of some things here:butter: 50 cents, tobacco: $2.00 to $2.50 per lb., crackers: 30 cents per lb., green apples (partly rotten): 5 cents each [and] good quality 3 for 25 cents, pickles: 5 cents each. As for tea, coffee, meat, sugar, rice and beans we draw all that we want from government. Also hardtack or square diet and sometimes we draw flour. So it is not really necessary for the soldiers to buy mutch trash from sutlers at such exorbitant prices.

Perhaps you you think I do not say enough about the baby in my letters. Well, I will send you part of a story that will partly make up for the deficiency. [not included in the letter] So I will close for this time. Yours as ever. Write often.

T. J. Davis

Camp near Carthage, Louisiana, May 7th, 1863

Dear Lucinda,

I again sit down to write you a few lines in answer to two letters I received from you last night, one dated April 16th, the other the 19th, and was glad to learn that you was well. I am as well as usual. The wether is getting rather uncomfortabley warm here, though it is cooler today than usual. We have not suffered mutch from heat yet.

We are still in camp where I last wrote you on the 3rd but I do not think we will remain here but a few days longer. Our forces has taken Grand Gulf and about six hundred prisoners. We sent 450 of them up to Milliken's Bend day before yesterday and we have 150 more here at the Landing that were shiped up from Grand Gulf last night. Many of the prisoners are good-looking men and intelligent enough to be engaged in a better cause. There was quite a number killed and wounded on both sides at Grand Gulf but I have not heard the peticulars.[3] There is large bodies of our troops still coming down here and I think there will be a move made on Vicksburg before many weeks.

I have not seen Jabe yet. I don't know whether Foster's Battery was in the fight or not, though I do not think it was.

You said you saw Mrs. Johnson and that she said she meant to pay them notes when Johnson sent her the money. I do not think he will send her a great deal more for her [man is] at Memphis in the hospital trying to get his discharge and probably he will succeed. I will probably write to Baker if he does not pay them before June.

I saw John Greenman, John Smith, and Hank Allen of the 8th Regiment last night. They were well and in good spirits. Their regiment went on down to the [Grand] Gulf this morning.

I would not write any more if I were you about the old man Hunt as it does not interest me enough to pay for writing it and I shall take no part in their quarrels.

I do not think you have time or take time to read or study your books mutch as you do not spell or compose but little if any better than you did a year ago. I am afraid that you do not turn your attention enough in that direction to take an interest in it. I know you have not time to make a business of studying like a person would have at school, but there is scarcely any woman, unless they have a verry large family and

---

3. Grand Gulf was not abandoned by Confederate forces until the night of 7 May 1863. Grant's troops had defeated a Confederate force at nearby Port Gibson on 2 May 1863 and the battle and prisoners that Davis mentions were probably the Port Gibson fight and its attendant casualties. Federal losses were 875 while Confederate losses were 832 battle casualties and 1,000 southern soldiers captured following the battle. [Faust, p. 595–596]

no help, but what has some odd spells of leisure time during the day. Even after a person has been at work while sitting down to rest the body, they can at the same time refresh the mind by reading some useful book. A few minutes time well-employed at home in study is worth a whole day idled away at school. In most all your letters I find quite a number of words misspelled and phrases of uneducated people wrote in to express language. Bad language, and especialy bad spelling, is the first thing noticed by educated people. To know good language a person must study it and not borrow it from uneducated people that do not understand it. You can improve yourself mutch by selecting well-written peices from books and writing them off. At the same time pay peticular attention to the meaning of each word and how it is spelled. By frequently writing this way you will get it impressed on your memory. I wrote a little on the same subject to you some time ago in answer to which I received a long string of excuses of being so busy. But I did not think them sufficient excuses to give it up altogether. We may think that we already know as mutch as some other folks and think that will do. We must learn to rely on our own resourses and knowledge in our worldly affairs and the better we are informed the better we are prepared to meet obstacles.

T. J. Davis

[Attached to this letter was the following]

We should learn to be self-possessed, self-reliant, not too self-important, or too weak and giddy. I have known married women, many of them who would spend near half their time in visiting through the neighborhood and be verry prominent in telling how many bad neighbors and how many mean acts she had known them to do etc., etc., and who went home with Sally Jones from the last meeting and who got the mitten, and who got cut out, and who had lately got married, and who was promised to be married; and who lately had babies and who soon would have one and a thousand and one other things too numerous to mention, at the same time had plenty of good books at home or could easily get them but did not know whether the earth rolled around or whether it stood still and the moon drove the sun around it or whether the sun was mad to obey the dog star by its continual barking. Perhaps I have said too mutch on this subject but I do not mean to be stringent. I like to see people aspire to learning while they are young and can retain it in their minds, especially one that is so near to me as yourself. I am ignorant and unlearned myself and I know enough of ignorance to understand the value of education and sound judgement. If you pick errors in my composition and spelling and recite me to it, I will take it all in good part and try and profit by it.

I supose that Silva will be six months old tomorrow and will soon begin to teeth. While teething, there is considerable judgement to be exercised with children as well as care. If in warm weather, they should not be kept too warm, which is a fault with many mothers, for teething creates fever, more or less. And another fault is laying a child altogether on its back when put in the cradle or bed to sleep. For when teething there is a druling spittle that ejects from the gums and when lying on its back the child invariably swallow it, which is said to be very poisenous. A child when allowed to ly on the floor and sleep in its own way will mostly lay on its side or face though more often on the face in that position the drule will run out of its mouth.

Since I commence writing we have received orders to march. We will probably start in the morning. I think we are going over on the Mississippi side to guard a bridge on Black River.

It is getting late and I must close. Take care of yourself the best you can. I think I will be at home some time. I think that Jabe's and Robert's furloughs have played out. Tell Orla and Mary not to sit up nights and lose sleep looking for them for they might stand a chance to take cold and then not see them after all. It is better to take things cool especially in hot weather that we may not get over-heated in the summer time or get gray before we are old.

I received a letter last night from sister Elisabeth and one from brother Isaac. They were all well. I thought that Elisabeth would have written to before now but she has verry bad eyes and has a great many letters to write to friends in the army. If I were you, though, I would not write to them until they did to you. I did not think to write so mutch when I began but I kept scribling ahead so the second sheet is full. Direct as before. Yours as ever, good-bye.

Thos. J. Davis

Camp Near Vicksburg, May 24th, 1863

Dear Lucinda,

I again try to write you a few lines to let you know that I am as well as usual. I do not intend to write but little this time. I have not written a letter to you for over two weeks because I had no chance to send it.

We left Carthage on the 9th Inst. We have had a long and active march. We crossed the river at Grand Gulf on the 10th. We then took up our line of march for Jackson, at which place we arrived and took by storm on the 14th. We then turned about the next morning and started for Vicksburg. We met the regiments from Vicksburg under General Pemberton on the 16th on Black River and had a big fight and cleaned the Rebels out and took four thousand prisoners. We have taken 83 pieces of canon from the

Rebels. Since we left Grand Gulf, we have drove them back into their fortifications at Vicksburg.[4]

I have not had a letter from you since I wrote to you before. I expect one
this evening. The captain is going with the mail in a few minutes. You
must not be uneasy until you hear from me again. Yours as ever,

Thos. J. Davis

Camp Near Vicksburg, Mississippi, May 26th, 1863

Dear Wife,

I again sit down to write you another epistle to let you know that I
am still well and that I still think of you though many miles separate us.
I received a letter from you yesterday dated May 2nd, 5th, 6th. I was
verry glad to hear from you and to hear that you was well. I wrote you
a few hasty lines a few days ago but I had not time to give any peticulars.

I will give you some of the peticulars of our campaign since we crossed
over in Mississippi. We crossed over the river at Grand Gulf on the 10th
of May. Grand Gulf is at the mouth of Black River and is on a high eleva-
tion of bluffs and was a splendid place to fortify against our river forces.
But our gunboats proved too mutch for the Rebel works there. They took
the place and captured most of their artillery and a quantity of prisoners
of which I mentioned before on the 11th.[5]

We left Grand Gulf for Jackson and camped at night at a little town
called Cayuga. On the 12th our troops ahead of us had a fight with the
Rebels 3 miles west of Raymond and repulsed them with considerable
loss.[6] We come up with the advanse of our troops in the evening.

The next morning our division went in the advanse. The morning of the
13th we marched into Raymond which, by the way, is quite a respectable
town and the county seat of Hinds County. We halted about 2 hours at
this place and replenished our provision wagons with Rebel supplies that
we captured here. We then marched on 9 miles farther and camped near
a town called Clinton which is ten miles west of Jackson and on the railroad from Jackson to Vicksburg.

---

4. After crossing the Mississippi River, the 18th Wisconsin marched to Raymond, Mississippi, where they transferred into Sanborn's (First) Brigade,
Quinby's Division, 17th Army Corps. Under Sanborn, the 18th Wisconsin participated in the capture of Jackson (14 May 1863) and the Battle of Champion's Hill
(16 May 1863) [Brown, p.191–194, 202–204]

5. Contrary to Davis' information, efforts by Federal gunboats to subdue Grand
Gulf were unsuccessful on 29 April 1863. [Long, p.343]

6. The 18th Wisconsin was not involved in the fighting at Raymond. Casualties
at Raymond were approximately 500 killed or wounded on each side. [Long, p.
352]

It rained hard during the night but we were all ready on the morning on 14th and at 4 o'clock in the morning we took up our line of march for Jackson. About nine o'clock it again commenced raining. About the same time our advance cavalry & artillery commenced skirmishing with the enemy, our skirmishers gradually driving the Rebel skirmishers back. About ten o'clock our advance came upon the main Rebel force about three miles from Jackson. Our infantry was ordered forward on double quick. Our division was ordered to make a bayonet charge on the Rebel batteries and infantry about half past ten. We charged on them with two lines of battle for a few minutes. They tried hard to check us but they could not stop us and when we broke their lines they soon began to skedaddle and scatter in every direction and after charging them a mile and a half at double quick we came to a halt and straightened up our lines. By this time the Rebels were all out of sight. The Rebels run on through town and never halted but told the citizens as they passed through that the Yankees were coming hell-bent for election. We marched on into town and camped for the night.[7]

The boys, though wet, weary, and worn felt jubilent over the capture of the Sesesh capital. They lost no time in helping themselves to anything they wanted to eat and drink and all the tobacco they could carry with them. Jeff Davis' residence is in Jackson and I learn that it was burned since we left there together with most of the city.[8]

In the charge at Jackson our regiment lost 23 men killed and wounded.[9]

On the morning of the 15th we about-faced and started back towards Vicksburg and on the 16th we met General Pemberton with all his Rebel forces from Vicksburg about half way between Jackson and Vicksburg on Baker's Creek. We had a general engagement with the enemy and after a hard and determined battle, we repulsed the Rebels with a heavy loss on both sides of killed and wounded. We captured about 2,000 Rebels as prisoners of war.[10]

---

7. Casualties in the fighting at Jackson were approximately 325 Federals killed or wounded and 200 Confederates lost. [Long, p. 353]

8. Jackson was a manufacturing city. Before turning around to move on Vicksburg, Grant ordered the burning of machine shops, factories, foundries, and warehouses as well as the destruction of all railroad facilities. [Grant, Ulysses S., Personal Memoirs of U.S. Grant, Vol. 1. New York, Charles L. Webster & Company, 1885, p. 507]

9. Casualties were six killed and sixteen wounded, none from Davis' Company C. (Quiner, E.B., The Military History of Wisconsin: A Record of the Civil and Military Patriotism of the State in the War for the Union, Chicago, 1866, p.662)

10. General John C. Pemberton was placed in command of Vicksburg in October 1862. In the ill-coordinated, give-and-take Battle of Baker's Creek (usually called Champion's Hill) on 16 May 1863, Grant's Federals finally pushed Pemberton's Confederates back toward Vicksburg. Federal casualties were about 2,500; Confederate losses were 3,850 including 1,700 prisoners. [Long, p.353–354]

The Rebels retreated back about 5 miles to Big Black River and made another stand and thought to repulse us there but our forces crossed the river higher up and attacked the Rebels in the rear. This was on the 17th and after another hard fight the Rebels again fled leaving twenty-six hundred prisoners and 17 pieces of artillery in our hands.[11]

The Rebels retreating towards Vicksburg on the 18th, our forces followed them up closely and kept up a skirmish in their rear. On the 19th the Rebels were driven into their fortifications at Vicksburg and Haines Bluff. Haines Bluff is 12 miles northeast of Vicksburg on the Yazoo River. The Rebels made strong works here to prevent our gunboats from runing up that river. General Sherman attacked and capured [captured] Haynes' Bluff with all their artillery and a large number of prisoners on the 20th.[12] On the 23rd and 24th our regiment skirmished all day both days with with the Rebels in front of their batteries at Vicksburg.

Our regiment lost several killed and wounded. Alvin Caulkins received a slight wound in the leg, the ball glancing around the shin bone and making quite a scar. But the wound is not deep. It does not prevent him from walking around. He will be fit for duty again in 2 or 3 weeks. In all the fighting in this campaign so far our regiment has lost 42 men killed and wounded but, strange to say, not one man of company C has received the mark of a bullet.

Captain Jim Burnett of company G, 30th Illinois, cousin to Al Burnett, was killed at Baker's Creek [Champion's Hill]. He was wounded and taken prisoner once before. Jim Ditto, a second cousin of mine, was shot through the brain while skirmishing at Vicksburg on the 23rd. He lived about an hour.

We have orders to march and I must close for the present

Haynes' Bluff, Mississippi, June 1st, 1863

Well Lucinda, after so long a time I will try and finish my letter. On the evening of the 26th of May while I was writing we received orders to

---

11. At the Big Black River on 17 May 1863, a small Confederate holding force of about 5,000 troops was left behind to keep a bridge open for one of Pemberton's Confederate divisions from the Champion's Hill fight. The division never arrived, having escaped in another direction, but 10,000 Federal troops attacked at 8 o'clock in the morning and quickly overwhelmed the Confederate position. Casualties were light: 279 Federals, mostly wounded, and 1,700 Confederates captured along with eighteen cannons lost. [[Long, p. 354]

12. Davis misunderstood the situation at Hayne's Bluff. Confederate troops abandoned the works as they withdrew into the Vicksburg defenses. Sherman's XV Corps simply took possession of the works on 18 May 1863 as they marched toward Vicksburg. [Grant, p.527–528]

march forth with seven days rations on an expedition under General F. P. Blair.[13] Our forces numbered about twelve thousand men. The object of the expidition was to ascertain the whereabouts and strength of the Rebel General Joe Johnson who it was thought was between Yazoo City and Jackson collecting his scattered forces together that we whiped at Raymond and at Jackson.[14] And it was rumored that he intended to attack our forces in the rear at Vicksburg.

We started from Vicksburg about ten o'clock on the evening of the 26th and marched out 8 miles and camped 'til morning. On the 27th we marched to Bear Creek where we drove away a squad of guerrillas. On the 28th we kept on towards Yazoo City our cavalry occasionally runing into squads of Rebel cavalry. On the 29th we resumed our march toward Yazoo City. In the afternoon we come upon a force of about four thousand Rebels at Mechanicsburg. They did not stand mutch of a fight for they fled before our skirmishers and skedaddled to the east side of Black River. So Joe Johnston had to take up a position farther in the interior of the state. Yazoo City is 60 miles northeast of Vicksburg on the Yazoo River. On the 30th we turned about and came down the Yazoo River and and burned most of the cotton and cotton houses along the valley and we arrived here at Haynes' Bluff on 31st of May, yesterday evening, making a trip of nearly a hundred miles.

The day is quite warm and the boys are pretty well run down. I don't think, however, that we will march mutch for sometime to come. Our forces are closed up snugly around Vicksburg so that the Rebels can't get out and our batteries are shelling them every day. They must sooner or later surrender.

T. J. Davis

June 1st/63

Well Lucinda, I will write a few lines more as the other paper would not hold it all. I expect we shall get another mail in a day or two then I shall look for another letter from you.

---

13. General Francis P. Blair Jr. commanded a division in Sherman's XV Corps during the Vicksburg campaign. The Mechanicsburg Expedition (26 May–4 June 1863) was ordered by Grant to protect the rear of his besieging army at Vicksburg. Blair's force dispersed small Confederate forces, burned bridges, obstructed roads, then confiscated livestock on their return to Haynes' Bluff. [Welcher, pt.2, p.894]

14. General Joseph E. Johnston was the third ranking officer in the Confederate Army. Transferred west in November 1862, Johnston was given the formidable task of supervising two armies in difficult situations, Bragg's forces in Tennessee and Pemberton's forces in Vicksburg. [Davis, William C. (ed.), The Confederate General, Vol. 3., Harrisburg, Pa., National Historical Society, 1991, p.193–197]

John M. Stokes, musician, Company C, 18th Wisconsin. Fifer Stokes died at Jefferson Barracks, St. Louis, in May 1862. (Photo courtesy of the Rosma Rathbun Limbeck Collection, U.S. Army Military History Institute)

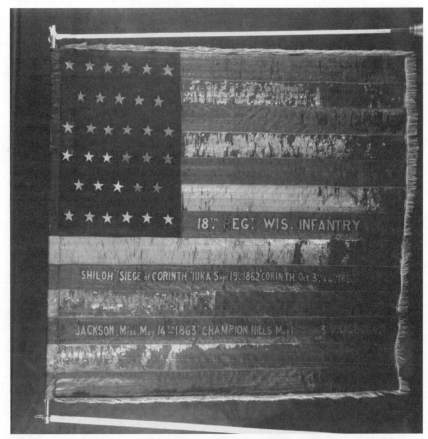

Federal colors of the 18th Wisconsin Infantry. The federal colors note battles in which the unit participated through the Siege of Vicksburg in 1863. (Photo courtesy of the Wisconsin Veterans Museum)

State colors of the 18th Wisconsin Infantry. The colors feature the Wisconsin seal. (Photo courtesy of the Wisconsin Veterans Museum)

Lucinda Spaulding before her marriage to Thomas J. Davis. She was 17 when she married the 29-year-old Davis.

Lucinda Davis and baby, Silvie Mae. This is the portrait referred to in T. J. Davis's August 27, 1863, letter.

Thomas J. Davis, circa 1864

Thomas J. Davis, circa 1912, wearing a fiftieth anniversary Battle of Shiloh veterans badge.

Ransom J. Chase in his captain's uniform, 1865. Chase rose to lieutenant in the 18th Wisconsin before resigning on account of disability in January 1863. He reenlisted as a captain in the 42nd Wisconsin in 1864 and participated in President Lincoln's funeral in Springfield, Illinois.

Ransom J. Chase as he appeared in an 1891 history of Woodbury County and Sioux City, Iowa. Although an extremely successful postwar law practice was curtailed by ill health in 1883, the county history noted that "his work has been crowned with that degree of success implied in the fact that he is one of the millionaires of the city."

Captain Robert S. McMichael commanded the Badax Tigers in 1864–65. A justice of the peace before the war, he officiated at the wedding of Thomas J. and Lucinda Davis on October 6, 1861.

Wisconsin soldiers monument, Vicksburg National Battlefield Park. Mounted on the monument walls are regimental tablets and rosters of all Wisconsin soldiers who participated in the campaign.

Detail of the 18th Wisconsin Infantry plaque on the Wisconsin soldiers monument, Vicksburg National Battlefield Park. Thomas J. Davis is the seventh private listed in Company C.

Colonel John B. Sanborn's brigade, including the "Badax Tigers," was accorded the honor of occupying Vicksburg, Mississippi, upon its surrender. The 4th Minnesota Infantry (pictured), with whom the 18th Wisconsin served for most of the war, led Sanborn's brigade into the captured city on July 4, 1863. (4th Minnesota Regiment Entering Vicksburg, July 4, 1863, by Francis Millet, courtesy of the Minnesota Historical Society)

I received a letter from Belle and Ida, David Ingersoll's sisters the same time I got yours. They wrote that little Charlie and the rest of the folks were well. Ida said she had written a letter to you.

That candy heart you sent me come through without being broken but the cookey you sent was all ground into powder. In return I will send you a paper of pins and some steel pens that I captured at Jackson.

You say that you supose that I think you are the poorest writer that I receive letters from. You are altogether mistaken if you think so but I would be glad to have you a better writer than any I get letters from. I only thought you did not take interest enough in trying to develop your natural abilities. I know that you have a good intellect, mutch above ordinary women, if you would just confidence in yourself to bring it out. And you are of the age now that the general run of mind and character is forming which will follow you through after life. You can now write a better letter both in composition and penmanship than any of my sisters. You write a better letter than Jabe and as good as any of your sisters that I have received letters from. You say when I come home that I must do all the writing for you do not like to write. Perhaps that accounts for your not trying more to improve.

I wish you to learn to like to write and compose so that you would not be ashamed to write to anybody, if necessary, on any kind of business. It is not that I wish you to write a correct and proper letter to me in particular but more to show your abilities when you have occasion to write to others. And a love for study and learning generally refines a person's general run of mind and character. If I was at home I should be just as anxious for you to improve as I am now. I should [have] been glad if it were so that you could attend school all the time I was gone. I do not wish you to think me too hard and exacting. I think in a few years you will agree with me.

We passed Foster's Battery about 9 o'clock in the evening after the battle at Baker's Creek. I spoke to Levi Noble but Jabe was at one side and we was in a hurry so I did not see him. Levi said he was well.

This is Sesesh paper I am writing on and I will send it in a Sesesh envelope.

Blackberries and plums are getting ripe and I have had two or three messes of new Irish potatoes. Green apples are getting large enough to stew. On this last march I saw several fields of new wheat out and in the shock and fields of corn as high as my head.

As my paper is growing short I must close. Write as often as you can and give me the news, generally. I have scratched this over in such a rough way I don't know as you can read it. You must not be uneasy if you do not get mail regular but I think it will be more regular than it has the last month.

I remain yours as ever,

T. Jefferson Davis

Camp near Vicksburg, June 11th/63

Dear Wife,

I will write you a few more lines today as I am somewhat at leisure for I often do not have an opportunity to write when I wish to do so. I received a letter from you last night dated May 28th and was glad to hear from you again and to hear that you was well. I am still as well as usual.

The weather is quite pleasent today. We had a heavy rain yesterday and last night which was mutch needed to allay the dust and cool the air.

Military affairs remain about the same as when I last wrote you. The Rebels are still in their works and we are still holding them there.

Tomorrow is your birthday when I believe you will be 19. I hope I shall be at home before you are another year older and I think I will if I live. Next Sunday, the 14th, little Charlie will be seven years old. I have not seen him since two years ago last April. It seems that I am almost getting lost to a civilized world.

I think if Silvie weighs 20 pounds she must be a large and healthy child, notwithstanding the number of times you wrote to me that she was sick or unwell. You must not think she is going to die if she happens to get the b__y [belly] ache or cholic or happens to sneeze and cough a few times. Silvie is the propper way to spell her name. At first I unthoughtedly spelled it wrong though there is no great diferance.

You said you wished to know what interest I was to have on them Baker, Johnson & Co. notes. I thought I wrote that to you before. Both notes, when given on the 21st of June, 1861, amounted to one-hundred-and-eighteen dollars and 33 cents. The notes simply state with interest which means seven per cent lawful interest of the state of Wisconsin from date until paid. On the 21st day of June, 1863, they will then have been drawing interest two years. On the 21st of this month the interest and principal of both notes added together will amount to one-hundred-and-thirty-four Dollars and 93 cents. As for Mrs. Johnson, I do not depend on her paying anything. You say you think Baker can pay the notes anytime if I would receive his money. I am still of the same opinion in referance to it that I was before and if Mr. Baker has got Wisconsin money that is worth its face dollar for dollar it will not cost him but little to get greenbacks for it for there is a vast amount of greenbacks in circulation in the North and where there is mutch trading done. I can't think greenbacks are hard to get so don't receive his Wisconsin money. I will write to Baker today.

You say that Susan wrote again for you to go out there and live with [them.] I supose she is just blarneying. She knows that you will not go but she wishes to flatter you by making you believe that she is verry liberal and affectionate.

I did not intend to write this mutch when I commenced, though I could write more. I have not received but three or four full written sheets from you for three months. You generally say you have not time to write but little. You may look for small letters from me until you get time to write larger or at least a few of them. Then again you say you have no news to write. Of course, I do not look for great stiring events to transpire in the Badax Valley every week. Why, tax your inventive faculties and originate something yourself. It certainly must be a slow thinker that can't fill one sheet of paper in a week.

I received the ring you sent me. It is too large for my little finger and to [too] small for the rest but I can fix it. I shall keep it to remember the donor. I will send you some more Sesesh steel pens. Write soon.

I remain yours as ever for several days,

Thos. J. Davis

Camp Near Vicksburg, June 19th, 1863

Dear wife,

I sit down this morning to write you a few lines to let you know that I am well and hope this will find you the same. I have not received any letter from you since I last wrote. We had quite a large mail last night but I did not get any letters at all. The last letter I got from you was dated 28th of May. I shall certainly get one from you the next mail.

Jabez and and Levi Noble was up here to our regiment last Sunday. Jabe has been unwell for some time but he is getting stout again. Levi looks hearty and is as full of gas as ever.

We are still where we was when I last wrote. Vicksburg is not taken, yet, but it is about as good as taken for we have got them in there and they can't get out and as soon as their grub runs out they will be compelled to surrender. Our skirmishers and the Rebel skirmishers talk to each [other] every night. Sometimes our men and the Rebels will meet between the two lines and talk as long as they wish and then return each to his place. Night before last we was out on the skirmish line. We hollowed over to the Rebs and told them to come over and have a chat and we would let them go back again. Several of them come over to our company and talked a couple of hours and then returned to their fort. They said we had them tight in there; that they could not get out nor we could not get in there. They said if we would remain as we are, that they must surrender when their provisions is consumed. 'Tis one month today since they were driven into their works so they have one month less provisions now than when we drove them in.

The Badax boys are all well.

The wether is pleasant, not so warm as a week ago. We have been having some good rain. We, however, look [for] hot weather mostly until September. The time seems to pass rapidly and the summer will soon pass if we ly in camp. I have nothing more at this time to write. Write soon and often.

Yours as ever,

T. J. Davis

[On the back of the last page in a large scrawl Davis wrote:]
Nothing more. I can't think of nothing.
[At the bottom of the page:]
Just as I finish Levi Noble and E. Caulkins come up to see us. They say the battery boys are well.

Camp near Vicksburg, June 24/1863

Dear Wife,

I sit down on my bunk this evening to write you a few lines to let you know that I am as well as usual. I received a letter from you last night dated June 7th & [10]th. I was sorry to hear that you and the baby was sick but I hope before this reaches you that you both will be well again.

The wether continues pleasant, not cool, neither verry hot.

The boys are all tolerable well.

Foster's Battery is a good fighting battery and do good execution for they have good guns. Foster was wounded and has gone home. Foster is a verry good fighting man but no doubt there is thousands in the army that are just as good as he.

We are still in our old position. Vicksburg has not surrendered, yet, but our cannons are battering away at the Rebs every day. It is beyond our knowledge how mutch provision they have but they must certainly give up sooner or later and the sooner the better.

The battery boys are all well. Jabe, Levi, Calvin, and E. Caulkins were up here the other day.

We had a nice rain last night.

I have not had any letter from neither Sarah, Susan, or Hariet for some time. I also wrote to James about two months ago and have received no answer from him. I have received but few letters lately.

I will close for this time. We will get paid two months pay in a day or two.

Yours as ever,

T. J. Davis

Write soon.

Camp Near Vicksburg, June 29th, 1863

Dear Wife,

I sit down this morning to write you a few lines to inform you that I am as well as usual and hope this may find you well. I have not had a letter from you since I wrote before, but will look for one in a day or two.

Jabe was quite sick night before last but considerable better yesterday. I am going down to the battery as soon as I get through writing to see him. The rest of the boys, I believe, are as well as usual.

I got a letter from Susan Wilson the other day. I will send it to you. It is not a verry long one and does not contain mutch news. I have not had a letter from Sarah for a long time,

We are still at our old camp, yet, and our forces are shelling away at Vicksburg every day as usual. It is thought that the garrison cannot hold out mutch longer. There was two rebel mails intercepted a few days ago, one going in and the other coming out of Vicksburg. The one going in was from Joe Johnston which stated to Pemberton that that he, Pemberton, must do his own fighting as it would be impossible for him, Johnston, to help him. In the mail going out there was several letters from Rebel officers, certain colonels and generals, some of which stated their supply of meal was exhausted and they had to live on meat and beans. These letters were sent to their families and several of them said they expected soon to take a trip up north as they would soon be compelled to surrender but thought they would soon be exchanged again. Then they would come home and see the folks. I hope they may soon take the notion to give it up for we have had quite a long siege of it.

In my other letter it stated that we would soon get two months pay but I think we will not get any pay 'til sometime in next month and then get four months pay.

Write soon and often and write the news.

Yours always,

T. J. Davis

[On the last page was the following:]

I will send you some verses that Susan sent me.

I went out blackberrying yesterday and got all the nice ripe blackberries I could eat and sold $1.65 worth besides and got my hands pretty well scratched up to boot. I sent Susan some verses and I sent the same ones to you but you did not say you ever got them.

T. J. D.

[The letters of July 2nd and 3rd were part of one continuous letter]

Camp near Vicksburg, July 2nd/63

Dear Wife,

I again sit down this afternoon to write you a few lines to let know that I am as well as usual. I received a letter from you last night dated June 17th and was glad to learn that you and the baby was better.

I went over to the battery last night to see Jabe. He was quite sick for a few days but is getting much better. Levi Noble stuck a cane stub in his lame arm near the shoulder. It lames him so that he is off duty for the present. The rest of the battery boys are well.

We received two months pay today. I think I will send some to you in a few days by express. If I do, I will write when I send it.

Things around Vicksburg remain about the same as when I last wrote to you.

I was somewhat surprised to hear that Mrs. Johnson had paid one of them notes as I did not think she would pay anything while Johnson was in the army but I am glad she was able to pay it. I wrote to Baker some time ago in reference to it.

The 25th [Wisconsin] Regiment is at Haynes' Bluff. There is two men from company A down here today they say the boys are in pretty good health. I would like very well to see the boys but they are too far away to go visiting. Perhaps I will get to see them after Vicksburg is taken so that we will have a chance to run around a little, which I hope will not be long.

July 3rd, 1863

Well, tomorrow is the 4th of July which I do not expect [they] celebrate as many of the citizens do up North, by making a large dinner and get together old and young, large and small, maids & matrons and belles and beaus to listen to long and learned speeches, vocal & martial music, and the sound of the blank charged cannon. But we will perhaps amuse ourselves with the sound of our cannon shelling the Rebels inside their works to let them know that the Yankees still remember the 4th of July.

Robert McMichael has just gone to the express office to send some money home. I sent 20 dollars with him. Mrs. McMichael will get it from Viroqua and you will get yours of her. You will pay your part of the express fee when you get the money.

I don't feel like writing today, I am so nervous. I don't know as you can read this after you get it. You said that Mrs McMichael had got three letters from Robert since you got any from me. I don't see the reason of it for I am sure that I have written as often since we come to Vicksburg as he. You will begin to get them before this time. I have have got your letters for two or three weeks in advance of Mrs. McMichael's letters.

Since writing the above the Rebel General Bowen came out to General Grant's headquarters with a flag of truce.[15] Firing has now nearly ceased

---

15. General John S. Bowen commanded a division of Confederate troops at Vicksburg. He was a pre-war acquaintance of General Grant's and was a natural choice to deliver General Pemberton's communications to the Federal commander. [Grant, p. 557]

all around the line. I do not know yet what they want. It may possibly be for a stipulation for a surrender of Vicksburg. I hope it may be so, but fear it is not.

My paper is out. Yours verry truly,

T. J. Davis

Vicksburg, Mississippi, July 5th, 1863

Dear Wife,

I sit down this morning to write you a small epistle to let you know that I am as well as usual and I believe the rest of the boys are well. I wish this may find you in the best of health and spirits. The wether continues quite warm and is getting dry.

I saw Levi Noble yesterday. He said that Jabe was getting quite smart again.

I suppose you will wish to know how I enjoyed the 4th yesterday to which I can say that I never enjoyed a fourth so well in my life for yesterday we took possession of Vicksburg and all the Rebel works with between twenty- and thirty-thousand prisoners. I wrote to you on the 3rd that the Rebels had come in to Grant's headquarters with a flag of truce. I was pretty certain that the Rebels was about surrendering then but I did not wish to say mutch encouraging about it untill I was sure. The capture of Vicksburg is by far the largest and most important victory of the war.

At about eleven o'clock yesterday forenoon, the Rebels come outside of their fortifications and stacked their arms and then retired behind their works again and about twelve o'clock our army corps under McPherson marched forward with the brass band playing "Dixie" and took possession of the center while the other two army corps under Sherman and McClernand took possession of the right and left. And thus, on the 4th of July the long sought Rebel stronghold fell into the hands of the Yankees amid loud and prolonged cheering and the firing of blank carterages from the Yankee cannon.

I have not time to write many peticulars today. I will write more hereafter.

The capture of Vicksburg will relieve the minds and bodies of many soldiers of much care and their folks of a great deal of suspense and anxiety concerning them. Our ears have been saluted nearly every day for 48 days with the discharging of firearms in battle and during that time we had more or less men killed and wounded every day and since night before last the stillness that prevails so far as fighting is concerned seems almost strange.

I do not know the exact number of prisoners we took here but our officers say there is 28,000 including the sick and wounded. During the siege the Rebels lost a great deal heavier than we which the marks of our rifles and cannon inside of their works abundantly show. Their provisions were about all exhausted and they had been on short rations for sometime. They seemed to be in quite a hurry for Grant to issue them something to eat.

There is some talk that as soon as Grant gets things straightened around there will be a few furloughs granted from each regiment for a limited number of men to go home. If so, and I can get a furlough, perhaps I may come home the latter part of summer or next fall.

I received a letter from Sarah McLain yesterday. I will send it to you. This letter will not be news to you for you will hear of the surrender of Vicksburg long before you get this letter. I will close for this time. I will write again soon. I remain truly your obedient husband. Write as often as often as convenient. So good-bye,

T. J. Davis

Vicksburg, Miss., July 10th, 1863

Dear Wife,

I sit down this morning to write you a few lines in answer to your letter dated June 22nd which I received last night. I was verry glad to hear from you and to hear that your health was improving. I am as well as usual, though not stout. There is mutch of the time that I am not really able to do duty but still I do it. I am again troubled with nerviousness and dyspepsia this summer. Though not dangerous, it is verry disagreeable. Sometimes it is dificult for me to write with any degree of decency. However, by taking care of myself I succeed in getting along tolerable well. The wether is quite warm, yet, and we cannot expect any more cool wether until September.

I have not seen Jabez since I wrote before but Levi Noble was over here the other day and said he was getting well rapidly.

Captain Layne is quite unwell. He is run down with chronic diarrhea. He thinks of starting north in a few days. He is getting verry poor and I don't think there is mutch hopes of him getting well while he remains here.[16]

Major Jerry Rusk of the 25th [Wisconsin] is here. He came a few minutes ago. His regiment is still up at Haines Bluff. He says there is a great deal of sickness in his regiment, there being nearly three hundred on the sick list at the present time. Jerry himself does not look so fat as when I saw him in Milwaukee.

I received a letter yesterday from brother Isaac and my sister Mahala McIntire and also one from Elisabeth and one from David Ingersoll and

---

16. Layne never recovered from his illness. His resignation was accepted in January 1864, and he subsequently died in Wisconsin on 29 February 1864.

Ida and her man. They all wrote that the folks were all well but that there was considerable sickness in the county. Ida said she had received a letter from you. David said while he was writing that Grandma and Charlie was hulling peas for dinner and that Charlie was throwing pea hulls at him so that he could hardly write.

I went up to Young's Point day before yesterday on a steamboat after our tents that we left there in April. We will perhaps have our tents pitched tomorrow.

We are now camped inside of the Rebel fortifications about half a mile from town. I have been all over the city. It has been quite a nice place before the siege but it is battered to peices now so that it is a hard looking place now. There is hardly a house in town but what has a cannonball hole in it and some of them are literally battered to peices. The ground is verry hilly in and around the city. The citizens, men, women, and children were driven out of their houses by our cannon. They were obliged to dig holes in the hillsides and live in the ground like gophers. It was rather a hard pill for the chivilrous belles of proud Mississippi to digest. But they were compelled to take it notwithstanding.

The prisoners that we took here are now all paroled and will be marched out of our lines today. We have kept them guarded inside of their own fortifications since they surrendered and they have been at liberty to go all around town as they chose. Our men and the Rebs mix up promiscously together and talk about the war and joke about past battles. I will get more paper

T. J. Davis

Vicksburg, Mississippi, July 11th, 1863

Well, I commenced writing you a letter yesterday but did not get through with it. Since the capture of Vicksburg our army corps has been in possession of the place and we have kept the prisoners coralled inside the outer lines of their old works and have been allowed to run loose so that they kept inside the lines. The Rebs and Yankees mixed up together and as a general thing talked as friendly as if they had always been good friends. I am pleased to see our men treat the prisoners so well for it will have a good effect on them in future in our favor. Manny of them say they have been deceived into the war if what we tell them be true and they think the Yankees are not such a hard lot after all.

The number taken here as near as I can learn is thirty-one-thousand and-eight hundred. They have all been paroled except some that have taken the oath of allegiance and wishes to remain with Uncle Sam. Today we guarded about half of the paroled prisoners through the lines and let them go towards Jackson. We will probably pass the remainder through our lines tomorrow.

Vicksburg was getting to be quite a hot place for the Rebels before they surrendered. The city is badly torn to peices with our artillery and our rifle balls was thrown in all parts of city. Both citizens and soldiers were compelled to live in holes in the ground to protect themselves from our fire. Over a thousand mules and horses was killed during the siege. They were killed both by our artillery and infantry. The Rebel General Green was killed by one of our Infield [Enfield] rifles at a distance of over a mile.[17]

I have not been to the 30th [Wisconsin] Regiment lately but it is here. Jim Wells is driving a team and was well when I last heard from him. Also, Munt Candor, O.C. Richardson, and W. Curry.

O.C. Richardson felt verry bad about the death of James Ditto and told me that he never regretted anything in his life so mutch as he did to report his death to his father. All the company, while talking of his death, seemed as mutch affected as if he had been a near relative. They all give him great praise as a brave soldier & that he was brave even to rashness and I have no doubt that too mutch daring was the cause of his death. I saw him the evening before he was killed as our regiment was marching out on the skirmish line. He rode along and talked to me for sometime. He told me that his battery was out of ammunition and that he had been out skirmishing that day with a rifle. I cautioned him to be verry careful while engaged in such business and advised him not to go out anymore as it was dangerous and also that skirmishing was not his business. But he replied that he liked the fun and I doubt not that he did. I heartily cympathize with his parents in their bereavement but I can console them that he fills the grave of a brave soldier and his loss is most deeply felt by those who knew him best. I will have to get more paper

T. J. Davis

[To George and Elisabeth Ditto]

Vicksburg, July 11th, 63

3rd Epistle

Captain James Burnett was killed while his regiment was supporting ours on the left at the battle of Baker's Creek on Champion Hill. He was not more than a hundred yards from me when he was killed but I did not see him nor hear of his death 'til the next day.

Captain Rogers of McAlister's Battery was killed just at our left on the line of our forts in front of Vicksburg. A surgeon of the 17th Illinois was killed about the same time & and at the same place. He lived in Monmouth.

---

17. Confederate General Martin E. Green was wounded on 25 June 1863, then killed instantly by a sniper's shot in the head on 27 June 1863. There is no historical evidence to indicate that the shot was made at the distance of a mile. [Davis, v.3, p.31]

We have seen verry hard service for the past two months. I have not slept in our tents since the 26th of April but we have got our tents now and we will put them up in a day or two. After Port Hudson has fallen in our hands we will have the entire control of the Mississippi River and effectually cut off Rebel supplies from Arkansas, Louisiana, and Texas which is now a material item to them. If the Army of the Potomac could succeed in giving Lee's army a good cleaning out I think the Rebels would begin to think their day of grace was about passed.

I was glad to hear from Mother. I will write to her soon.

Cousin Jack Vanosdol is captain in the 59th Ohio Regiment. I saw John Trannum the other day he is in the 16th Iowa. Harris Trannum got away from the Rebels in Texas last fall and come through to Cairo and joined the 87th Illinois Regiment. He is here but I have not seen him.

I have not had a letter from William since I wrote to Isaac.

I received a note from the postmaster at Memphis the other day stating there was a letter stoped there at the office for the postage and said if I would send him three cents he would forward it to me. I think it is from Will for he has franked several letters to me and the postmaster had no business to stop it.

You say you do not know what a Copperhead is. From what you wrote I thought you did. In my other letter I told you what Copperheads were or what I understand them to be. I think you have been swallowing some polittical arguments that you did not understand for I see you like many others are too ready to call everybody abolitionist that are not strictly democrat. Men that are loyal, both Democrat and Republican, I make no distinction between them. I respect and honor them both alike. I am not an Abolitionist, neither am I a Copperhead, but as the Rebellion has gone as far as it has, I am strictly a Proclimation man and that is what's the matter. If polittical parties understood each other better, there would not be so mutch contention between people that had a disposition to do right.

Perhaps I will tire your patience with what I have written so I will close. Tell George I would like to hear from him. Give my best respects and well wishes to all my friends. I remain yours truly as ever.

Thos.J.Davis

Direct to Vicksburg Miss.

Company C, 18th Reg. Wis. Vols.
Vicksburg, Miss., July 13th, 1863

Dear Lucinda,

I will while away a few leisure minutes this afternoon in writing a short epistle to you in answer to your letter dated July 1st which I received last night. I was glad to hear that you was well. I am as well as usual.

We had a nice shower of rain last night and the wether is cool and cloudy today. We have got our tents again. Last night was the first time we slept in them since the 26th of April, though we have not suffered for the want of them.

Robert got a letter from his wife last night dated the 28th of June. For three or four weeks past your letters have come ahead of Mrs. McMichael's but before that hers were generally several days ahead of yours.

All the paroled Rebel prisoners were passed through our lines yesterday and day before. The whole number of prisoners that we took here was 31,800 so our officers say. They made quite a long string at any rate.

This is Sesesh paper. It is not verry good but still I can write on it so it can be read if you do not undertake to read too rapidly. I bought ten quire of a Sesesh prisoner for a dollar.[18] Articles are verry dear among the Confederates. I will give you some of their prices as their soldiers tell me. Such paper as this $2.50 to $3.00 per quire, army butternut pants $9, common Stoga[19] shoes $8, common watches $50 to $60. Here in town [a sign] which read: shaving 50 cents, shampooning $1.00, hair cutting $100 & a soldier told me that before Vicksburg surrendered he paid $5.00 for a beef's liver but the others are common prices. Corn is worth from two to four dollars per bushel, wheat four to six, coffee and tea is scarcely known in the Confederacy; and many other articles that we use in the North are not to be had in Dixie. Several soldiers told me that they never saw any white beans until they saw them in our camp.

I have several letters to answer today so I have not time to write you a long letter today. I will send you a letter from Elisabeth. She promised to write to you last summer but has neglected it and I give her fits for lying so mutch about it.

I saw Levi Noble yesterday. He Said Jabe was sent North the day before. He Said Jabe was getting well verry rapidly. Before he started he will perhaps go to Memphis until he is thouroughly recruited up. Foster's Battery has gone out on Black River.

Alvin Caukins leg is about well again. It is not healed up but he is not lame. I will close for this time. Write often and give the news. Direct your letter to Vicksburg. I remain yours ever truly faithful,

Thos.Jeff.Davis

I would like verry mutch to have your likeness if you can get it taken conveniently. I think I shall get mine taken again shortly.

T. J. Davis

---

18. A quire is a set of twenty-four sheets of stationary paper.
19. This is probably a reference to Conestoga shoes, a style of heavy shoe or boot named for Conestoga, Pennsylvania.

Co C., 18th Regiment Wis. Vols.
Vicksburg, July 24th 1863

Dear Lucinda,

I sit down this evening to write you a few lines to inform you that I am as well as usual. I received a letter from you today dated July 7 & 8th. I was verry glad to hear from you and to hear that you & little Silvie was well. I am glad to hear that the baby is so healthy. I think it is altogether likely that I will not know her when I get home and perhaps she may forget me, but I guess she will soon get acquainted again. Perhaps I may come home on a furlough by the time she is a year old and, by that time, I supose that Silvie will begin to walk.

I wrote to you several days ago that Thos. Decker would start home on a furlough the next day but he did not start until yesterday evening. I intended to have sent $20 home by him but I was off with a team drawing water when his furlough come from headquarters so he started as soon as he got it.

We was paid 2 months pay last week. I think I will express 20 dollars to you in a few days. I wrote to you before that I had some idea of going home on a furlough this fall. I do not know as I shall go but if I get a chance to go when I want to, I think I shall if I think the war will not be over by next spring. If I do come, I want to start the last of October or first of November.

The Lake Superior boys arrived here to the Regiment last night; there was 7 of our company, viz: H. Cleary, Jasper Powell, Nelson Mills, Peter Campbell, Joseph Ross, Harvy Lindly, and William Loucks.[20] Also Mr. [Thomas] Stevenson of Company D. They all look well and seemed glad to get back and see the company again. Some of those prisoners blowed a great deal about the hardships thay have endured since they were taken prisoners but after they have been in active service in the field as long as the rest of us and been through such marches in heat, mud, and dust and been through as many dangerous fights, I do not think, until then, they will have any room to brag of their hard treatment and bravery over the rest of the regiment. There is two more Shiloh prisoners, John Merrill and John Dickson, that did not come back.

The wether has been verry warm here for sometime. Men cannot exercise but little in the middle of the day.

I received a [letter] from Susan Wilson today dated the 12th Inst. She wrote that her folks was all well. She did not say anything about Hariet's folks. She said she had just received a letter from you.

---

20. "Lake Superior duty" refers to camps near the villages of Superior and Bayfield in northern Wisconsin. Members of the 18th Wisconsin Infantry, paroled after the Battle of Shiloh, were not allowed in combat or to support combat troops. Consequently, they were sent to these parole camps to await exchange for Confederate prisoners. [OR, II-4- p.542]

If Mr. Baker received that letter from me, I think he might do so mutch as to tell you what he could do or write and tell me. He seems to act verry careless about it. If he does not give any satisfaction on the subject, I am afraid I shall have to give him some trouble about it. I shall not receive any wildcat Wisconsin money that cannot be trusted overnight. If I was at home where I could use money and knew what money was good, it would be some different. I see in many cases how loyal Union men assist soldiers' wives, though perhaps Baker thinks you are not in need of money. But that is none of his peticular business. I do not like to be hard on any person that I think intends dealing on the square.

I have not heard from Jabez since I wrote to you before. I do not know where he was taken.

I should be very sorry indeed if your mother had gone crazy again. I was in hopes she had got intirely over it.

Peaches are now getting ripe. Tomatoes and roasting ears are now fit for use but there is so manny of us here and the country around Vicksburg so badly overrun that we cannot get many vegetables to use. I hope by next summer that I will be up north where I can raise my own garden sauce.

Port Hudson was taken by General Banks on the 8th Inst. with several thousand prisoners.[21] So now the Mississippi River is open to Yankee boats from Itaska Lake to the Gulf of Mexico and I don't think the Rebs will ever be able to get another strong position on the river.

I think I shall get my likeness taken again and send to you but I do not want any gun or cartrage box about it. I have soldiered so long that guns has ceased to be an ornament of attraction to me unless I wished to look like a savage. Though some people think it makes a man look brave and sedate. But I have seen so many cowards that can never be got into a battle getting their likenesses taken with their guns that it almost disgusts me to see a picture taken with a gun.

I have received two letters from Burnett since last winter. I have been looking for another one from him for sometime but I think he is almost ashamed to write back to the regiment.

The Rebel General Joe Johnston has evacuated and left Jackson and I don't know where he is gone. I don't think he will stop verry near Jackson to stand us another fight. There is now a large number of our troops now coming in from Jackson and some of them are going down the river. I think we will probably remain here the rest of the summer. We are kept pretty steadily on duty here but I would rather do that than to march this hot wether.

21. Port Hudson, Louisiana, was the last fortified position on the Mississippi River held by Confederate troops. The 7,000-man garrison under command of General Franklin Gardner surrendered to General Nathaniel P. Bank's 33,000 Federal troops on 8 July 1863. [Long. p.381]

Friday, July 25th, 1863

Well Lucinda, I am going on picket this morning so I will finish my letter and put it in the office before I start. Alvin Caulkins received a letter from home July 9th. He says the folks are well. Alvin's leg is getting about well. He is doing duty again. I don't hear anything from Ike Odell. I don't know where he is. Well Lucinda, I received a good long letter from you yesterday, so I will send you a long one in return. If there isn't mutch in it, I don't know of any more news to write this time.

So I will close. Write often and tell how the crops are &c. &c. I remain yours always,

Thos. J. Davis

Co. C, 18th Regiment, Wis. Vol.
Vicksburg, Miss., July 30th, 1863

Dear Wife,

I sit down this morning to write you a few lines to let you know that I am as well as usual. I received a letter from you yesterday dated the 16th of July. I was glad to hear that you was well. I am glad that little Silvie is so hearty and smart. I am in hopes she will continue so until I get home. From what you say I think I can immagin how she looks sitting on the floor playing and laughing and, once in a while, crying. But crying is natural for all children.

Captain Foster has got back to his battery. Robert McMichael was at the Battery [last] night. Levi Noble has been sick but is getting smart again. They had just received a letter from Jabez. He is at St. Louis. He wrote that he was nearly well again. I hope he will not come back here until the wether gets cool in the fall. The talk is that Foster's Battery is going up the river soon.

I received a letter from Susan Wilson yesterday. She said the folks was well. She says she thinks I am quite a poet, though I supose she wants to flatter her new brother a little. I sent some verses to my brother in Kentucky. He had some of them printed. He sent me two of the verses. I will send them to you. I sent you a copy of them some time ago but you never said that you received them. [not included in this letter]

I received a letter the other day from brother William but it had been a month on the road. I am looking for another letter from him soon. He said that he was well and in good spirits. You say that Ida Snyder must be a verry affectionate woman or else deceitful from the letters she writes to you. I think she is a verry good woman though she may be a little deceitful withal. I have known her since she was a child and she always thought a great deal of me. Perhaps that accounts for her being so free with you.

You think that I have rather beat you on writing short letters. Well, I rather think I did when I took a notion to do so. You had got into a habit of writing two or three sides of a small sheet and then say you could not think of any news to write. So, I thought I would make you think that I could not think of mutch news though for the past month I have written full twice as many letters to you as I have received from you.

You say that I have no child to occupy my leisure hours. I know I have no child but I have many other things, instead. I know that a small child occupies mutch of the mother's time, but certainly you must have time to write one sheet of paper a week. Though, as I said before, you may have more work to do than I thought you had to accomplish and, I say again, I don't want you to work hard. I would rather pay your board for you can afford to do without work as well as those that would have you work hard for them.

You say you have some time now that you could read if you had some good book and say you wish to send to Milwaukee and get a history of the war. I have no objection to it but if I wanted a history of the war I would wait until the war was over and then get a good history of all of it. All good reading is useful and more or less instructive.

It would be verry advantageous to you to take lessons in grammar and dictionary. It will assist you mutch in talking, writing, and spelling and if you should neglect it a few years longer, it will never do you much good for people as a general thing do not improve much after they are twenty-three or -four years old. Any useful book that you would like to read I have no objection to you buying it. When I get home I think I will let old Mr. Hunt understand where he lives. Do you keep your watch runing? Well, my paper is out and I must close. Yours always,

T. J.Davis

Co. C, 18th Regiment Wis. Vol.
Vicksburg, Miss., August 6th, 1863

I sit down this afternoon to write you a few lines to let you know that I am as well as usual hoping this will find all well and in good condition. I received a letter from you yesterday dated July 19th, 22nd, and 23rd. I was glad to hear that you was well for I feel uneasy whenever I hear that you are unwell.

The wether continues quite warm yet. We occasionally have a shower of rain but it does not seem to cool the air but little. It is raining a little this afternoon.

We are kept pretty closely on duty at present. We have to go on guard about every other day. We are not relieved from guard until ten o'clock in the morning, then go on again the next morning. So you see we do not have a great deal of extra time to play on for we have to police. That is, we have to sweep and clean up our campground everyday removing everything that may be thrown around such as meat or anything that is subject to rot or contaminate the air so as to make it unhealthy. I was at work all this forenoon picking up and burrying old Sesesh clothes that was left on their camps. They were half-rotten and dirty. So you may supose it was not a verry pleasant job. We are having all the ground inside of the Rebel fortifications thoroughly policed and cleaned up. About the time Vicksburg surrendered there was so many dead animals and men and filth scattered around that there was a large number of buzzards sailing around over Vicksburg every day. The boys used to say that the buzzards had a mortgage on Vicksburg that they were calling for a foreclosure. Our regiment is in verry good health considering the time of year and hot weather.

I have not received any letters since I wrote to you before but I will look for some soon. Alvin Caulkins received a letter from Mary dated 18th of July. Of late, you forget to state the date of my letters you receive so I cannot tell how long it takes you to get them after they are written.

You wanted to know whether or not we had plenty to eat, &c. Yes, we always have plenty to eat and if it is not cooked to suit me I can cook what I want myself. I have got to be a pretty good cook. I have cooked for the company considerable but I do not like the business so I refuse to cook any more. Peaches are now ripe here. I wish I had room in my letter. I would send you a peck to eat. Tomatoes and watermellons are ripe.

Levi Noble, Calvin Hagerman and E. Caulkins was here night before last. They were well. They said they expected to go to Natchez in a few days. Alvin went down to their camp today and said he could not find the battery. He thinks they have already gone down the river. I supose before this time you have had a letter from Jabe since he went to St Louis.

We have first rate beds now. We make them of reed cane as there is plenty of it here. We cut them 6 or 7 feet long. We drive down 4 forks and put on a crosspiece at each end and then lay on the cane close together as wide as we want it, then put on our blankets. It is the best substitute for a bed that I ever tried. It springs and gives to pressure so as not to make a man tired or sore as solid boards do. We have our tents again. We raise them up 2 or 3 feet from the ground so the air can circulate through and under them. Well Sis, my paper is about out so I must close for this time. I remain truly yours as ever,

Thos. J. Davis

Company C, 18th Regiment, Wis. Vols.
Vicksburg, Miss., Aug 14, 1863

Dear Wife,

I received your letter last night dated July 30th and was rejoiced to read that you was well. Therefore, I while away a leisure hour this afternoon in answering your letter. I am as well as usual at this time though the regiment is not quite so healthy now as it has been the fore part of the summer. The wether is still verry warm and we do not look for any cool wether until the middle of next month. We have a light shower of rain every day or two but still the wether clears up hot. I am afraid there well be considerable sickness this month and next though I do not feel mutch uneasy about myself for I think I can take care of myself so as to prevent sickness unless some contageous disease gets in camp.

I received a letter from your mother a few days ago dated July 25th. Tell John I will write an answer to his letter soon. I received a letter a few days ago from Elisabeth Ditto. She says the folks are all well. I have not heard from Jabe since I wrote to you before.

Ed. Crandall saw Levi Noble in town yesterday. He said that Levi had a furlough and was going to start home on the first upriver boat. I went downtown today to see him but I could not find him for I wished to send some money with him. I supose that Thomas Decker has about started back for his regiment by this time. Furlough business goes slow. There will be a few more men furloughed from this regiment.

Company C, 18th Regiment Wis. Vols.
Vicksburg, Aug 24th, 1863

Dear Lucinda,

I received your letter yesterday dated Aug 5 & 6th and this morning I sit down to write you a few lines in reply. I am as well as usual considering the warm wether. We had three days last week of cool nice wether but it had turned of hot again. But by the middle of next month the wether will begin to grow cooler when it will be mutch more pleasent. Soldiering down here It is not so healthy here as it was a month ago. The diseases are principally diurrhea, billious & typhoid fevers. Old Mr. Moody and Henry Cleary are quite sick at this time. The most of those Lake Superior boys have had a brush of sickness since they come to the regiment.

I received a letter from brother William. A few days ago he wrote that he was well and I supose he is for he sent me his likeness and it looks as though he was hearty.

I would get my likeness taken and send it to you and one to him but I want to wait until cool wether so I will be more fleshy. I am a little too lantern-jawed now to take a good portrait now. I am not verry fat here in this country in warm wether. I only weigh 144 lbs. this summer but as soon as the wether gets cooler I will gain in flesh

You said that you understood that Robert McMichael wrote to his wife that I was going to start home on a furlough in two days after he wrote his letter. You or somebody else was laboring under a mistake. He probably wrote that Tom Decker was going home at that time and somebody probably understood it to be Tom Davis and perhaps that is the way the story started. I have not applied for a furlough, yet, and would very probably not get it if I had. If I go home on a furlough at all I shall probably not go untill October or November. I have never written anything to encourage you to look for me before that time, if at all, and if you had heard as manny false and groundless stories as I have since I have been in the army you would cease to have any confidence in them. Robert did not write that I was coming home and you should not believe any report to that affect no matter who circulates it. I would be verry glad, indeed, to go home but I am in hopes of seeing some turning point in the war in which even I am in hopes that we will all get to go home for good before our three years is out, which would suit me mutch better than a temperary furlough. I know that you must endure a great deal of suspense and anxiety for in your case you hardly feel like a married woman or a single one. In one sense your situation is like a girl that had unhapily been seduced, deceived, and deserted by a false lover as you have a child but no husband. But I hope that circumstances may yet bring things out all right.

We are still here as we was when I last wrote. I think we will stay here until cool wether but it is uncertain how long we will remain here. At least I don't think I will march more than a thousand miles while the weather is as hot as it is now.

Thos. J Davis

E. Caulkins is here. He looks hearty. He says that some of the battery boys got a letter from Jabe a day or two ago and that Jabe said he was about well again and would soon return to the battery.

I have been speculating a little since we come into Vicksburg. I have made over fifty dollars to send home. I would have sent some money home by Thomas Decker but I was not in camp when he started.

Some of the boys just come up from the landing and say that Tho. Decker had landed but he had not come up to camp yet. His furlough [ended] on the 22nd Inst.

I have no particular news to write today and there is so mutch noise around and I have some work to do. So I will bring my epistle to a close.

Oh, I forgot another one of our company by the name of Cox will start home on a furlough in a day or two. Furloughing goes verry slow. Write as soon as convenient. So goodbye for the present,

Thos J Davis

Company C, 18th Regiment Wis. Vols.
Vicksburgh, Miss., Aug 27th, 1863

Dear Lucinda,

I received your letter today dated August 12th and was verry glad to hear from you again and to hear that you was well. I have not been verry well for some time. I have been a little afraid of getting the ague or billious fevers but I have commenced taking quinine and I think I will drive it away. Thomas

Decker came to camp that evening after I mailed my last letter to you. He brought me your likeness. Your likeness looked quite natural though you do not look so fleshy as you did when I left home. I don't hardly know whether Silvie looks natural or not but she was so fat that the picture machine could not get to her eyes though I think it is a first rate picture for a small chile.

Ben Alison's wife and Tom Decker's wife come down with Tom. They are here now. They will start for home again in a day or two. Ben's wife come down to try to take Ben home with her. He has been sick for some time but I guess he will not go now. Tom Decker was verry foolish for bringing his wife down here and she was certainly foolish for wanting to come. It is a verry poor place to bring respectable women to visit unless they have special business. And besides, it is verry expensive. Tom Decker's expenses going home and coming back and bringing his wife down here and sending her back will cost him more money than he has saved in the last year, to say nothing of a small amount (but I don't know mutch) of reputation for his wife by bringing her in such company.

The wether is not quite so warm as it has been and I hope that the hot wether is pretty well passed.

Aug 28th

Well Lucinda, it was late yesterday evening when I commenced this letter so I will finish this morning before I go on guard. Old Mr Moody and a Dutchman of our company started home on a sick furlough yesterday morning. H. Cleary is not able to be sent north yet. Nearly half of our regiment are sick or more or less unwell at this time. Lieutenant Carter has the intermittent fever; the principle diseases are fever and ague, billious and intermittent fevers, and chronic diarrhea but I hope the wether will soon get so that our soldiers will grow more healthy. There is now quite a number of convalesent soldiers being sent home on sick furloughs. William Cox of our company started home on furlough two days ago he and Tom Decker is the only ones that has got furloughs yet. I can't tell you anything about when I can or shall get a furlough to go home. Only one furlough a month makes verry slow work towards getting around. I hope we will be able to get a final furlough before another summer comes round. Well, I will have to go on [on] guard in a few minutes so I will have to close. Write soon and often. I remain yours as ever,

Thos. J. Davis

Company C, 18th Regiment Wis Vols.
Vicksburg, Miss., Sept 1st, 1863

Dear Lucinda,

I sit down this afternoon to write you a few lines so that you would get a line from me every week. Anyhow, my health is about the same as when I wrote to you last.

The wether continues comfortably cool, yet, though it is quite warm in the middle of the day. I have no news of importance to write today.

I will send a letter to your mother in this. You can read it and send it to her the first oppertunity. I wrote her all the news so I will not write mutch to you this time.

I don't want you to look for me home until you see me coming but if I get a chance I think I will come within a month-and-a-half or two months. I don't want you to think that I slighted you because I did not write more to you.

Henry Cleary is getting better and will probably be discharged soon. I asked Will Cleary about that overcoat but he did not say whether he would sell it or not.

Well, you must be a good girl until I write again. Sometimes I almost wish you had not sent me your picture for I have to be looking at it every day and it makes me want to come home worse than I did before. I remain yours ever and anon.

Thomas J. Davis

CHAPTER SEVEN

They Have Kept Us Jogging Pretty Good

On 11 September 1863, the 18th Wisconsin boarded a riverboat with other units from their brigade, now under the command of Colonel Jesse Alexander, and steamed north to Helena, Arkansas. The move was intended to reinforce a Federal column that had marched westward to threaten Little Rock. The Vicksburg troops landed at Helena on 14–15 September only to learn that Little Rock had already been surrendered to Federal troops on 10 September.

The Badgers remained in Helena nearly a fortnight before embarking again on 26 September and moving upriver to Memphis. Their division, previously part of the 17th Corps, was attached to General William T. Sherman's 15th Corps to replace a division that Sherman had left behind at Vicksburg. The 15th Corps had been ordered to begin a gradual movement toward Chattanooga to reinforce the struggling Army of the Cumberland, recently defeated at the battle of Chickamauga. The 18th Wisconsin remained in Memphis from 27 September through 5 October when they were moved by rail to Corinth, Mississippi. From that location they marched eight miles east to Glendale where they bivouacked to guard the Memphis & Charleston Railroad.

Picket duty was uneventful and on 22 October the Wisconsin boys were moved eastward once again, this time to the end of the railroad line near Bear Creek, Mississippi. After a week on Bear Creek helping to repair the railroad, the Badgers broke camp and marched with the division northeastward to the Tennessee River. Following winding country roads, rough mountain trails, and fording cold streams, the Eighteenth marched with their division from 29 October until 20 November, when they finally made a muddy camp in Chattanooga.

Chattanooga, Tennessee, was a city under siege in November 1863. A Confederate army threatened the city from atop nearby Lookout Mountain and Missionary Ridge. Southern cannons threatened to sink steamboats carrying supplies up the Tennessee River and Confederate cavalry units struck at wagon trains bringing supplies overland. The Federal Army of the Cumberland, defeated two months earlier at Chickamauga, Georgia, was safe within Chattanooga but found small comfort in starvation. With the arrival of fresh and confident Northern troops from other theaters, however, the balance began to shift in favor of the Union forces. Food and forage supply lines were reopened and, with General U.S. Grant's arrival, an offensive was planned to dislodge the entrenched Confederates.

On 24 November, the 18th Wisconsin, with Sherman's portion of the Federal army, moved quietly from their campsites under cover of darkness and, crossing the Tennessee River in pontoon boats, seized the northern end of Missionary Ridge near Tunnel Hill. Confederate opposition stiffened on Sherman's front later in the day and his progress against the Southern line was halted. The "Tigers" suffered no casualties, however, as their brigade had dug into a hilltop taken early in the campaign and was held in reserve.

Sherman's halt notwithstanding, Federal successes elsewhere on Missionary Ridge turned the tide of battle in favor of Grant's army and forced the entire Confederate line into a general retreat on the evening of 25 November. The "Tigers" joined in the pursuit the next day. Marching from Tunnel Hill across country, they picked up Confederate stragglers and discarded equipment before giving up the chase near Graysville, Georgia, on 27 November. On returning to Chattanooga cold and hungry, Colonel Gabriel Bouck found that the lieutenant left in charge of preparing rations for the men was sleeping comfortably in his tent. According to a witness, "As soon as Bouck ascertained where the delinquency was located, he proceeded, in his peculiar way, to roast that officer and for a few minutes their was a perfect storm of profane expletives heard there, the likes of which has probably never been equaled."[1]

Except for the brief and decisive Chattanooga campaign, the autumn of 1863 was a peaceful period for T. J. Davis and his comrades. Davis' correspondence during this three-month period included several lengthy passages regarding the family's finances. When Lucinda wrote to T. J. about neighbors who had approached her for loans, he mixed a bit of solid advice with a full measure of praise for Lucinda's common sense. Davis also found ways to stretch his $13-per-month pay, mostly through loans to men in the regiment on whom he could rely for a prompt return plus interest. He found other ways to earn money, including sale of blueberries, beer, and newspapers. In one passage, he claimed to be able to come up with $50 to $75 if he needed it; an impressive amount, indeed, for a lowly private.

---

1. Brown, p. 272–273.

Davis also made it clear that he was looking out for himself in other respects than finances. He was well aware of the ill effects caused by the harsh and unrelenting army diet of salt pork, hard crackers, and coffee, not to mention army whiskey. He substituted healthier rations when he could do better than what the army offered and he occasionally fasted in order to give his digestive system some relief.

Finally, Davis took advantage of the opportunity to transfer into another branch of the service. The Pioneer Corps was an experiment of sorts in that the Pioneers were neither West Point-led, as were regular army engineer battalions, nor were they volunteers who had been originally recruited to do construction duty, as were the 1st Michigan Engineers & Mechanics. It appears that Davis stepped forward as a volunteer and that he found the new duties quite to his liking. He appreciated the healthy construction work, the regular hours, and the reduced combat risks. He was also able to put down his rifle for a time and concentrate on building rather than on destroying.

Company C, 18th Regiment; Wis. Vols.
Memphis, Tennnessee, Sept 28th, 1863

Dear Lucinda,

I sit down this evening to write you a few lines to let you know that I am as well as usual hoping this may find you well. I have not received any letters from you since the 16th of this month, the day after we landed at Helena. The reason of it is I supose that several of our mails went on down the river to Vicksburg and will have to be sent back up the river again before we get it.

Well, we are beginning to get back towards the north again. We started from Helena night before last and arrived here at Memphis yesterday evening.[2] We remained on board of the boat last night and this morning we marched out to the upper end of town and camped in a nice grove. It was just eight months and seven days from the time we left Memphis 'til

---

2. The fifteen-day Helena expedition was graphically described by artillerist Jenkin Lloyd Jones whose 6th Wisconsin Battery accompanied the 18th Wisconsin, 4th Minnesota, and 63rd Illinois infantry regiments aboard the freight boat "Illinois." Upon arrival in Helena, the division learned of the surrender of Little Rock to Federal troops on 10 September 1863. No longer needed in Arkansas, the troops from Vicksburg were left in Helena until river transports returned for them. Jones takes the gloss off soldiering as he observes his comrades "raising 'ned,' breaking into saloons, drunk, etc . . . helping themselves to anything or everything they want and march on, putting provost guard at defiance." [Jones, J. L., An Artilleryman's Diary, Madison, The Wisconsin History Commission, 1914, p. 93–99]

we returned to it again. Memphis has been repaired up, cleaned out considerable since we was here last winter. It is now quite a nice looking and interprising city. It reminded me mutch of home. This morning while marching through town as we passed a schoolhouse where there was about a hundred children collected for school. This is the first school I have seen in opperation in the South.

Colonel Bouck has returned from home and rejoined us here last night. He brought us down a new stand of colors for our regiment with all the battles we have been into inscribed on them, viz: The Battles of Shiloh; Siege of Corinth; Iuka; Corinth; Jackson, Mississippi; Champion Hills; and the Siege of Vicksburg.[3]

The hot wether for the season has passed and the nights are getting quite cool. The time has now arrived when military operations will be vigorously resumed. I look for a lively campaign this fall. I don't know how long we shall remain here. We may stay some time and again we may soon be sent to reinforce Rosencrans at Chattanooga. All military eyes are now turned with marked attention to Rosencrans' army.[4] Rosencrans has had a verry hard fight and suffered severely from far superior Rebel numbers but from what I can learn the Rebels have suffered as bad or worse than our own army and now I suppose that Rosencrans has got a position so that he can hold the Rebels until he can receive reinforcements enough to whip them out. We look anxiously every day for important news from that quarter. General Hurlbut's [XVI] army corps will leave here shortly for Rosencrans and Sherman's corps is arriving here from Vicksburg for that quarter. Brother William was in one of Rosencrans corps that was badly cut up. I shall feel verry anxious about him until I hear from him.

The health of our regiment is improving. The Badax boys are all well.

I wrote to you in two other letters that I sent you some money from Helena by express. Perhaps it has got through by this time. I think it is likely

---

3. In most of the United States Volunteer regiments, a stand of colors consisted of a national flag and a regimental flag. The 18th Wisconsin's regimental flag was the state seal on a solid blue background. Battle honors could be inscribed on either flag and were placed in the red and white stripes of the 18th Wisconsin's national colors. A newspaper story was published in 1936 about Bouck's attendance at a ball while home on furlough. Bouck was asked to lead the mayor's wife in the grand march at the start of the ball during which a louse appeared on his uniform coat. "Why colonel, there is a louse on your coat!" said the horrified woman. Calmly, the Colonel took the offending parasite in his fingers and placed him inside his coat saying, "Get back where you belong." [Lord, p. 174–175; "Oshkosh Northwestern," July 3, 1936.]

4. At the Battle of Chickamauga, Georgia, 19–20 September 1863, General Braxton Bragg's Confederate Army of Tennessee defeated General William S. Rosecrans' Army of the Cumberland. However, Rosecrans' beaten army retreated into the fortified city of Chattanooga to await reenforcements. [Long, p. 410–412]

that there will not be many more furloughs granted again for some time. At least I don't make any calculations on getting one soon. Well, it is getting so dark that I can hardly see the line so I must quit for the present. I will write again in a few days. If we remain here we will get letters several days quicker than we did from Vicksburg. Please write often and give the news. I remain yours truly as ever. Goodnight,

T. J. Davis

Company C, 18th Regiment Wis. Vols.
Memphis, Tennessee, Oct 2nd, 1863

Dear Wife,

I take up my pen this morning to write you a few lines in answer to your letters dated September 16 & 17th which I received yesterday and was verry glad to hear that you was well. I have not received a letter from you before since the 16th of September and it was dated the 2nd. There is probably one letter you have written that I have not received. It probably went on down to Vicksburg but it is time that it should come back.

We are still at Memphis but it is uncertain how long we will remain here. Some reports say we are going to Chattenooga and others say we will soon return to Vicksburg. But our regimental officers know but little more about it than I do. It makes but little differance where we are for our three years is going on all the while. We can get mail quicker and more regular here than we could at Vicksburg and if I had my choice I would some rather remain here the ballance of my time. But military affairs are uncertain and full of changes and we must learn to take things as they come.

The wether is now cool and pleasant and the nights are too cool for comfort for we left our tents at Vicksburg and only brought one blanket each to keep us warm outdoor. But our tents and knapsacks will probably be here today or tomorrow. The health of the regiment is mutch better than it was a month ago. My health is only moderat. Part of the time I feel verry well and again for several days I don't feel so well again. But I go to the doctor as little as possible.

In your letter you said that Jabe & his wife and yourself went over to the store and got weighed but that was all you said about Jabe being at home. You say that you weighed 132 lbs. Well, that is considerably less than you weighed when I left but perhaps you may feel just as well for you was quite fleshy then. A reasonable amount of flesh is necessary for strength and vigor but too mutch is a burden to a person and worse than useless. I think probably you was heavier when I left home than you will ever be again. 132 lbs. is a verry good weight for a woman, at any rate. I have not been weighed for several days. I don't think I weigh any more than 144 lbs., yet, but I think I will begin to flesh up some shortly.

You said October would soon be around and then you would begin to look for me home and you did not want to look until the last of November before I come. I do not wish to disappoint you and I have never given you mutch encouragement that I should be certain to come home this fall at all. It has been over a month now since any furloughs have been granted in our regiment and we have not more orders from headquarters to grant any more, as yet. I am not certain that any more furloughs will be given this fall. But if I get an opportunity it is probable that I will come, but don't look for me until you are sure that I am coming or until you see me. I am sure you do not wish to see me worse than I wish to come but as it is I endevor to take the world as it comes.

You wanted to know how I like my officers. As to that I don't know as it would be propper for me to give the peticulars of private affairs. Some of them are gentlemen and many of them are not but I always do my duty and ask no favors of them.

Four days more and it will be two years since we was married, although I have been [gone] the most of that period. Yet the time seems short but I hope I will be with you more in the next two years than in the two years past.

I received another letter from Sarah McLain. I will send it to you and it will tell its own news.

Since I commenced writing some of our boys that was left at Vicksburg just come and say all our tents and knapsacks are at the landing. They will all be brought up this evening. I will look for that odd letter from you when the things come up.

We have three months pay now due us and probably we will get two months in a week or two. If we remain here that long the most of the boys are straped and clean of money and wishing the paymaster every day. Many of the officers as well as privates have been runing to me to borrow money. I don't allow myself to get out of money entirely. I generally keep enough to buy all necessaries that I need and have a dollar or two in my pocket on pay day.

Since we come to Memphis again it seems as though we was getting pretty well back towards home and I think more about going home now than I did when we was at Vicksburg. If we could go home from here we could save six or eight days in going and coming less than we could from Vicksburg.

Well, I don't know of any peticular news to write that would interest you more than I have written. If Jabe is at home I should think he might have afforded to write me a line and let me know that he was still alive. At any rate, if nothing more I received the letter that you wrote speaking of Johnson paying that other note. I supose you will have the money I sent you from Helena by the time you get this letter. With these lines I will close for the present. I will write again in a few days. I remain yours as ever.

Thomas J. Davis

When shall our hopes be realized for which we went to war,
And left our friends and families away from us so far.
When shall the cannons mouth be closed and peace reign again supreme,
How joyous is the soldier's heart to think of such a theme

T. J.D.

Company C, 18th Regiment, Wis. Vols.
Memphis, Tennessee, Oct. 4th, 1863

Dear Wife,

I sit down this morning to write a few lines before we leave here. My health is about as usual.

We have orders to be ready to get on the cars this evening preparatory to going to Corinth. I received two letters from you since I wrote one dated August 25th and the other September 9th. They had been [to] Vicksburg. I expect another letter from you today as news boys are pedling papers in camp and say that a large mail come down the river but has not been distributed, yet. The next time you hear from me I will probably be at Corinth or between there and Chattanooga.

The wether is cool and windy. Last night was rather too cool for comfort.

I got a letter from brother Isaac. He wrote the folks were well. I have no news to write today of interest.

Thomas Decker's wife started home from here yesterday evening. She will probably get home by the middle of the week.

One year ago today we finished the battle of Corinth, a day that will long be remembered by the 18th. Two years ago day after tomorrow we was sworn to live together but we have not done mutch of it yet.

I expect you are begining to have some cool days in Wisconsin by this time. You must excuse this pencil writing for I lost my pen and all the other boys are using theirs so I thought I would write a few lines with a pencil.

I don't hear anything more about furloughs. I supose they are played out so you must not look for me soon.

When you write direct your letter to Memphis, Tennessee. I have nothing more to write at present. I will write again when I receive a letter from you. I remain truly yours as ever

Thos. J. Davis

Co C, 18th Regiment; Wis. Vols.
Glendale, Miss., Thursday, Oct. 8th, 1863

Dear Lucinda,

I sit down to write you a few lines to let you know where I am and how I am getting along. Well, we left Memphis on the 5th inst. and arrived at Corinth by railroad the same evening. We remained all night at Corinth and marched from Corinth to this place on the 6th and at morning I was detailed to go on picket so you see I have not had time to write until now. Glendale is 8 miles east of Corinth on the railroad between Corinth and Iuka. We had been down about Vicksburg so long that I never expected that we would get back on our old stomping again.

There is considerable differance between the climate here and at Vicksburg but it would have been full as pleasent to have remained at Vicksburg this winter. But this is as far south as I wish to spend another summer. I hope I will not be compelled to spend another summer south of Wisconsin though it is quite likely that I will.

We have not had any mail since we left Memphis so you see I have not had any letter from you since I wrote on the 4th. The latest letter I have received from you was dated September 16 & 17th. I expect another letter from you as soon as we get a mail.

My health is not verry good. I am considerably troubled with the dyspepsia and rheumatism again. The nights are getting quite cold which makes it worse on my rheumatism.

It is said that this part of the army is going to repair the railroad from here to Chattanooga to open supplies to Rosencrans from Memphis. So probably we will remain on the line of this road all winter. At present the cars only run to Iuka. The distance from here to Memphis is 100 miles and is about 200 miles from here to Chattanooga so it will be quite a long road to guard when it is opened clear through.

The most of the boys in our company are getting quite stout again. Those that were left at Vicksburg sick have been sent north and will probably go home on sick furloughs. I hear that Mr. Moody was at home and had got worse and was not expected to live.

Well Lucinda, I just received a letter from you dated September 23rd. The mail come while I was writing. I was glad to hear that you was well. I supose that Silvie is eleven months old today. It is nearly time that she should begin to think about walking but as a general thing verry fleshy children do not walk so young as others do that are more lean. But I suppose that she will begin to walk probably by the time I get home.

I see in the papers as I predicted sometime ago that further issuing of furloughs has been suspended for the present and I don't think they will be renewed this winter.

So you see that my furlough for this fall has played out unless I play off and get home on a sick furlough. How would you like for me to come home that way?

It certainly takes a long time for letters to go from Vicksburg to Wisconsin but they will not go from here as quick as they did last summer for then the mail went from Corinth to Columbus by railroad and now the mail must go to Memphis and then go up the river from there.

I received a letter today from brother William but it was written on the 16th of September, three days before the Battle of Chickamagua so I don't know whether he come through battle all right or not. I see in the papers that the division that he is in was considerably cut up and scattered. I am still anxious to hear from him. I will write to him today. I understood from one of your letters that Jabe was at home. I understood from your letter that Jabe and his wife and you went over to the store and got weighed and I thought it strange that you did not say something more about him. I burned the letter or I would get it and see if you wrote it by mistake or I read it by mistake.

Well, my paper is about out and I must close. I remain yours for ninety days or over.

T. J. Davis

Company C, 18th Regiment, Wis. Vols.
Glendale, Miss., Sunday, Oct. 11th, 1863

Dear Wife,

I sit down this morning to write you a few lines in answer to your letter dated September 27th & 28th which I received last night. I was glad to learn that you was well and in good spirits and I hope you may be blessed with good health until I return home. My health is some better than it has been for several weeks past though I am not stout. You must not feel uneasy about my health. I have not been really stout but little of the time since I have been south and I don't expect to have real good health as long as I remain here. But I don't intend to give up and die as long as I can help it. I always have had good hopes of going through the war and getting home but if I did not have any such hopes I would have but little to encourage me to action. I was not stout when I come into the service and I have endeavored to be as careful of my health as circumstances would permit. But in the army there is mutch exposure that cannot be avoided.

Robert McMichael is sitting by my side writing to his wife. You said that Mrs. McMichael had received a letter from Robert dated September 15th but you had not received any from me since the first. I wrote to you on the 15th the same time Robert wrote at Helena and I wrote two letters to you from Vicksburg since the first of September. I think you have received several back letters from me before this time. Since we come back as far north as Memphis I get letters from you nearly in half the time that I got them at Vicksburg and I hope you will get letters quicker and more regular from me. You said you counted the letters you had received from me since I had been in the service and it did not quite amount to one per week. There has been many times while we was marching that I did not have an oppertunity to write as often as once a week. But a good share of the time the past summer I have written twice a week. This is the 7th letter I have written to you since the 15th of last month and the tenth one that I have had no answer from.

The wether is cool and pleasant and the nights most too cool to be comfortable standing picket.

You said that you thought that I must have made more than fifty dollars speculating if I sent as mutch money home as Robert said I had. Well, I did make more than fifty dollars and when we get paid again I think I shall have fifty dollars more to send to you. So you see that I don't spend all my wages like many poor fellows I know of in the army while their families at home are really in need of it. When I get home I want to be able so that we can live above the hand of poverty, which I am satisfied we can do, and I am proud of you to see that you take so mutch interest in laying up what you get for future use. But I don't wish you to be too miserly to keep yourself comfortable and respectable. I wish you to keep yourself and the baby comfortable even if takes more than your state pay to do it. When I get out of the war I think I can soon get myself in shape so that I can make a good farm on some of the western prairies and be as independent as some of our poor relatives who would give us kind advice how to make a living and think they was conferring on us a great favor.

I received a letter last night from sister Elisabeth Ditto. She said the folks were all well in that part of Illinois. She said that Mother had returned from Ohio. She has been out there on a visit for 7 or 8 months. She said that Mother received a letter from me just before she left Ohio and she meant to answer it soon.

I expect a letter from David Ingersoll soon. I wrote to him over a month ago. I saw a young man a few days ago who was just from my old neighborhood in Illinois. He said he seen little Charlie and said he was well and full of fun and mischief as ever.

We are still here at Glendale but it is uncertain how long we shall remain here. We may go on to Iuka or farther east in a few days and we may stay here for several weeks.

I don't know when we will get our pay again. The last of this month there will be 4 months pay due us. The most of the men in the regiment are out of money and are verry anxious to be paid. I would like to see the men get their pay, but as for myself, I have enough to last me for spending money for some time yet. Speculating is all dried up because the soldiers are all out of money. The most speculating I done was by making and selling small beer but the wether is getting too cool for that business now. Even if money was more plenty I have not sold any whiskey except my rations that I drew and didn't want to drink it. Selling whiskey for money is an occupation I was always opposed to for it generally runs into such degrading consequences.

There is plenty of persimmons in this part of the country. They will soon begin to get ripe. They will hang on the tree all winter. I don't supose you ever saw any of them. I wish I could send you some of them. They would be quite a curiosity to many folks in Badax. Besides they are quite a nice fruit when ripe. But while green they will draw the widest blubber mouth into a whistling attitude in a very short time by merely tasting them.

We don't hear anything from Rosencrans' army lately. Things are working verry still. We shall look for important news from that quarter soon. A movement is also in progress on the Potomac and will soon look for news from there. The Rebels seem to be trying to make a desperate strike somewhere for they know their cause is growing more hopeless everyday. So they concentrated their forces [on] Rosencrans with the hope of destroying his army and breaking our advanceing columns. Rosencrans lost heavy but so far the Rebels have suffered the most.

Well Lucinda, I don't know of any more news of importance except that the Lieutenant just come along and ordered us to sign the payrolls which is some indication that we will get paid before long.

Well, I have written quite a long letter this time whether there is mutch interesting matter in it or not. Well, I guess I will close for this time. I have to answer Elisabeth's letter today. Now I want you to be a good girl and take care of yourself the best you can until I can get a chance to come home and see my Sis. I Remain yours sincerely and faithfully as ever

Thos. J. Davis

Company C, 18th Regiment. Wis. Vol.
Glendale, Miss., October 15th, 1863

I sit down this morning to write you a few lines in order to let you know that I am still here and my health is about as usual of late. I have not received any letter from you since I last wrote and will probably not get another one from you for two or three days. As it has only been about three days since I wrote and your last letter was wrote on the 28th and mailed on the 30th of last month.

We are still at Glendale doing picket duty. There is some talk that we will go back again towards Memphis to strengthen the guards on the railroad as the Rebels persist in making raids on trains and tearing up the track occasionally. A little fight occured at Collierville,15 miles this side of Memphis last Sunday. The Rebels undertook to intercept as they thought a passenger train but it happened to be loaded with soldiers and General Sherman was also with them. Sherman got the men out in line of battle and a sharp fight ensued for several hours which resulted in the repulse of the Rebels and and the capture of some prisoners.[5]

The wether still continues cool with considerable [rain] for several days past and things generally begin to have the appearance of real fall weather. Frosts and cold nights are becoming frequent. The 25th of October last year we had quite a little snowstorm at Corinth but we have no indication of such an event yet this fall.

There is no news to write today. I have not had any letters from anybody since I received yours nor have we had any mail. Since we will perhaps get mail today we shall expect to hear stirring news from Rosencrans army soon. The Rebels have a large force collected in front of him and will probably try to drive him out of Chattanooga. But the Rebels cannot keep their forces away from other escential points long enough to stand Old Rosey mutch of a siege.

I wrote to you before that we would probably get paid in a few days but we have not been paid yet and probably we will not be paid until after we move from here or at least so says report.

It seems mutch more lonesome out here on the railroad than it did when we was here last year. I don't know why it seems so unless we have been so long with a large army. I think we will remain on this railroad the coming winter unless we are sent back to Vicksburg in case we should be needed there which is not unlikely, though not verry probable.

I have not had a letter from Jabe since he left Vicksburg. Probably he has more letters of interest to write home when he feels like writing. I guess he is not mutch of a hand to write anyway. I hope he may get a furlough and go home before he has to come back to his battery. The battery is now at New Orleans and will perhaps remain a long time as they have 30 pounder guns which are not easily moved on a march. Well, I guess I have nothing more to write this morning. I will close until I hear from you. I remain your husband and lover as usual. Write soon.

Thomas J. Davis

---

5. The Collierville, Tennessee, railroad skirmish of 11 October 1863 did indeed involve General William T. Sherman. When his train from Memphis to Corinth was attacked by Confederate cavalry, Sherman directed a defense of the Collierville train station for four hours by a 600-man force until rescued in the evening by Federal troops marching from twenty-six miles distant. [Lewis, Lloyd; Sherman: Fighting Prophet. New York, Harcourt, Brace and Company, 1932, p. 310–311]

Company C, 18th Regiment Wis. Vols.
Iuka, Miss., October 20th, 1863

Dear Wife,

I take my pencil this morning to write you a few lines in answer to your letter of [?] th Inst. that I received yesterday. We are now on the march and at Iuka. We will leave here to day at 11 o'clock and march out as far as Bear Creek seven miles from this place. Bear Creek is as far out [as] the cars run at present. I don't know how far east we will go. There is talk, however, that we will go through to Chattanooga but I don't mutch believe that we will go so far as that.

We was paid two months payday before yesterday but I will not send any money home at present or untill I hear from what I last sent. And I may not send any until next payday.

My health is some better than when I last wrote to you.

Thirteen months ago today I was in Iuka before. That was the day after the battle and it has changed hands between the Rebels and Unionists several times since then.

You must excuse a short letter today as I have but little time to write today. I will try and make it all up some other time.

The boys are all improving in health slowly that has been sick. Ed Crandall is healthier now than he has been since he has been in the service. Alvin got a letter from E. Caulkins the other day and Ed Crandall got one from C. Hagerman at the same time. The battery was at Brashear City, Louisiana, and the health of the boys is improving.

The wether is cool and pleasent today with some appearance of rain though we had a heavy rain last night.

I will write again when we stop for a few days. I remain yours as ever,

Thos. J. Davis

Company C, 18th Regiment Wis. Vols.
Camp Near Bear Creek, Miss., October 22nd, 1863

Dear Wife,

I sit down this morning to write you a few lines to let you know where I am (as we advance). We are camped on Bear Creek, 8 miles east of Iuka and not far from the state line between Mississippi and Alabama and I suppose another days march will take us into the State of Alabama. We did not leave Iuka on the 20th as I wrote to you in my last. We layed over on the 20th and marched here yesterday, the 21st.

The country is quite rough and broken in these parts, not verry thickly settled. But we have good water and plenty of wood.

We are now as far east as the railroad is in runing order. There is a large bridge to build over Bear Creek before the cars can proceed farther which will require several days before it is finished. We will probably stay here a day or two before we march again.

I wrote you in my last that I would not send you any money at present but some of the other boys made up a package to send home so I put in and sent with Robert McMichael and Ed Crandall. Ed sent fifteen dollars, Robert sent twenty dollars, and I sent fifty dollars. Mrs. McMichael will get it from Viroqua of Mr. Lincoln and you will get your fifty dollars of her after paying your share of express fees and Lincoln's charges for his trouble.

We had quite a hard rain yesterday in the fore noon which made it verry unpleasent marching. The air is cool this morning and the sun is partly obscured by clouds but I don't think we will have any rain today.

I have not received any letter from you since I last wrote but I will look for another from you next mail.

My health, I think, is slowly on the gain but I am considerably troubled with nerviousness and dyspepsia yet. I think I will get along pretty well, however, and I don't want you to feel uneasy about [me] for that would not help me at all or do yourself any good. My time is considerable more than half out and if I live through the rest of it, I will then come home anyhow independent of furloughs or anybody else. I have always thought that I would come through the war and get home all right but so long as I stay in the service I will try and make myself useful and do as well for myself as I can consistently. Well, Lucinda I have nothing more to write this morning so good bye for the present. Yours as ever,

Thos. J. Davis

Pioneer Corps, 2nd Division, 17th Army Corps
Winchester, Tennessee, November 12th, 1863

Well Lucinda,

After so long a time I will now finish my letter. My health is considerable better than it was when I last wrote. I have used two letters from you since I have had a chance to send you any. The last one was dated 18th & 22nd of October. We have had a long and weary march. We crossed the Tennessee River the last day of October and we arrived here at Winchester last night and we will march again this afternoon and I have not time to write a long letter. Winchester is in middle Tennessee about 75 miles from Chattanooga and about 85 miles south of Nashville. I don't know exactly where we will march from here.

I received a letter from brother William a few days ago. I will send it to you. You said that Hartwell Allen wanted to borrow some money and you wanted to know what I thought about it. I wrote to you sometime ago not to loan money and that is all I have to say about it.

I have been detaild into our division Pioneer Corps. When you write direct your letters to Pioneer Corps, 7th Division,17th Army Corps. I may remain in this corps until my time is out. Our business is to fix roads and build fortifications &c.[6] When we stop and get into camp I will write you a longer letter.

It has been three weeks since I have sent you a letter before I sent you fifty dollars from Iuka. I supose you have probably got it by this time. In your last letter you said you had received the money I sent but did not say when it was sent nor how much.

T. J.Davis

Pioneer Corps, 3rd Division, 15th Army Corps
Bridgeport, Alabama, November 17th, 1863

Dear Wife,

I sit down this morning to write you a few lines to to let you know that I am in moderate health hoping this may find you well. I wrote you a letter on the 12th while at Winchester. We left Winchester the 13th, traveled all day, and camped on the Cumberland Mountains and arrived at the foot of the mountains at noon on the 14th and arrived at this place at noon on the15th. We have had a long and tedious march with rough and rockey roads. We are at Bridgeport, Alabama, 30 miles below Chattanooga.

We received orders a few minutes ago to be ready to march at a half hours notice. One division of our corps is crossing the river today and we will probably cross tomorrow and go to join Hooker[7] on the right flank this side of Chattanooga. We are now near enough to the front to

---

6. "As the supply of technically educated military engineers were entirely inadequate to the demand, recourse was had to the rank and file for officers and subordinates possessing the necessary qualifications; thus were formed our "Volunteer Engineer Corps," or as a more familiar term to us, "Pioneer Corps" generally working under the . . . direction of some competent civil engineer, detailed for this duty from the troops serving with the command and assigned to staff duty." [Hickenlooper, Andrew; "Our Volunteer Engineers"; Sketches of War History, 1861–1865; Cincinnati; Ohio Commandery of Mollus; 1890, p. 303]

According to Special Field Order 22 dated in 13 December 1862, each division of the Federal Army of the Tennessee was to recruit 150 men who were good mechanics or builders. These men were to form a Pioneer Corps or combat engineer unit to serve the needs of the divisions. The Corps was further subdivided into detachments of twenty-five men each under the command of an officer competent in mechanical and engineering work such as bridge-building, road repair, and building construction. [National Archives and Records Service, Summary of Pioneer-Corps History, Correspondence from E. O. Parker, 1973]

7. General Joseph Hooker had been relieved of command of the Army of the Potomac at his own request in June 1863, during the early stages of the Gettysburg campaign. After the defeat of the Federal army at Chickamauga in September 1863, Hooker was called upon to lead two army corps (XI and XII) from the Virginia theater to Chattanooga to help break the siege of that city. [Warner, Generals in Blue, p. 234]

hear occasional cannon shots. Hooker has been gaining some advantages over the Rebels in position and I think when we get around ready to attack them they will pack up what loose traps they have and make a retrograde movement towards the south for I don't believe they will stand us another big fight here for there is more Yankees here now than they will be able to handle. But they have quite a large force, too. Our forces are begining to work around in their rear. In my last letter I told you to direct your letter to Pioneer Corps (Core), 2nd Division, 17th Army Corps but our number has lately been changed. You will now direct to Pioneer Corps, 3rd Division, 15th Army Corps.

I received another letter from Sarah McLain yesterday dated October 27th and also one from sister Elisabeth Ditto. There [is] not mutch interesting matter in either of them. I will send both of them to you.

I saw Ben Pulver yesterday. He looks well and hearty. He belongs in the 92nd Illinois Regiment. He was in the Battle of Chickamauga. I am now only about 30 miles from where brother William is. Probably I may get a chance to see him. You will see by Sarah's letter that I wrote to her that Jabe was at home so I supose I will have to take it back. I have not received any letter from you since I last wrote. I shall expect another the next mail. I have several letters to answer today so I cannot write as mutch to you as I otherwise would. I hope we will get into camp before long so we will have more chance to write.

I was over to the regiment this morning. The boys are all well. They told me that there was to be one man from each company sent home to recruit and that Robert McMichael was going from our company.

This is the best watered and healthiest part of the south I have been in yet. The health of [the boys] is getting much better. I am yet troubled more or less with rheumatism and dyspepsia but I feel better than I did a month ago. I must close. I remain yours as ever.

Thos J. Davis

Direct your letter via Nashville, Tennessee

Pioneer Corps, 3rd Division, 15th Army Corps
Chattanooga, Tennessee, November 22nd, 1863

Dear Wife,

I sit down this evening to write you a few lines in answer to your letter dated October 25th & 28th which I received yesterday. My health is still slowly improving and appetite is as good or better than it has been since I have been in the south and if it still improves as it has the past two weeks for two weeks to come, I am afraid I will have to get two haversacks to carry my rations.

We left Bridgeport on the 19th and arrived here at Chattanooga on the 20th. This is the hilliest you ever saw. The Badax hills are quite small in comparison to these. I was up on top of a big hill where I could see the camps of any amount of Rebels on the surrounding hillsides. I think there will be some fighting or runing done here before a great while but I believe it will be more runing than fighting.

We had quite a heavy rain night before last and yesterday fore noon but it is a verry clear and pleasent day to day.

I saw brother William as we came up from Bridgeport. His regiment is guarding the railroad about halfway between Bridgeport and Chattanooga. He looks well and hearty he was rather surprised when I called at his shanty for he was not looking for me for he suposed that I was yet out near Corinth. He says they have seen a little of all kinds of times in the mountains this fall. His brigade is now in what they call the Reserve Corps.

I wrote to you before that Robert McMichael had got a chance to go home on a recruiting tour. He left Bridgeport on the 16th. I had wanted to see him before he went but he started before I really knew it. If you see him, tell him goodbye for me and that I will see him again in the spring. I supose he is at home by this time.

I will now soon begin to feel saucy as I am now begining on my last year of of soldiering. I think I will finish up the present contract before I take another one.

This is mutch the healthiest country we have been in in Dixie. The water is good and plenty of it and the air is fresh and bracing from the mountains. I supose we will have some pretty cold weather here if we remain in the mountains all winter. I am in hopes that this winter's campaign will close up the war so that all the soldiers may have a chance to return again to their homes in civil life. But we must now abide the fortunes of war and bear it with as good grace as possible. I shall not attempt to give mutch news this time as I know of but very little to write. When you write, direct to Pioneer Corps 3rd Division, 15th Army Corps in care Capt. McBride.[8] Tell Robert McMichael to write to me and I will answer it. Please to write often. I remain yours always,

Thos.J.Davis

Pioneer Corps, 3rd Division, 15th Army Corps
Chattanooga Tennessee, November 30th, 1863

Dear Lucinda,

I sit down this morning to write you a few lines to inform you that I am as well as usual and truly hope this may find you in good health. I have not received any letter from you since I last wrote to you. The last letter I

8. Captain Edward J. McBride 59th Indiana Volunteer Infantry Regiment, directed the 7th Division, 17th Army Corps (later transferred to 3rd Division, 15th Army Corps) Pioneer Corps. [Archives, Parker, 1973]

received from you was dated 25th & 28th of October over a month ago and I have anxiously looked for a letter from you every mail for nearly two weeks. I don't know why I do not get letters from you for I have received letters from Illinois as late as the 18th of this month. There is railroad communication from here to the North so that should come from Wisconsin in 5 or 6 days.

I received a letter a few days ago from David Ingersoll. He said that the folks was all well and that they had heard that I was dead. I will send you the letter.

We have had quite an interesting time here since I wrote to you last. Our army corps (Sherman went up on the west or north side of the Tennessee River on the left of our lines 4 miles above Chattanooga) and after 12 o'-clock in the morning of the 24th of this month we launched over a hundred pontoon boats into the river and went to work crossing our troops right in the face of the Rebels for the purpose of getting possession of and holding Missionary Ridge which was strongly held by the Rebels. It was really interesting to see our men crossing. We had about a hundred and fifty boats runing at once, each boat carrying about 30 men. The river was full of boats, some going one way and some another. They looked like a lost flock of geese swiming around blinded with a light and not knowing where to go. We crossed two divisions or about ten thousand troops in less than three hours and again [at] daylight.[9]

We had a line of breastworks thrown up two miles in length and men in them to hold them. The first three regiments that crossed the river went out and captured about two miles of the Rebel picket guards that was in front of us. Among the number was a captain officer-of-the-guard and a lieutenant colonel acting officer-of-the-day. At daylight the pontoon (company) went to work throwing a pontoon bridge across the river and by ten o'clock the bridge was finished and from that until night there was a steady stream of infantry, cavalry, & artillery crossing the river.

During the day our front lines advanced several times and by night they had thrown up three lines of works. During the night a heavey line of battle was formed around the left and in front of Missionary Ridge and on the morning of the 25th Sherman's corps advanced on the enemy and there was heavey fighting on our left all day and afternoon General Thomas attacked in the center with a heavy charge taking a large quantity of artillery and some prisoners.[10]

---

9. The movement Davis described in his letter was the crossing of the Tennessee River above Chattanooga by Sherman's Army of the Tennessee in the early morning hours of 24 November 1863. [Long, p. 436–437]

10. The successful Federal attack up Missionary Ridge on 25 November 1863 by General George H. Thomas' Army of the Cumberland resulted in the capture of thirty-eight cannons and more than 4,000 Confederate soldiers. [Long, p. 437–438]

The 2nd and 3rd Brigade of our division made a charge on a heavy line of Rebel artillery and infantry in the afternoon. The Rebel position was so strong that they had to fall back losing several hundred men. I have not time to give you the details of the battle but we have badly defeated the Rebels here scattering them in disorder. We followed them to Grayville in Georgia 18 miles from Chattanooga skirmishing and taking prisoners from them all the way and part of our forces are after them, yet. We came back to Chattanooga yesterday.

The talk is that we will remain here for some time to guard the place while it's reserve troops will go forward. The wether is quite cold today. Last night the ground froze quite hard. Ice froze some half-inch thick.

I found one of my uncles the other day in the 5th Ohio Cavalry that I had not seen for 11 years.

I will write again in a few days. Yours as ever,

Thos. J. Davis

Well Lucinda,

I will write you a few more lines before the mail goes out. It is sprinkling a little of rain. I will not attempt to give you any war news. The Rebels are all whiped out of this vicinity and I supose that some of them are runing, yet. We captured several thousand of them. There is a large corrall full of them here in town and they are being sent off to Nashville as fast as the cars can take them.

This is Rebel paper that I am writing on and it is verry poor stuff. We burnt a large Rebel arsenal in Georgia the other side of Chattanooga while we was following the Rebs after the battle. There was a large number of gun barrels and new locks and stocks that had not been put together yet. They will not make any more guns at that [place] again verry soon.[11]

We was paid two months pay on the 2nd of this month. I don't think I will send any money home for a few days, yet. I want you to tell Robert McMichael to be sure and write to me, that is, if you see him. I don't think there will be any more furloughs granted this winter but another year will give me a final furlough and then I will not have to come back. I am still in the Pioneer Corps and I think it is an easier place than it is in the regiment. Direct your letters as I last wrote.

The boys in the company is all well.

---

11. There is no evidence of a Confederate arsenal being located near Chattanooga. However, the destruction of a Confederate supply depot at Chickamauga Station is prominently mentioned in several campaign histories and may be the "arsenal" that Davis saw. [Cozzens, Peter, The Shipwreck of Their Hopes. Urbana, Ill., University of Illinois Press, 1994, p. 363]

Well, Lucinda, I will close for this time and I will write again in a few days.

I remain truly yours as ever,

Thos. J. Davis

Pioneer Corps, 3rd. Division, 15th Army Corps
Bridgeport, Alabama, December 5th, 1863

Dear Wife,

I again take my pen to write you a line in answer to you letter of 15th of November which I received last night. I was very glad to hear from you and to hear that you was well for I had not had a letter from you for over two weeks. The last letter I received from you before this was dated 25th of October so they were over two weeks apart.

My health is still improving slowly and my appetite is getting quite good, though I am not yet free from dyspepsia & rheumatism and Uncle Sam's board is bad medicine for dyspeptics; the principal diet being hard bread, fat meat, and coffee. We sometimes have fresh beef but verry seldom get any vegetables because the transportation line is occupied with more substantial food that is really necessary for the support of the army.

We are now at Bridgeport, Alabama, again. We left Chattanooga day before yesterday morning and arrived here last night. I stoped overnight with my brother, Will, at his regiment between here and Chattanooga night before last.

It is reported that we will go into camp here or at Huntsville until our division recruits up from their fatigueing marches. The wether has been quite pleasent for the past three or four days but is cloudy today and has the appearance of rain. But we have got our tents again and are prepared to keep dry. So let the rain come if we don't have to march.

You did not say whether you had received the fifty dollars I sent you from Iuka or not.

You again wrote to know if I had clothes enough and enough to eat &c. We was a little short of provision while we was at Chattanooga because there was so many of us and the roads was so bad that the teams could not supply us from Bridgeport, the end of railroad transportation. We have always had plenty of clothes and blankets. I have more than I like to carry on a march. I have got a good pare of boots that will last me all winter. I mean to have enough to keep me comfortable while I am in the army if money or stealing, either one, will get it. So don't write that old story over so many times.

I would like to hear something new and original, anything [from] yourself. I would like to see you show some spirit and force of mind of your own. In most of your letters you have something to say about Jabe's wife and Odell's folks and somebody's baby &c. Jabe's wife nor Odell's folks, either you know are no peticular playthings of mine and if I hear from them once a month, it will do me verry well.

I don't know anything about Ike Odell. I have not heard of him for six months but if I was allowed to judge of Odell's facilities for supporting babies, I would say it was time for him to saw off and quit the business.

I have not received a letter from Susan Wilson since I left Vicksburg. I wrote to her since I received a letter from her, though she may not have received my last.

My paper is out. Write soon,

Thos. J. Davis.

Pioneer Corps, 3rd Division, 15th Army Corps
Bridgeport, Alabama, December 11th, 1863

Dear Wife,

In accordance with my usual custom I sit down this morning to write you a few lines to inform you that my health is as good as usual and I truly hope this may find you in good health. I have been waiting patiently for several days to get another letter from you but it has not come yet. The last letter I received from you was dated the 15th of last month and I received a letter from Madison several days ago dated the 30th. Your letters seem to come verry slow of late. They should come here quicker than to Memphis for there is railroad communication from here all the way to Wisconsin.

We are still at Bridgeport but we will probably not remain here long. It is said we will go from here to Huntsville.

The wether is quite pleasent here for winter but 2 or 3 days ago we had some verry heavy rains and as a matter of consequence made the roads quite juicy. The mud here is not more than 14 inches deep on an everage but up towards Chattanooga it is said the roads are quite muddy. But the mud is drying up quite rapidly and will soon be ready for another rain.

We will soon begin to look for a letter from Robert if he don't forget us when he gets home. The boys in the company are all in their usual health. John Lippin of Company K, [formerly] of our company, died on the 8th Inst. He had deserted at Memphis and went home and was arrested there and sent back to the regiment. He was a man that was verry fond of whiskey and while he was up north I suppose he got an overdose of it. He was unwell when he got back and it finally run into the typhoid fever.

I don't think we will do mutch more hard marching this winter, at least I hope not, for they have kept us joging pretty well this fall. There is not mutch news to write from here. All is comparatively quiet in the neighborhood of Bridgeport and Chattanooga.

I have received but few letters lately. It seems that something is wrong somewhere.

The last accounts report the Rebels leaving Knoxville in a mutch greater hurry than they went there and if they don't watch their corners, some of them will get hemed. Sherman is in command of the forces that went from Chattanooga to Knoxville. The Rebels in this part of the country since their defeat at Chattanooga seem quite chop-fallen and down at the heal.

I was on guard last night and I feel too drowsy to write so you will overlook a short letter. I will write more when I get a letter from you. I remain ever truly your unworthy husband,

T. J.Davis

Pioneer Corps, 3rd Division, 15th Army Corps
Bridgeport, Alabama, December 21st, 1863

Dear Wife,

It is with great pleasure that I take my seat on my bunk this evening with a bayonet for a candlestick to write you in answer to your letter of the 30th of November and 2nd Inst. and I was glad indeed to hear from you (for letters come verry slow here) but I was sorry to hear you was so unwell. I hope however that your illness did not last you long and that you [are] all well 'ere this. My health is about the same as when I last wrote. The dyspepsia still troubles some but I feel tolerable well otherwise and like you I have been troubled with the toothache ever since I was at Chattanooga. I have two teeth that are aching and both of them could be pluged and do good service, I think , if I could get a good dentist to work at them. But there is no dentist here so I will try and get along with them the best I can until I get where there is one. If you have not had your tooth drawn yet you had better get it examined and if it can be saved by a dentist you had better have it done if you have to go to Viroqua or LaCrosse to get it done.

The 18th Regiment, with the rest of the 1st Brigade, left here for Stevenson this morning and we (the Pioneer Corps) have orders to follow tomorrow morning at 8 o'clock and I supose that our division will go to Huntsville and we will probably be stationed along the railroad the remainder of the winter.

Well Lucinda, I have not burned any of your letters since the one I mentioned before. But I still I remember the most that was in it. Now I did not mean to hurt your feeling by what I wrote. I always endeavored to write to you in a plain and candid manner though sometimes, perhaps, I write too plain. At that time I was quite unwell and was easily put out of patience. The first time you wrote to me you said that old Mr. Hunt wanted to borrow $15 Dollars to pay Stevenson, as he had a mortgage on a pair of steers, and that he wanted to lift the mortgage and give you a mortgage in turn and asked me what I thought about it. And so I told you. And then you wrote that you let him have 25.00 dollars to pay taxes on the land and he wanted you to take a mortgage on the same steers. So I thought it looked like twisting the thing around a little. The old man never seemed to have any disposition to accommodate me and and I always thought there was not mutch prospect of him ever doing mutch for anybody or himself, either. As for your mother or John, I am willing to help them to anything they may need but I will use all the means in my power to keep Mr. Hunt from getting that place into his own hands. But I don't know exactly what condition as to taxes the land is in. If you don't know you had better test Robert McMichael to see about it while he is at home. I wrote to you not to loan any money unless it was in cases of extreme charity for I knew that if you commenced to loan any money and folks found out you had any, that you would soon have more customers than you could supply. So I thought best not to loan any. You said that you had sent for your state money again and that you was going to replace with it the 25 dollars you loaned. Now I don't want you to do any such thing. I hope you do not think I am so narrow-hearted as to grudge you what money you need. I always told you to use enough money to keep you comfortable and it is my wish for you to do so even if it required all that I could send you. But as we are poor, if there is any left prudence requires us to save it. I consider what is your interest is also my own and what is my interest is yours. And you I consider the greatest earthly interest I have. Let the 25 dollars go to grass. I have two or three more $25s in my pocket I could send you if you needed them. I feel proud to say that but few women have been as prudent as you have, especially with your experience. And I hope we may yet live many happy days together after so long a time of suspence and anxiety and what I may have said to you or asked of you that is unreasonable, ungenerous, or unkind I most humbly ask your pardon and when I get home I will let you whip me for being a bad boy if you wish.

I sent to Louisville 3 or 4 days ago for a gold pen for you. I gave the man your address and told him to send it to you by mail from there. Ink wants to be thin. Writing fluid is the best to use with a gold pen. If you get it let me know if it is a good one.

Well, it is getting late and I must close for tonight and I supose we will go to Stevenson before I finish this letter.

T. J. Davis

Stevenson, Alabama, December 23rd, 1863

Well, this morning finds me at Stevenson. We broke up housekeeping and burnt most of our furniture yesterday morning and left Bridgeport. We will stay here today while a pontoon bridge is being laid across Duck

River so that we will probably proceed on towards Huntsville tomorrow. I feel verry well today after my days march yesterday. The mud is verry deep in places and makes slow marching with heavily loaded wagons. It is cool and cloudy today and has some appearance of snow.

You asked me what was the cause of my leaving my company or if I was compelled to go into the Pioneer Corps. I left the company with my own free will because it was my choice. I would mutch rather be here than in the regiment for I have more natural exercise in the daytime and less exposure at night. I have no guard to stand here and no drilling to do and less restricted by orders, while in the regiment I would have to stand picket from once to three times a week and I feel better to do two days work than to stand one disagreeable night on picket. It is not hard work here. Sometimes there is several days that we will not have anything to do. It is quite fashionable for men to do the best they can for themselves in the army and I mean to do so myself the rest of my time, though I never was so successful at kissing officers' a__s,s for small favors as some others no more worthy than myself. My paper is out goodbye,

Thos. J. Davis

Pioneer Corps, 3rd Division, 15th Army Corps
Larkinsville, Alabama, December 29th, 1863

Dear Wife,

It is with much pleasure that I again sit down to write you in answer to yours of the 13 & 15th Inst. I was verry glad to hear that your health was better than when you wrote before. It came through quicker than any letter I have received from you for a long time.

Day before yesterday I was helping to fix the road through a bad swamp and it rained all day or nearly so and I took cold and was quite unwell yesterday and last night. But I feel considerable better today I still have a hard cough but I think I will be all right again in a day or two.

Well, Christmas is over and do you want to know how we spent Christmas? I immagine I hear you say yes. Well, I will tell you. We left Stevenson on Christmas morning and by some mistake our brigade quartermaster neglected to draw the propper rations for the first two days march. Consequently, most of the boys were out of rations for dinner and towards night the boys made many joking remarks about our Christmas festaval: one would yell out, "Christmas gift", and another one, "Hardtack?" and another, "Sow belly." And some of the boys would scatter out on the road sides and shoot any hogs or cattle they could find runing loose. But the supply was inadequate to the demand. Some of the boys would jokingly suggest that they boil their dirty greasy haversacks and make a kettle of soup. As for myself, I happened to have a few crackers and some ground coffee left in my haversack and I gave a citizen 25 cents for enough side pork for my supper and that is the way we passed our Christmas.

We seem to have rather hard luck on Christmas in Dixie for on Christmas a year ago we were on short rations at Holley Springs having had our supplies cut off. We, however, have plenty of rations now and will probably fare more suptiously on New Years. It seems a little hard for soldiers to march a day or two on little or no rations but it is really a benefit to many of them for the most part of soldiers food is strong and hard to digest and to fast a day occasionally relieves the stomach for a while and gives the digestive organs a chance to gather strength. Under my own observation I have seen that too mutch eating & too little exercise have killed many soldiers or at least was the causes of diseases that did kill them. Twenty soldiers have died from eating too mutch of impropper food where one has starved to death with those in Southern prisons included.

The old soldiers are begining to enlist in the veteran [regiments] quite rapidly but I have not enlisted yet and I don't think I shall for several days. I enlisted on my own responsibility the first time so I will not enlist again unless you are willing. If Robert said all the 18th would re-enlist if necessary, I supose he was trying to instill into some of them home patriots a disposition to come down here and help some of their old neighbors do a little fighting.

I must stop and help build a chimney.

December 31st, 1863

Well Lucinda,

I commenced writing this letter day before yesterday but we have been so busy fixing up camp and one thing and another that I have not had time to finish it until now. I have not got over my cold yet but I feel better than I did two days ago. I still have considerable cough yet but I think it will wear off again in a few days.

Well, we have got another little shanty built with a nice little fireplace in it and all muded up tight and our tent stretched over the top of it. It looks some like the shanty you spoke of only it is not quite so large as ours. It is only about 7 by 9 feet. When I get home I think I will build one a little larger for us to live in.

Today is the last day of the year. The next letter I write you will be dated in 1864. One of the boys of my tent just come in with a couple of geese that he bought of a citizen out in the country so you see we will have a stew fry for New Year's.

Two years ago tonight we was together at a watch meeting at Springville and I would be glad if the war was over and we was there tonight. But I don't think the war will last more than another year longer. I would be glad if the war would end before my time is out for I don't want to hear of war after I go home for I want to enjoy peace for a while.

Today is muster day and a verry wet one at that for it has been raining nearly all day that is up to this hour: 2 o'clock. I have not seen any of the boys in the regiment since they left Bridgeport. They went on ahead of us to Huntsville which is 36 miles west of here. The division may not get all together again for sometime as the brigades are scattered along the railroad at different places.

You wanted me to write what my mothers name is if you write to her direct: Mrs Nancy Kiddo, Keithsburg, Mercer County, Illinois. I have not had any letters of consequence for several weeks but I think the mail will begin to go more regular so that we will get our mail more promptly.

Well, I will have to stop to go out to muster.

Well, we just mustered for two months more pay but I don't know when we will be paid. It may be sometime. I am in no hurry, however, for I have all the spending money I will need, I supose, untill we are paid.

Well, I believe I have nothing more of importance to communicate this time. So I will close for the present. Write soon. I remain as ever your obedient servent.

Thos. J. Davis

P.S. Direct your letters as I last wrote

CHAPTER EIGHT

An Open Confession
Is Good for the Soul

With Chattanooga secured and the Confederate army miles away in Georgia, the 18th Wisconsin Infantry was ordered west again, down the Memphis & Charleston Railroad and across the state line into Alabama. A casual march took the troops through Bridgeport, Stevenson, Larkinsville, Jonesboro, and finally into winter quarters at Huntsville, Alabama, where they arrived in mid-January 1864. The regiment was quartered in the county courthouse and drew provost guard duty in Huntsville while Davis and the others who had volunteered for the Pioneer Corps worked on projects along the Tennessee River.

During this winter encampment, the men of the Eighteenth were assembled on several occasions to conduct important business. Effective 20 December 1863, the entire division in which the Badgers marched was permanently transferred from their old 17th Corps to General John A. Logan's (formerly Sherman's) 15th Corps and the new unit was designated the 3rd Division.

Also, beginning in the last week of December, reenlistment was brought up for discussion among the troops. The 18th Wisconsin was about to finish the second year of a three-year contract and victory over the Southern Confederacy was still a distant goal. Federal authorities were anxious to secure as many reenlistments as possible in order to keep veteran armies in the field. To sweeten the reenlistment offer, each man was guaranteed a $302 bounty, a thirty-day furlough, and special designation as a Veteran Volunteer. If enough men from the regiment reenlisted, the unit would retain its numerical and state identity and would be listed in perpetutity as a Veteran Volunteer Regiment. In time, 178 Badgers agreed to the terms and the 18th Wisconsin remained on the rolls as a fighting unit.

A shock to the regiment was the fact that the popular Colonel Gabriel Bouck announced his resignation from the 18th Wisconsin on 4 January

1864. A demanding man with his regiment, Bouck, had used his legal-administrative background to train and drill his officers while skillfully using a "rough-and-ready," hard-swearing facade with which to awe the enlisted men. On several occasions, Bouck had even served as brigade commanding officer. But he had also served nearly three years since enlisting in April 1861, and he was determined to return to Oshkosh to revive his political fortunes in Wisconsin. His resignation was accepted on 16 March. With Bouck's departure, Major Charles H. Jackson was promoted to lead the regiment as lieutenant colonel and Captain J. P. Millard was appointed major.

As an officer, a colonel has the option of resigning from his military service. As an enlisted man, T. J. Davis was bound to his three-year contract unless discharged for cause. Davis' faced a real dilemma when confronted by the choice of serving out his time or reenlisting for another term. Completing his service would have allowed him to return home to his family, a young wife with whom he had spent less than two months before leaving for the army and a child he had yet to hold in his arms. Yet, the army's offer was a tempting one; a thirty-day furlough to go home to see loved ones, plus a generous bounty of nearly two years pay with which to plan for the future, and the satisfaction of a rebellion suppressed in the company of comrades and friends. Davis understandably wrestled with the alternatives and, in the end, explained with no little eloquence in several letters his reasons for making his choice.

In addition, the letters in this chapter focus on the quieter, relatively peaceful winter encampments experienced by the soldiers on both sides. In the absence of barracks facilities, each mess group of four to six men was responsible for building and equipping its own winter quarters, usually a wooden shanty with a small fireplace. Of course, there were no guarantees that a change of base wouldn't undermine a soldier's efforts to construct a comfortable shelter. Winter quarters also meant that the mail finally caught up with soldiers who had often marched far ahead of letters and boxes from home. As well, with the Christmas and New Year holidays to celebrate, the opportunity to receive holiday parcels filled with sweets and gifts was a great benefit to the morale of many Civil War soldiers. Others found relaxation in the company of local women. One brigade diarist remarked, "Many of our men became intimately acquainted with some of the ladies of this town [Whitesburg]."[1]

Although Davis spent the winter of 1864 with the Pioneer Corps moving up and down the Memphis & Charleston Railroad line repairing bridges, he also spent time visiting several of the towns along the road. Most impressive to him was Huntsville, about which Davis left a compli-

---

1. Brown, p. 283.

mentary description although his views of Southern society were some-what less than complimentary.

With the coming of spring 1864, the several Northern armies that were gathered under General William T. Sherman's command prepared for a new campaign. The "Tigers" remained in Huntsville until 1 May, when they were moved a few miles south to guard a ferry crossing at Whites-burg on the banks of the Tennessee River. Returning to Huntsville on 19 June, the 18th Wisconsin rested for two days before marching for Chat-tanooga. They had, at last, been called up for the Atlanta campaign.

> Pioneer Corps, 3rd Division, lath Army Corps
> Jonesboro, Alabama, January 8th, 1864

Dear Wife:

I sit down this evening to write you a few lines in answer to your letter dated December 23rd which I received this morning and was glad indeed to hear from you and to hear that you was well. My health is only mod-erately good. I have had the worst cold for the last two week past that I ever had in my life but I am getting considerably better, though I have quite a hard cough, yet, but I think it will wear away now in the course of a few days.

For the past three days we have had the coldest wether I have seen in the south. It looks considerably like Wisconsin wether. The ground is frozen so that it will bear the wagons and teams except in verry deep mud holes. It tried to snow last night but it only snowed enough to make the ground look white. We are now at Jonesboro ten miles East of Huntsville. We left Larkinsville on the 4th Inst. and marched verry slow, only making ten miles the first two days. We arrived here last night at dark.

The last letter I wrote to you was the 31st of December. I would have written again before this but I was on the road and did not have a chance.

We will probably remain here at this place a week or ten days and build a bridge across Flint River before we go on to Huntsville.

The 18th [Wisconsin] is at Huntsville. I have not seen any of the boys since they left Bridgeport and perhaps I will not have a chance to see them for a week or two to come.

There has been considerable excitement here lately among the troops about enlisting in the Veteran Service. I don't know how many of the 18th has gone into it as they left Bridgeport just as the excitement commenced. As for myself I have not enlisted yet and you need not be afraid that I will. I did not come to war for money and when my time is out and I think I have served my country my share. I am then going to quit and go home and money cannot hire me to stay longer. I am now on my last year and the time will soon roll around if we keep our health.

You said I promised to send you my picture after I got fatted up a little and that you would soon begin to look for it. I had a chance to get it taken at Bridgeport but there is no daguerrian artist [photographer] here and I am afraid if I should send it to you that you would think I looked poorer than I did when I sent my picture last winter.

If Tom Stevenson had to borrow money of me to clear him from the draft, he would be pretty sure to go to war for instead of loaning him money to keep him out I would give 25 dollars to force him into the army for he is one of the few that I would like to see "come to Limerick."

I have plenty of clothes or, in fact, all that I can carry and a soldier wants no more. You need not put yourself to any trouble to send me anything by Robert unless it would be a pair of socks if you had them as the government socks are generally poor things and you need not put yourself to mutch about them.

My paper is out and I must close I remain yours truly as ever,

Thos.J.Davis

Pioneer Corps, 3rd Division, 15th Army Corps
Jonesboro, Alabama, January 15th, 1864

Dear Sister,

I sit down this morning to write you a few lines in answer to your letter dated December 27th which I received two days ago. I was very glad to hear from you and to hear that you was in your usual health. My health is about as good as usual though I am not verry tough. I am still troubled more or less with rheumatism and dyspepsia but I still do my share of duty as the detail comes around. My health is however considerable better than it was when we came up to Memphis from Vicksburg.

I have not heard from William since we came back from Chattanooga on the 4th of December. His regiment was then about half way between Bridgeport & Chattanooga. I stoped and staid all night with him and cousin Aaron Davis. They were both well and talked of enlisting in the Veteran Service but I advised Will not to do it. But I have not heard from him since.

We have had verry cold wether here since New Year's, that is, for this country. The ground has been frozen for two weeks so that wagons and teams would not break through in the muddiest places. But it has been getting warmer the last two days and begins to look like the opening of gentle spring in Illinois and probably in a few days more the wagons cannot find any bottom in the roads.

We left Stevenson, Alabama, the day before Christmas and on Christmas Day and the day after we traveled muddiest roads that I ever saw in my life and without rations, at that. The boys thought it was a rough old

Christmas party. Many poor mules gave completely out and could not be brought along and they were knocked in the head and left on the roadside. We layed over at Larkinsville a week and spent New Year's. We had more to eat New Year's than we had on Christmas. I had fresh pig and roasted goose and plenty of hardtack and sow belly. We are about 75 miles west of Chattanooga on the Charleston & Memphis Railroad and 8 miles east of Huntsville. My regiment, the 18th, is at Huntsville and I have not seen any of them since the 20th of last month.

When you write to me again, don't write the 18th Regiment on it at all for your letter went to the regiment at Huntsville and was sent to me from there by a teamster and I was probably a week later in getting it in consequence. Several others that I have told to change directions have directed them the same as you did and they all go to the regiment and I have to get them from there.

We are now at work building a railroad bridge over Flint River and when we get it finished we will go on to Huntsville and probably stay there the rest of the winter. Well, I have not time to write a long letter today. I will write more when I hear from you again. I remain as ever your humble brother,

Thos.J.Davis

To H.W. & Elisabeth Ditto
Write soon.

Pioneer Corps, 3rd Division, 15th Army Corps
Jonesboro, Alabama, January 17th, 1864

Dear Wife,

Today is Sunday and I am not on duty so I will occupy part of this evening in writing you a few lines to let you know that I am in my usual health. I have not received any letter from you since I last wrote. The last letter I received from you was dated December 23rd and mailed 25th.

We are still at Jonesboro working on a railroad bridge and we will go on to Huntsville when we get it finished. The 18th is still at Huntsville I have not been to the regiment for about a month but I hear that over half the regiment has re-enlisted in the Veteran Service. I think I hear you ask: "Did you you enlist, Thomas?"

To which I reply, "Not mutch, Mary Ann." I did not go to war for money (though I need considerable of it) and when my three years is out I think I will bid Uncle Sam's service farewell for several days. Not that I am tired of the cause but I want some others that have not been to war to come out and try it a whack. And after they have been in the field as long as I have they will know what civil law is worth.

We are having quite pleasent winter weather now since the cold spell has passed.

I received a letter last night from Belle and David Ingersoll. They wrote that the folks were well. They sent me little Charlie's picture. It is a good picture and looks quite natural, only he has grown considerable since I saw him. I have my family altogether now. I keep them in my writing book where I can look at them every day and think how glad I will be when I get home and have an opportunity to sit down and talk with them. If you should go to LaCrosse again I wish you would go to a good artist and get your ambrotype taken, small size in a case, and send it to me. Those you had taken in Viroqua were poorly done. Ben Rantz is not mutch of an artist, anyhow. I think I will get my picture taken and send to you when I get to Huntsville. If you can conveniently, you might have your picture taken in one side of the case and Silvie's in the other, though you need not put yourself to too mutch trouble about it.

I have not much news to write this time. I will write more when I get another letter from you. From what I hear I supose you have had some verry cold wether in this month but I hope it will not remain so cold all winter. Well, I believe I will close for the present. Please to write soon. Direct your letters as before: Pioneer Corps, 3rd Division, 15th.A.C via Nashville, Tennessee

Thos. J. Davis

Pioneer Corps, 3rd Division, l5th Army Corps
Jonesboro, Alabama, January 23rd, 1864

I sit down this morning to write you a few lines to let you know that I am in my usual health and hope this may find you well. I received a letter from you the same evening after I mailed my last letter to you. It was dated December 30th and the next day I received another one from you dated December 9th and last night I received another one from you dated November the 8th. So you see how the mail matter has been arranged for sometime past. I was however verry glad to read them if they were old letters. I received the lock of Silvie's hair. I think her hair looks verry much like yours. I think I will have a chance to see her inside of another year. Then I will see if her features resemble you.

I received a letter from brother Isaac dated Jan [?]t. He wrote that the folks were well and the wether verry cold and that Mother was at a protracted meeting. I received a letter yesterday from Clara Wilson, your niece. She wrote in place of her mother as she has been sick a long time. Clara writes a verry good letter for a girl of her age. I will send it to you.

The wether is quite pleasent here now it looks more like spring than winter. We have clear, frosty nights and bright, warm, sunny days which almost give one the spring fever that has work to do.

There is considerable excitement here about the Veteran Service and many of the old regiments are going into it strong and the 18th is going in about as strong as any of them. All of Company C has re-enlisted except Len Davis, Lorn Decker, and myself. But I don't think the Veterans of our regiment will get a furlough home this spring. They have to stay here until those that are going now shall return and by that time I think the spring campaign will begin and then there will be use for the veterans here.

I have not been to the regiment since they left Bridgeport but I see some one of the boys nearly every day. I think I will go to the regiment tomorrow.

We have got this railroad bridge nearly completed and when we get it done we will go on to Huntsville and probably the other side.

You wanted to know what pretty name I sent S. McLain's boy. I did not send any name. I thought if she could not think of anymore names, she had better quit having boys (that's all). I have not received any letter from her for sometime. I never got a letter from her yet that she did not write that she was sick, or had been verry sick, and sometimes expected soon to be worse. I think she must be troubled with the hypo mixed with the blues, and it takes spells of striking in. I gave her a pretty hard rub in a letter last fall about complaining so mutch and the last letter I received from her she appoligised about it. I seen verry plainly that she understood the rub. I expect to die sometime myself but I don't want to make other folks miserable grumbling about it all the time.

There is not mutch going on here at present. Rebels are still deserting and coming across the Tennessee River into our lines and and taking the oath under the President's grant of pardon.

You said that you would send me some newspapers if you thought I would get them. I can get papers here when the mail comes all right, at least a week later date than you could send to me. Isaac has sent me several papers from Illinois and they came through all right, though considerably behind time.

The veteran soldiers are being mustered in at Huntsville and will soon be paid. It is reported that those that did not join the veterans will not be paid until next pay day but I think it is only a joke to get them to enlist in the Veterans.

I heard the other day that Robert McMichael had got 16 recruits but I did not believe it.

I am on commissary guard today and the mail goes out at 1 o'clock so I will not have time to fill the sheet today.

If you would fold your letters crosswise of the paper only it would be less bulky and the paper less wrinkled up. you double the paper four time when twice is all that is necessary.

Well, I will close for this time. You must take care of yourself the best you can, and if you are dissatisfied where you are perhaps you could get some good place to stay where there is no children or at least not so many.

I would mutch rather pay your board than to have you imposed upon or have you work too hard. So goodbye. Ever remain your faithful husband,

Thomas J Davis

[A portion of the following letter was destroyed by insects. Consequently, much of the content was reconstructed by the editor.]

Pioneer, 3rd Division, 15th Army Corps
Huntsville, Alabama, January 29th, 1864

Dear Wife,

I sit down this morning to write you an epistle in answer to your letter dated January 10 & 13th which I received last night and I was glad indeed to [hear] from you and to hear that you [was] good as [usual].

We have verry nice wether at present. It is the most warm [spell] of wether now that I ever saw at [this time of] the year though it is cloudy today [and has the] appearance of rain. I don't think we [will get mutch] more cold wether here this winter. [We finished work on] the railroad bridge I wrote of before. [We came] into Huntsville day before yesterday. [It is] one of the prettiest towns or cities I [have seen] anywhere. It is nearly twice as large as [?] and mutch nicer buildings. [The] largest portion of the citizens have left it.

[I went to see] the boys in the regiment yesterday. They are quartered in the courthouse and are doing provost guard duty in town. They have good comfortable quarters and they put on more style than Regulars. They say that each man is on duty nearly every other day and must answer to five roll calls each day and drill two hours in the forenoon and two in the afternoon of each day.

Those that have joined the Veterans expect to be mustered in a day or two. Ed Crandall just received a letter from Sarah. She told him to be sure and not join the Veterans. But from the appearance of things now I firmly believe that the war will end by the time our three have expired and I am in hopes that the boys will make a good thing of it for the old soldiers have stood the long tug of war and I think that [they will] now be partly rewarded for it. Our [regiment was one of] those of them that has joined Veterans Service but they [have] great hopes that they would get home on a [furlough by the] first of next month. But I don't think [they will] get a furlough this spring or until the [fighting] is over.

I sent the money to Louisville [to pay for] a gold pen and gave the [man the Wisconsin] address and told him to send it to [you. You did not] write of receiving it. Perhaps it has [been delayed] by the snow blockade. I don't know when [or whether we are suposed to] get our pay when the veterans do or not [?] but I wish we would get it for it would [help in] trading with the boys. I don't know how [long we will] remain here. We don't have much to do now, though they may start us out on some railroad before long. I would mutch rather stay here in the Pioneer Corps than in the regiment. (Won't you be awful mad if if the Veterans of Company C should come home this spring on furlough and me not with them or not a veteran either?)

I supose that Robert McMichael [will] soon start back to the regiment. You said that you sent a letter to me by George Rogers. I expect it will be some time before I get it.

Well, these other two sides of this sheet is so dirty that I will not write mutch more. I will look for another letter from you in a few days. You say you have written two letters to your brother, James, since last spring and that you were looking for an answer. I think if it has [been that] long since he wrote that you would [give up] looking for a letter by this time. I don't [know if his] writing propensities are verry extensive. [He sent me a] short letter about a year ago and I [answered] it immediately on receipt but I [have not] heard from him since, though he may [have not ever] got my letter.

[Well, Lucinda,] I have nothing more to write [of importance] so I will close.

[Please] to write soon, Your husband,

T. J. Davis

Pioneer Corps, 3rd Division, 15th Army Corps
Whitesburg, Alabama, February 6th, 1864

Dear Lucinda,

I sit down this morning to write you in answer to your letter dated January 17th & 20th which I received yesterday. I was very glad to learn that your health was so good. I hope it may continue as good. As for myself my health is better than it has been for sometime and I hope by propper care to still improve during the spring.

The weather today is cloudy, cool, and chilly and it rained considerably last night. It has been pleasent so long that we may now expect some foul weather.

I received the postage stamps you sent me. They come in good time for I was just out of that article. I was pleased to learn that you had received the gold pen I sent you and I was glad that it suited you but I see the ink you used is too thick to write well with a gold pen.

We are now at Whitesburg on the Tennessee River ten miles south of Huntsville. We came down here on the 30th of January and have built some small boats and have also built some fortifications on the north bank of the river. The Rebs have a fort and some breastworks right oposite us on the other side of the river. We talk with the Rebs across the river every day. The first day we came here we was building two boats on the river bank and when we had them nearly completed the Rebs begun to fire at us and drove us from our work. We then took our guns and got behind rocks and returned the fire until they quit shooting. We been exchanging shots nearly every day until yesterday. We agreed not to shoot at each other across the river. None of our corps got hurt by shooting.

I am writing this by a fire in a deserted Rebel house on the bank of the river and I can look out of the door and see the Rebs walking around their fort. I think the Rebel Confederacy will soon rapidly begin to play out.

Robert McMichael and his recruits had not arrived at the regiment when we left Huntsvil!e, though they may be there by this time. We will probably return to Huntsville in a few days.

I don't expect to get home until my time is out for I will now soon be a nine month's man and then my time will soon wear away. I would have tried to get a furlough this spring but we are not paid yet and I have nearly a hundred dollars trusted out among the soldiers until payday and we may not be paid for two months yet and I want to be here so as to collect it when they get their pay. I should like the best in the world to come home before my time is out if I could conveniently, but I should dislike the idea of coming back so soon worse than to stay while I am here. But now I can begin to see the end. Then I will be permitted to come home to stay and then I don't think I will ever go away and leave you so long again.

You did right in buying that tax certifficate and when I get home I will try and have the place relieved from taxes.

You wrote that Lid Powell got married and her man had enlisted. If he had enlisted before he married her I should thought him to be more sensible.

T. J. Davis

Feb. 6th 1864

Well Lucinda,

As I cannot mail my letter until tomorrow I thought I would write a few more lines as I got a good lengthy letter from you. This is about 4 o'clock in the evening and the wind blows quite cold from the north and, from appearance, I would supose that the wether today is quite cold in Wisconsin and I immagin I see you sitting close to the stove trying to keep your feet warm and keep Silvie from freezing. But I feel glad for you that the winter will soon be over and by the time another begins I hope to be at home where I share the cold and fireside with you, perhaps, in a shanty of our own.

Little Silvie will be 15 months old day after tomorrow and I supose she will soon be runing alone. I immagin that I see her now runing around with her little curly flaxen hair and making considerable noise and getting into considerable mischief when she finds an oppertunity to do so. And I supose she will be walking before I get home.

We have a good house with a good fire place in it to stay in while we are here. I think we will remain in the vicinity of Huntsville until the begining of the spring campaign. I think we will spend our next summer in Alabama and Georgia. I don't know whether our regiment (the 18th) is yet sworn into the Veteran Service or not. It had not yet been mustered when I left Huntsville. I think the prospect of them getting a furlough this spring is doubtful and, you see, if they do go I will be left here because I am not a Veteran. I would like if the war would end before my time is out but I don't wish to stay any longer than my time in the army. When my time is out and I wish to come back to the army, I can do so and make more money than I can by enlisting again, unless the war ends by that time. Well, I am tired sitting on the floor writing on my knee so I will close for the present. Write soon. I remain ever faithfully yours. Goodbye,

Thos. J Davis

Pioneer Corps, 3rd Division, 15th Army Corps
Huntsville, Alabama, February 12th, 1864

Dear Lucinda,

I take my pen this morning to write you a few lines in answer to your letter dated January 27th. I was verry glad to hear that you was well and the wether was not so cold as it had been the first of the month. My health is getting quite good again. In fact it is better than it has been for over a year and I begin to feel quite saucy again.

Robert McMichael's recruits arrived here three or four days ago. I was at the regiment and seen them all. I received two letters by mail that you had written since that one you sent by George. The boys were all well when I was at the regiment yesterday but the recruits was grumbling they thought that there was something wrong about the mail as they did not get letters as soon as they expected. But they will learn a lesson of patience if they remain in the army any length of time. They all seem to be verry well satisfied.

I received a letter from Sarah McLain the other day. She wrote that her family's health was mutch better than it had been. She puts on considerable agony about Susan Wilson's accomplished girls, especially Clara. I will send you the letter so you can read it. I also received a letter from David Ingersoll dated February 1st. He said that the folks were all well and that little Charlie had received your likeness that you sent him. David said that his broken arm was quite lame so that it was dificult for him to write (he had his arm broken when a boy).

The wether here is quite pleasant though the nights and mornings are cold enough to make fire desireable. Our Pioneer Corps came back to Huntsville yesterday.

Well Lucinda, I have something to tell you that I am ashamed to write but as it is said an open confession is good for the soul I supose I may as well make the confession. I have enlisted in the Veteran Service with what I have written to you to the contrary notwithstanding. I hope you will forgive me for it as well as for breaking my promise that I made you that I would not. Now, I do not wish you to think because I enlisted that I lack any devotion towards you. I reconsidered the prospects of military affairs together with my own private affairs and I came firmly to the conclusion that it was the best thing I could do for you and myself, too, as under my old enlistment I could be held 'til the 20th of next January and I firmly believe by that time the war will be over and probably before. And if the war holds out longer than that I am quite certain that I can get discharged if I choose (though say nothing about that to anyone). If the regiment goes home this spring on furlough I will probably go with them. I wish you to get ready (so if I should come) to make a visit with me down into Illinois and if you like the country and people and you are willing, perhaps I will leave you in Illinois as mail would be more convenient there and if not you can go on a visit to Michigan if you choose. Our colonel gave me the promise that I should remain in the Pioneer Corps as long as it remained organised and General Smith and General Logan said the organisation of the Pioneer Corps would be kept up.[2] And I would much rather stay here than in the regiment.

T. J. Davis

Pioneer Corps, 3rd Division, 15 Army Corps
Huntsville, Alabama, February 18th, 1864

Dear Lucinda,

I once again sit down to write you a few lines in answer to your letter dated 3rd inst. and was glad to hear that you was still well and in good spirits. My health is as good as it has been for sometime. The wether has been verry pleasant until yesterday and last night it was quite cold with a northwest wind and I expect you are having a good cold time in Wisconsin about now. But one consolation is that the winter cannot last a great while longer.

We are now about 6 miles west of Huntsville building another railroad bridge. The 18th has not yet been mustered into the Veterans and will

2. General John E. Smith commanded the 7th Division, 17th Army Corps. The 18th Wisconsin was assigned to the 17th Corps at Corinth, Mississippi, in January, 1863. The division was later transferred and designated the 3rd Division, 15th Army Corps, under Smith's command until he was transferred in April 1865. [Welcher, pt.2, p. 304–307]

probably not be until the 1st of March. I don't think the regiment will get furloughed until after the spring campaign. I don't think any more troops will be allowed to go home until those that are at home gets back, for our line here has been weakened to strengthen Knoxville as Longstreet is endevoring to besiege that place again. But I think he will be obliged to leave there as quick as he came.[3]

The 18th is still doing provost duty in Huntsville and will probably remain there until the opening of the spring campaign. The boys are quite impatient for their expected furloughs for most of them expected to be at home before this time when they joined the Veterans. But as for my part, I am just as easy as an old shoe and take things as they come. I have not been mustered into the Veterans nor been examined by the doctor and I don't know but that I may be rejected on examination, though I think not.

I received a letter from Isaac last night dated February 7th. He said the folks were well; no news of importance. I have not received a letter from brother Will since I came from Chattanooga, though I have heard from him several times. You said that your mother was going to write to me again. I would like to hear from her verry well. I have not had a letter from her for a long time.

The gold pen I sent you cost 1.50 cents. I sent to the same place and got six verry large pens at 3.50 cents. each. I sold four of them at $5. 00 each and I have two yet. The Pioneers has not been paid yet and perhaps will not be until next payday. I wish they would get paid. Not that I need money myself but then I could collect what the boys owe me. I have not made any beer since we left Vicksburg as the wether has been too cool. I have not had any chance lately of speculating mutch and I can't tell how it will be next summer.

Some of the citizens around here are preparing to go farming but there is many farms that will have to be refensed before a crop can be put in and, in most cases, no niggers to do it. So let the world jog as best it can and let the Confederacy get out of its own hobble or else fall and give in or by waiting a little longer the Yankees will cave it in for them.

I will close this short epistle hoping to hear from you again soon. I remain ever faithfully yours,

Thos. J. Davis

Lucinda. M. Davis and Silvie

---

3. Confederate General James Longstreet had unsuccessfully besieged and attacked Knoxville, Tennessee, during November 1863, while the Chattanooga Campaign was also being fought farther to the south. After Grant defeated Bragg at Chattanooga, he sent several army corps to help General Ambrose E. Burnside's Federal garrison at Knoxville. Longstreet withdrew and went into winter camp some sixty miles distant at Greenville, Tennessee. He never threatened Knoxville again. [Welcher, pt.2, p. 643–656]

Pioneer Corps, 3rd Division, 15th Army Corps
Huntsville, Alabama, February 22nd, 1864

Dear Lucinda,

I sit down this pleasant afternoon to write you a few lines to let you know that I am in my usual health hoping this may find you well.

We are now repairing the railroad between Huntsville and Decatur and we will probably have the cars runing from Nashville to Huntsville via the Nashville and Decatur Road in a few weeks. We have had considerable cold wether here for about a week but the wether has changed again and today it is so warm that I am sweating as I sit in [the] tent writing. I think we will have rain soon as the air seems so soft and heavy.

I have not received a letter from you since I wrote before but I thought I would write so that you would get a letter from me every week anyway.

The 18th has not yet been mustered into the Veteran Service but will probably be in a few days. But I hardly think they will get home on furlough this spring.

February 25th 1864

Well Lucinda, I will now finish my letter. I was called on duty while writing the above so I did not finish it. I received a letter from you on the 23rd dated 7th and mailed 12th Inst I was verry glad to hear that you was still well. I think I feel better this spring than I have since I came to Dixie but still I am not as stout as I should wish to be.

I was at the regiment yesterday. Jim Kingston and John Chaney has got to the regiment. Jim Kingston was sick with the measles but the wether is pleasent and with the propper attention he has I think he will soon get over them.

The officers were fixing to have the regiment of the Veterans mustered. They still think they will get their furlough this spring but I think it is yet doubtful so you need not look for me until you see me coming. And do not be frighted if you do see me coming.

I received a letter yesterday at the regiment from brother William. He is at Cleveland, 40 miles east of Chattanooga, on the Knoxville Railroad. His regiment has gone the Veteran ticket and gone home. Will would not go the Veteran so they put him into the 75th Illinois Regiment while the 59th [Illinois] went home on furlough. He wrote that he was well and thought he could stand it the remainder of his term.

The wether continues warm and pleasent and leaves are begining [to] put forth denoting that spring is approaching. Our corps was paid last week and I collected part of the money I had standing out but I will not send any home until I know whether or not I will go home this spring. We got the bridge finished that we was working at and we have moved 2 miles farther from Huntsville.

I see that some of the first veteran regiments are returning to the army but those that left our division furloughed will not be back until about the 15th of March. There is no military movements of importance going on here at present but we will have a large field of opperations in the spring.

I must close. I remain ever your faithful husband,

T. J. Davis

Huntsville, Alabama, March 5th, 1864

Dear Lucinda,

I sit down this afternoon to write you a few lines to let you know that I am in moderate health hoping this may find you well.

I am now at the regiment in Huntsville. I came here on the 2nd inst. for the purpose of being mustered into the Veteran Service but the regiment has not yet got their necessary papers ready and it will probably be two or more days yet before the regiment will be mustered. They will be paid shortly after muster. I will go back to the Pioneer Corps which is 16 miles west on the railroad as soon as mustered. I have not mutch idea when the regiment will get their furlough but the officers say they think we will start home the last of this month—but I would not be surprised [if] we would stay until after the spring campaign. The 4th Minnesota Regiment started for home today.

I have not received a letter from you since I last wrote but I expect there is a letter for me from you at the corps and will probably be two by the time I get back there. The boys in the Company are all well except Jon Kingston and he is now over the worst of the measels and is able to be out of his bed part of the time. Alvin Caulkins received a letter from his mother yesterday. She said if Alvin got furlough she wanted him to come home and not to go to Wisconsin to see the girls for there was plenty of as good girls in Iowa as those in Wisconsin and not many of them had beaus.

The wether is quite pleasent now though we had two or three days rain the first of this month. Indications now show that spring is really here and the military spring campaign is maneuvering and in motion. There was considerable fighting near Dalton, Georgia, last week and the regiment that brother William is in, the 75th Illinois, was engaged and lost 70 men but I don't know whether William was hurt or not. I will feel anxious until I hear from him.[4]

---

4. A reconnaisance toward Dalton, Georgia, by Federal troops during the week of 22–27 February 1864, caused sporadic fighting near the town. The Federals finally withdrew after determining that the Confederates held Dalton in force. Davis was right; Dalton was the start of the spring campaign to take Atlanta. [Long, p. 467–469]

I am not so crazy about a furlough as some of the men, not even so mutch as some of the boys that have no wives from the fact that I do not allow myself to fret about it. Though there is none of them that I think would enjoy themselves any better than I would with you. Two of the regiments of our division that went to Chattanooga has returned.

Ed Crandall received a letter from Cal Hagerman the other day. He said the boys were all well in the battery. He also said that more of the Badax boys had enlisted in the Veterans.

I have written twice to Jabe but have not received a letter from him since he left Vicksburg.

I expect you will give me fits when you hear that I have re-enlisted but I will bear it all in good humer and try and make it all right when I get home. I have pretty good hopes that another year will wind up the war, then we can settle down in a peaceful home of our own with nobody to molest us or make us afraid when swords shall be exchanged for pruning hooks and plowshears and our avocation will be to build up a country instead of tearing one down. When even Rebels will cease to be law breakers and become tired of opposing the strong arm of justice and seek protection under the power they have sought to break down. War cannot always last. The South cannot afford to ruin their own country and starve their inhabitants. They are human flesh and blood the same as the rest of mankind. Therefore, they cannot live in a fruitless desert like the prairie dog or the sage hen. They must and will and I long to see them offer terms of peace to save them from ruin. When that time comes no man will be more glad to return to the comforts of home and the smiles of family than myself. Your presence will be a source every day [of] comfort. Your kind nature would soothe my indiscreet wanderings of mind when little reverses would cross my path. My hopes for the future are hopes for you and our wellfare and happiness and to that end is my aim. I know that I have neglected you in writing and have written things that I should not have written and at other times my mind has been taken up by other things that I could not convey my feelings with the pen. But you are at liberty to enquire of my army associates as to the faith of morals and virtue you reposed in me. I am sorry to say that some men in the army, on investigation, would show a spotted record and many of that same kind have been cut down by disease.

Sunday morning, March 6, 1864

Men & women to live happy, must obey the laws of nature both in morals and in health. To retain a clear conscience, a person must do what they know to be right and just, one to another, and [not] betray trust or honor that have or should be pledged and even the laws of health require that men should be moral, temperate, virtuous, and honest to enjoy the health which they are entitled to enjoy. And whenever these laws are violated, punishment is sure to follow in some shape or other. What can man enjoy when his health is gone, his character gone, and deserted by his honest friends? They are a curse to themselves and a neucence in that and to be avoided by honest people. But when a person has the feeling in their own heart that they have done honor to themselves they can meet their friends with open arms and smiles of virtue and innocence and be appreciated as a friend, indeed, the value of whom could not be enumerated in price.

Well Lucinda, there is not much news to write this time. News just came in town that 14 men was killed by a railroad collision last night between here and Stevenson, which is probably true.[5]

I will close for this time. Believe me. Ever yours,

Thomas J. Davis

Huntsville, Alabama, March 15th, 1864

Dear Wife,

I sit down this afternoon to write you in answer to two letters that I received from you yesterday, one dated February 23rd and the other 28th. The first I have received from you for three weeks and I was very glad to hear that you was well but was sorry to hear that the baby had been so sick. But I hope it will get over it and not have the diptheria again. Diptheria is generally hard on [young] children. I am in as good health as usual.

I am still with the regiment at Huntsville waiting to be mustered into the Veterans. The mustering officer has been sick is the reason that we have not been mustered before this. He is getting better now and we will probably be mustered this week.

The boys in the regiment are as well as usual except Will Cleary. He has been having a few chills.

I was sorry to see that you was so mutch out of heart in reference to my re-enlisting in the army. I know it looks like a long time and a hard road to travel to soldier three years longer but I don't intend that I shall serve three years longer, even if the war should last so long as that. I thought as long as I had soldiered so long that I ought to get some pay for what I had

---

5. Once again, Davis' news sources were accurate. A brother regiment from the same brigade as the 18th Wisconsin, the 4th Minnesota Infantry, had departed for home on their reenlistment furlough on 5 March 1864. The train on which they were riding had stopped at Anderson Station, eleven miles beyond Stevenson, Alabama, when it was struck from behind by another train. In the collision, seven soldiers and civilians were killed, twenty-two were injured, and twenty-one cars were badly damaged. [Brown, p. 284]

done. I see from Elisabeth's letter that you sent me that she thought I had soldiered long enough for one man. I hope after being lucky so far that I may get through safe. But as far as that is concerned, life is uncertain any place and we must run our chances.

You wanted me to let you know when I should be at home on furlough so you would know when to look for me. That would be impossible for me to tell you though we will probably come home sometime this spring. If not this spring we will come as soon as the spring campaign is over. I think however we will come this spring but don't disappoint yourself looking untill you see me coming.

Robert McMichael has not got back to the regiment yet and probably he did not start when you thought he did.

There is not mutch news here of importance. Sherman has returned to Vicksburg from his raid into Mississippi.[6]

The wether is somewhat cooler today than it has been for several days but the season for frost is now about over this spring. I have no more news to write so I will close for this time.

I ever remain yours,

Thos. J. Davis

P.S I will send you a song. [not found]

Huntsville, Alabama, Thursday, March 22nd, 1864

Dear Wife—

It is with great pleasure that I once more have the privelige to write to you again. In answer to a letter I received from you last night dated 9th inst. and was glad to learn that you was well. My health is as good as usual with the exception that I have had a bad cold for a few days past but nothing serious.

The wether has been quite cool for several days and last night we had quite a snowstorm. Last night there was 4 or 5 inches of snow on the ground this morning but it will be nearly all gone by night. I think after this squall is over we will not have any more cold wether this spring.

I am at the regiment in Huntsville. The regiment was mustered last Saturday and we expect to be paid in a few days but I don't know how soon. The Pioneers returned to Huntsville yesterday having finished the railroad bridges between here & Decatur.

---

6. General William T. Sherman led a Federal infantry column from Vicksburg to Meridian, Mississippi, 3 February–4 March 1864 to destroy Confederate rail and supply resources. Though a parallel cavalry raid was judged a failure, Sherman's infantry destroyed millions of dollars worth of railroad equipment and cotton while they "lived off the land." The Meridian Campaign is considered by some historians to have been a practice expedition prior to Sherman undertaking his famous "March to the Sea" in November–December 1864. [Faust, p. 488]

I received two letters yesterday from brother William. He was in the late fight at Dalton, Georgia, but did not get hurt. I also received a letter from David Ingersoll notifying me that he was married and that the folks was all well. His letter was dated March 10th.

I have been here ever since the 2nd of this month. I have not been doing duty but I believe I would rather have been out in the country with the corps working a little than be laying around town, though I have been trading around a little trying to make as mutch money as I spend.

We will probably start home about the last of this month if we go at all. But affairs may be so arranged that we may not go this spring at all. But I think the prospect is pretty good, though you must not look until you see us coming.

You seem to be considerably discouraged on account of my reenlisting. I hope however you will not think I will stay three years longer for I don't mean to do it, even should the war continue. But I don't intend to desert, either. I will get out honorably on account of my health. But as things are now, I don't think I could do any better than to stay in the army a while longer. I expected you would give me a good scolding for enlisting but I see you cannot scold worth a cent. But if you are mad when I go home I will quarrel you out of it. I have thought sometimes that probably it would be better for me not to go home this spring for the boys joke me considerably about my other furlough. So I supose I must be careful next time.

I would like it well if it was so you could go to school the ballance of the time I am in the service. But probably Silvie will be too mutch in the way.

Well Lucinda, I have not mutch news to write today but if I come home this spring I expect I will make you tired with with hearing so mutch talk out of me and all this sort of thing. Robert McMichael's commission of first lieutenant came to the regiment from Madison a few days ago. J.H. Brightman, a private in our company got a commission a few days ago as 2nd lieutenant in the 37th Regiment Wisconsin Volunteers.

Well, I believe I have no more news this time. Tell Mother and John they must excuse me this time. I will write to them soon or else come and tell them about it.

I remain always yours,

Thos. J. Davis

Pioneer Corps, 3rd Division, 15th Army Corps
Huntsville, Alabama, Sunday, March 26th, 1864

Dear Lucinda,

I sit down this plesent Sabbath evening to write you a few lines to let you know that I am in my usual health. I have not received any letter from you since I last wrote but I will look for another letter tomorrow.

The Pioneer Corps has returned to Huntsville having finished the railroad bridges and I have come back to the Corps though both the Corps and Regiment are in town not more than a quarter of a mile apart. So I come to the regiment every day if I choose. I don't know how long the Corps will remain in town. Probably not long as we have orders to get ready for the spring campaign. General Sherman & General McPherson arrived here yesterday and it is thought that a forward movement will be made shortly.[7] The 48th & 59th Indiana Regiments that have been home on Veteran furlough are now on there way back marching through from Nashville to Huntsville on foot. They left Nashville yesterday morning. It will take them six or seven days to march through.

We have no assurance when we will get to start home though there is talk that we will be allowed to go when the Indiana regiments get back.

We have had quite rough wether for the past two weeks for this time of year until yesterday and today. The wether has been clear and pleasant and I think that spring has now fairly commenced.

I still tell you as I did before not to look for us home until you see us [as] we may have to go through the spring campaign before we get our furlough. I know that there have been several of the boys writing home a month ago stating that the regiments would be at home in a few days. I have been in the army long enough to learn a little military and regiments as well as men must wait and let things take their regular cource. When we get ready to start home you will find it out soon enough so it is not nesessary to look on uncertainties.

The veterans have not been paid yet and will probably not be for several days. Now Lucinda, I hope you will not think hard of me for reenlisting, although perhaps I may have done wrong. But I studied the matter over thoroughly and it was for your good as well as my own that I done so. The more we save during the war, the better start we will have when we set up housekeeping and I thought I could not do better for [the same] length of time. Neither do I believe [the war] will last three years. Of course I could enjoy myself better at home with you. But then I should have to be in the spring and fall campaign this year anyway and I think that will end most of the fighting. The war cannot always last. It must conclude some way inside of two years. You say that I should come home and let others go that have been at home. That would be all right, I know, but if they stay at home, let them pay for it. I was credited to Milwaukee as there was no one in the town[ship] of Jefferson that I wished to shield

---

7. On the day Davis penned this letter, General James B. McPherson succeeded Sherman in command of the Federal Army of the Tennessee to which the 18th Wisconsin was assigned. [Warner, Ezra J., Generals in Blue. Baton Rouge, Louisiana State University Press, 1977, p. 307]

from the draft. James Lowrie wrote to me that I could have $125 dollars if I would be credited to Jefferson but I think I can get more from Milwaukee (so let her want, if I don't.)

Well Lucinda, I have no great amount of news to write today and hoping this may find you in the best of health and spirits and hoping that I may 'ere long be permitted [to be with] you again and spend a happy [month in] your society. I bid you an affectionate goodbye.

T. J. Davis

Pioneer Corps, 3rd Division, 15th Army Corps
Huntsville, Alabama, April 1st, 1864

Dear Wife,

As this is April Fool Day, I thought I would sit down and write you a short epistle in answer to your last letter dated March 16th which I received yesterday and was verry glad to hear that you was well. My health is as good as usual though I don't brag of being entirely well, but reasonably well for me. I have had a cold nearly all through March but it is getting better now. The wether still continues unsettled it is raining today and the air is damp and chilly.

We are still at Huntsville and don't have mutch to do, only sit around the fire and haul wood and lope around town, though the latter is not mutch amusement.

I received a letter from brother Ike today he wrote that the folks were well. He said that Elisabeth and Louisa had both just received a letter each from you. I received another letter from Clara Wilson. I will send it to you. I sent you one of hers before but you never wrote that you received it.

The [5]th Iowa Regiment started home this morning on Veteran furlough and the 80th Ohio will start this evening and the 63rd Illinois will start tomorrow. I don't think our regiment, the 18th, will go home now until the other regiments get back and that will be the middle of May or the [not legible] answer. I have no news more to write today. Hoping to hear from you soon. I close. I remain ever truly yours,

T. J. Davis

Pioneer Corps, 3rd Division, 15th Army Corps
Huntsville, Alabama, Sunday, April 10th, 1864

Dear Wife,

I sit down this morning to write you a few lines in answer to your letter dated 24th of March which I received several days ago but I was sent out in the country on detail and I did not have a chance to answer it until now. My health is tolerable good at present. I had quite a hard cold for over a month but I have got nearly entirely over it now.

The wether is cloudy and quite cool today, not any too warm to wear my overcoat as I sit in my tent writing. We are still in Huntsville. Our Corps is going to work building fortifications and we will probably remain here for sometime. We are camped within a ¼ of a mile of the 18th Regiment. I am at the regiment nearly every day when I am in town.

You wrote that you was anxious to get a letter from me hoping that I would tell you when we would be at home. If I should write to you a dozen times and try my best every time I could not then tell you when we would come. The officers of the regiment does not know any more about [it] then I do. However, they have been telling the boys all a long that the regiment would surely start home in a few days but I was satisfied that we would not go until our turn come, like going to mill. I am confident that we will not go home until the 4th Minnesota returns and that will be the last of May or first of June and then we may be kept until fall if we are needed. But I think it is probable that we will go home about the first of June. You must not look for us, however, until you know we are coming.

I read a letter that Rosene Morley wrote to Ed Rogers concerning the sickness and death of his wife. She wrote a verry good letter. She said she wrote at the request of Elias's folks. I received a letter last night from Sarah McLain. She says her folks are quite well (something new, however, for her to write) and that her boys were at work by the month. She said she had just received a letter from you and had answered it so I supose you have got before now. She makes it appear that she is a verry swift writer for she says she was about 5 minutes writing her letter. I will send it to you. Her excuses and quick writing don't corespond. I will answer it in a few days. I received a letter from Ida and Bennett Snyder a few days ago. The folks were all well. No news of importance

Our regiment has been mustered three weeks but they have not been paid yet. You say that James wrote that he had not heard from me for a long time. I think it will be a long time yet before he hears from me unless he writes. I wrote to him nearly a year ago and have not had an answer. I can't afford to do all the writing and receive no letters. Well Lucinda, I have no news to write today so I will close. I shall look for another letter from you to day or tomorrow. So goodbye for this time. I remain ever yours,

Thomas J. Davis

Pioneer Corps, 3rd Division, 15 Army Corps
Huntsville, Alabama, April 16th, 1864

Dear Wife,

I sit down on my bunk this afternoon to write you a short epistle in answer to your kind letter dated March 30th which I received two or three days ago. I was verry glad to hear that you was well. This leaves me in as good health as usual. The wether continues quite cool. I may say nearly cold for an overcoat is yet quite a requisite article.

We are still in Huntsville fixing to fortify the place. The regiment (18th) will move out of the courthouse day after tomorrow. They will camp outside of town. I don't hear as mutch talk of the regiment going home now as I did a month ago.

Merrick Rogers has got the smallpox but it is thought he will only have it lightly.

I received a letter yesterday from Jabe & Cal Hagerman dated March 26th. They said they were in moderate health but neither of them really stout. E. Caulkins was tough and rugged. They said the wether was beginning to get quite warm at New Orleans.

There is not mutch news of military character worth mentioning. There was quite an accident occured here in town a few days ago. One company of the First Illinois Artillery was going out of town to drill and as they was crossing the railroad near the depot the captain gave orders to close up and in order to do so the guns in the rear was brought up on a trot and as one of the caisons or (amunition) wagons struck the railroad iron which exploded a percussion shell, igniting the rest, and blowing the whole caisson to atoms killing four men and one horse, tearing them litterally to pieces and wounding three other soldiers and one citizen. It was a horible sight and will learn others to be more caustious in future. It was, however, a lesson of prudence verry dearly bought.

I supose you are wondering when the 18th will come home but it would be best for you to think as little about it as possible for that will not bring us any sooner.

E. Warner stayed all night with our regiment a few nights ago on his way to the 25th. The 25th is at Moorsville about 20 miles from here.

We will probably not start for home before the first of June. Don't look for us any before that time. I should not wish to keep you in suspence looking for us when I know there is no probability of us getting started from here. How mutch better it would suit me if I could walk over and see you every week and talk with you and tell you what I wished to say instead of conveying my thoughts such a distance to you by making crooked marks on this paper. But the process as slow as it is, I am glad there is one medium by which I can converse with you. No circumstance can better serve to cause a person to appreciate the value of a friend (especially a husband or wife) than that of being seperated from them. But true faith of the virtue and integrity one to another is worth more than gold. "I wonder if my husband has kept sacred his vow of single love or has he sought or been won by other female smiles?" has been a querry in the mind of many a wife since this war began. "I wonder if my wife retains her propper affection for me and carries herself above suspicion in my absence or has she given herself up to her passions?" is the query of many soldiers in the field and I am sorry to say there is too mutch ground for these suspicions in many cases on both sides. My paper is out. I must close. Yours always,

T. J. Davis

Pioneer Corps, 3rd Division, 15th Army Corps
Huntsville, Alabama, April 24th, 1864

Dear Lucinda,

I sit down on my bunk this Sabbath evening to write you a short epistle to let you know that I have not forgotten you if I cannot get letters from you. This is the third letter I have written to you since I received any, your last being dated the 30th of last month and the boys in the regiment has received letters two weeks later than that. You have always been so prompt in writing that I begin to feel uneasy for fear you are sick, though I hope my fears are groundless for there is times when the mails are delayed on the road.

My health continues tolerable good for me. So I don't complain.

The weather is quite pleasent now but the spring has been unusually backward for this climate but now the balmy breeze under an Alabama sun has driven the chilling blast to more colder shores and nature once more is assuming her mantle of green. Citizens talk of farming but alas, mutch of the country is laid waste by the ravages of war. Many plantations are fenceless, houseless, slaveless, and no horses wherewith to farm as in the proud days of southern chivalry.

The news is unimportant in this department at present. I was over at the regiment today and signed the pay rolls. We will probably be paid in a few days. I am glad of it for I have loaned myself nearly [out] of money though I always manage to have a little for necessary use.

I have wrote so often about the 18th's furlough that I am almost ashamed to mention it anymore but, if not called into the campaign before, the regiment will probably start home about the first of June. If I come this spring I will bring you a present for you to remember me by but I don't know what it will be yet. You may be sure that I will be glad to meet you at home as soon as I have an opportunity to do so. We having lived together so short a time and been separated so long, it would almost seem (if it were not for our constant correspondence by letter) that your idea of having a husband would be only immaginary. Yet I hope we may after so long a time make our weded life real and spend a happy life together as a reward for our long suspense and care for each other's welfare. "Hope on, hope ever" is a motto for success. With hope the heart will surmount great obstacles and without hope it will break at trifles.

Well Lucinda, I will close for this time hoping to hear from you soon. I remain as always. Yours,

Thomas. J. Davis

Pioneer Corps, 3rd Division, 15 Army Corps
Huntsville, Alabama, April 30th, 1864

Dear Sis,

I endeavor this evening to write you a short epistle in answer to your letter dated 13th inst. which I received two days ago. I was glad to hear from you and to hear that you was feeling so well. My health is tolerable good for me. The last letter I received from you before this was dated March 30th so there must be one or two letters that you wrote that did not come through. You write every time that you are anxious to know when I am coming home. I have not yet given you mutch encouragement when I should be at home and wrote for you not to look for me for I do not wish to keep you in suspense. But I will surely, gladly come when I can get the oppertunity to do so.

I received a letter from Mother last night. She wrote that she and the folks were all well. She said she had received a letter from you and had answered it. I also received one from Elisabeth and Ike and Elisabeth spoke of getting a letter from you and she said she had been waiting for a letter from me before she answered it but would soon answer it as she did not get any from me.

The weather has been quite warm this week and vegetation is growing rapidly with alternate thundershowers and sunshine.

Our regiment was paid yesterday, that is, the Veterans got their bounty of $175.00 and the regiment will probably get their monthly pay before long, perhaps before they go home. I will not send any money home at present until I find out whether we get furloughs or not this spring.

The 4th Minnesota Regiment will be back here sometime next month and it is said we will go when they return. But I don't know that that is the case and if true it will be June before we get away from here. So don't look for us until you know we are on the road.

The 3rd Brigade of our division will go from here to Decatur tomorrow and the other two brigades will probably remain here for sometime, at least that is the present impression. We are kept quite buisy at work now in town building fortifications and ordinance and commissary buildings so I don't get mutch time to write. I don't work hard, however, for I have learned like many other soldiers to shirk or play-off pretty effectually. I will look for another letter from you in a day or two and will try and write more next time. Yours always,

T. J. Davis

To Sis. Davis
Pioneer Corps, 3rd Division, 15th Army Corps
Huntsville, Alabama, Thursday, May 5th, 1864

Dear Lucinda,

It affords me mutch pleasure to have the privelige to write you again. I have not received any letter from you since I last wrote, the last one being dated April 15th, though I have been looking for one every mail for several days. I will probably get one tonight or tomorrow night. I am as well as usual except that I fell from the 2nd story of a building that I was at work on last Saturday and struck with my left hip and back across the edge of the floor which has disabled me from working probably for several days. I can hobble around on crutches a little but such a bruise is slow getting well.

The regiment went to Whitesburg down to the river ten miles from here last Sunday. I don't know how long they will remain there, probably several weeks. You said in your last letter that John Carpenter wrote that the 18th would start home in a few days. He had no reason to write such a report but perhaps it is chargable to his limited knolege of military affairs. He will soon learn not to pick up all frivelous reports and write them home as truths. But I should think you had been bored with reports so often that your confidence in them would be weak by this time. I have nothing to write today about coming home, as I don't know anything about it. Why therefore should I tell you I was coming? I have not seen any of the boys of the regiment since they went to Whitesburg.

I received a letter last night from D. Ingersoll and his wife. They wrote no news. The folks [was] well and the weather was wet was the most it contained. Dave is a verry poor hand to write letters, anyhow, and he don't try to improve mutch from appearance.

The weather is quite pleasent, not so warm as last week. But as I write at ten o'clock the sun shines through the tent so that a coat is not essential to comfort. I feel somewhat lazy and lonesome and my ideas are scattered so that I hardly know what to write today. Though if I was present with you, I could relate many little naratives which might be interesting, yet seemingly of not enough importance to take up the time and space it would require to write them. Here I sit thinking of home and friends, the War and its cause, wrong and justice, life and its crooked windings almost at one thought without any peticular conclusion on either. If our thoughts could be read as they proceed from the brain what a volume of scattered matter would the reader obtain. Many secrets of corrupted persons would then be devulged to the disadvantage of bad purposes and more restraint would be thrown upon thoughts as well as actions. We should therefore confine our thoughts to pure motives and apply them to moral, intellecual, and useful purposes.

For while the mind is employed in digesting evil thoughts, the hands are not likely to be doing good works. Idleness of mind and body beget vice and crime.

Well my paper is about out so I will close for this time. Please write soon. I remain ever your faithful husband,

T. J. Davis

Pioneer Corps, 3rd Division, 15th Army Corps
Huntsville, Alabama, May 10th, 1864

Dear Lucinda,

I again take this method of a short discourse in answer to your letter dated April 24th which I received yesterday. I was glad to learn that you was well but hope you may not again have occasion to use yourself up fighting fire.

I am getting considerable better of my hurt but it will probably be several days before I will be able to work.

It is raining this morning and will probably rain all day but it is nice growing weather and an occasional rain is more desireable than otherwise at this time of the year.

I have not received any letters but yours since I last wrote and your letters have been coming verry slow of late. I have not received but two letters from you that was written in April, one dated the 10th & 13th and the other the 24th & 27th. So I don't think you have written every week lately for my letters generally come through pretty correct.

You wished to know if I wanted you to get ready to go to Illinois. Of course I do. If it does cost money we can stand it to spend some once in a while.

Our regiment is still at Whitesburg and I think that we will have a chance to go home about the first of next month, as I wrote you before, for that will be about our time. The regiments have to take it by turns like going to mill, though if we are verry mutch needed we may not start so early as that. We will, however, without a reasonable doubt, get our furloughs before fall. I would rather go home in warm wether than to go so early in the spring.

You said you was uneasy for fear I would get the smallpox. There has been a few cases of it here but I have been several times amongst it where it was mutch worse than it is here since I have been south. I am not afraid of it for I have been vaccinated before and since I came in the army, and I don't think I will take it at all.[8]

---

8. Vaccination was a common and effective method of preventing smallpox among troops at the time of the Civil War. [Adams, p. 219]

You said Jabe wanted to reenlist if his health would permit. He wrote in the letter I received from him that he had no notion of going the Veteran ticket.

We have just received news here that there has been some big fighting on the Potomac and that Grant has used the Rebels quite rough and has got their communications cut off from Richmond. I hope it may all be true and the move successfully followed up. Grant has a large army there and knows how to use it and I think this summer and fall will pretty well use up the Confederacy.[9]

You said you thought if our officers were as loyal as they should be the war would long since been over. It is true we have had some officers which perhaps were not verry loyal but we have suffered many defeats through the ignorance of our officers not knoing their duty properly. But at the same time the Union army has had mutch more to contend with than most people at the North have any idea of. I have seen many peices in newspapers censuring our generals for bad management and telling how such and such movements should have been made and to read it you would think the writer was a better general than any in the field when at the same time perhaps he had never been south and didn't know enough military tactics to shoulder arms propperly.

I will send you some flowers in a day or I will put them in a newspaper. They will perhaps several days behind this letter well I must close. I remain ever yours

T. J.Davis

Pioneer Corps, 3rd Division, 15th Army Corps
Huntsville, Alabama, Sunday, May 15th, 1864

Dear Wife,

I again take up my pen to write you a short epistle in answer to your welcome letter dated May 4th which I received this morning. I was verry glad to hear that you was well. I am getting considerable better of my hurt though I am not able to work yet and will probably not be for sometime yet for my hip and back is slow getting stout again.

The weather is quite pleasent now. It rains every few days. It is cloudy today and the air is cool.

---

9. While Sherman led his army against Atlanta, General U.S. Grant supervised the Virginia Campaign by accompanying General George G. Meade's Federal Army of the Potomac. Heavy fighting occurred against General Robert E. Lee's Confederate Army of Northern Virginia in the Wilderness region of central Virginia on 5–7 May 1864. [Long, p. 491–494]

I wrote you a letter last week and sent you some flowers in a book the same day. You will probably, however, get the letter a week in advance of the flowers.

I have not been to the regiment since they went to Whitesburg but I saw one of the boys the other day and he said that Robert McMichael had got back to the regiment. We have been looking for a raid in here from Forest or at least we was expecting one last week and we made arrangements to give him a warm reception but he did not come for he turned his course another direction.[10]

The Veterans of our division will soon all be back from their furlough and unless we are kept for emergincies, which I don't think will be the case, we will start home about the first of June. So I think we will be at home about the10th of June. However, circumstances may possibly keep us untill fall but I think not. So I think you can look for us about the 10th of June.

I do not wish you to think from what I wrote in my letter of the 16th of April that it was through any jealousy on my part but it was from what I have heard from many soldiers' wives and saw of many soldiers since I have been in the Army. It is not my disposition to be jealous for if I had a wife who I had reason to believe to be other than honest, I should give her all the chances in the world to show her real character for a woman's virtue that must be guarded and watched is truly a bogus article and not worth the price it costs And to me the sooner such a one was known, the better it would suit me.

I have not received many letters lately from some cause or other. I received one yesterday from one of my cousins in Illinois and it had been on the road just a month.

Last week has witnessed the heaviest fighting of the War and many thousands on both sides have fell in mortal combat. General Grant is meeting with good success and so far the Rebels have been mutch harder used than ever before on the Potomac and it is generally believed that this time Richmond must surely change owners. Sherman is pushing the Rebels hard at Dalton, Georgia, and good news is soon expected from that quarter. We soon expect to hear of a victory or two which will more than overballance all the little Rebel raids this spring and shake the rebellion to the verry center. But still we quake for fear that some unforeseen calamity

---

10. General Nathan B. Forrest was the most successful Confederate cavalry raider in the Western theater but during the spring of 1864, Forrest campaigned in west Tennessee and Mississippi, not in north Georgia. His reputation, however, may have caused Federal soldiers like Davis to expect him to turn up anywhere. [Faust, p.79]

may befall our army just as victory seems within its grasp. Yet our hopes are for the better and we must wait to see them realised.

I have no news of importance to write more than I have written today and I don't feel in mutch of a thinking mood to write so I will close this hoping to talk a letter or two to you in a few weeks. I remain yours as ever,

T. J. Davis

Pioneer Corps, 3rd Division, 15th Army Corps
Huntsville, Alabama, May 21st, 1864

Dear Lucinda,

I sit down this morning to answer your letter dated May 8th & 11th which I received last night and I was verry glad to hear that your health was so good this spring and I hope it may continue. It is three weeks ago today since I fell from the building and hurt myself. I am now able to walk around considerable but I will probably not be able to work for several days yet.

We had quite a little scare here a few days ago. There was a force of Rebels crossed the Tennessee River between Whitesburg and Triena and it was thought they were coming to attack this place but they turned to the left and struck the railroad ten miles west of here at Madison Station and drove away part of the 13th Illinois Regiment that was there. The Rebs burned the depot. We sent out troops from here and chased them back across the river. There was a few prisoners taken on both sides but there was not mutch fighting.[11]

During the excitement the 18th [Wisconsin] was ordered up here from Whitesburg. They was here two days and then went back again. I saw Robert McMichael. He is looking quite well. He had on his uniform and captain's straps and looks considerably officerlike. The rest of the boys were well. I heard from Merrick Rogers the other day. He is getting well from the smallpox.

There no news different from what I wrote in my last about going home. Lieutenant Colonel Jackson told me that he did not want to take the regiment home before the first of June as he [wants] to have them spend the 4th of July at home. All the regiments that have been home on furlough from our division have returned except the 63rd Illinois and their time has been up several days.

---

11. An attack by Patterson's (Confederate) Cavalry Brigade was made at Madison Station, Alabama, on 17 May 1864. The Confederates captured sixty-six men of the 13th Illinois Infantry, cut the telegraph, and burned the railroad depot filled with cotton bales and equipment belonging to the 13th Illinois. The pursuit of the raiders resulted in the capture of twenty-four Confederates. [OR-I-38-pt.3-p.271–272]

There was 14 more came into the Pioneer Corps from our regiment a few days ago. Ed Rogers and Jesse Smith came from my company.

I received a letter from Ida and Bennett Snyder last night. It was the same date of yours the folks were well. Ida said she had just received a letter from you informing her that I had reenlisted. She did not know it before for I never wrote it to anyone in Illinois. Ida said she was mad at me for reenlisting for she thought I had been in the service long enough for one man. Perhaps I was foolish for doing so but I do not regret it for I think I will be out nearly as soon as if I had not gone in again. The most I regret is to have you discouraged about it though I hope you will not get the blues and think I will never get out of the service.

The weather is quite warm to day and looks mutch like summer. The woods look as green as they do in July in the North and it is getting to be a good time for bushwhackers in the South.

General Sherman's given orders that no mail shall go north of Nashville for the present. I supose that some of my letters are there yet that I wrote to you but I will continue to write and perhaps you will get them after a while.

I am glad you like the present I left you so well and I think I shall think a great deal of it myself but that is not the kind of a present I had illusion [sic] to in my letter and I don't know as another one of that kind would be altogether advisable under the circumstances if I should come home this summer. I did not think you had forgotten me or ever would forget me but I wish to make myself worthy of esteem as well as simple rememberence. I must close as my paper is exhausted. Yours always,

T. J. Davis

Pioneer Corps, 3rd Division, 15th Army Corps
Huntsville, Alabama, May 28th, 1864

Dear Lucinda,

I sit this evening to write you a few paragraphs in answer to your letter which I received last night dated May 16th and mailed 20th. I could hardly term it letter, either. It might more appropriately be called a note. But as you asked me, of course, I will excuse you as you said you was in a hurry. But if you had worked on it 4 days more until the mail went out you might have got in some of the news you spoke of. I [will] not grumble, however, for we should do good for small favors. I will try and write you a longer letter than I received. Your letters of late come through mutch quicker than they did three or for weeks ago. Your last one was mailed the 20th and I received it on the 27th. I received a letter from you a few days ago dated April 6th. I supose it had laid over someplace on the road.

My health has not been verry good since I got hurt. I have been a little dyspeptic again but I am getting better now. I have not worked any yet and probably will not for sometime yet, though, I can walk about now without the assistence of a crutch and I think I will get along now verry well. I was glad to hear that you was well and I hope you may continue so.

We still continue to have fine weather and somedays are quite warm. I sent you some flowers in a book about two weeks ago. I supose you have got them by this time if they went through.

I had thought that I would be at home before your next birthday but I hardly think it probable now that I will for all of the Veteran regiments of our Division that went home on furlough have got back [and] are posted on duty at diferent places and our regiment is still at Whitesburg. I hear nothing more of them being relieved to go home and know of no regiment here at present that can be spared to relieve them. I did have some idea that we would go about the first of June but I did not think we would go before that time. But now I supose we must wait until we can be spared and it is dificult to tell when that will be. But still I think we will go this summer. I hope, however, we may all have a good time when we do get home.

We are still at Huntsville and I don't know how mutch longer we may stay here. There is some talk that we will be relieved from here by another division and that our division will be sent into Georgia, but I don't believe it. If they are relieved from here I believe our regiment will go home before they go to the front.

I received a letter from Elisabeth Ditto and one from Louisa a few days ago. They were all well except Mother. She had been verry sick but was getting a little better when Elisabeth wrote.

I will give you a little sketch of Huntsville what it is and has been. Huntsville has one of the largest and best springs in the south.[12] It forms a large creek at its very head and has a water power that froces [forces] the water through a large pipe nearly half a mile uphill into a reservoir 20 feet deep and 80 feet across and from the reservoir the whole town is supplied with water through iron pipes and small streams of water urns down each street fed by force pumps stationed on the various streets.

It has two churches with spires over a hundred feet high and several others of less dimentions. It has one ceminary which we now use for a hospital and a female college, a three-story brick and a splendid building where the rich men educated their daughters at considerable expense and, as there was no public schools in the South, poor men's children

---

12. Huntsville, Alabama, was founded at the Big Spring, a blowing spring from which twenty-four million gallons of fresh water flow each day. [Hamilton, Virginia Van Der Veer, Seeing Historic Alabama. Tuscaloosa, Ala., University of Alabama Press, 1982, p.10]

grew up like the Negros, uneducated, and the poor people were thought even less of in the south than Negros from the fact that they were less profitable. They were, however, used as dupes by the rich who induced them always to vote for men and measures contrary to their own Interest.

Huntsville was also a verry fast place in the days of Slavery the King when the rich were rocked in the cradle of luxury, vice, idleness, and crime when no Yankee would dare to say that a nigger had a soul and wasn't a brute or say that slavery was anything less than a divine institution ordained and blessed by the Deity. In those days lived many of the elite chivalry here who dwelt in princely houses and were clothed with bad consciences and fine linen and fared sumptuously every day that the nigger was obedient to his master. He talked politics and drank mutch bad whiskey and kept women that were less virtuous. And he waxed verry rich so that he became a mighty man in the earth and his fame went abroad in all the land.

He had man servents and maid servents and more especially maid servents who, by a bell in each room in the house, they could at any time be summoned to do any servile labor for her sainted lord that might promote his comfort or lust. Many of the maid servents, especially body servents, by an admixture of blood from one generation to another, are about as fair as their white owners. Many of these chivalry also owned oxen, sheep, and asses and made asses of themselves by braying abolition and amalgimation to the Northern Yankees when at the same time they wished amalgimation to be kept monopolized by the South. Oh consistency, thou hid thyself.

But now behold the Lincoln hirelings have rose up, a mighty host, and have overspread the land. The chivalrys soil is polluted by their intruding feet and [they] desolated the land and break down many high places and caused many of the proud, yea, hauty chivalric soul drivers to the house of refuge in some more remote corner of the earth who, no doubt, is now praying to God to protect slavery, his divine institution, as it is failing in the hands of man and so may it be well for the present.

I will close hoping to hear from you or see you soon. I remain as ever yours truly,

Thomas. J. Davis

Pioneer Corps, 3rd Division,15th Army Corps
Huntsville, Alabama, June 4th, 1864

Dear Lucinda,

I sit down this morning to write you a few lines in answer to your letter dated May 22nd & 25th which I received last night and was glad to hear that you was well and in good spirits. I am still gaining slowly. I can walk around town some but I have not done any work since I was hurt and perhaps I will not do any for sometime to come. I will not work untill I get stout enough to stand it, anyhow, if it is six months. I have been otherwise unwell for sometime but I am now feeling better and I think I will be all right in a few weeks.

We had a nice shower of rain last night and one night before last and the air is nice and cool today. I received a letter from brother Will night before last. I will send it to you. I also received one from D. Ingersoll noted 22nd of May. The folks were all well but no news, as usual, for he never writes mutch.

I hear nothing more definitely about our regiment going home but I think we will probably start by the first of July. The 18th is still at Whitesburg. I see some of the boys nearly every day. I have not seen Robert but once since he came back. I think I will go down to regiment soon and stay a few days.

You say that you have not received any state money since the first of January on account of our company not being reported which fault I would say is not the captains. All the companies are reported as a regiment by the Colonel and I supose it has been neglected on account of expecting to report soon at Madison verbally. But then I suppose you need not be in a hurry as you have what money you will need and it will all be good when it comes. I have only been paid to the first of January but I have money to last until I will get it and some besides. If I had not got hurt I should have been trying to make a little more money by this time but as it is, I must do the best I can.

Your birch bark letter was a verry good substitute for paper. I have shown it to a number of the boys. A few of them knew what it was but the most of them did not. It was considered quite a curiosity by all of them. They wondered how it could be peeled off to look so mutch like paper. I think considerable of it and I will keep it as a curiosity. Your letters have come quite regular for the past few weeks but sometime ago they came irregular. But I supose it was mostly in fault of the mail somewhere. But the mail comes in from the North every day now. We [get] daily papers everyday and keep posted about Grant's movements on Richmond. He is moving slow and sure and is progressing as well or better than could be expected under the circumstances.

The guerrillas and bushwackers are getting somewhat saucy and troublesome around here since the woods have got so green. Some of the 10th Missouri boys caught three of them on the railroad between here and Woodville last week. They tried to make them tell where the rest of their gang was but they swore they would not tell on their own men. So the 10th boys told them if they would not tell on their own men they should not tell on ours. So the guerrillas was placed on the heads of three barrels under a limb of a tree with ropes attached to the limb and their necks. The barrels were kicked from under them and, of course, they died for they could not get any foothold. So bully for them. That is the way they all should be served when caught.[13]

Well, Lucinda, as I have no great amount of news to write I will close for this time hoping to hear from you soon and hoping to see you before a great while and talk over things thats past since we parted and prospects of a future life together. It seems truly hard that we must be seperated and not permitted to see or enjoy the society of those that are the most near and dear to us. But we must live in hopes of a better future. Yours always,

T. J. Davis

Pioneer Corps, 3rd Division, 15th Army Corps
Huntsville, Alabama, Friday, June 9th, 1864

Dear Wife,

I sit down this afternoon to write you a few lines so that you may hear from me as often as possible. I have not received any letter from you since I wrote before but I will look for another in two or three days.

My health and lameness is still growing better though slowly. I went down to the regiment at Whitesburg last Monday and came back this morning. Company C are all well except Jim Kingston. He has been quite sick but is getting better. Merrick Rogers is getting pretty well over the small pox but he will probably be discharged on account of his old scrofalus complaint.

The 18th likes to stay at Whitesburg verry well though they are willing to go home on furlough when they can get a chance to do so but it is not known when that will be. I had been in hopes that we would get home before your next birthday, which is next Monday. If I was there then don't you believe you would get a good whiping, though perhaps you may think though that you can handle me now as I am not verry stout. And sometimes I think it would be hardly worthwhile for me to go home on a furlough for I may not be able to do a man's duty and that would be more of an aggravation than to not go, perhaps. But under such circumstances a furlough now may not be as dangerous as heretofore and as the furlough then was not long enough for a boy, I don't know what could be produced now. I have said enough on this subject now so I will wait and tell you the rest when I get home.

---

13. Guerrilla hangings were not at all out of line with General William T. Sherman's campaign policies. In July 1864, Sherman wrote an open order to officers commanding troops along his railroad supply line, "Show no respect or mercy to guerrillas or persons threatening our road or telegraph." [OR I-38-5; p.140–141]

I received a letter from Mother a few days ago. She was getting considerable better but not well, yet. She said that her and Elisabeth was going to write to you soon snd that she had meant to have written to you sometime ago.

There is nothing of importance going on here. Sherman has been doing some big fighting down in Georgia lately and a prospect for considerable more soon.[14] I will not write mutch today and will write more when I get a letter from you again. You must not be uneasy in looking for us to come for it is uncertain when we will get started. But the longer time we stay now the less we will have to stay when we come back. Be a good girl and I will bring you some candy. Yours always,

Thos. J. Davis

Pioneer Corps, 3rd Division, 15th Army Corps
Huntsville, Alabama, June 14th, 1864

Dear Wife,

I sit down this afternoon to write you a few lines in answer to your letter dated 5th Inst. which I received last night and I was glad to hear that you was well. I am still slowly improving though I have not done any duty yet. I may, however, be able to go to work before long but I shan't do mutch until I feel like it. The wether is quite pleasent now we still have a good shower every two or three days and yesterday was quite cool but it is warmer today.

You say you heard that Jabe, Calvin and E. Caulkins was killed. Such may be the case but I don't believe it from the fact that their battery belonged to the defensive force of the city of New Orleans and I don't think they have been in a battle at all. I saw John Carpenter yesterday. He said the boys were all well in the company except Jim Kingston and that he was improving.

I received a letter from Elisabeth and Mother of the same date and at the same time I did yours. Mother was mending slowly and the rest of the folks were in moderated health. They wrote no news of importance. Mother said that her and Elisabeth was going to write to you that day but they had been talking about that same thing for a long time.

You wrote as though you was expecting us [to] come home soon but by the time you get this, I supose you will think we have not come yet. It

---

14. During May 1864, Sherman's army had fought and maneuvered Johnston's army out of north Georgia and across the Etowah River at a cost of 9,000 Federal casualties. Those losses were replaced with the arrival of the 17th Army Corps in early June 1864, as Sherman faced Johnston near Kennesaw Mountain. [Bailey, Ronald H. Battles for Atlanta, Alexandria, Va., Time-Life Books, 1985, p.60]

seems that all the troops are needed in the field now and I think that none will be furloughed now, only those that they cannot hold without. Our regiment can be held till the first of November before being furloughed if we are needed here and I should not be surprised if we would be kept until that time or until the two great campaigns of Richmond and Atlanta is decided. I was not expecting to start home before the first of June nor did I feel sure we would start that soon for I had a pretty good idea that all available forces would be needed in the field and I thought after the campaign had commenced that we would be kept as long as they could keep us. I still hear a report among our officers verry frequently to the effect that the regiment would go home in a few days but I don't pay any attention to it. So I don't expect to write mutch more about coming home until we get ready to start. But when Robert gets home on furlough, you can tell him that I will be along in a few days, that's all.

The 10th Iowa starts home on furlough tomorrow but their old time is nearly out so they can't be kept any longer.

There is nothing new going on here at present. There has been some talk lately that we would be sent to Atlanta, Georgia, but I don't think we will go soon if at all this summer.

I hope you will not keep yourself uneasy looking for me to come home. You don't know how glad I would be to see you that we may again spend a pleasant month together. But still, I don't allow myself to worry about it for I think we will have a pleasant time when I do come. In the mean time, I wish to receive letters from you regularly for after I begin to look for a letter from you I feel uneasy about you until I get one. I supose that you think as you are all the time at one place that I would be careless about hearing from you every week but when I don't get one I feel disappointed. I have always tried to write to you as often as once a week but I have several times been situated so that I could not do so on account of being away from mail communication. I was always anxious to hear from you every week if only to hear that you was well and, of course, I thought that you had the same concern for me. The war cannot always last and if we both live, I hope we may yet add many days of comfort to each other's lives. Hope is the only stay that supports the heart and if we dispair we are already miserable. How many should-be-happy lives have been sacrafised on the alter of fate by giving up all flattering hopes for the future. A good share of our happiness consists of immagination as well as reality. But happiness in immagination without reality is a vain shadow. True happiness consists in obeying the laws of nature, of health, and of justice. A person cannot always judge their friends by what they appear to be. How disgusting it is to look through the thin gauze of a vain and fickle person, a pretended friend, and see there is no support of reality behind the scene. Confidence nor money should be trusted to rogues or strangers lest it should [be] squandered and exposed at the expense of the lender.

Well, Lucinda, I have already written more than I intended to when I commenced so I will close for this time hoping to hear from you soon. I remain ever truly your husband and lover.

T. J. Davis

Pioneer Corps, 3rd Divisison, 15th Army Corps
Huntsville, Alabama, Sunday, June 19th, 1864

I again sit down to write you a few lines to inform you that I still think of you. My health is about the same as when I last wrote. I received a letter from you this morning dated May 31st but I got one a week ago dated June 5th so I did not get mutch news today. I was afraid those flowers would get mouldy before they got through to Wisconsin. The regiment came up from Whitesburg yesterday. Our division are now under marching orders and will probably join Sherman at the front soon.

Some of the boys sent home part of their money yesterday. I sent two hundred dollars. It will go to Lincoln in Viroqua and you can get it there. Ed Rogers sent some to Elias so you can go or send an order with Elias when he gets Ed's money. You will have to pay the express charges there. I loaned Robert McMichael a hundred dollars or else I would have sent three hundred. Robert did not draw his pay last payday.

The boys in the Company are as well as usual. Will Cleary is lying beside me on the bunk as I write, indulging in a sound sleep and from appearance is dreaming of the girl he left behind him.

Will and Mary have been coresponding again by letter for some time and he intends going to Iowa when he gets his furlough and probably he and Mary will tie up before he comes back. Joy go with them so say I. Mary wrote to Alvin that she thought I was joking in what I wrote to her about Will over a year ago. It was nothing however to me and, of course, she can exercise her own judgement but she may yet see the point of the joke in a different direction. None of Caulkins folks have sent any word to me by Alvin for a long time. Perhaps they don't thank me for what I wrote. But if they don't, I did not charge anything for it so it will cost them nothing. I received a letter from Isaac yesterday the folks were well. No news of importance. I have no news to write today.

In your two last letters you seemed to be looking for me home but we have not started and I will now put off the time to the first of November. So you can again begin to look for us about that time. Our regiment is generally at the tail end of everything except in a fight and there it is generally put in ahead. But our time will come after a while. I remain ever yours truly,

T. J. Davis

CHAPTER NINE

Sherman Is Slowly Driving the Rebs

General William T. Sherman had been engaged with Confederate forces since the second week of May as he maneuvered south from Chattanooga toward Atlanta. The division to which the "Badax Tigers" belonged was called up from their winter quarters near Huntsville about a month after the start of the campaign. Most of the division was sent ahead by rail while the 18th Wisconsin and several other units were kept in Chattanooga. On 5 July the Eighteenth departed Chattanooga guarding the division wagon train and a 1,000-beef herd on its way to Sherman's front near the Chattahoochee River. The procession passed through Dalton, Kinston, and Cartersville before delivering the wagon train to a railroad supply depot at Allatoona on 13 July.

Guard duty on the railroad near Allatoona occupied the regiment's time for five weeks before a call for help came from Tennessee. Confederate cavalry raiders threatened the Federal army's supply line north of Chattanooga and troops were needed to protect that vulnerable road. From 22 August until 19 September, the Badgers marched up and down the rail line patrolling between Chattanooga and Nashville before the crisis passed. The Eighteenth returned to Allatoona, now a huge supply depot, to rest and relax. While the Wisconsin boys had been in Tennessee chasing raiders, Sherman's main force had fought several pitched battles outside Atlanta. They had finally succeeded on 1 September in forcing the Confederate army, under the command of General John B. Hood, to evacuate Atlanta. For Sherman and his troops the capture of Atlanta was a signal military victory. For President Abraham Lincoln, facing a national election within two months, it was a vital political victory.

Although the 18th Wisconsin never directly participated in the Atlanta fighting, Sherman's victory was as much a triumph of logistics as force of arms. Though he commanded a numerically superior army, Sherman's greatest challenge during the Atlanta campaign was in keeping his troops fed and supplied with ammunition while campaigning in a hostile territory. To troops like the 18th Wisconsin fell the inglorious task of guarding the extended supply line from Kentucky to the fighting front. Sherman addressed this very situation in his war memoirs when he stated:

"The Atlanta campaign would simply have been impossible without the use of the railroads from Louisville to . . . Atlanta. Every mile of this 'single track' was so delicate that one man could, in a minute, have broken or moved a rail, so our trains usually carried along the tools and means to repair such a break. That single stem of railroad, four hundred and seventy-three miles long, supplied an army of one hundred thousand men and thirty-five thousand animals . . . by carrying 1,600 tons daily, which exceeded the absolute necessity of the army. Therefore, I reiterate, that the Atlanta campaign would have been an impossibility without these railroads; and only then, because we had the men and means to defend them."[1]

While most of the "Tigers" were protecting Sherman's lifeline, T. J. Davis remained in Cartersville with the Pioneer Corps. His correspondence continued without interruption through the summer of 1864 and reflected the varied fortunes of Sherman's campaigners. Davis liked the Georgia countryside through which he marched, noting that the men were much healthier than they had been in Mississippi and Louisiana. There was a spirit of confidence that, regardless of opposing Confederate troops, Sherman and his western boys were bound to take Atlanta. The Confederate evacuation of Atlanta in early September was cause for some comment but Davis treated the event with only a casual mention, as if it was only to be expected that the city would fall to Sherman. Davis spent more time commenting positively on Robert S. McMichael's promotion to captain of the "Tigers" and on the marriage of a Federal soldier to a Georgia girl, an act of which he did not at all approve.

His letters during this period were not simply camp reports, though. They showed the degree to which soldiers kept attuned to war and political news through letters, newspapers, and the military telegraph system. The naval campaign at Mobile Bay was a source of some curiosity to Davis as was the attempt by Confederates to influence the course of the war through peace negotiations at the Canadian-American border near Niagara Falls. He followed the political campaign between Lincoln's Union-Republican Party and General George B. McClellan's Democrats and was well enough informed to note, with some pleasure, the death of Confederate cavalry General John Hunt Morgan. Most of the soldiers of the Civil War period had probably grown to manhood with limited travel and school opportunities but they were men who had been raised in a lively, politically vibrant society. They cared a great deal about the na-

---

1. From "Memoirs of General William T. Sherman," vol. 2, pp. 398–399.

tional events in which they were playing a role. Davis' letters provide an intriguing glimpse into that interest and involvement.

Chattanooga, Tennessee, Sunday, June 25th, 1864

I sit down this Sunday evening to write you a short epistle to let you know that I am still in Dixie. My health is better than when I last wrote to you but still I have not done any duty yet. Our division left Huntsville last Wednesday morning to march through to this place but I was not able to march so I staid at Huntsville until Thursday evening and got on the cars and got here Friday forenoon. The division camped ten miles the other side of Stevenson last night and will get here about next Wednesday. They are having verry warm weather for the march and I learn from some men that came in on the cars from the division last night that there had been ten or twelve men sunstruck since they left Huntsville. I am glad that I did not attempt to march with the division for I am quite sure I would have fizzled out before this time.

I have not received a letter from you since I last wrote and I will not get any until the division gets here. The last letter I received from you was dated 5th of this month so I will expect two when the division comes up.

There is no news of great interest from the front for a few days. There was some heavy fighting in Sherman's army on the 18, 19, & 20th of this month and many of the wounded have been sent here and to Nashville.[2] Our division will probably go on to Marietta, Georgia, when they get here but I will write to you again before we leave here.

It is so warm that have to stop and wipe the sweat off my face every few minutes and my hand is so unsteady that I don't know as you can read this. It rained a little about noon but the sun has come out hot again and I think it will rain again to night.

I received a letter from brother Will the other day. He was well and in the rifle pits in front of the Rebs and his regiment [59th illinois Infantry] has since been in two or three fights but I don't here anything about him.

I had a letter from D. Ingersoll a few days ago. He said the folks was well.

You must excuse a short letter today and when I get a letter from you and I can write better, I will write more. I wrote to you the last time that I sent you two hundred dollars. You will get it of Lincoln in Viroqua. Well, my paper is about played out so I will close for this time. I remain ever truly yours,

Thos. J. Davis

---

2. The fighting to which Davis refers in this letter was stubborn, rain-soaked combat as Federal troops fought their way toward the strong Confederate Kennesaw Mountain defense line. [Long, p. 519]

Pioneer Corps, 3rd Division, 15th Army Corps
Chattanooga, Tennessee, July 1st, 1864

Dear Sis,

I will endeavor to while away a few leisure moments in writing you a few lines in answer to your letter dated June 12 & 15th which I received yesterday. I was glad to hear that you was well and I hope this may find you the same. I am considerable better than I was two weeks ago though I have not got entirely over my fall yet and perhaps will not this summer. I think I could have been sent to Nashville from here last Saturday if I had tried and probably got furloughed from there but I did not want to go until the regiment goes home. I have always had a great horor of being around hospitals and don't want to go into one as long as I can keep out.[3] I don't want you to feel uneasy about me for I think I will get along verry well or at least as well as I can until the regiment goes home.

The regiment got here last night. They marched from Huntsville to Stevenson and came from Stevenson here on the cars. We will wait here until the division wagon trains gets through and then we will march on to Kingston which is in Georgia 56 miles from here by railroad. We will leave here about the 4th so I won't be at the Springville celebration this year. I shall always remember the celebration we had last year and I would like to celebrate the capture of Richmond this 4th but I am afraid it will take Grant the most of the summer to take Richmond. But I believe he will hammer away at Richmond until he does take it.

The weather is quite warm now and several boys in our division got sunstruck on the march but I don't think there was any killed from our regiment. We had a good shower of rain yesterday but it is quite warm again today. Merrick Rogers has got the rheumatism in his knees and is in the hospital here. Jim Kingston is also in the hospital. Robert McMichael told me sometime ago that his wife was going to Platteville to stay with her folks.

I don't think that Robert's shoulder straps gives him the big head any, yet, nor I don't think it will. Robert was a good man before he came into the army and I think he will remain so. A man that is a man at home can be a man in the army but take a person that could get no office at home and who generally managed to keep in debt to the tailor for his clothes and felt too important to work and if he can get a commisson in the army, he will be a bigoted swell-head like a bloated set of bowells contain noth-

---

3. Civilian hospitals were frightening enough to 19th-century citizens who often considered them simply way stations on the road to death. Doubtless, army hospitals held even greater horror for soldiers who had watched many a sick or wounded friend die in their cheerless confines. [Wiley, p.129–148]

ing but offensive wind and will always command the disrespect of sensible men. I suppose that Robert can afford to pay more now towards keeping his wife than when he was a sergeant. I loaned him a hundred dollars a few days ago to send home to his wife. I have made more money so far since I been in the army than he has and I used to hire him for a dollar a day last summer to sell beer for me. But that was all right enough.

I don't think that our division will be put in the extreme front in this campaign. It is said we will relieve another division at Kingston so they can go to the front. Our regiment will not now get to go home until after this campaign if it takes all summer. There is more or less fighting in front every day and every day there is more or less wounded brought in here from the front. Our division has been extremely lucky this spring in not being called into battle, though they had enough of it last year.

There is a great deal depending on this year's campaign and will go a great way towards deciding the result of the war. I cannot see that the war can possibly last three years longer and I should not feel altogether satisfied to be at home while the war is going on and I hope how soon it may close, for a few years longer would bring our whole country to a mass of debt which would require manny years to regain as prosperous a condition as before the war.

Wish you to live as contented as you can and in hopes of a better future for I still feel in hopes that we may yet be permitted to spend manny pleasent days together. I know that soldiers' wives see a hard time to get along and they are not given half the credit that they deserve for if they have a husband that they love and respect as such they are in almost constant suspense lest they should hear in the next mail that he is either sick, killed, or wounded. I always feel anxious to hear from you every week and when I don't get letters I feel uneasy about you and I know I should feel mutch more uneasy if our positions were reversed. I have only received your letter since I wrote before. I suppose you will get the money I sent you before you get this as I expressed it on the 18th of June.

I see from the papers that the weather is verry dry all over the Northern states and unless rain comes soon the crops will be verry light. I would like verry well to go with you to Michigan if I was at home but I shall not promise now when we will get home. I have not had a letter from Susan for a long time and Hariet has not written to me since she was in Wisconsin though I believe I have written to her twice since.

I want you to keep up good courage and I will call around and see you one of these days and stay a day or two. I believe I will close for this time write soon.

From your soger boy. Goodbye, Sis.

T. J. Davis

Pioneer Corps, 3rd Division, 15th Army Corps
Chattanooga, Tennessee, Sunday, July 3rd/64

Dear Lucinda,

I sit down this afternoon to write you a few lines before we leave this place. We are going to start for Kingston tomorrow. Our regiment and the Pioneer Corps is going to guard the division wagons through. It will probably take us eight or ten days to go through. We have not had any mail since I wrote you last. Our mail has been sent on to the front and we will not get any more mail until we get through which will be sometime yet. I begin to feel considerable better since I left Huntsville. I am going through with the Corps. We will not march more than ten or twelve miles a day.

The weather continues quite warm though we have had several showers of rain during the past week. Blackberries are now getting ripe here and we have picked all we wanted since we have been here and early apples are getting ripe but there is not enough of them to be any object. I could get to stay here in the convalescent camp if I wanted to do so but I would rather go with the Corps so I can get my mail once in a while. I don't know as I will have a chance to write anymore until we get through but I will do so if I have an oppertunity. There will be three of Company C left here: H. Baker, P. Mooney, and D.Caulkins. They are unwell and will not be able to march.

There is no war news of interest since I wrote to you before. There is still more or less skirmishing going on every day. We are camped about two miles from Lookout Mountain. There is an officers' hospital on top of it. I should have went up there for curiosity but it is too warm for such an excursion of curiosity.

One year ago today Pemberton and Grant held their consultation preparatory to the surrender of Vicksburg and I don't think I shall ever forget that time. It was full warmer weather than we have here. I don't think we will have mutch of a celebration tomorrow but probably Sherman may give Johnston some music by way of amusement.

Well, as I have nothing more of Interest to write I will close. Write soon, direct as before. I remain as ever yours truly,

T. J.Davis

Pioneer Corps, 3rd Division, 15th Army Corps
Dalton, Georgia, Thursday, July 7th, 1864

Dear Wife,

I sit down this evening to write you a few lines to let you know that I am in tolerable good health and on the march. We left Chattanooga on the 5th and arrived at this place this afternoon. This is 40 miles from Chattanooga. We will start on in the morning for Kingston and I will probably not write again until we get there. It will take us about three days more marching to get to Kingston. I have not had any news from the front since we left Chattanooga. So far we have got along verry well. The weather has not been so warm since the 4th as it was two weeks previous.

Dalton is the place where Johnston's Rebel army wintered last winter. The town is about the size of Viroqua or a little larger. The country around here is quite rough but there is plenty of good water. Seven miles north of here is where the Rebels had their strongest defences on some verry rough hills and there is many acres of different hillsides that are now covered with dilapidated shanties that the Rebs quartered in last winter.

Our force consists of the 18th Wisconsin, 5th Ohio Cavalry, 3 Companies of the 23rd Missouri, and the Pioneer Corps. We are guarding through the division wagons and about a thousand head of beef cattle. I don't think we will go clear through to the front for the rest of our division that has gone ahead are on the railroad this side of Big Shanty.

I have not had any mail since I wrote before and we will probably not get any until we get to Kingston. I think that Sherman will soon get possession of Atlanta for he drove them south of the Chattahoocha River several days ago. When they left there they gave up the best defences they had. You must excuse a short letter this time. I merely drop you a line to keep you posted as to my whereabouts. It is getting so dark I cannot see the lines so I must quit. Be a good girl and write often. I remain ever yours,

T. J. Davis

Pioneer Corps, 3rd Division, 15th Army Corps
Kingston, Georgia, July 11th, 1864

Dear Wife,

I sit down this morning in answer to your letter dated 19th & 22nd ult. which I received yesterday and was glad to hear that you was well. I am getting in pretty good health again for me. I walked the most of the way from Chattanooga to this place but I did not carry any load and we did not make verry heavy marches. We was five days coming from Chattanooga, a distance of [78] miles. The weather was not so hot on this march as it was two weeks previous. We had a heavy rain on Friday evening and another good rain yesterday (Sunday) evening. We are about 30 miles from the Chattahoochie River where Sherman's army are but we cannot hear what they are doing now. It is reported that our army has crossed the Chattahoochie River but it is only a report.

I expected to get several letters when we got here but I did not get but one and that was from you. John Carpenter got one from Marcia dated the 26th. He said you wrote a few lines in it. I notice that Marcia's letters are from two to four days later than your's and your letters that are mailed at

Hockley are generally mail marked from two to four days after they are written. I wish you was at a place where the mail went out every day.

We had a verry good trip through from Chattanooga. Our train was not attacked on the route but our cavalry captured 30 guerrillas and fourteen horses back near Calhoun on Saturday morning. I think they will be used pretty rough. They will probably be hung as our generals are coming down on such characters verry strict of late.

The 18th is also at this place. The boys in the company, I believe, are all well. We do not know yet how long we shall remain here. We may stay until the campaign is over and we may not stay but a few days. Our regiment will be verry likely to go home as soon as this campaign is over but it is useless to conjecture when that will be. So I don't trouble myself about it but wait with patience hoping soon to hear that our men have possession of Atlanta. I don't think there is any regiments going home now but as soon as the campaign is over I think all the veteran regiments that have not been home will be permitted to go then. So you need not look for us verry soon but be contented to wait until we do come and we will talk about it then. Well, for this time I will close. I remain ever your husband in Union,

T. J. Davis

Pioneer Corps, 3rd Division, 15th Army Corps
Cartersville, Georgia, July 15th, 1864

Dear Wife,

I again endeavor to write you a short letter to let you know that I am in reasonable health and hope this may find you in good health. I have not received any letters from you since I wrote to you on the 11th inst. while at Kingston. I expected several letters that I did not get. I think that I had several letters burned on the trains that the Rebels lately destroyed for us. The last letter I received from you was dated June 19th & 22nd and letters have been received here written from Wisconsin as late as the 6th inst.

We left Kingston last Tuesday and came to this place. This is 14 miles south of Kingston and on the Etowah River. Cartersville is 24 miles from Marietta and 47 miles from Atlanta. The 18th went on to a station seven miles south of here and will probably remain there for some time. Our division general's headquarters[4] are at this place and the Pioneer Corps will probably remain here until the division again moves. We hear nothing of unusual note from the front for a few days. Only Sherman is slowly driving the Rebs and we look ere long to hear that he has possession of Atlanta.

---

4. General John E. Smith.

The weather continues pleasent for this climate but rather warmer than a week ago.

This is a verry rough rugged and rocky country and what farms there are are deserted and left and trampled under the feet of our army and the fensing destroyed. We have verry good water here. This is a great country for blackberries. They are now ripe and we have had all we could use ever since we left Chattanooga. We find more apple orchards in Georgia than we seen in Mississippi or Louisiana. We have plenty green apples to cook and we get some that are ripe which make a verry good change with our army rations.

I shall not attempt to write a large letter today but I will try and write often so you will know where I am. I will send you a Georgia flower. I don't know the name of it but it is verry pretty but I suppose it will be spoiled before it reaches you. Hoping to hear from you soon, I remain as ever your affectionate Tom. Write soon,

T. J. Davis

Pioneer Corps, 3rd Division, 15th Army Corps
Cartersville, Georgia, July 21st,1864

Dear Wife,

I sit down this morning to write you a short letter in answer to yours bearing date July 6th & 7th which I received this morning and was verry glad to hear from you but sorry to learn that you was not in good health. But I hope this may find you well. My health is tolerable good for me so that I don't complain. I received a letter from you dated June 28 & 29 a few days ago but I had written to you the day before so I thought I would wait until I got another before I answered it.

The weather here continues pleasent but rather warm for comfort but not so warm as it was three weeks ago. We have not had any rain for over a week and we begin to think about rain again.

I went out foraging day before yesterday and I helped to cut oats for our mules it was the first harvesting that I have done in Dixie. Wheat harvest is over here but the oats are just fairly ripe.

I have not been to the regiment since we came to this place. They are stationed on the railroad 8 miles south of here.

I received a letter from Louisa a few days ago she said the folks as well as usual though she said they were scared on account of the smallpox being in the neighborhood. She said she had not answered your letter yet but intended to soon, and then excused herself by saying it was a burden to her to write as long as she could help it conveniently. I wrote her that if she neglected to write she had no cause to grumble because she did not receive letters.

This is my birthday but I did not think of it until I commenced writing. If I was at home today wouldn't you give me a stick of candy if I would be a good boy? I would like verry well to get your picture. I intended to have had mine taken and send to you before we left Huntsville but I was so lantern-jawed all spring that I did not think you would like the picture and we was also thinking of going home and in that case I thought I would carry my picture with me.

Night before last our forces in front was within 4 miles of Atlanta and was then making a move and there is a report in the Chattanooga paper of yesterday that Atlanta was taken with 15,000 prisoners but I don't put mutch confidence in the report, yet. But still I think Atlanta will be ours soon if it is not now taken. Our troops in front are verry much fatigued from their long campaign and they verry much need rest.

I made a keg of beer last night, the first I have made this season. If you was here today I would treat but I don't think it would make you mutch intoxicated; at least I can't get drunk on it when I try. It is dificult to get material to make it here so I don't think I will make but little of it this season.

I received Clara Wilson's letter you sent me. She may probably wait some time if she don't answer my letter until I go to see them but I would like to go verry, verry well if I had time and oppertunity. Well, my paper is about spent and I will close. Write soon I remain ever your boy,

T. J. Davis

Pioneer Corps, 3rd Division, 15th Army Corps
Cartersville, Georgia, July 26th, 1864

I employ a few leisure moments to day in writing you a short epistle in answer to your letter dated July 17th & 18th and mailed at Lacrosse the 18th. I was verry glad to hear that you was well as you had wrote a time or two before that you had been somewhat ailing. Your last letter come through mutch quicker than any letter I have received from you for a long time. My health is about the same as when I last wrote you last.

The wether is quite pleasent at present. The days are not so warm as in June and the nights are cool enough to sleep under two blankets. We are yet at Cartersville and will probably remain here for some time. We have not had much to do since we came here and, in fact, I would not do much if we had.

There has been some verry heavy fighting at Atlanta a few days ago with heavy loss on both sides. Among the killed was Major General McFerson, one of the ablest generals in our army. We have been under him nearly two years and his loss is mutch regretted by all the troops of his command. He commanded the Army of the Tennessee which consisted of the 15th, 16th and 17 Army Corps.[5]

We don't hear any peticulars from the front. It is generally believed that our forces hold Atlanta for there was heavy fighting all round it and we could verry distinctly hear the canonading here on Friday, Saturday, and Sunday. I am verry anxious to hear from the front and hear from Will as I have not heard from him for sometime.

I supose you received the money I sent you in your letter of the 6th. You said it was at Viroqua but in your last letter you did not say anything about it.

You say that Elias Rogers says that the war will last seven years. As to prophesying as to the duration of the war, I never pretended to know. Neither do I think that Elias knows any more than I do. One thing I am confident of and that is it cannot last four years longer from the fact that neither side will be able in money and men to carry it on long for both sides are now rapidly becoming bankrupt.

I notice in the last two papers we received that there were some men at Niagra Falls in Canada purporting to be Rebel commissioners and wishing to come to Washington to negotiate for terms of peace. But I think it is only a sham arrangement between the Copperheads and Rebels to make a show for peace for the sake of trying to defeat the Union or National Party at the November election. That is my opinion at present but it is to be hoped that a better design is at the bottom of it.[6]

Since writing the above a train of cars came in from the front with some Rebel prisoners. The men on the cars say our forces are not yet in possession of Atlanta but are nearly all round it.

I received a letter from Mother and Elisabeth a few days ago. The folks were as well as usual.

There is no other news of importance to write at present. You must be good children and don't cry nor play in the dirt. I remain as ever your soger boy.

T. Jefferson Davis

---

5. General James B. McPherson was killed on 22 July 1864 in the Battle of Atlanta when he mistakenly rode into a line of Confederate skirmishers. He was the highest ranking Federal officer killed in the Civil War. [Faust, p. 466]

6. The 18 July 1864 Niagara Falls peace conference was indeed an effort by three Confederate emissaries to influence the approaching national elections by politically embarrassing President Lincoln and ruining his chances for reelection. Lincoln recognized the scheme for what it was, however, and his offer of peace only with the restoration of the Union and the abolition of slavery was rejected by the Confederates. The Union Party was the name used by the Republican Party during the 1864 electoral campaign. [Long, p. 541]

No.2 Pioneer Corps, 3rd Division, 15th Army Corps
Cartersville, Aug 2nd, 1864

Dear Wife,

Being at leisure today I thought I would write a few lines for pass time even if it is not interesting for your perusal. But if I had time I would write a little every day although I have no news of interest to write. But I can write something else. The weather is cool and pleasant today. We still have showers every few days which makes it mutch more pleasent than if it continued dry and hot.

We have not had any newspapers for two or three days. I learn that they are not allowed to be sold along the line at present which makes times verry dull for news.[7] I think there is some important move going on in front but we cannot hear anything definitely what is being done, but we will probably hear in a few days.

Friday Aug 5th

Well, I will finish my letter this morning. We moved camp day before yesterday and have been buisy fixing up or I would have finished it before. We received our pay yesterday. I have not been to the regiment since we came here. I don't know whether they have been paid yet or not. I will not send any money home at present as there is no express office here.

I think I will go down to the regiment and see the boys in a few days. We do not get any papers yet and we still know but little of what is going on at the front. I think that Sherman can take Atlanta whenever he wishes to do so but is figuring to try and take part of the Rebel army and waiting on Grant's movements East.

I received a letter two days ago from brother Will dated the 24th [of] July. He was near Atlanta and was well. He has had a verry hard campaign since the first of May though he seems to be in good spirits. I have not received any letter from you since I commenced this. I received your letters no. 1 and 2 so I will no. my letters after this if I don't forget it.

The 10th Iowa has returned from furlough. Sam Coe was in Viroqua the 4th of July. He said they had a good time there.

---

7. General William T. Sherman was no friend to Civi War-era newspapers or reporters. He felt strongly about the need to conduct the Atlanta campaign without the security leaks that reporters represented. The simplest way to accomplish that end was to keep the number of newsmen following his army to a minimum and to restrict the circulation of newspapers within his jurisdiction. [Marszalek, John F., Sherman: A Soldier's Passion for Order, New York, The Free Press, 1993, 270]

Yesterday was the day set apart by the President and Congress as a day of national humiliation and prayer.[8] I went to church last night and heard the chaplain of the 63rd Illinois make a sermon. I got tired, however, and went to camp before the sermon was concluded. I hope that those who offered prayers did it with the right spirit and pure motives.

My health [is] as good as usual though I feel too nervous today to write good. I hope this will find you in good health and in good spirits and remain so until I get home this fall and then I will tell you a great many long, windy stories (not of my bravery, however) about soldiering in general and Southern life. As I have no important news, I will close. Write soon. I remain ever your soger boy.

T. J. Davis

No. 3, Pioneer Corps, 3rd Division, 15th Army Corps
Cartersville, Georgia, Aug 8th, 1864

Dear Lucinda,

This is Sunday morning and I sit down to spend a short leisure time in writing you a short epistle in answer to your letter dated 26 & 27th of July which I received yesterday and was glad to hear that you was well. My health remains as good as usual. Your letters of late have come through verry prompt and in good time quicker than they came to Huntsville.

We had quite a heavy shower of rain last night. We have a shower about every other day though not enough to keep the ground muddy. The weather is warm though not excessivly hot.

I have not received many letters since I came down here besides yours. You said you would like to have my picture again if I could get it taken to see if I looked any better then I did in the last picture I sent you. I don't think I could get a verry hansom one taken now unless I would get a good looking man to sit in my place. But I think I will not get one taken until I come home and then I will bring my picture to you so you can then tell which is the best looking person, me or the man that left you and went to the army. Probably you had best not send your picture until I go home. It may not get here before we start. We may start in a few weeks but it is uncertain when but it will probably not be a great while.

---

8. President Lincoln issued several proclamations throughout the war calling for days of prayer or thanksgiving. In addition to his well known designation of the last Thurday in November 1863 as Thanksgiving Day, he had also earlier proclaimed the first Thursday in August (6th) 1863 a day of thanksgiving for recent victories. The designation of the first Thursday, 4 August 1864, as a day of humiliation and prayer appears to be a repetition of the 1863 proclamation. [Long, p.395]

I have not been to the regiment yet but I think I will go down there to-morrow as some of the boys in the regiment is owing me some money. I think they were paid yesterday.

I look at your picture and Charlie's verry often but I think you are good enough looking to make a better picture than the one you sent and when I get home I will have you try it over again and see if there cannot be an improvement made. I like to see women appear well, especially one who I have as mutch regard for as yourself, both in manners and dress. By manners I do not mean good or bad behavior but a free and easy and an attractive appearance. It is not the one that has the finest apparel that looks the best but one that has her clothes properly made, fited, and kept neat. A person should always think him or herself as good as anybody else and no better than other good folks and be free to act when the motives are good.

A person should study their own nature and cultivate deficiencies and subdue excesses of the mind wherever they are found to occur. Improve language as well in conversation as in writing. Study the force of words and learn to use them in their propper place. The mind should be more occupied in high intellecual thoughts, problems, and suggestions than in neighborhood frivolities in which there is but little knowledge to be gained. I do not write this as a censure but only to attract your notice. If it had not been for Silvie, I should have made arrangements to have you gone to school the most of the time I was in the army.

Well, I have filled this sheet so I must close. I remain as usual, verry truly your obedient husband,

T. J. Davis

No. 4, Pioneer Corps 3rd Division, 15 Army Corps
Cartersville, Georgia, Aug. 15th, 1864

Dear Wife,

I sit down this morning to write you a short letter to let you know that I am as well as usual hoping this may find you well. I have not received a letter from you since I wrote before. The last one received from you was dated July 26 & 27th but I think I will get another one today or tomorrow.

The weather has been quite warm for three or four days which makes the boys feel quite lazy so far as working is concerned. We still continue to have showers every day or two.

I went down to the regiment last Wednesday and came back on Friday. The boys are all well except Sam Moore and George Rogers. George is crippled up with the rheumatism but he is not in the hospital. The company does not seem to be verry proud of their recruits so far as the Rogers boys are concerned.[9] Jim Kingston is nursing in the hospital at Rome. He wants to come back to the company. Alvin Caulkins is well and hearty. He is considerable larger than I am. He weighs about 170 lbs. Robt. McMichael is in good health and seems to be enjoying well in the dignity of Captain. This is, however, a mutch healthier country than Mississippi or Louisiana for our Division is in mutch better health now than they were a year ago.

I received a letter from Louisa Wagner dated July 29th. She did not write mutch news, only the folks were as well as usual.

We had a little excitement here yesterday. There was 1500 Rebel Cavalry reported about 18 miles from here who intended to try and take this place and tear up the railroad. We had our cartrage boxes filled up with the needful and was ready for them but they did not come. We have a force [of] cavalry now out in persuit of them. All is again quiet this morning.

Affairs at the front remain about the same as when I last wrote you. Fighting and skirmishing is going on every day to a greater or less extent. I will not write a long letter today. I will write again when I receive a letter from you. So be a good girl and don't cry and I will bring you some candy. Please to write soon. I remain ever yours.

T. Jefferson Davis

No. 5, Pioneer Corps, 3rd Division, 15th Army Corps
Cartersville, Georgia, Aug. 22nd, 1864

Dear Wife,

I sit down this morning to write you a few lines by way of informing you that I am in my usual health and spirits. This is the third letter I have written to you since I received one. The last one was dated the 27th of last month but the reason I have not received any was that the Rebel raiders in Sherman's rear have attacked the railroad in several places and stoped the runing of trains for several days. The Rebs did no great deal of damage except that they took two companies of the 17th Iowa prisoners. But they paroled them and let them go after taking their arms from them. We expected an attack at this place but they did not come.[10]

---

9. At this stage in the Civil War, many recruits who were sent forward to join veteran regiments were reluctant replacements. Some had been drafted, others had joined as substitutes for drafted men, and still others had joined primarily for substantial bounty money being offered by Federal, state, and local authorities. [Wiley, p.343–344]

10. General Joe Wheeler's fast-moving force of 4,000 Confederate cavalry tried to disrupt Federal rail communications between Chattanooga and Atlanta in an August 1864 raid. The surrender of sixty-five men from the 17th Iowa Infantry at a railroad blockhouse between Tipton and Dalton, Georgia, occurred on 15 August. [OR I-38-3; p.276–277]

The cars have resumed their regular trips but as yet I get no mail. I felt certain I would get a letter from you last night and was very mutch disappointed when I found there was none for me. But I think I will get one tonight for as a general thing when I wait several days to get a letter from you before I write and then give it up and write anyway, I then generally get a letter from you the next mail.

The weather is not so warm as when I wrote to before. We had a heavy rain yesterday and last night and today the atmosphere is quite pleasent.

Ed Rogers received a letter from Joe Johnston a few days ago. He was with his regiment at Petersburg and was well. He wrote rather a desponding letter. He thinks he has been misused.

We have had but little war news for several days but we learn that Farrigut's forces used up the most of the Rebel fleet at Mobile and that our forces are now in possesion of some of the Rebel forts near the city. Affairs around Atlanta remain about the same as when I last wrote. More heavy fighting has been going on. Two trains of Rebel prisoners passed here yesteday going north. I will not write mutch today. I will write more when I receive a letter from you. I remain ever your affectionate husband and admirer,

T. J. Davis

No. 6, Pioneer Corps, 3rd Division, 15th Army Corps
Cartersville, Georgia, Sunday, Aug 28th, 1864

Dear Wife,

I sit down this pleasent Sabbath day to pen you a few lines to inform you that I have not forgotten you. Though I begin to feel as though I was forgotten by you or else that you are sick and not able to write. The last letter I received from you was dated July 26th and that was received over three weeks ago. Ed Rogers has not received any letter from home since I have. So I don't get any word from you at all. I have not been so long without a letter from you since I been in the service where the mail comes so regular. The mail comes in every day and every day for over two weeks I have anxiously listened for my name as the list of letters was called off, only to be disappointed when they were all given out to find there was none for me. I wrote to you last Monday and told you that I had been looking for a letter from you so long that I expected to get a letter from you next mail but another week has passed and no letter yet. So I can now assure you that I begin to feel quite uneasy about you. But I hope I may soon receive a letter from you which will relieve my anxiety.

I got my picture taken a few days ago but I will not send it until I get another letter from you.

Part of the 18th went up to Cleveland, Tennessee, several days ago and have not returned yet. They will probably be back in a few days. My company [C] went with them.

I will not write much today but will write again as soon as I get a letter from you. This leaves me in tolerable good health and I hope this may find you well. I remain as ever your husband,

T. J. Davis

No. 7, Pioneer Corps, 3rd Division, 15th Army Corps
Cartersville Georgia, September 3rd, 1864

Dear Wife,

I sit down this evening to write a few lines to inform you that I am in as good health as usual and hoping this may find you well. I have waited another week but I have received no letter from you yet, though I have looked anxiously for one every mail. But, however, there has been an interruption on the railroad between here and Nashville and we have not had any mail for three days and It is uncertain when the cars will come through. But it seems that I certainly will get a letter the next mail. I will not send this out until tomorrow and if I get anything in the mail line before this goes out I will mention it before I send this.

The 18th has not returned yet and I understand they are on the railroad between Chattanooga and Nashville. The Rebels are yet prowling along the railroad in considerable numbers trying to interrupt our communications in Sherman's rear.

We had quite a heavy shower of rain last night and another one today and the weather is not so warm. I think our hot season is about over for this year.

We had a telegraphic dispatch from the front this morning stating that our forces took possession of Atlanta at ten o'clock yesterday morning but the dispatch gave no peticulars. But that mutch is verry good without any peticulars. I wrote to you once before that Atlanta was reported taken but this time I am quite certain that Atlanta is ours.[11]

Sunday, September 4th

Well Lucinda, I will finish my letter. The mail train came in this morning and I received a letter from you after waiting so long. It was

---

11. Sherman took possession of Atlanta on 2 September 1864 after General John B. Hood's Confederate army was forced to evacuate the city on the night of 1 September. [Long, p. 564–565]

dated August 18th, No 6. I think the last one I received before was No 3 so there must be some yet behind as the last one I received before was dated July 26th. I had begun to feel quite uneasy and you don't know how glad I was to receive another letter from you and to hear that you was well. You say you weigh 136. Well, that will do verry well and perhaps you feel better than you would if you was more fleshy. I was on the scales a few days ago and weighed 146 so I yet have the advantage of you ten pounds.

I also received a letter from Elisabeth & Mother this morning. They were in moderate health. They had just received a letter from Brother Will near Atlanta. He was slightly wounded in the shoulder on the 27th of July but was still doing duty.

I will send you my picture in this letter so you can see how hansom I am growing.

You said that I wrote as though we were coming home soon. I only wrote for you not to send your picture for fear that we might go home before it came. I expected we would go soon after Atlanta was taken but I hear that our regiment has taken the place of some 100-day men whose time are out.[12] So it is hard to tell when we will get off. My paper is out and I must close. Expecting soon to hear from you again, I ever remain yours truly,

Thos. J Davis

No 8, Pioneer Corps, 3rd Division, 15th Army Corps.
Cartersville, Georgia, September 10th, 1864

Dear Wife,

I again endeavor to write you a short letter to inform you that I am as well as usual truly hoping this may find you well. I have received nothing later from you since I last wrote you. I received one of your back letters this week dated Aug 3rd. It had passed on to the front and had been laying at Marietta for sometime. We have had no through-mail from the North since I wrote you before. The Rebel cavalry have been interrupting the railroad and I understand that there will be no through mail for several days to come.

---

12. Terms of enlistment varied widely in the Federal army during the Civil War. Early war volunteers enlisted for ninety days. After the battle of First Manassas (Bull Run), terms increased to one-, two-, or three-year tours of duty. Anticipating hard-campaigning in the spring of 1864, Lt. General U. S. Grant accepted an initial offer of 100,000 one hundred-day recruits from a group of Northern governors saying, "As a rule I would oppose receiving men for a short term but if 100,000 men can be raised in the time proposed . . . they might come at such a crisis as to be of vast importance." [OR, III-4- p. 239]

I received a letter this week from D. Ingersoll's wife dated the 9th of August. She said the folks were all well. She said that Charlie was going to school. One of her brothers was wounded near Atlanta not long since one of my old neighbor boys in the same company was killed.

The great guerrilla raider John Morgan was killed in Greenville, Tennessee, about ten days ago so that he will trouble our borders no more.[13]

There has been over a thousand Rebel prisoners passed here for Chattanooga this week. They were taken at Jonesboro, 20 miles south of Atlanta. There are several thousand more at Atlanta yet to be sent north.

As the railroad has been interrupted, perhaps you will not receive letters verry regularly from me but I will continue to write even if I don't get letters from you.

The regiment has not yet returned and I don't know where it is but I think they are after Wheeler up in Tennessee someplace. Part of Sherman's army has returned to Atlanta and part of them are still chaseing Old Hood.[14]

I hear but little of our regiment being furloughed. The way things look now we may be held until our old time is out, then they will be obliged to let us go home. I have heard so mutch talk of furlough that I am almost sick of hearing it and I don't think as mutch of going home as I did last spring although I would like first rate to go. You don't know how anxious I am to see my sis and babies for I think of you every day and feel as though I shall surely see you 'ere long and I endeavour to make the day pass as lightly as possible. Silvie by this time must be large enough to be quite a plaything. Sometimes I try to immagin how she looks and fancy I see her sticking the broom handle in the stove, upsetting the wash basin on herself, putting sticks in the churn, and trying to put the cat into the slop pail and other such mischevious sports.

I supose they have been drafting in Wisconsin before this time but we have had no Northern papers for nearly two weeks and I feel lost without the news and I hope the mail will soon become regular again.

---

13. Confederate cavalryman, General John Hunt Morgan, was surprised and killed by Federal troops in Greenville, Tennessee, on the morning of 4 September 1864. [Long, p. 566]

14. General Joe Wheeler's Confederate cavalry had raided deep into Tennessee after the early August attacks near Dalton, Georgia. Though the raid accomplished little, Federal troops were kept busy chasing the elusive horsemen. General John B. Hood's Confederate Army of Tennessee withdrew twenty-four miles to Palmetto, Georgia, after evacuating Atlanta. Hood lingered on Sherman's flank, resting his 40,000 men and awaiting a chance to strike Sherman's supply line at some vulnerable point. [Dyer, John P., From Shiloh to San Juan. Baton Rouge, Louisiana State University Press, 1989, p.152–156]

We have had considerable rain in this month and the weather is gradually becoming cooler and the approaching fall season is becoming apparent. Well Lucinda, I will close for this time hoping to hear from you soon I remain as ever yours,

Jeff. T. Davis

No. 9, Pioneer Corps 3rd Division 15th Army Corps
Cartersville, Georgia, September 15th, 1864

Dear Lucinda, T

This pleasant morning I take up my quill to write you a short letter in answer to two letters that I received this week, one was dated August 25 and the other September 1st. Your letters begin to come through more regularly again and I hope the mail may not be interrupted again this fall. When you don't get letters from me you may be sure that the fault is in the mail and not in me for I everage more than a letter a week but I supose you have not received my letters regularly of late on account of Wheeler's raid in our rear.

All military arrangements are quiet in front. There will probably be no fighting in front for sometime to come. The army will probably be reorganized for the fall campaign. The Regiment has not returned yet but I think it will be back here in a few days. They are near Winchester, Tennessee. Ed Rogers is in the Pioneer Corps with me. I see him every day. He don't get many letters from Elias.

You say the Copperheads are making boasts and threats what they mean to do. I know there is considerable excitement in the North in reference to political matters but I apprehend no serious war in the North. I think those sneaking peace men and Copperheads are too cowardly to fight for anything. They may talk saucy to a woman or a verry old man or a small boy but they won't fight. For if they were brave enough to fight at all they would fight for an honorable cause. Peaceism, in my opinion, is only a pretence for an excuse to stay at home. I am but little afraid of Copperheads. There is but verry few soldiers that I have talked with say they are going to support "Little Mc". They are most all going for Old Abe & Andy: The Railsplitter and Tailor.[15]

I have not received many letters lately. I don't write as mutch as I used to. Susan Wilson has discontinued writing to me so I don't write any more to her.

---

15. The 1864 presidential campaign pitted the incumbent Lincoln ("The Railsplitter") and Tennessee unionist war governor, Andrew Johnson ("The Little Tailor"), against the ticket of George B. McClellan ("Little Mac") and George H. Pendleton, a vehement Ohio peace Democrat. [Long, p. 594]

Our regiment will probably go home between now and Christmas but they have no orders yet so I hardly think anything more about it, only as somebody mentions. I have no more news to write today so goodbye from your boy,

T. J. Davis

No. 10, Pioneer Corps 3rd Division, 15th Army Corps
Cartersville, Georgia, September 21st, 1864

Dear Lucinda,

I take my pen this morning to write you a short letter to inform you that I am in my usual health and in good spirits and I hope this may find you well. I have not received a letter from you since I wrote last but I am look-ing for one every mail. We are still at Cartersville and nothing of note has transpired since I wrote.

The regiment has not returned from Tennessee yet but it will probably be back here in a few days. We are now having a rainstorm and this morn-ing it is raining verry leisurely as if it had commenced for a week's work. As the campaign of Atlanta is over this army will now rest and recruit for the fall campaign and when our regiment gets back here from Tennessee I think it will be sent home on furlough, but you must not look for us too soon. But I hope it will not be verry long.

Perhaps we will be at home in time for the election in November. I think I will give Ole Dabe another lift this fall. As the war commenced under his administration, I want to see it end before Old Abe leaves the White House and I think the prospect for Lincoln's reelection looks verry flattering.

Oh, I had like to forgot to tell you I was at a wedding yesterday. Well, I was and a gay affair it was. The bridegroom was a member of the 16th Missouri Regiment whose term of service has just expired and the bride is a native, backwoods Georgian of the lowest order. Neither of them has sense enough to enjoy good health and I really pitty the boy to think he is making such an ass of himself as to carry such a thing home with him for a wife after soldiering three years in such a God-forsaken country as this when there is plenty of nice girls at home where he might have chosen one that would have been a credit to him, though I don't think a man that will marry the refuse trash in this country is worthy of a good woman at home.

But I find that the girls in the North have great cympathy and feelings of more than friendship for the soldiers. Many a girl's ambition is to be-come a soldier's wife and I am sorry to say that manny girls have mis-placed confidence in soldiers who lead a profligate life of debauchery in the army who are not worthy of being husbands of decent women. But again I find that men who are men of principal and integrity who have enough brains and self-respect to controll their brutal animal passions will act just as decent here as they will at home. If a person has a disposition to act mean, low, and degrading they are sure to do so as soon as an oppertunity presents itself that will conceal their shame from their friends. A few become so bold and reckless that they care nothing for their own character or their friends' feelings and will even boast of what they should be ashamed to disclose.

Well, as my paper is used up I will close. So goodbye. I remain ever yours,

Thos. J. Davis

No. 11, Pioneer Corps, 3rd Division, 15th Army Corps
Cartersville, Georgia, Sunday, September 25th, 1864 Dear Wife,

I again assume the privelige this fine Sunday morning of writing you a short letter in answer to yours of the 7th inst. which I received last night. Your letter finds me in as good health as usual as I hope this in turn may find you. We have had verry wet weather for over a week but the clouds have cleared away and the air is quite cool so that the fall weather is verry appearant.

Our regiment came back last Wednesday. I saw the Company as they passed here on their way to Alatoona. The boys were all well but they had been marching through middle and west Tennessee for a month and they looked quite rough and dirty. The Regiment will probably be paid this coming week and they will probabily start home next week or at least that seems to be the calculation now. I think we will be at home about the 15th of October.

The 1st Wisconsin Cavalry came here from the front on the 12th of August. I am acquainted with several men in it and have been to the regiment several times and I could have seen your uncle's son if I had known he was there. I saw the boys get on the train when they went home.

All seems quiet in this department at present. The Rebs tried hard to tare up the railroad in Sherman's rear but they did not affect [effect] mutch damage to the road. They were around us quite thick for a while but they were quite careful about attacking our forces along the road.[16]

Ed Rogers has not received a letter from Elias for more than a month. He thinks Elias is very slow about writing. I heard that Burnett died of the

---

16. Since Hood's infantry was still resting and refitting at Palmetto, Georgia, Davis was probably referring to Wheeler's earlier cavalry raids.

wound that he received at Petersburg. Some of the boys got that news in a letter from Viroqua. I have not received many letters lately but I don't write as mutch as I used to. I sent you my likeness sometime ago but I supose you had not received it when you wrote. I think I will bring you a picture before long. As I have no news of importance to write today I will close until another day. Ever remaining yours truly,

T. J. Davis

CHAPTER TEN

We Dosed Them with Blue Pills

The surrender of Atlanta to General Sherman in September 1864 marked a major turning point in the war. But the Confederate army that had been forced to yield Atlanta was not defeated. They retreated southwest of the city to regroup. On 1 October, the Southerners swung north of Atlanta and cut General Sherman's railroad supply line at several points. Moving north at a rapid pace, Confederate infantry and cavalry posed a real threat to Federal troops along the rail line.

As a division of 2,000 Confederates approached the supply depot at Allatoona on the night of 4 October, 150 men of the 18th Wisconsin stood in their way with 1,800 Federal comrades. General Samuel French's Confederates had a slight advantage in numbers, superior artillery, and maneuverability. General John Corse's Federals held the high ground, were well entrenched, and expected reinforcements within twenty-four hours.

Southern skirmishers moved on Allatoona in the early morning hours of 5 October and drove pickets from the 18th Wisconsin into the safety of the post. As the sun rose, Confederate artillery blanketed the Union troops holding twin hilltop forts. The forts were within supporting distance of each other but were separated by a narrow 150-foot-deep gorge that allowed for the railroad's passage through the hills. Only a footbridge connected the two commands. On the west side of the gorge were four artillery pieces and most of the Union troops, including four companies of the 18th Wisconsin, to defend against a likely attack up that slope. Three companies of Badgers held the fort to the east along with other infantry regiments and a two-gun section of artillery.

As the Confederate artillery fire lifted, Southern troops charged from surrounding cover and up the slopes of both hills. The attack on the east fort was driven back before it reached the entrenchments. To strengthen that fort, the four companies of the 18th Wisconsin in the west fort were sent to the east side as reinforcements. Attacks on the west fort continued

281

and were much heavier. The Confederates came close to breaking the Union defense throughout a morning of bitter attacks and counterattacks. Shortly after midday, however, timely Union artillery fire disrupted yet another Confederate assault and a surprise counterattack by desperate Federal troops drove the Southerners from the slope and into full retreat.

Among the casualties at the Battle of Allatoona were two killed and twelve wounded from the 18th Wisconsin. However, on the evening of the battle it was found that a battalion of eighty men from the 18th Wisconsin's companies E, F, and I had been captured defending a railroad blockhouse two miles from Allatoona. The losses at Allatoona reduced the 18th Wisconsin's strength to less than one hundred men, including twenty men on detached service in the Pioneer Corps.

> No. 12, Pioneer Corps, 3rd Division, 15th Army Corps
> Cartersville, Ga., Oct 4th 1864

Dear Wife,

I again attempt to to write you a short letter to inform you that I am in as good health as usual truly hoping that this may find you well. I have received no letter from you since I last wrote. Oh, yes I did, too. I received one dated August 10th containing Mr Keyes' death and also the story of Cutter the Spy which is a verry good story.

Well Lucinday, we are still at Cartersville and it is dificult to say how long we will remain here. In my last letter I wrote you that we expected soon to go home on furlough but Rebels are again interrupting the railroads. So that it may be mutch longer now before we start than I expected. It is a verry disagreeable thing to be kept in such suspense expecting to go every few weeks and then to be disappointed every time. If I knew we was not going I would not trouble my head about it. I hope now that they will not let us go until my old time is out and then they will have good time getting me back here again. Not that I wish to do anything wrong but I don't mutch fancy a bargain that is all on one side and myself one of the party and have nothing to say in it. You must not think that I am disspirited for I keep perfectly cool but hereafter I mean to look more after "No. One" as that is every man's business.

We have had no mail for over a week. The last letter I received from you was written September 10th. That is the latest date and perhaps it may be sometime before the mail will again become regular. When I fail to get mail regular and it is two or three weeks before I get a letter, I become more anxious to go home. But when I get letters regularly from home I feel more satisfied. I don't wish you to get uneasy about me but keep perfectly easy and I will be along home to see you after a while.

I have no news to write today. I will look for a letter from you the next mail that comes. So be a good girl. I remain your anxious husband,

T. J. Davis

P.S. Two years ago today was fought the second days battle at Corinth and the weather was mutch warmer then than it is today and the dead on the battlefield produced the worst oder I ever smelled. It turned me quite sick several times. Today is alternate sunshine and rain. It has rained nearly every day for over a week.

TJD

No. 13, Pioneer Corps, 3rd Division, 15th Army Corps
Cartersville, Georgia, Oct. 8th 1864

Dear Lucinda,

Once more I attempt to write you a few lines to let you know that I do not forget though I receive no letters from you. I have not received any letter from you since I wrote on account of the railroad being torn up. Neither do I think that you have received letters regularly from me of late.

Hood's Rebel army seems now to be broken into colums and trying to destroy the railroad in Sherman's rear. The Rebels attacked Alatoona last Wednesday, the 5th inst., with a large force when a heavy battle ensued and after about five hours heavy fighting the Rebels were defeated with heavy loss. We lost about six hundred men killed, wounded, and missing and the Rebels lost between twelve and fifteen hundred killed and wounded. We only had about two thousand men engaged and the Rebels had between six and seven thousand but our men had the advantage of breastworks and literally strewed the hillsides with the Rebel dead and wounded.[1]

I was not there during the battle but I could hear the fighting here five miles distant verry distinctly and those that were there say it was a verry hard fight for the number engaged. Luckily, the 18th did not sustain as heavy charges from the Rebels as some other regiments and consequently theirs was not so great. The 18th lost two killed and about 20 wounded. Company C. lost one man killed (John H. Singles) and five wounded (viz) Wm Loucks, Joseph Ross, Jasper N. Powell, Elijah Frasier and David Caulkins. Caulkins and Frasier were wounded very slight and are both doing duty. Caulkins had the tip of his thumb shot off and Frasier was

---

1. Fearing an approaching Federal relief column, French finally retreated with losses of 800 killed, wounded, and captured. General John Corse's Federal casualties totalled 700 men. The entire command was cited by Sherman for their bravery in defending the crucial supply center. [OR-I-39-p. 761–766]

creased with a ball across the hip. The other three are more seriously wounded but with care all will recover.

Three companies (viz) E, F,and I were stationed at a bridge 2 miles south of Alatoona and were taken prisoners. They will get their Veteran furlough in a bad shape.[2]

The Regiment will not probably start until the transportation becomes again regulated, which may be several weeks. Some of the boys think if they are not sent home soon they will not come back again as their old time is nearly out, but I don't know how it will be arranged but try and content myself as well as I can. The sergeant of my squad and myself have built us a snug little shanty out of lumber with two glass windows and fireplace and are very well prepared to stand the winter if we stay here.

I don't have mutch to do now as I am acting bugler for the Pioneer Corps and the most of my work is blowing and I would now as soon stay here until my old time is out and be mustered out if they want we should stay. They can't keep us longer than the 20th of January without sending us home anyway. Well, my paper is about out and I must quit. I remain as ever yours,

T. Jefferson Davis

For the N.W. Times
FROM THE 18TH WIS. V.V.I.[3]

Alatoona, Ga., Oct. 10th, 1864

Mr. Editor:—We had a very warm engagement at this place on the 5th inst., which resulted in another victory of our arms.

The following is a list of casualties in "C" Co.:

Killed
John H. Singles—Private

Wounded
Private John J. Ross, in leg,	slight
Wm. Loucks, in hand & breast,	"
Elijah S. Frazier, in side,	"
David Caulkins, in hand,	"
James Kingston, in mouth,	"

---

2. The three companies of the 18th Wisconsin guarding the bridge over Allatoona Creek took shelter in a blockhouse for forty hours until French's artillery set the fort afire. The smoke and flames finally forced the Badgers to surrender. [OR-I-39-p.751–752]

3. Since reenlisting as a unit, the Eighteenth was entitled to the honorary designation of "Veteran Volunteer Infantry."

Corp'l. J.N. Powell, in left shoulder, severe.

The men of "C" Co. fought well and determinedly.
Very Respectfully, your Ob't Servant, W.N. Carter 1st Lieut., 18th Wis. inf.
[NW Times, Nov. 16, 1864, p. 2]

For the N.W. Times
FROM THE 18TH R., W.V.V.I

Alatoona, Ga., Oct. 10, 1864

Mr. Powell, Esq.

Sir, In accordance to promise, I avail myself of this opportunity to write a few
lines to you to inform you of the condition and nature of the wound received by
your son Jasper, in the Right Shoulder, in the battle of Alatoona, Oct. 5th, inst.
I am happy to inform you that his wound is not a dangerous one although it will
be painful for some time; luckily for him there are no bones broken. The ball
passed through his shoulder near the joint that connects the arm to the body but
it is nothing more than a flesh wound, which I think will soon heal up. I am
sorry he was wounded but we ought to feel thankful that it is no worse than it
is. I can inform you that when he was wounded he was fighting the enemies of
our country; he was under my eye all through the battle, until the time he was
struck, which was about one hour before the battle ceased. You have reason to
feel proud of your son; he is honest, brave and kind, and loved by all his associates. I do not speak thus to flatter you, but speak what I think just and right.
He left here on the 7th for Rome, Ga., but I understand they are moving the hospital from that place farther north. If this is true, which I have no doubt is, he
will probably go to Nashville.

This was one of the hardest contested battles I have ever been engaged in.
I never saw men fight with more coolness and determination than they did
here. We had only between 1500 and 1600 men [here] all told; the rebs attacked us with 8,000 troops under command of Gen. French—they with the
intention of capturing us and our rations (which we had stored here) without
much of a fight, but they were badly fooled for we gave them a reception that
they will long feel and remember. I consider this one of the most glorious
and successful defenses of the war considering the numbers engaged. If we
had lost our rations here, Sherman's army would certainly have suffered for
the want of them. We have issued two days rations to five army corps since
that time that could not be obtained at any other place under the circumstances.

This was a bloody affair. Our loss in killed, wounded, and prisoners is
706; the enemies 2250, or nearly a man and a half for every man we had
engaged in the fight. The rebel prisoners say that they brought along 200
wagons with them to haul away our hard tack in (but they had to go away

without.) They say this was where they were to get their next supply of rations and that was one reason why they fought so hard. I am proud of the Co. I have the honor to command. They behaved well and fought like heroes. I never saw men fight harder in my life than they did. They were bound to never surrender as long as we had men to fight. I think that I can say with truth that I have not got a coward in my Co. There were six men wounded and one killed in Co. C. John H. Singles was shot through the head and died instantly.

There are some great military movements going on here, the particulars of which I presume you have seen in the papers. Hood has marched with his army northward and is threatening Rome and Kingston, but Sherman is wide awake for him. I have no fears for the result.

Excuse my long letter and answer it and let us know how the battle is going in Vernon County, for we can, with propriety, call this Presidential campaign a battle for the Union and liberty. I hope the friends of the Union in the North will stand fast to their posts and fight the enemies of our country at home with ballots while we fight them at the front with bullets. We have more to fear from our enemies in the north than we have from Southern traitors in the field. I think that if Lincoln can be re-elected to the Presidency for another term that this war will soon come to an honorable termination. Nothing would discourage the rebs more than this. They are building their hopes upon his defeat at the coming election and the success of a party that are pledged in their favor, for what is the Chicago Platform but a pledge to them that there shall be no more fighting if they are successful for they plainly tell us that the experiment of war to restore the Union is a failure and they recommend a cessation of hostilities to see if we cannot settle it some other way.

Now if they fail to restore the Union in their way, what then? Why, the war is a failure & there is no use of fighting any longer. So we have no alternative but to let them go on their own terms, which as Jeff Davis and his Cabinet plainly tell us, are the recognition of their independence. I know they try to cover up their Chicago platform with McClellan's letter of acceptance but this, in my opinion, is only a trick to get votes. I hope every friend of the soldier will stand by the President's administration and show us that you do not think that all of the blood and treasure that has been spilled and expended in this war has been a failure. Are we who have suffered almost every hardship and privation for the last four years for the preservation of our glorious Union, to have the lie put to us, and say that after all the glorious victories that we have gained, that it is all a failure? The platform is an insult to the brave soldiers in the field. Now, when our arms are victorious, when we are pressing the enemy to the wall, let us hold fast our grip and the contest will soon be ended, and the soldiers who have stood the heat of battle will be permitted to return to their homes with honor to themselves and friends.

Yours Truly, R. S. McMichael Capt. of Co. C., 18th Wis. Inf't. [NW Times, November 23, 1864, p. 1]

For the N. W.Times
FROM THE 18TH REGIMENT

Alatoona, Georgia, Oct. 12th, 1864

Mr. Editor:
   Dear Sir, allow me the privilege of addressing you a few lines in regard
to our Regiment. Since my last there were seven companies of our Regiment
(with the exception of a few that were left on picket duty) started after Old
Wheeler. On the 22nd of August they went up to East Tennessee and then
to Middle Tennessee; they say that they had a good time; they were gone till
the 22nd of September before they returned back to Alatoona. The boys
looked well and felt well. I was one of the lucky ones to be left behind —
it was a very lonesome time while the boys were gone & time passed off
slow.
   Our Regiment is in pretty good health; there are a few cases of the chills; also
a few wounded which were wounded at this place on the 5th of this month —
we had one of the biggest fights here that was ever on record for the amount of
men engaged. They commenced firing on our pickets about 1 o'clock at night
an kept up a steady firing on the skirmish line till they drove in our skirmishers and pickets. We were drove back into our works at ½ past 3 o'clock a.m. and
then the rebs charged on us; but we held them in check until ½ past 3 o'clock
[p.m.] when they broke and run in every direction. They came here for the express purpose of taking our rations and the place. It would have been a good
[thing for them] if they had succeeded in taking what supplies we had here for
what we had on hand would have lasted them a long time; but in place of our
hard tack, we dosed them with Blue Pills[4] and they operated to a charm on
them.
   Our loss in killed, wounded, and missing was 709 — their loss was (as near
as we can ascertain) ??00. Our Regiment did not loose very many in killed nor
were there but a few wounded; however, three of our Companies were unfortunate enough to be taken prisoners, to wit:
   Companies E, F, and I, they were guarding a bridge which crossed the Alatoona Creek two miles from where we are stationed. The rebs left one piece of
artillery and two regiments there to work on them while they were fighting us
here. After we gave them a darned good whipping here they went back to the
bridge and opened on us with the balance of their artillery. [They], however,
smoked them out so they were obliged to surrender. They held their position
till nearly sundown before they surrendered. The three companies lost 1 killed
and two wounded — our company lost 1 killed and 1 wounded — the killed was
John H. Singles, a brave and good soldier and one that will not be missed only

---

   4. "Blue Pills" was slang for bullets but was also a jesting reference to the blue
pills of mercury and chalk that were so commonly prescribed to soldiers by army
doctors. [Wiley, p. 137]

by his Company, but by the Regiment. He had nearly served his three years and reenlisted as a Veteran to help close this rebellion and to return home to see his friends, but failed to obtain his furlough as the Regiment has never been sent home on a furlough. The wounded were Jasper N. Powell, through the shoulder—John J. Ross, in the leg—Wm. Loucks, through the hand—E. Frazier, in the side slightly. The amount engaged on our side was only about 1500 and the rebs was between 8 and 10,000. They had 12 pieces of artillery and we had only 6. Old Hood is making his was back to Tennessee and Sherman is following him—he has a force on each side of Hood and one in the rear of him, driving him up—he has a trap fixed for him at some place or other and I hope that it will catch him and his whole army.

Yours Respectfully,

Harrison Sayre Co. C, 18th Reg't. Wis. Vet. Vol. Inf'y [NW Times, November 16, 1864, p. 1]

No. 14, Pioneer Corps, 3rd Division, 15th Army Corps
Cartersville, Georgia, October 13th, 1864

Dear Wife,

I sit down this morning to write you a few lines in answer to your letter No. 12 dated Sept 25 & 28 which I received last night and I was verry glad to hear from you and to hear that you was well for I had not received a letter from you for two or three weeks. I think there is yet two or three of your letters that are yet behind. Last night we received the first mail we have had for over two weeks the railroad is getting pretty well repaired again.

From appearence of present movements we will soon evacuate this road from Atlanta to Dalton. Our troops have been going back past here towards Chattanooga ever since day before yesterday morning and they are still going by, yet. The 4th, 23rd, 14th, 16th, and 17th Army Corps have passed and the 15th Corps will pass today. We are under orders to be ready to march at any moment so we will probably follow up soon. The reason of such a move as near as I can learn is that Richmond is taken and that Lee is marching part of his Richmond force into East Tennessee with the intention of geting into our rear and cut off our army.[5] But it they come in about Chattanooga or Knoxville they will get waked up good and strong. The 20th Army Corps is still back at Atlanta. If Sherman does evacuate the railroad, the 20th Corps will probably burn Atlanta and follow up in a few days and destroy the railroad

---

5. Davis may have remembered that a year earlier, Longstreet's Corps from Lee's Army of Northern Virginia had tried to take Knoxville, Tennessee, by siege. There was no such repetition of that strategy in 1864.

as they come. We will, however, [know] more about the movements in a few days.[6]

We are now having very pleasent weather. We had a light frost day before yesterday morning and it is about cool enough for pleasent marching. We came to this place three months ago yesterday and I have got tired enough of it now to go someplace else. All I regret is that we have to leave our comfortable little house. But then we can build another where we stop again.

Ed Rogers has not got verry stout yet and he has not yet received any letter from Elias. He thinks Elias is verry slow about writing.

I don't hear any more talk of the regiment going home soon and it will soon be too cold for us to go so far north after being south so long and many of the boys seem verry indifferent about going home now. For all having orders to be ready to march we may not leave here for a long time yet. So I never prepare to go until we have orders to pack knapsacks. If I had thought we would not went home before this time, I should like to had you sent me your picture. But as we was looking to go soon I was afraid that I would not get it I am glad that you got mine that I sent you.

After the drafted men leaves, I think the town of Harmony [Wisconsin] will be pretty well thinned of men.

Well Lucinda, I will close for this time and write a few lines to Marcia. Keep in good spirits and don't get discouraged and do the best for yourself that you can. Perhaps there is better times coming. Write often. I remain ever faithfully your,

T. J.Davis

No. 16, Pioneer Corps, 3rd Division, 15th Army Corps
Cartersville, Georgia, October 28th, 1864

Dear Wife,

I sit down this afternoon to write you in answer to a letter I received from you yesterday dated 12th Inst and was glad to hear that you was mending and I hope this may find you entirely well. My health is tolerable good at present and time passes off quite lively. I have got quite a comfortable shanty built and feel at home as long as we remain here though there is talk of our leaving here in a week or ten days. But we may remain here sometime, yet. The boys at the regiment are all well or was yesterday. The weather begins to be cool though we have had but verry little frost yet this fall.

---

6. Davis' view of the situation regarding Atlanta's future was remarkably accurate. One month later, on 15 November, Sherman did, indeed, leave the safety of the railroad supply line, burned Atlanta, and started his March To the Sea. [Long, p. 597]

The railroad, I believe, is again repaired between Atlanta and Chattanooga and I supose our mail matter will be received with more regularity.

Ed Rogers has got the yellow jaunders [jaundice] but he is doing verry [well]. They will probably not last him long.

Refugees mostly women and children continue to go North on the cars. Some of them are pittiable looking objects being destitute of nearly everything. These southern women as a general thing are not very attractive to northern men. They are mostly long-necked, thin-faced, sharp-featured and discontented looking beings. From their appearance they don't look verry amorous but many have given themselves up to prostitution and will hang around our military post among the soldiers when they are permitted to do so.

The most of the Southern women chew tobacco and dip snuff, as they call it. But you will ask me what dipping snuff means. Well, I will tell you. They take a piece of hickory wood or dry hickory bark and whittle it about the size of a pipe stem and 4 or 5 inches long. They then bruise one end which they usually do by chewing it, thus making a kind of brush or swab. This they wet in their mouth and then opening their snuff box dip it into the snuff when quite a little bunch of the dry snuff will adhere to the wet stick. They then put it into their mouth and with the bruised stick they will rub their gums and teeth and give their mouth a general moping, occasionally dipping the stick back into the snuff until the mouth becomes full of snuff and slobbers. They then commence spitting and a goose in the summertime makes a decent appearance in comparison. That is what they call diping snuff and it is the most disgusting habit I ever saw.

I will send you a ring that I made and I wish you to tell me what fingers it will fit the best. You must excuse a half-sheet today as I wrote you a long letter last week. I will write again before long and tell you if anything new turns up. Write often. I remain as yours &c.

Thos. J Davis

(No. 17), Pioneer Corps 3rd Div 15th Army Corps
Cartersville, Ga, November 3rd, 1864

Dear Lucinda,

I sit down this rainy morning to write you an epistle in answer to your letter dated October 19th. I was glad to learn that you was well. My health is as good as usual. It has rained considerable the past two days and the wind blows raw and disagreeably cool.

Affairs at Cartersville remain about the same as when I last wrote you. We have been expecting to march for a week or two but we seem no nearer marching now than a week ago. Harrison Sayers was here from the regiment yesterday evening. He said the boys were all well. The regiment expects to be paid soon and it is said by some of the officers that the regiment will go home sometime this month but I don't want to go now until my old time is out and then be discharged for after keeping me this long without a furlough, I cannot see how by any legal right I can be held as a Veteran. My old muster would hold me until the 19th of January but my three years from enlistment expires on the 19th of this month and we was promised 30 days furlough inside the state before the expiration of our term of enlistment. Now I am willing to stay until the 19th of January and I am not willing to stay any longer. As it is I am resting perfectly easy about it and waiting to see what they intend trying to do with us.

I am sitting before the fire in my shanty this morning while I write and if you was here with me I would feel almost at home. Yet I do not wish you to be here for this is no fit place for a woman. But as for myself, I get along verry well.

You wrote that Silvie got hold of my picture and used it pretty rough. I suppose she wanted to see her Old Ba's likeness as she had not seen him for a long time and it seems hard for her to be spanked for that. She will soon be old enough to know how to take better care of a likeness and then I will give her another one to keep.

Wouldn't you like to see me cooking and keeping house if you would? Just call in some day but I am afraid you would not be much captivated with my neatness as a housekeeper. You might find a dirty shirt under the bed and probably ashes scattered over the hearth, although I keep a broom. You would see two guns hanging up overhead and our cartrage boxes, haversacks, and canteens, and a bugle hanging against the wall. I do some of my own cooking, that is, such articles as I get hold of that we do not draw from the commissary. Persimmons and pumpkins are the staple fruit of the season since blackberries and apples and peaches have disappeared, though we occasionally get some sweet potatoes and fresh pork.

Ed Rogers is still getting better. He went down to the regiment night before last and came back yesterday.

In my last letter I sent you a ring which I supose you will get if it does not get broken on the way. As there is no news to write from here I will close for this time. Hoping to hear from you again soon, I remain as ever your Soldier Boy,

T. J.Davis

CHAPTER ELEVEN

The News Is Glorious
and the Future Is Bright

With the Atlanta Campaign concluded and the Confederate Army in Georgia in retreat again, the 18th Wisconsin was finally sent home on veteran furlough. All reenlisted officers and men were allowed thirty days leave. Most of the "Tigers" departed Georgia on 28 November 1864. Nonveterans and new recruits were assigned to the 93rd Illinois Infantry Regiment and participated in General William T. Sherman's March to the Sea and the subsequent Carolinas Campaign.

The "Tigers" spent the holiday season with their families and friends, then rendevouzed at Camp Washburn at Milwaukee. By 5 January enough of the 18th Wisconsin veterans were present that the regiment departed by train for Chicago. After a one-day layover in Chicago the unit traveled through Indianapolis and Louisville to Nashville where they arrived on 11 January. There the Badgers were loaded onto the paddleboat "Nightingale" and were sent back north. From the Cumberland River they steamed up the Ohio River to Pittsburgh, where the Eighteenth disembarked on 29 January. By train, the men were sent from Pittsburgh to Baltimore and then on to Annapolis where the men boarded the steamer "New York" on 6 February. Four days later, the 18th Wisconsin landed at Beaufort, North Carolina, and boarded a train to New Bern where they established a camp.

On 4 March, assigned to a brigade in General Jacob D. Cox's Provisional Corps, the "Badax Tigers" joined a column pushing westward into North Carolina. The Federals repaired the railroad track as they marched. Skirmishing, and then fighting, broke out on 8 March as Confederates attempted to keep Cox's Corps from uniting with Sherman's army coming up from the southern part of the state. The three-day battle of Kinston or Wise's Fork failed to stop the Federals and the Confederates finally retreated toward Goldsboro. The 18th Wisconsin suffered no casualties in the fighting.

Cox's men entered Goldsboro on 21 March 1865 as Sherman's army was fighting the battle of Bentonville a few miles to the southwest. Sherman's divisions prevailed over the smaller Confederate force, which retreated from Bentonville on the night of 21 March. Sherman and Cox's command, now led by General John M. Schofield, united on 23 March at Goldsboro. The 18th Wisconsin rejoined their comrades in the 1st Brigade—3rd Division—15th Corps after an absence of nearly four months.

Sherman's army, rested and resupplied, departed Goldsboro on 10 April 1865 for Raleigh. Southern cavalry scouts fell back before the advancing Union troops, who occupied the North Carolina capitol on 13 April with little resistance.

As the Eighteenth entered Raleigh, they received news of General Robert E. Lee's surrender to General Ulysses S. Grant in Virginia. Within days, rumors of Confederate capitulation in North Carolina were fired by reports that flag-of-truce couriers had been seen carrying messages between Sherman and Confederate General Joseph E. Johnston. On 18 April, a preliminary agreement was signed between the generals, effectively ending the war for the boys of the 18th Wisconsin Infantry.

Once the surrender agreement was signed at nearby Durham, orders were received that the division in which the "Tigers" had been serving since Vicksburg was to be broken up. According to the 4th Minnesota boys who marched alongside the Eighteenth, "General [John] Smith, with his staff officers following, rode along our front uncovered, hat in hand, saying: 'God bless you all!'" Two days later, on 28 April, spirits were lifted when General John Logan, 15th Corps commander, was serenaded by a large group of soldiers at his tent. Logan stepped out with a smile and told the gathering that within forty-eight hours, many of them would be marching homeward. The crowd went wild. Rifles were fired into the air, canteens were filled with powder and exploded, and signal rockets were sent skyward in celebration. Except that the men were eight months behind in receiving their pay, they were a happy army.[1]

Perhaps because T. J. Davis had just returned from a veteran furlough, his letters from January 1865 and onward reflect less concern about home issues and include more descriptive passages about his return to the seat of war. The rail and river journey from Chicago to Nashville to New Bern was the trip of a lifetime for many of the "Tigers" and Davis logged every phase in his letters. Once he had arrived in North Carolina, he assured Lucinda of his safety and of his intention to return to the Pioneer Corps.

Unique among the letters during this period was a poem that Davis composed for Lucinda, "In Camp Alone Today." But although Davis expressed his loneliness with some eloquence, he also admitted to Lucinda

---

1. Brown, p. 409

several letters later that he had not enjoyed his furlough as much as he had hoped he would. The prospect of returning to the army had left him unsettled throughout his stay at home. Clearly Davis longed for an end to his service and a return to the peace and quiet of civilian life.

The end came quickly as Davis and his comrades learned in mid-April 1865. One week after Robert E. Lee surrendered to Ulysses S. Grant, the Confederate army in North Carolina asked for terms. Davis' reaction was candid : "Much more has been accomplished than I had reason to hope for this early three months ago." Celebrations and homecoming plans were cut short when news of President Lincoln's assassination reached the Federal troops but, interestingly, Davis spends little time mourning the slain President. Surrender activities were moving so swiftly that even so tragic an event as Lincoln's death could not keep the Davis and his comrades from anticipating the end of hostilities and a return to their loved ones.

The 18th

is home on furlough for 30 days. Capt. Robert S. McMichael and Lieut. Carter, and 16 men of Co. C have arrived at home and three wounded men belonging to the company, not veterans.

Capt. McMichael made us a call on Monday. He is in excellent health and says the company are all well.

We are glad for ourselves and for the people of the county to welcome back on their veteran furlough the war worn veterans of the 18th Wis. Vols. and long will we remember and cheer the gallant men who were victorious on the bloody field of Allatoona. [NW Times, November 30, 1864, p. 2]

Oyster Supper

Capt. R.S. McMichael, Co. C., 18th Wis. Vols, who, with the veterans of his company have been enjoying a furlough at home, gave a superb oyster supper to his officers and men and invited guests last Monday evening.

The supper was given at the North Star and gotten up in the best style. The oysters were well cooked and the accompaniments all right and well served.

These brave men of the 18th were conspicuous among the brave and gallant defenders of Allatoona only a few weeks ago and helped to win that great victory.

Capt. McMichael has been the happy recipient of a splendid sword, belt, sash and gauntlet Gloves from his men.

The dancing portion of the company retired to Lincoln's Hall and enjoyed a few figures.

Co. C. started again for Milwaukee this morning.

Swiftly may our enemies waste away before the sturdy blows of these gallant men and their companions. [NW Times, December 28, 1864, p. 3]

Milwaukee, Wisconsin, Dec 30th, 1864

Dear Wife,

I will write you a few lines this morning to inform you that I am as well as usual. I arrived here yesterday at half past one p.m.and found that only three of my company [was] here viz. Lieut. Carter and Jasper Powell and Christopher Koher. This morning Capt. McMichael, T. Decker, N. Mills, J. J. Ross and E. Crandall came in. They say that all on Badax remains about as we left it.

We are in camp at Camp Washburn and not half of the regiment here yet. I don't know when we will leave here but I think not before the first of next week. Milwaukee looks about as it did when I was here before so I have nothing new to write about the city so I shall not write but little this time. I shall look for a letter from you in a day or two for I am anxious to hear how you got through. I will write again in a few days. Yours as ever,

Thos. J. Davis

Milwaukee, Wisconsin, Jan. 2nd, 1865

Dear Wife,

Well, New Year's Day has passed and I will write you a few lines to inform you that we are still here. The regiment has not more than half come in yet but probably the most of them will be in tonight. We will probably not leave here before Wednesday. I wrote you a letter last Friday but I have not received any from you yet, though I will expect one before we leave here.

There is tolerable good sleighing here and the sporting gentry seem to be enjoying it verry well. The weather is pleasent for winter. The folks say it is not so cold as it was last winter.

Just as I finished writing the other side of this sheet, one of the boys came in from the post office with a letter from you. You may guess I was glad to get it for I was anxious to hear how you got through. Your letter was written on the 30th, the same day I wrote to you, and you will probably get my letter today. I am verry glad that you got through all right. Tell Hariet to write for I believe I wrote last.

Bill Cleary has not come yet. Probably his getting married has gone back on him. Robert McMichael said that Henry Johnson was arested before he came away. He was arrested for desertion and also for stealing. He will probably have a pretty rough time of it.

When you write again direct as before for if we are gone, the letter will follow the regiment. We will go to Nashville when we leave here.

I have no news to write today. Please write soon. I remain yours as ever,

Thos. J. Davis

P.S. Excuse a bad pen.

Soldiers' Home, Chicago, Illinois, Jan. 5th, 1865

Dear Wife,

I will write you a few lines today to let you know where we are. We left Milwaukee this morning at 8 o'clock and got here at half past twelve and we expect to Start for Nashville at ten o'clock tonight. All of our company is here except four; viz. John Kingston, Peter Campbell, Frank Harris, and Wm. Loucks and I am afraid they will have some trouble getting to the regiment. Will Cleary and Alvin Caulkins have got back. Will and Mary was married on the 10th of December. Will took him a homestead of 80 acres in Iowa and also bought a piece of timberland.

We have a hundred recruits with us that are assigned to our regiment. They are mostly substitutes and drafted men and we have to keep them under guard.[2]

The weather is quite pleasent. It is thawing considerable today.

I will send you a ring as a New Year's present but I don't know as it will fit you.

I will not write mutch today. Direct your next letter to Nashville. Give my respects to Hariet's folks and tell them to write. I remain as usual yours,

Thos. J. Davis

Indianapolis, Indiana, Sunday, Jan. 8th, 1865

Dear Wife,

I will write you a short letter this morning to let you know that I am in tolerable good health and hope this will find you well. I wrote you a letter while I was in Chicago and sent you two rings which I supose you have received before this time. We left Chicago night before last at 9 o'-clock and we arrived here yesterday morning at half past nine. We meant to have left last night for Louisville but we failed to get transportation. So we will be obliged to lay over here until tomorrow morning as there is no trains runing on Sunday.

There is more snow here than there was in Chicago but it will not last long as the weather is mild and thawing, though it is too cold to sleep comfortable in barracks. I went to a hotel last night and had a good bed to sleep in.

Jake Clear was arrested in Chicago for murdering a Norwegian by the name of Leng [Lange] who kept store on Coon Prairie. Leng was going to LaCrosse for food about the time Jake's furlough was out and, as they had

---

2. Guarding drafted men was necessary late in the war as they were known to escape from marching columns, troop trains, and riverboats. [Wiley, p.344]

formerly been old friends, Jake started to ride with him as far as LaCrosse on his return to the regiment. The Norwegian was found murdered (with his skull broken in with an axe) near the road on the prairie about 2 miles below LaCrosse. After Jake was arested, he confessed to the murder and said that he got two-hundred-and-twenty-five dollars from the murdered man but expected to have got a mutch larger amount. Jake's photograph was found near where the dead man was lying. It was one of the most brutal, reckless, and shocking murders I have known. Jake was taken back and lodged in the LaCrosse jail to await his trial. [3]

I have no more news to write today so I will close. I will write again soon. Direct your letters to Nashville. I remain your Soger Boy,

T. J. Davis

Nashville, Tennessee, January 11th, 1865

Dear Wife,

I will write you a few lines today to let you know that we are at Nashville and I am in as good health as usual. We left Indianapolis on Monday morning the 9th and got to Louisville the same evening and left Louisville the next evening at one o'clock and arrived at Nashville at 2 o'clock this morning. We probably leave here in a few days for Savannah, Georgia, via Indianapolis and New York so we will retravel part of the same road we have just come over.[4] If we get back to our old division I will probably go back to the Pioneer Corps again. I don't know how soon we will start but it will probably be several days before we get our regiment all together and ready to start.

We have not received any mail since we left Milwaukee and I don't know whether we will get any before we leave here or not, but I think we will. I wrote to you when I was at Chicago and also at Indianapolis. There was more snow at Louisville than there was in Milwaukee but there is none here and I think there is none in Louisville by this time as it was raining when we left.

---

3. The murder of Lange by Jacob A. Clear was a shock to his former comrades of Company C, 18th Wisconsin. According to one news account, Clear took $225 from the dead man and continued on his way to Chicago to join his unit. He paid off a $50 loan to Captain Robert McMichael, loaned money to several of his comrades, then went on a spending spree. He had only $1 in his possession when arrested. He was subsequently sentenced to life in prison, the first five days each year to be spent in solitary confinement. [North Western Times, 18 Jan. 1865, p.1; 10 May 1865, p.2]

4. At the time Davis was writing this letter, Sherman was still in Savannah which had fallen to his Federal army on 20 December, 1864. Sherman ordered his troops to begin their march northward through the Carolinas in 19 January 1865. [Long, p. 626–627]

I have no news to write today. I will write again before we leave here. I will look for a letter from you this evening if our mail has not been sent to Savanah. I want you to write how you like the country and also how you like to stay there and all about it. I will dry up for this time. Direct to Nashville until further notice. I remain ever yours

Thos. J. Davis.

P.S. What does No.165 Porter Sv. mean on your address?

Nashville, Tennesse, Jan. 15th, 1865

Dear Wife,

This Sabbath afternoon I sit down to write you a few lines in order to inform you that I am in as good health as usual. Hoping this may find you well. We are still in Nashville and I can't tell how long we will remain here but I don't think we will leave here for several days to come. I see from the Chattanooga paper that the detatchment of the 15th & 19th Army Corps will soon be sent to Savanah and we will undoubtedly go with them. Those of our company that we left at Chattanooga are at Louden, Tennessee, and we expect them here in a few daze. I supose they will come with the detachment above mentioned. I hope we will go to Savanah as I would mutch rather go back to our old division than to go in to any other one.

There is not mutch military in this vicinity. Things appear to be quiet in General Thomas' Department.[5]

I have not received any letter from you since I left Milwaukee. There was a large mail here for us when we came but it was sent to Savanah early the next morning before it was known at the post office that we was here. We have had two or three mails since but nary a letter for me. I have written several letters to you and I think you have received all of them before this.

The boys have all returned to the company from furlough except Frank Harris and I don't know whether he intends coming or not.

The weather is quite pleasent here today. The sun shines bright and the muddy roads are drying up. The Cumberland and Tennessee Rivers are up bank-full and steamboating is verry lively now.

I have not written any letters, only to you, since I left you but I will write some soon.

---

5. General George H. Thomas had been detached from Sherman's army after the fall of Atlanta. He was sent north to Nashville, Tennessee, to defend that region from Hood's Confederate army while Sherman made his famous march through Georgia. On 15–16 December 1864, Thomas' troops nearly destroyed Hood's besieging army in the decisive battle of Nashville. [Long, p. 610–612]

Jim Moody's wife has been arrested on suspicion of being concerned with Jake Clear in that murder as she was runing around with Jake the most of the time while he was at home while Jim Moody is in the army, (another case of nuptial fidelity).

I have nothing more of interest until I hear from you. Direct to Nashville. I will write again in a few days. I remain affectionate soger boy,

Thos. J. Davis

On Board the Steamer "Nightingale" off Troy, Indiana, below Louisville, January 20th, 1865

Dear Wife,

I sit down today to write you a few to let you know where I am. We are now on our way to Savannah. All of the detachment of the 15th & 17th Army Corps are with us. They came to Nashville two days before we left. We left Nashville on the 18th at noon we are on board a fleet of steamers and will go up the Ohio River as far as Pittsburg unless we meet too mutch ice but as yet we have found none but perhaps we will find ice by the time we get to Cincinnati. The weather is quite cool to travel on the river. It freezes considerably at night but it is more pleasent in the day time. But the farther we go up the Ohio River the colder it it will get until we get to Pittsburg. We will take the cars at Pittsburg for New York and steamers from there to Savanah. It will take us five or six days more for us to run to Pittsburg on these boats and the boys will be glad enough to get off when we get through.

I have not received a letter from you since I left Milwaukee though I have written quite a number to you. It must be that you did not receive my letters. I expect I have been directing them wrong. You wrote for me to direct to No. 165 Porter Sv. but I suppose you meant it for a "t" in Stead of a "v". You should always write your directions verry plain when you are in a strange place to me. I will direct this to 165 Porter Street as I suppose that is what you meant.

We will get back to Louisville tomorrow morning. It is five hundred miles from Nashville to Louisville by water. Direct your next letter to New York with the company and regiment though I will probably not get any mail from you until we get to Savanah. Those boys that we left were verry glad to get back to the regiment. They were all fat, tough, and dirty except Merrick Rogers and Nat Shepard. They were left at Loudon, Tennessee, sick.

I sent you two rings in a letter from Chicago but I don't know as you got them. If you did not, inquire for letters marked Lucinda M. Davis, No. 165 Porter Sv. The boat shakes so that it is dificult to write so you can read it but I guess you will make it out some way.

As I have no news of importance to write will close. I will write again when we get up to Cincinnati. I want you to write and let me know how you enjoy yourself and how you like to live in Michigan. I will feel verry anxious about you until I get a letter which will probably be sometime. I remain as ever yours,

Thos. J. Davis

On board the steamer "Nightingale", Sunday night, 7 o'clock, Jan. 22/65

Dear Wife,

I will write a few lines tonight as we are steaming up the Ohio River between Madison, Ind., and Cincinnati. We are now within fifty miles of Cincinnati and if we run all night we will be there before daylight. We had to tie up last night on account of the fog and tonight the river is thick with floating ice but still we are traveling with moderate good speed. We left Louisville yesterday about 3 o'clock. We would have been to Cincinnati before now if we had run all the time.

I wrote you a letter day before yesterday and mailed it at Cannelton, Ind. I will probably mail this in Cincinnati tomorrow.

We begin to see considerable snow on the river banks up here though it is not verry cold for it has been thawing yesterday and today. We had considerable rain yesterday while coming through the locks in the canal at Louisville. We have had a reasonable good trip so far for the time of year but it is rather too cold for comfort for so many on the boat. The 23rd Army Corps is one day a head of us. They came out of the Tennessee River. They are going to Grant. The 23rd Corps and our detachment will number about 25,000 men. Enough to help the Eastern army to a considerable extent.[6]

We have not received any mail yet or at least I have not. But some of the boys have had letters from home as late as the 10th before we left Nashville.

I will quit for tonight and will write more tomorrow before I mail this. So goodnight.

T. J. Davis

Ohio, Monday morning, Jan. 23rd, 1865

Well, we are at the wharf at Cincinnati this morning and it is snowing quite briskly. The ice is getting quite heavy in the river and we will

---

6. The 23rd Army Corps, sometimes called the Army of the Ohio, had served it's entire existence in east Tennessee and north Georgia. It was not en route to Grant's army but to coastal North Carolina to assist in the capture of the port city of Wilmington. [Welcher, pt.2, p. 346]

probably go from here to New York by the railroad, but it may be several days before we get away from here as there is too may of us to all get transportation immediately. I wish we was through for this is the wrong time of year for pleasure riding in the north and it makes things somewhat disagreeable where there is so many together.

I have not been out in town yet but I am going when I finish this letter but I don't feel mutch like getting on a drunk this morning. Well, I believe I have nothing more to write this morning so goodbye,

Thos. J. Davis

[This letter was written on stationery provided by the Cincinnati Sanitary Commission]

"Our Country !"   "Our Homes !"
FROM CINCINNATI BRANCH U.S. SANITARY COMMISSION,
TO OUR BRAVE SOLDIERS.

Cincinnati, Ohio, Thursday Evening, January 26th, '65

Dear Wife,

This evening still finds us in Cincinnati and no better prospect of getting away from here than when I last wrote. The weather is verry cold today. The mercury has been below zero all day with a keen wind and heavy ice in the river. So heavy that boats are not runing today. We will probably have to stay here until we can get transportation to New York on the cars and there is about 25,000 troops that will probably go before we will. I hope however that we may go soon as it is too cold here to soldier in the winter time.

We have not received any mail since we left Nashville. All our mail, I supose, has been sent to Savanah where we are expected to go.

There is some talk of us going out to Camp Denison to wait until we can leave on the cars but it is hard to tell what we will do and when we will do it.[7] We are still on board the boat that we came from Nashville on and we are piled on so thick that we cannot all cook or keep warm and the boys in the regiment are nearly all straped for money, officers and all, so that they cannot get on many benders as many of them would like to do. I have had something like a hundred and seventeen aplications to borrow money since we left Milwaukee but I intend to keep enough for my own use, though I have loaned considerable to the

---

7. Camp Dennison was located in eighteen miles northeast of Cincinnati, Ohio, and was named for William Dennison, the Republican war governor of the state from 1860 until 1864. [Cromie, Alice Hamilton, A Tour Guide to the Civil War, Nashville, Tenn., Rutledge Hill Press, 1992, p. 214–215]

boys and I have bought three boxes of tobacco and sold to them on credit.

I supose that you have received the first letter I wrote since we came here before this time. I wish you to write to me as soon as you get this and direct your letter to Cincinnati, Ohio. Don't put on the company or regiment and perhaps I will get it before we leave here.

I have been through the city considerable since we came here. Cincinnati is a larger city than Chicago and there is quite a government business passes through this city but I think Chicago [will] overtake Cincinnati in population and in wealth in a few years.[8] I will not write mutch today and I will hope for an answer from you before we leave here. So be a good girl and write often. Yours as ever,

Thos. J. Davis

Baltimore, Maryland, January 31st, 1865

Dear Lucinda,

I will write you a few lines this evening to inform you that I am as well as usual and I hope this may find you well. We left Cincinnati on the 21st and arrived at Pittsburg, Pa., about 3 o'clock on the 29th. We were well received at Pittsburg and given a good dinner by the citizens. Pittsburg is mutch of a business city, there being a great many manufacturing establishments there and the people seem verry loyal.

We left Pittsburg at half past six o'clock on the evening of the 29th and arrived here in Baltimore this morning at 4 o'clock. Baltimore is a mutch nicer city than I expected to find. The streets are kept clean and the buildings look neat the most of which are made of brick. Baltimore is a larger city than Cincinnati containing over two hundred thousand inhabitants and it being a seaport city. Its commercial business in times of peace have been verry considerable.[9]

We came through Columbus, Ohio, and we stoped there several hours and I went out and took a look at the capitol building which is a magnificent one. It is the best state capitol building in the U.S. We also came through Harrisburg, the capitol of Pennsylvania. It is quite a nice town but the statehouse is not so good as that of Ohio.

We found plenty of snow all through Ohio and Pennsylvania but by the time we got here there was but little snow and today being the warmest day we have had since we left Nashville what little snow there was here most all melted off today. Tonight we are in good barricks at the

---

8. Cincinnati's 1860 population was 161,000; Chicago's was 109,000. [Andriot]
9. Baltimore's 1860 population was 212,000. [Andriot]

west edge of the city and we have orders to start for Anapolis tomorrow morning at 8 o'clock and there we will probably take shiping for Savanah, Georgia

We did not go to New York as we expected. We expected to go to New York until we got to Harrisburg, Pennsylvania. There we received orders to report to Anapolis, Maryland.

I have not received my letter from you yet nor I don't expect until we get through. It is a month ago today since I received a letter from you and I believe that is the longest I have been without one since I been in the service except when I was at home with you. Then I did not care for letters.

Oh, I must tell you. There has been considerable talking about peace for the past few days and today we had a telegraph dispatch from Washington to the effect that Jeff Davis had sent two peace commissioners to Washington and that they had got as far as Fortress Monroe.[10] The news in New York caused gold to fall from $2.20 to $2.05. I don't want you to think that I believe that the war will be over in a week or two and that I will be at home for in the first place the news wants confirmation and the next place, if it is true, the commissioners may want better terms than we will give them and go back without peace. But I believe that peace is not far distant and that we can whip peace out of them in from three to six months. But I will be glad as well as the whole country to see peace come as early as possible and as McCawber says, "We will wait patiently for something good to turn up." [11]

Well, my paper is about out and I must quit for tonight. I will write the next oppertunity. Direct via New York. I remain ever your obedient husband,

Thos. J. Davis: To Sis (Kiss Silvie for me)

On board the Steamship "New York", Annapolis, Md., Feb 3rd, 1865

Dear Wife,

I sit down this morning to write you a few lines to let you know that I am as well as usual and hope this may find you well. We came down from Baltimore to this place day before yesterday and last night we came on board this steamer. We will leave this place for Sherman's army this evening or tomorrow. The weather is pretty cold today and there is con-

---

10. On 28 January 1865, three peace commissioners from the Confederacy were named by Jefferson Davis to propose negotiations for a settlement of hostilities. President Lincoln sent Secretary of State William H. Seward to begin talks with the commissioners aboard a riverboat in Hampton Roads, Virginia. [Long, p. 629]

11. Wilkins Micawber was a Charles Dickens character from the 1850 novel, "David Copperfield."

siderable ice in the bay and the wind off the saltwater feels disagreeable, though we have a warm place in the ship to stay so we can keep comfortable. This is a great place for oysters and those that are fond of such fruit have been improving their oppertunity.

We have heard nothing of importance in refferance to the peace question. Since I wrote last I have but little faith in it at present but I think the Rebs will be compelled to come to a settlement before many months.

I shall not write but little today but I will write more when we get through I am getting verry anxious to hear from you and hope we will get where we can get some mail before long. I will close for the present. Please to write soon. I remain as ever yours,

T. J. Davis

New Berne, North Carolina, Sunday, Feb. 12th, 1865

Dear Wife,

I take my seat in the pine woods on the sand near New Berne, N.C., this pleasant Sabbath afternoon to write you a short epistle to let you know that I am in tolerable good health and hoping this may find you well. The last letter I wrote to you was while we was on shipboard in the bay at Annapolis, Md. We left Annapolis on the morning of the 6th inst. and arrived at the mouth of the harbor at Beaufort, N.C.,about noon on the 9th. We lay out at sea 24 hours in a storm, the sea being too rough for us to make the harbor. The most of the boys got well seasick as the ship would roll and heave. Some of the boys would lean over the railing and heave Jonah for all that was out. Others would be too sick to stand up and would lay down and roll with with the ship and vomit. Some were swearing, others praying, and some [wishing] they had died before he went for a soldier. As for myself, I did not get seasick at all for I used precautionary means to prevent it and I came through all right.[12] But there was one day that the thousand men that was on our boat ate but little rations and chewed but little tobacco. They all got over their sickness, however, and was glad they were not dead.

I did not know when I wrote you last where we were going but suposed we were going to Savanah. But before leaving Anapolis we were ordered to New Berne. It is thought that part of Sherman's army is going to join us here from Savanah and make a raid into the interior of North Carolina. We landed off the ship at Beaufort on the 10th and came out 2 miles and camped on the bay and remained there until 2 o'clock yesterday when we

---

12. Davis never revealed his precautions but there were many folk remedies that claimed to mitigate seasickness including bicarbonate of soda, dry toast, morphine or opium, stuffing the ears with cotton, and breathing into a paper bag.

took the cars for this place 36 miles from Beaufort on the Neuse or News River. New Berne is a much larger town than I expected to find and it is really a pretty place but the country between here and Beaufort is for the most part low, wet, and sandy the timber being nearly all pine.

We have heard nothing of importance about the peace movements since we left Annapolis so we don't know anything about it. But I don't look for peace for some little time yet. But, of course, I would not object to have it as soon as possible on honorable terms.[13]

We will probably remain here at New Berne for several days, at least probably several weeks.

I have not yet received a letter from you since I left Milwaukee for we have received no mail since we left Nashville. When you write again direct to the company and regiment, New Berne, N.C. Our mail I suppose has gone to Savanah and I think it will be sent back before long. I hope so, at least, for I am verry anxious to hear from you and to know how you are getting along.

The weather is quite pleasant today though somewhat windy. It is clear and the sun shines warm and has the appearance of spring and I see some citizens preparing for farming though this is not so warm a country as Southern Mississippi or Georgia. We have had a long and tedious journey and I am glad that we have found a stoping place, if only for a short time. Please to write soon and often and may heaven protect you. From your ever affectionate husband,

Thos. J. Davis

Company C, 18th Regiment Wisconsin Volunteers
New Berne, N.C., February 26th, 1865

Dear Wife,

Another week has passed away and I again sit down to pen you a few lines as a weekly message to the loved ones at home in whose wellfare I am most interested and who are most interested in me. We have not yet received any mail and it seems verry uncertain when we will get any. But one thing is verry certain, that is, we have been grossly neglected in our mail matter and somebody is to blame for it. But I don't know who it is. [We] have been here over two weeks so that the authorities should know by this time where we are and where to send our mail.

The weather is pleasent today. It is warmer than any day we have had since we came here, but it has been raining for several days until this af-

---

13. President Lincoln and Secretary of State Seward had met with the Confederate commissioners on 3 February 1865 and had reiterated their expectations of reunion of the states and abolition of slavery. The Hampton Roads talks were cordial but unsuccessful in the end. [Long, p. 633]

ternoon. It has now cleared off warm and pleasent and I am now sitting in my shanty in my shirt sleeves without fire and am warm enough at that. We have got our shanties completed. Mine is 12 by 14 feet and nine men occupies it including myself.

There is nothing of importance as yet transpiring in this vicinity. Only a few Rebel deserters come into our lines most every day.

Since I wrote to you last we have official news that Sherman has taken Charleston and Columbia, South Carolina, and is still stiring the Rebels up at several other places.[14] I say, "Bully for Sherman". Let him drive them clear out of Rebeldom. Charleston, the Birthplace of Cecession, has now fallen into our hands and I would be glad if the town could be burned to the ground and the ground sunk underwater so that Rebellion could never get a foothold there again. But as it is, the Rebellion is fast playing out so that their leaders are now appealing to God and the niggers for divine and physical aid in this their terrible and last struggle. May God forsake their cause. Their niggers all run away and their leaders leave the country. And the sooner the [better] it will be for the country.

Our army as far as I have saw of late are in best spirits that I have saw them during the war and all seem to concur in the opinion that the Rebellion cannot live many months longer. But I don't write you this to try to make you believe that I am coming home in a few days. For I expect to stay in the army until the war is over but believe that next fall will see the end of the war and I hope the end of the service for me and all the rest of the soldiers who have as mutch to call them home as I have.

Perhaps I was to blame for going Veteran but I hope it will turn out the best for us both and I hope we may hereafter not regret it, though sometimes I regret that I went home on furlough at all for I only remained with you long enough to put me in a good notion to wish to stay longer. But I am not homesick. However, neither do I intend to be for I do not suffer myself to give way to my feelings. But you don't know how anxious I am to hear from you. It seems almost a year since I saw you because I have been anxiously waiting for a letter so long. You may tell Susan and Hariet that they expect me to write to them anymore. That they must write to me first as I have written last.

If I had known the route that my regiment was going from Milwaukee I should have went with you to Michigan and stayed with you a month longer for we was doing no good for that length of time. Then I could have caught the regiment at Baltimore before they left.

---

14. Columbia, the capital of South Carolina, was surrendered to General William T. Sherman on 17 February 1865 and was badly damaged by fire that night. Charleston, the birthplace of the Secession movement, surrendered the next morning but did not suffer the devastation visited on Columbia.

This is the most curious looking country that I was ever in. The principal production of this part of the state is rosin, turpentine, and tar which in times of old was considered a legal tender for all dues, state or national and the collectors would procure himself a third class mule and lash on his back a pair of large gourds and proceed through the country and gather the taxes due from the inhabitants. I should not like to live here as well as I would in Tennessee or North Alabama but North Carolina is considered a verry healthy state though the land is generally poor and, like most of the southern states, the poor people are verry ignorant as a general thing.

Well Lucinda, I will close this sheet hoping to hear from you soon. I remain your devoted husband,

Thos. J. Davis

On this side I will send you a few verses of rhyme that I ground out with my old machine:

In Camp Alone

Today in camp I sit alone, no company to greet,
With thoughts steadfastly fixed on home and those friends I hope to meet.
The soldiers are lounging in their tents to protect them from the sun,
The wether now is quite too hot to sport in outdoor fun.

Some talk of furloughs, some discharge, and some the end of war,
With longing hopes of getting home which in future seems afar.
They talk of diferent things and themes with many contrasting tone,
There's many soldiers round in camp but yet I seem alone.

The summer's sun of Dixie's clime pours down her heated rays
In contrast to the northern breeze I've enjoyed in former days.
Sometimes domestic cares arise and my thoughts are all at home,
But when aroused from reverie, I find myself alone.

Thomas. J. Davis

Company C, 18th Regiment Wisconsin Volunteers
Camp near Crow Creek, N.C., Sunday, March 5th, 1865

Dear Wife,

Well Lucinda, as this is Sunday and my day to write I will endeavor to write you a few lines to inform you that I am as well as usual and I truly hope this may find you in good health and spirits. We left New Berne yesterday morning at 9 o'clock and marched out to Bachelor's Creek and this morning we marched to this place. This place is 18 miles west of New Berne and on the railroad from New Berne to Goldsboro and Raleigh.

The 23rd (Schofield's) Corps is with [us] and we are now repairing the railroad to Goldsboro, which is 45 miles from here, and we will probably meet Sherman at that place. There is but a few Rebels in our immediate front and they fall back as we advance.

We have had considerable rain the past week and it is still cloudy today and the air is cool. We have not received any mail yet but I think we will surely get mail before many days, at least I hope so for I have not been so anxious to hear from you since I have been in the service. I have written to you every week since I have been here and I should probably have written oftner. If I could get letters from you. I have no news of importance to write today so you must be content with a short letter and I will write you a longer one when I get one from you. So good-bye for this time. I remain as ever cincier and affectionate husband.

Thos. J. Davis

Company C, 18th Regiment Wisconsin Volunteers
No. 18, Camp Near Kinston, N.C., March 13, 1865

Dear Wife,

I sit down this morning to write you a letter in answer to three I received from you yesterday; one dated February 20th, one 27th, and the other March 1st and you don't know how glad I was to hear from you and also glad to hear that you was well. I think all the letters that you directed to Savanah, Georgia, went there and are perhaps with Sherman's Army. I wrote you a letter a week ago yesterday but I had no chance to send it back to New Berne so I have it yet and I will send it with this.

We left New Berne on the 4th and we came up to the Rebs on the 7th and we commenced on the 8th and had a four days fight with the Rebs. The fighting was not general nor so hard as some we have been in for during most of the time our army was maneuvering and getting into position. So on the night of the 11th the Rebs left our front after getting the worst of it and finding we was too strong for them. We lost some prisoners and captured some but I don't know how many. Our regiment was under fire several times but luckily had no men killed or wounded. We had two men captured while on the skirmish line. Neither of them were from my company.[15]

---

15. The fighting described in this letter was the Battle of Kinston (or Wise's Forks). Confederate troops under General Braxton Bragg attacked Union troops moving west out of New Bern, North Carolina. The sporadic fighting lasted for three days (8–10 March 1865) until the smaller Confederate force withdrew. Casualties among the Federals were 65 killed, 319 wounded, 953 captured. [Welcher, pt. 1, 68–69; OR-I-47-1-p. 62]

Byron Johnson is dead. We left him at New Berne in the hospital with the typhoid fever. He died on the 4th inst. the same day he was taken there. There is no other news of importance.

Robert McMichael has not received any letter from home since he left. Yours are the only letters that I have received. Yet I suppose others have written but the letters have gone to Sherman. I have not numbered my letters since I left home but since I left you I have written you 17 or 18 letters but I have not wrote only about once a week since I came to New Berne. I will, however, write as often as convenient.

You say that you are getting anxious to leave Detroit and want me to find a place for you. I expected you would want to stay with Susan and Hariet until April or May. I have not made any arrangements for a place for you but I think you had better go back to Wisconsin when you get through your visit. You could stay with my folks in Illinois but they are all strange to you and part of them Copperheads. So I think you would injoy yourself better on the Badax among your acquaintances. I supose you can get as good a place as I could get for you so do the best you can. I want you to get a good place if you have to pay a good price for your board. When you start back your best route will be to go to Chicago and from there through Galena to Dunlieth opposite Dubuque and there take a steamboat up the river and land at Badax City and you can get from there on the Badax most any day.

I sent my overcoat and a blanket home with some things that George Rogers and John Carpenter sent to Elias Rogers. John wrote to Elias to [leave] my coat and blanket at Lewis Smith's.

Well Lucinda, I have nothing more to write today. I know you will be looking anxiously for a letter from me for more than a weeks before you get this. You must do the best for yourself that you can. I remain as ever your soldier boy,

T. J. Davis

Company C, 18th Regiment Wisconsin Volunteers
No. 19, Kinston, N.C., March 17th, 1865

Dear Wife,

This evening I take my seat in my tent to write you a short letter and tell you that I am in tolerable good health and I hope this may find you well. I have not received any letter from you since I last wrote (on the 13th) but I will expect one the next mail. We had a small mail last night but nothing for me. We have mail here every two or three days.

We are now in Kinston. We moved across the river into town night before last. The Rebels have left and gone towards Raleigh to see what Sherman is doing and we will probably follow on after them in a few days or as rapidly as we can repair the railroad. It will be repared from New Berne to this place in two or three days more. The Rebels had the railroad in runing order from here to Goldsboro when they left but I don't know how bad they destroyed it as they fell back. They did not injure the road near the town.

The country begins to improve in appearance out this way though there is but little captivating about it, yet. The land is generally sandy and the most of the timber is pine and there is yet plenty of swamps to raise all the frogs that a person needs.

We have not had many newspapers to read lately and we begin to get behind the news. You wrote that you heard that Sherman had got defeated. The last we heard from him was a few days ago he was then near Raleigh so I don't think he is whiped mutch yet.

The Rebels got considerably worsted in this fight here. Our loss was verry light in killed and wounded from the fact that the Rebs charged on us as we were behind works. The Rebs left eight hundred dead on the field. We had no way of ascertaining the number of their wounded as they got the most of them away with them. The Rebels confess a loss of twenty-two hundred. The Rebels, however, took more prisoners than we did. They captured about a thousand of Massachusetts & Connecticut troops on the first days fight and we captured five hundred from them.[16]

John Dickson (a brother to Hi) has received a 2nd lieutenant's commission in the 46th Wisconsin and he is going to start for the state tomorrow and I will send this letter by him to New Berne and let him mail it there. I will continue to send letters to Detroit until you tell me to change directions.

I had hoped to hear how you liked your visit but you did not say anything about it until you wrote that you was tired of Michigan and wanted to evacuate the state. But I supose you are a little like [me] in not wishing to depend too mutch on relations or stay too long with them. I like to go and see my relations occasionally verry well, yet, I wish to be independent of them. You will continue to direct my letters to New Berne as the mail must come that way.

We will work our way on into the interior of the state and join Sherman about Goldsboro or Raleigh.

---

16. According to reports filed after the Battle of Kinston, at about noon on 8 March 1865, the 27th Massachusetts and 15th Connecticut infantry regiments were attacked in force by General Robert Hoke's Confederate division. The two Federal units were captured almost to a man, losing a total of 889; 828 as prisoners of war. [OR-I-47-1-p.62; OR-I-47-1-p.998–999; Barefoot, Daniel W., General Robert F. Hoke: Lee's Modest Warrior. Winston-Salem, N.C., John F. Blair, Publisher, 1996, p.286–288.

The weather has been quite warm for a few days past until last night. It turned colder and it is quite cool yet tonight but not enough so as to freeze. I have been troubled for several days with the rheumatism and I may have to be left behind but I don't want to if I can travel.

Well, I will close for this time hoping to get another letter from you soon. So goodnight. I remain yours as ever,

Thos. J. Davis

Company C,18th Regiment Wisconsin,
Kinston, March 23rd, 1865

Dear Wife,

I sit myself down this afternoon to write you a few lines to inform you how I am and where I am. Well, I am in the hospital at Kinston, N.C. I was left here on the 19th because I had the rheumatism so that I was not able to keep up with the regiment on the march. But I am considerable better now so that I am runing around considerably and will probably follow the regiment in a few days.

The regiment has gone on out towards Goldsboro which is 29 miles west of here. I understand that our forces from New Berne are joining with Sherman near Goldsboro. Part of Sherman's wagon trains is now here after supplies.

Our Colonel (Jackson) is here in town. He just came from New York. He is in command of seventeen hundred recruits and will take charge of Sherman's wagons for Goldsboro in a day or two. I don't know but what I will go with him when he leaves here.

I have been around town considerably yesterday and today and I find some folks that I really pitty their condition. Some of them seem to be good honest sort of people and say they were always opposed to the war although many were forced into it. Many people are reduced to poverty and no way to make a living. Those rich Rebels that have been broken up I cannot cympathise with at all and I like to see them brought to beggerry and I would assist in the work if nesessary.

The weather is quite pleasent today though the wind blows somewhat disagreeable. The peach trees are out in full bloom and the appeerence is verry much spring-like.

I received a letter from you the 19th dated the 8th inst. I was verry glad to hear from you and to hear that you was well but sorry that you had not received my letters lately. But I think before this time you have received letters from me informing you that I have begun to receive your letters. I have nothing important to write to you today so you will excuse a short letter this time. Direct your letters as usual to the regiment for I won't stay here many days. So good-bye for this time. Yours as ever,

T. J. Davis

Co. C 18th Regiment Wisconsin Volunteers
Goldsboro N. C., March 29th, 1865

Dear Wife,

I sit down this evening to write you a short letter in answer to one I received a few minute ago dated March 19th. I am verry glad to hear from you and to hear that you are well. I left the hospital at Kinston yesterday. I came up on the cars and joined the regiment last night. I am getting pretty well over the rheumatism again. I received five letters from you last night. They were all written in February. In one of your letters written at Marshall you said you was getting better of the mumps. That was the first that I heard you had them but I supose you have got well of them now. You still write that you are tired of Michigan. I wrote you a letter about the 13th of this month and told you that I thought it would be best for you to go back to Wisconsin and do the best you could there. I suppose you have received the letter before this time.

I received a letter from Lewis Smith dated the 5th of February, also one from brother Will Davis dated 3rd of February, and one from D. Ingersoll dated February 8th. So you see I got considerable February mail. I also got several letters that were written before I started home.

We are now back in our old division [3rd Division, 15th Corps] with Sherman and I am going back into the Pioneer Corps. I went over to see the Pioneer Corps boys last night and they had a great deal to tell me about their journey and doings the past winter, especially that portion of it in South Carolina. I supose that while the boys were in South Carolina they turned themselves loose in the destruction of every kind of property in that hotbed of treason.

March 30th. I will finish my letter this morning before the mail goes out. It is raining and has the appearance of a wet spell. The whole army is lying here round Goldsboro and we will probably stay here sometime to rest the army and draw clothing and perhaps pay.

You say you don't like to stay among so many Copperheads. If I was in your place I would not talk with them on politics at all nor pay any attention to them on that subject. It is raining through my tent so it wets my paper so I will have to close writing. Excuse a short letter. Write often. I remain ever yours. Direct: Pioneer Corps, 3rd Division, 15th Army Corps, Goldsboro, N. C.

T. J. Davis

No. 21, Pioneer Corps 3rd Division, 15th A. C.
Goldsboro, N.C., April 2nd, 1865

Dear Wife,

I sit down this pleasent Sunday afternoon to write you a short letter to inform you that I am as well as usual and hope this may find you the same. I have not received any letter from you since I last wrote. Your last was dated March 19th. I shall expect another one soon in answer to one I wrote at Kinston.

I supose you are getting anxious to go back to Wisconsin and perhaps you have gone before this time. I will, however, continue to write to Detroit until you tell me to change directions.

I received two letters yesterday, one from Green Sallee and the other from D. Ingersoll; one dated the 12th and the other the 15th of March. They both wrote that the folks were all well and they also both wrote that brother Will and Belle were married on the 2nd of March. That was an event that I was not at all looking for. Ida was living at Green Sallee's and Bennet was yet in the hospital at Quincy. David said they had received a letter from you about a week before he wrote but did not say they had answered it.

I received a letter from Will, written November 18th with his photograph in it.

I wrote a letter to Lewis Smith yesterday and I told him that you would probably be back there before long (that is to Badax). I also wrote to him that if he was not prepared to keep you again for him to assist you in getting a good place somewhere else.

We are still lying here and perhaps we will not leave here before the 10th or 15th inst. The army expects to be paid before we move. The army is in good health and good spirits and they think the Confederacy is getting pretty well used up. I don't want you to feel uneasy about me for I have a good place and my duty is not verry hard and I want to stay until this rebellion is wound to a close.

As far as comfort is concerned of course I would mutch rather be at home with you but I have hopes that the rebellion will play out before many months and we will once more have a peaceful country to live in and a good cause to live for and I think I will know how to appreciate a good home if we should be so lucky as to get one. Or even if our home should be poor, I know I have a good woman to live with which would make a humble home happy to me for happiness and contentment is a prize of far more value than money. I do not want any more furloughs for I did not enjoy myself while I was at home for the thoughts of coming back was all the time in my mind. I feel more contented now than I did while on furlough. I wish you to make yourself as contented as you can.

You did not say whether or not you received the two rings I sent you from Chicago. Well Lucinda, I will close for this time hoping to hear from you soon. I will try and write more often. I remain as ever your faithful husband,

T. J. Davis

Pioneer Corps, 3rd Division, 15th Army Corps
Goldsboro, N.C., April 8th, 1865

My Dear and Absent Wife,

I sit down this evening to write you a few lines in answer to your letter dated March 26th which I received last night and I was truly glad to hear from you and to hear that you was well and in good spirits. I am in moderate health at present. I was only in the hospital at Kinston a little over a week and I was verry tired with staying that long. It is a poor place for me to live and I don't think I was calculated to soldier in the hospital.

I am again with the Pioneer Corps so you can address your letters according. I have received the most of your letters that you sent me since I left home. About a week ago I received six or seven that was written in February and a few days after I got five that was written in January. I also received one from Clara Wilson and Sarah Kennedy that was written January 22nd and I answered it yesterday. I supose they thought I did not intend to write to them. Perhaps Sarah will think I am quite familiar on so short an acquaintence but then she commenced the joke.

We received official news yesterday of the capture and occupation of Richmond by Grant's forces which is hailed with great delight by this army and this evening Grant's official report of the Richmond affair. Also a report that Lee had surrendered 15,000 Rebels to General Sheridan.[17] To add more enthusiasm to the good news there was six thousand Rebels came into Goldsboro this afternoon and surrendered themselves to the 14th Corps. There is two brigadier generals and several colonels among their number.

I have not heard the peticulars of all the news that came in this evening but there is great excitement through all the camps of the different corps and if you was in hearing of us tonight you would think there was a battle going on here for the boys are out firing off their guns, bursting caps, filling their canteens with powder and blowing them up, and cannons firing all around the lines.

---

17. Sheridan's capture of Confederates refers to the battle of Sayler's Creek, Virginia, where General Robert E. Lee lost approximately 8,000 men and eight generals on 6 April 1865 during the retreat toward Appomattox. [Long, p.667–668]

It is generally believed here now that the Southern Confederacy is virtually gone up the spout. The news is indeed encouraging but still I shall be slow to believe all I hear until I get positive proof of its truith. The prospect of a speedy end of the rebellion never looked so bright and flattering as it does at present and I feel that peace is not far distant but I don't expect we will get to go home in a week or a month. I think this summer will wind the thing up for the thing is going about as I wrote you from Annapolis. I will write you more war news in my next.

We have orders to be ready to march on Monday morning but I don't know where to and I should not wonder if we did not march at that time.

I think I will write a letter to Mrs. Burnett soon. I have been thinking of it for sometime. I have not received any letters from any of my folks since I wrote you last.

I saw George and Ben Pulver and Star Waters this morning. They were all well. The 25th is camped within a half a mile of us.

I supose probably you will be gone from Michigan by the time this gets there. I hope you will get through without any trouble and I hope you will have a good visit with Sarah. I have been promising myself to write to your mother for sometime but I have not done it yet. Neither have I written to Elisabeth or my own mother but I must do so soon.

Well Lucinda, I have written you rather a hasty letter tonight but I hope and I supose it will interest you some. Well, goodbye for this time and I will write soon again. So be a good girl. I remain ever your husband,

T. J. Davis

Pioneer Corps, 3rd Division, 15th Army Corps
Raleigh, North Carolina, April 16th/65

Dear Wife,

Another week has passed and gone and another Sunday has come which finds me seated in my tent trying to pen you a few lines to let you know that I am in tolerable health and truly hoping this may find you well. This morning finds us in the Rebel state capitol of North Carolina which last Sunday was seeming held in comparative security by the Rebel General Johnston and his forces. We left Goldsboro last Monday morning and moved Raleigh-wards in three columns, our corps being on the extreme right wing. We came upon the Rebel advance cavalry about ten miles west of Goldsboro which we drove in front of us with but little resistance and on Thursday morning, as our colums came in front of Raleigh from the east, the Rebels left the city verry hastily to the westward.

We now have official information that Lee has surrendered the whole of his Virginia Army to General Grant and yesterday General Joe Johnson

[Johnston] surrendered his forces to General Sherman.[18] We sent several wagons laden with rations to the Rebels yesterday afternoon and they (the Rebels) will probably be marched in here this evening or tomorrow and paroled according to stipulations of surrender.[19] The news of Johnson's surrender went through the camps of the divisions and corps like wildfire and you may immagin that [it] caused great excitement and rejoicing throughout the army and everybody was anxious to learn the peticulars of the latest clothesline dispatches from the front. But we have not heard the peaticulars yet. We will get them this afternoon or tomorrow as Sherman with an escort and a number of other officers are out with Johnson now.

So the news is glorious and the future is bright and encouraging. Mutch more has been accomplished than I had reason to hope for this early three months ago. I think the rebellion is virtually at an end for after the capture of Lee's and Johnson's armies, I don't think they will be foolish enough to attempt to fight farther. I think I have seen my last battle in this war. When this news shall be fully known it will make many glad hearts, both North and South, and a general national rejoicing. In the mientime we must wait patiently to see what the next few weeks will bring forth. Although I believe the war is about over yet, you must not look for me home on every train for even when the war is over it may [be] months before we are all discharged.

Well, enough war news for this time. I have not received any letter from you since I last wrote for we have received no mail. You must excuse for writing a hurry this morning as the mail goes out at 7 o'clock. Please to write often. Direct to Raleigh, N.C. So goodbye for this time. I will write soon again. From your ever faithful soger boy,

T. J. Davis

Pioneer Corps, 3rd Division, 15th Army Corps
Raleigh N.C., April 19th, 1865

Dear Wife,

I sit down this morning to write you a short letter in answer to one I received from you last night dated April 3rd which I was verry [glad] to peruse and learn that you was well. My health is considerable better again and the brilliant prospect for an early peace makes me feel mutch better. Still I have no additional news of importance since I last wrote that we can

---

18. Although Lee surrendered to Grant on 9 April, Johnston's preliminary surrender did not take place until 18 April. [Long, p. 679]

19. The Federal army had shared rations with Lee's surrendered army at Appomattox and Sherman's men showed the same generousity toward the Confederates in North Carolina.

rely on as a certainty. General Sherman has been out with the Rebel General Johnson for several days and it is believed that Johnson is preparing to surrender all of the Rebel forces east of the Mississippi river and that the fighting is over. However, General Sherman for the present will not let the real state of affairs be made public for reasons of policy.[20] No doubt as everybody seems to think that the end of the war is near at hand if not virtually over. But we will wait patiently and not deceive ourselves with the idea of going home too soon. We can now begin plainly now to see the end and we can afford to be a little patient though there is a possibility that more hard fighting may be done but it is not probable.

I have seen quite a number of Lee's soldiers that surrendered at Richmond who lived here in Raleigh. They were paroled and have come home and all seem satisfied to give up the fight and are mutch elated at the prospect of peace.

We received verry bad news here night before last to the effect that [the] President was shot through the head by a Rebel desperado on the night of the 11th inst. in a theatre in Washington and about the same hour Secretary Seward's house was entered and the Secretary and his son were stabbed severly by another assassin. Neither Mr. Seward nor his son was dead but little hopes were entertained of the recovery of either. The news seems to throw a gloom over the whole army. The news is doubted by some who think the dispatch was sent in here by some Rebels who got possession of the telegraph between here and New Berne as the wires were cut a few days ago. It is to be greatly hoped that the news may prove unfounded [and] if it should prove untrue, it will relieve the minds of an anxious army here.[21]

I have received no letters but yours since I last wrote. I received a letter from you this week dated 8th of January which informed me that you received the rings I sent you from Chicago.

There is two newspapers printed here. They come out strong for the Union now since our army came in. There was three Rebel papers printed here. They left the city with the Rebel army. I have made ten or fifteen dollars this week selling papers. Probably I will sell some more. I have not been altogether idle since I left home and, if we get paid soon so I can get what is owing to me, I think I will have cleared a hundred dollars over my wages since I left home.

---

20. Sherman's initial terms had been sent to Washington, D.C., for final approval. He learned a week later that the terms had been disapproved and that General U.S. Grant was being sent to oversee new negotiations. [Long, p. 681]

21. The news of the President's death was believed by enough soldiers to force Federal officers to take extra precautions to safeguard the citizens and property of Raleigh, North Carolina. (Barrett, John G., Sherman's March Through the Carolinas, p. 235–236.)

Well Lucinda, I will close for this time. I supose you will be in Wisconsin by the time this gets to Detroit. So be a good girl and I will write again soon. So goodbye for the present. I remain as ever yours truly,

Thos. J. Davis

P.S. I found the following words Spelled the following way in your last letter; viz : pritty, citty, wring. Look at the dictionary.

Pioneer Corps, 3rd Division, 15th Army Corps, Army of the Tennessee
No. 23, Raleigh N. C., April 23rd, 1865

My Dear Wife,

I sit down this pleasant Sunday morning to write you a short epistle in answer to a letter I received from you last night dated 9th & 10th inst. which I was glad to receive and to learn that you was well, but sorry to hear that Silvie was unwell. But I hope she has nothing serious ailing her.

The weather here is verry pleasent now and the woods are getting quite green. Planted corn is coming up and appearance indicates that spring is here and summer soon coming.

I have been more dilatory about writing to my folks since I was at home than I was before though I have written quite regular to you. I have not written to my mother or any of my sisters since I left Ilinois but I think I will in a few days. I have intended writing to your mother but I have neglected her, also. But I will write to her soon.

We are now sure that the rebellion is intirely broken up and that peace is now being made and ratified and we will probably get home by the first or middle of July. But it is dificult to predict the exact time we will get home. Now that we have whiped the rebellion to death I can afford to be verry patient for two or three months until the government is prepared to muster us out and send us home. And I think you will be more patient waiting for me for we now can begin to see what we have been so anxiously hoping and looking for so long. I can now almost immagin myself at home and enjoying myself in the pursuits of civil life with my little family around me from whom I have been seperated so long. I think I will appreciate a home hereafter more than ever before and I hope it will never be nesessary for me to leave you so long a period again. Yet, I feel thankful that I have lived through the dangers and hardships of this most horrible and bloody of wars where so many have fallen victims on their country's altar and whose friends will miss them the more when the soldiers return home. Although this war has cost an inestimable amount of blood and treasure, yet we can see a bright future for our country in prospect with the assurance that rebellion and slavery is dead; the latter of which is the cause of all our troubles.

You wrote that you would soon start home so I will direct this to Hockley. Tell Mr. Smith that I think I will see him before harvest in a peaceful country.

I have no idea how long we will remain here. We are all encamped around the city and we have erected comfortable quarters and have but little to do. I have been selling newspapers every morning this last week. I am making verry good wages at it. It is said we will march from here through to Washington to be mustered out. The distance is two hundred and fifty miles. If we do march through I hope we will start before the weather gets too warm. We are now waiting for orders from the War Department but I can't tell when they will come or what they will be.

I supose there is a few letters you have writen that I have not received but I think I have got the most of them. I got the one you wrote to Cincinnati, Ohio. I have forgotten to number some of my letters. I think this one is about #23.

I have an idea that I will call and board with you a while this summer and perhaps if you don't charge too mutch I will stay all winter. Well, I believe that I have written enough this morning so I will close for this time. Write soon. Direct hereafter to the regiment. The Pioneer Corps may now be broken up at any time. I remain ever yours.

T. J. Davis

CHAPTER TWELVE

I Will Never Be a Military Dog

The 18th Wisconsin remained at Raleigh until 29 April when they began their northward march to Washington, D.C. Davis' correspondence ceased for three weeks as the "Tigers" departed North Carolina. The leisurely march the men had been led to believe they would make into Virginia turned into a foot race with another army corps. Twenty-five mile days were not uncommon and many men dropped by the roadside from fatigue and exasperation. The march to Virginia was more painful than triumphant. Nonetheless, upon crossing the state line into Virginia, a point marked by two large posts on either side of the Lawrenceburg Road, the regiments of the brigade gave a spirited yell as each crossed the line. The march continued through Petersburg and Richmond, then intentionally detoured through George Washington's estate at Mount Vernon before moving onward to the suburbs of Washington, D.C.

Under rainy skies, the 18th Wisconsin settled into a camp near Alexandria on 21 May. The weather cleared and warmed and the men were instructed to clean their uniforms, equipment, and weapons in preparation for the greatest parade of the war. The Grand Review, as it was dubbed, was a two-day event featuring General Meade's eastern armies on 23 May and Sherman's western troops the next day. The eastern and western troops were kept as far apart as possible, not just for logistical purposes but, as Davis mentioned in his camp correspondence, to keep the men from fighting with each other.

On 3 June the "Tigers" entrained for Parkersburg, West Virginia. At Parkersburg, the boys boarded a riverboat and proceeded down the Ohio River to Louisville, Kentucky, where they landed on 8 June. At Louisville the regiment went into camp with other regiments to await demobilization.

For a variety of reasons, including international tensions caused by the presence of a French puppet government in Mexico, the western troops

were held in camp in Kentucky throughout June. To keep the men occupied and fit for service, orders were issued to drill on a daily basis regardless of the summer-like temperatures. In at least one unit, the non-
commissioned officers declined to parade their companies and several
dozen men refused to fall in for drill. There was a distinct prospect of
mutiny among the veterans. Mild, but immediate, disciplinary action and
subsequent letters of apology from the offending noncommissioned officers calmed the troubled unit.[1]

T. J. Davis was among the disillusioned veterans in camp at Louisville.
The war was over in almost all parts of the South, he was anxious to start
for home, and he was angry at his commanding officer and the regimental surgeon. In a fit of temper, he left camp on 19 June 1865 and traveled
to Washington, D.C., to complain of his treatment to the President and to
the War Department.

Three days after Davis' last letter to Lucinda, on the evening of 19 July
1865, the 18th Wisconsin Veteran Volunteer Infantry Regiment was mustered out of the service at Louisville. The Badgers crossed the Ohio River
to Jeffersonville, Indiana, the next day and by 7:00 P.M. were rolling north
by train. After a breakfast stop in Chicago, the troop train continued north
to Milwaukee, where supper was served to the men. According to one diarist, "The Eighteenth Wisconsin Regiment and our regiment took supper
together, the Eighteenth doing the honors of the occasion and, with open
ranks, presented arms as our regiment marched through. . . . After supper
and a good and final visit together our boys and those of the Eighteenth
shook hands all around and bade each other farewell."[2] On 29 July 1865
the Badgers were publicly received in Madison, Wisconsin, and were then
officially disbanded.

The letters and articles that comprise this final chapter are a varied lot.
T. J. Davis enjoyed sightseeing in Washington, D.C., while awaiting the
Grand Review, although he left no record of his participation in the parade. Davis appeared to have been in good spirits as the "Tigers" prepared to depart Washington and, though he seemed to understand that
demobilization of the Federal volunteer regiments might be a lengthy
process, he also disclosed that he had his own plans to leave the service at
an earlier date.

Ransom J. Chase, missing from the scene for a year-and-a-half, reap-
peared, albeit briefly, in the pages of the "North Western Times" as a captain with the 42nd Wisconsin Infantry.

Four years of war had whittled the "Badax Tigers" from the boisterous,
confident company of "one hundred and sixteen better looking, better be-

1. Brown, p. 429–430.
2. Brown, p. 437.

haved, stronger physical or more patriotic and enthusiastic soldiers" who marched off to war in January 1861 to a mere handful of veterans. When mustered out in July 1865, only fourteen of the original "Tigers" remained in the ranks: three officers, six non-commissioned officers, and five privates.

When the "Tigers" returned to Viroqua after being mustered out they found their county, the tiny corner of Wisconsin from which they had volunteered, different in so many ways. Local leaders felt that as a result of the county name, their region had suffered from a poor public image even to the point of becoming the butt of crude frontier humor. So in 1862 the county fathers petitioned to select a new county designation. The name "Vernon" was selected for its suggestion of green farm fields. Its reference to George Washington's home, Mt. Vernon, didn't hurt, either. The only Bad Axe that remained on the map after 22 March 1862 was a river that drains the townships between Viroqua and the Mississippi River and a small village on the Mississippi River.

The "Tigers" also returned to an area devastated by a tornado that had struck Vernon County on 28 June 1865. Parts of Viroqua were literally swept away by the cyclone and there were but few buildings that did not show some damage from the wind. It would be years before Viroqua was back to normal but with the war over, the citizens of the county were able to turn their full attention to recovering from the disaster. Regardless of conditions in the county, though, the returning "Tigers" were happy to be home. Home from a war that had separated families, home from a war that had struck down friends and comrades, home from a war that had ended slavery, home from a war that had preserved the Union.

> Headquarters, 18th Wisconsin Volunteer Infantry
> Petersburg, Va., Monday May 8th 1865

Dear Wife,

I sit down this afternoon to write you a few lines to inform you how and where I am. Well, I am as well as usual and I think a little better than usual for I have just come through a march of about 175 miles. We left Raleigh, N.C., on the morning of the 29th of April and arrived here at Petersburg yesterday evening.

It has been two weeks ago yesterday since I wrote to you so I supose you will think I have been verry negligent in writing. The last letter I received from you was written on the 10th of last month. You will now get letters several days quicker from me now than you did when I was at Raleigh. I meant to have written about the time we left Raleigh but I could not find out the time we were going to start until we had orders to fall in.

We will probably leave here in the morning for Washington. So we still have another march of over a hundred miles ahead of us. We will go by way of Richmond which is 22 miles from here. Our army (Sherman's) will go into camp at Alexandria, Va., four miles [from] Washington and there be reviewed and mustered out of the service sometime this summer. You must not be in too mutch of a hurry in looking for me home for it may be two or three months before we can all be mustered out and paid. In the mientime though, you and I can both afford to be patient for awhile as the war is now over.

Well Lucinda, you must be content with a short letter this time and I will try and write more next time. I have matter enough to write a long letter but this ink is about as thick as gruel so I can hardly do anything with it.

We have had verry pleasent weather for marching. We had two or three showers while on the road. Just enough to keep down the dust and it is thundering this evening and I think we will have rain again tonight. When you write again, direct to the regiment to Washington, D.C.

Well Lucinda, I will close for this time hoping that 'ere long we will be permitted to meet again. I remain ever yours,

Thos. J. Davis

Company C, 18th Regiment Wisconsin Volunteer Infantry
Washington, D.C., Sunday, May 28th, 1865

Dear Wife,

I take this oppertunity of writing you a short letter in answer to two letters that I received from you yesterday. One was dated May 12th and the other May 19th. You may be sure I was glad to hear from you after being so long without letters. I was also glad that you had got home safe and without mutch trouble though your walk from Badax City I should think was anything but a pleasent exercise with Sylvie to carry. I was somewhat disappointed in not receiving that photograph you promised to send me and you did not mention in your letter that you had sent it. I received a letter from Mr. Smith dated April 23rd. Tell Mr. Smith that I will make one letter to you both for this time.

We are still encamped near the city and we now draw soft bread and pickles and begin to put on Potomac-style. The boys say we are now soldiering in Potomac-style and that we will soon draw paper collars, red neck ties, straw, and postage stamps and boot-blacking and have nothing to do and get furloughs every six weeks.[3] Our Western men and the Po-

3. Western regiments had been critical of the better supplied Army of the Potomac throughout the war. The red neckties had been adopted as a distinctive accessory by Brigadier General George A. Custer's Michigan Cavalry Brigade in 1863 and were worn by many in Custer's Third Cavalry Division, thereafter. (Wiley, p. 320; Urwin, Gregory J.W., Custer Victorious. Lincoln, Nebr., Bison Book, 1990, p.82)

tomac chaps do not agree verry well. They are having little petty quarrels and fights every day. But the quarreling and fighting is generally confined to men of weak minds and manners on both sides and in most cases under the influence of poor fighting whiskey and bad raising. There is too mutch of it, however, and it is all wrong and I don't like to see it going on. For if we have had a hard time and a long time fighting the Rebels and we have got them beautifully whiped and cleaned out, I should think that our soldiers ought to be satisfied without quarreling and fighting among themselves.

I received a letter from brother Will. He said the folks were all well. He was living with Isaac in the same house they were living when we was there. He said that Mother's broken leg was getting better but that she could not walk on it yet. From what you say it seems that Jabe and Mary have been trying to out do each other and both are worsted in the opperation. If that is the case they ought to make a draw game of it and recruit their strength and draw a fresh supply of amunition. Health demands moderation in all things, to say nothing of self respect.

I don't know as I have anything new to write today only it is a pleasent day. But yesterday and day before it rained all day. We are lying still here and awaiting future events. We expect that the army will be paid off in a few days which will come verry acceptable to me as I have several hundred dollars standing out which I will then collect.

Well Lucinda, I will close for this time hoping to hear from you again soon as we can get letters mutch quicker from each other now than when I was in North Carolina. I remain as ever your unworthy husband,

Thos.J.Davis

Company C, 18th Regiment Wisconsin Volunteer Infantry
Washington, D.C., June 2nd, 1865

Dear Wife,

I will attempt this afternoon to write you a short epistle in answer to your letter dated May 25 (which I received on the 31st) which came the quickest of any letter I have received from you for a long time. It does not take long for mail to go from here to Wisconsin. My health is as good as usual and I feel considerable better after recruiting up from our long march.

Well, we are stil encamped near the the Capitol City and where we can get news fresh from the War Department every morning. I have been nearly all over the City and have seen a great [many] things that I have wished to see for a long time. I have visited the Capitol, the Patent Office, the Treasury Department, the Washington Monument, General

Taylor's residince[4], and the White House (or the President's Mansion), and also Ford's Theatre where President Lincoln was assassinated. Yesterday was the day of fasting and prayer and the city wore a verry solemn appearance as nearly all the business houses were closed and all the public and most of the private buildings were draped in mourning.

You said in your letter that you heard that Sherman's army was coming home and you would not send your picture until I come home. You must not look for me too soon. It may several months before I get home but I have no idea of staying until my time is out. We will leave here tomorrow for Louisville, Ky., when we will go into camp and we will be mustered out and sent home from there when our time comes. But we will have to wait patiently until they get to us.

I will send you a couple of Washington papers that will give you more news than I can write. You are certainly not more anxious to see me come home than I am to come but it will not hurry the matter one minute to be impatient about it. So I mean to be just as careless about it as possible for I think I will get home before a great while. And then we will begin to think of living like married folks for the first time and as you say, I think that we both may have profited by being separated so long and I think hereafter I will appreciate a good home, a gentle-spirited, kind, and loving wife better now than I otherwise would. And I see no reason why we should not enjoy ourselves as well as any other folks in the world if fortune favors us with a comfortable living and good health.

All the men in our regiment that their time expires before the 31st of October next were mustered out of service day before yesterday but they have not been paid nor have not yet started home for they cannot get transportation yet. When you write again, direct your letter to Company C, 18th Regiment Wisconsin Volunteer, 2nd Brigade, 4th Division, 15th Army Corps, Louisville, Ky.[5] Write often and I will do the same. I must close as I am on guard today and my time is limited. I remain as ever yours.

T. J.Davis

---

4. Davis was probably referring to General Joseph P. Taylor, commissary general of the army until his death in June, 1864. Taylor had lived in Washington, D.C., since 1841 and must have owned a residence of some prominence for Davis to note it. General Taylor was also the younger brother of President Zachary Taylor. [Warner, p.494–495]

5. Upon the transfer of its commander, General John E. Smith, the 3rd Division was disbanded. The 18th Wisconsin was transferred to the 2nd Brigade, 4th Division. [Welcher, pt. 2, 290–291]

Review of the Troops at Washington

This splendid and extensively interesting parade came off at Washington two weeks ago. The President, Cabinet, Lt. Gen'l. Grant, and Secretary Stanton were posted on a platform in a conspicuous position, two weeks since, on which grand occasion the gallant and glorious army of the Potomac, led by Gen'l. Meade, passed in review. Correspondents represent the marching to have been with wonderful precision. Tremendous platoon reaching clear across the wide street, from curb to curb, with their ranks as straight as an arrow and their step as one man, came the victors of South Mountain, Gettysburg, Petersburg, and Richmond.

The Vernon County men will be here during the month of June.

On the next day came the veterans of the West, Sherman's Grand Army. Expectation was on tiptoe—all seemed to expect to see stalwart men, but poor marching and men clad in old, worn-out uniforms. But how egregiously mistaken the crowd found themselves. Gen'l. Sherman led his veterans by in the bright new uniforms that were issued to them in North Carolina and they marched through the city better, if there was any difference, than their brethren of the Army of the Potomac.

Each army consisted of nearly 75,000 men and nearly two whole days were occupied in their passage through Washington. The officers and men were hailed with showers of cheers and flowers. [NW Times, June 7, 1865, p. 2]

[Untitled Item]

Capt. R. J. Chase volunteered in Viroqua and went out from Viroqua as a private in Co. C., 18th Wis. Vols., Capt. Layne's company. He received a commission as 2nd lieutenant during the 2nd year the regiment was out. He resigned on account of the failure of his health. He went out as Capt. of a company in the 42nd last fall, raised in Dane and Vernon counties. We are glad to hear of the appreciation of his abilities.

Assigned to Duty—Capt. R. J. Chase of the 42nd Regiment of Wisconsin volunteers, and for some months past, Captain of the Provost Guard in Springfield, Ill. is assigned to duty to Rock Island as Judge Avocate of a court martial to be convened at that place on Tuesday. Capt. C. is an efficient and courteous officer and has won for himself the respect of the entire community.

We are pleased to learn that the present efficient provost guard are to remain for the present. Ed. [NW Times, June 7, 1865, p. 2]

Camp Near Louisville, Ky., June 9th A.D.,1865

Dear Wife,

I will attempt this afternoon to write you a few lines to inform you that we have again arrived in the Western Department. We left Washington last Saturday, the 3rd inst., over the Baltimore & Ohio Railroad. We came by way of Harper's Ferry, Va., Cumberland City, Md., & arrived at Parkersburg, West Virginia, on the Ohio River on the evening of the 5th inst. Parkersburg is three hundred miles above Cincinnati. We embarked on a fleet of steamers at Parkersburg on the morning of the 6th and tied loose down the river passing Cincinnati on the evening of the 7th and landing at Louisville on the morning of the 8th (yesterday).

When we disembarked we marched out five miles east of town where we are encamped. We had a verry pleasant trip and a verry quick one considering the low stage of water in the Ohio River. I was mutch surprised in passing through western Virginia and western Maryland to see the hearty welcome with which we was greeted by the citizens along the road. At nearly every house flags and white hankerchiefs were waved by the ladies and at nearly every station we found little girls and boys and men standing ready with pails and pitchers of cold water for the soldiers. And we would frequently hear them hurrah for Sherman and his western boys. It seemed to me like we were passing through a northern state. It must be remembered that there was a vast difference between the loyalty of eastern and western Virginia and that is the reason why western Virginia was so anxious for a separate state government, which it now has.[6]

I have not received a letter from you since I wrote to you on the 2nd but I think I will get one the first mail. I wrote to you to direct your letters to Louisville, Ky., which will probably be nesessary for the present.

We will probably get pay next week but I am unable to say how many months pay we will get, though it is verry evident that we will not get all that is due us. I have no more idea of what will be the future movement of this army than a man in the moon. you must, therefore, not expect us home as soon as you seemed to think we would be in your last letter. I think, however, we will ascertain in the course of a month from now.

We are encamped near a wheatfield. The owner is harvesting it with a reaper and the soldiers, through curiosity, are out in the field binding the wheat nearly as fast as the reaper cuts it.

The weather has been verry warm for several days, the thermomiter marking above 90 degrees in the shade, but it is a little cooler today with prospect of rain.

Well Lucinda, I will not write anymore until I get another letter from you, (that is) if I get one soon. Then I will write a longer letter. So goodbye for this time. Write often. I remain ever yours truly,

T. J.Davis

---

6. Western Virginia Unionists separated from Virginia in August 1861. The reorganized state adopted a new constitution in 1862 and was admitted as a state on 20 June 1863. [Faust, p. 816–817]

Louisville, Ky., June 15th, 1865

Dear Wife,

This morning finds me trying to write a few lines to a woman friend that I used to associate with before the war and whom I expect to see again before many months if there is no providential hinderance and no accident occurs. I received a letter from you yesterday dated June 1st which was a little behind time. Nevertheless, I was verry glad to get it. The mail we are getting now has all been to Washington and then re-mailed here but your letters will now come straight through here.

Robert McMichael has received his papers and started home yesterday. He has been verry anxious about home for some time. He sent in his resignation when we first came to Washington. I sent a silver fork and a set of teaspoons with him that came from South Carolina which he will deliver to you as a present from your soldier boy.[7] He also owes me thirty-seven dollars and 65 cents ($37.65) which he will pay to you and you will give him a receipt for the same.

The wether has been quite warm for several days but it is some cooler today. Wheat is now ripe and the people are buisy harvesting their grain.

You say that I have never written where I expected we would live after I got out of the army. I know that I never have and the reason is that I have not decided that question in my own mind and I will probably be guided by circumstances after I get out of the service for I think I will look around and see where I can do the best, which is hard to determine now. It will be early enough after I get discharged to seek a location to advantage.

Five companies of our regiment was paid day before yesterday but our company and 4 others are yet unpaid, but I supose they will be paid in a day or two. However, I have plenty of money for I collected two hundred dollars that the other companies owed me, which is more than I intend to spend soon.

The soldiers here are getting quite impatient to find out what is to be done with us as there is no orders from the War Department or anyplace else from which we have the least idea what is to be done with us in the future. And the men justly complain of being kept in such total ignorance and claim that we have at least the right to know whether we are to be discharged soon or kept in the service. If Robert McMichael wrote that we would all be at home soon, he only did so on his own impression without any authority more than supposition. But there was a great many who believed that we would soon go home after coming here.

---

7. Davis bought or traded for these souveniers of Sherman's march through South Carolina.

I have not received any letters since I wrote you last except from you and I have written but few of late. I will look for another letter from you now every day until I get one. Meinwhile I take every thing perfectly cool waiting for something to turn up in military affairs. You will please write often and I will do the same. I remain ever truly yours,

Thos.J.Davis

Coshockton, Ohio, July 16th, 1865

Dear Wife,

I will attempt this wet Sunday afternoon to write you a few lines to let you know that I am still in the land of the living and have not forgotten you. I expect you begin to feel uneasy about me by this time as I have not written to you since the 21st of last month.[Letter not included in collection] I left Cincinnati the next day after I wrote to you and went to Washington City. Perhaps you will wish to know what I went to Washington for. Well, I will tell you.

In the first place I believed that on account of my health I was entitled to a discharge from the military service. I made application to our doctor for an examination and he refused to pay any attention to me.

In the 2nd place, the Colonel[8] about the same time put me under arrest without any cause and had me on extra duty for several days. I then determined to go to Washington myself and see the President and see if there was no way that I could get a medical examination. So I went to Washington and remained there about two weeks but the President remained in his room sick and I could not get to see him.[9]

So I have got this far back and I have not yet made up my mind whether I will return to the regiment or not. For if I should go back now I would probably be court-martialed and mustered out without any more pay.

And another thing, I never wish to see our doctor or Colonel while they are officers in the army. I am not afraid of any punishment they may inflict on me but I will never be a military dog in time of peace to come at the whistleing of a few bigoted despots who have more impudence than common sense and who are to humanity a stranger.

Probably I have did a rash act but I am too sensative to bear abuse for nothing. I have not made up my mind what I will do. If I do not go back

---

8. Lieutenant Colonel Charles H. Jackson.

9. According to accounts, President Andrew Johnson suffered from headaches and general debilitation during July 1865. It is thought that his illness was brought on by a combination of long days of stressful audiences in the White House and the hot, humid July weather. (Bowers, Claude G., The Tragic Era. Cambridge, Mass., The Literary Guild of America, Inc., 1929, p. 21–22)

to the regiment I will probably be home by the first of September. I will write to you again in [the] course of a week. In the meantime you need not be uneasy about me.

I remain as ever your affectionate husband

T. J. Davis

P.S. Excuse bad writing for this ink is verry bad.   T. J.D

Co. C.

We had a call from Capt. McMichael the other day. His health was good but he was mourning the loss of his wife whom he had the misfortune to lose lately. First Lieut. Thomas Decker is now at home in good health and spirits. Second Lieut. Gould Hickok has located at Waukon, Iowa. The officers and men of this brave company are all at home and all in fine health and spirits. May our brave defenders never lack of anything. [NW Times, August 9, 1865, p. 3]

[Untitled Item]

In the notice of Co. C, 18th Wis. Vols. last week, we were laboring under the mistake that no capt. had been commissioned since the muster out of Capt. McMichael. The fact is that Wm. C. Carter, who went into the company a boy of 16 years of age, was mustered out after about four years service as captain of his company. Capt. Carter is one of the many honorable and worthy cases in our noble army of the rapid advancement of youthful soldiers. [NW Times, August 16, 1865, p. 3]

Postscript

Unable to obtain an audience at the White House, T. J. Davis never did return to his regiment. He bought eleven army mules at auction and returned to his wife and baby daughter in Wisconsin. Listed as a deserter from his unit, Davis' military record was cleared, as were thousands of others, by a general amnesty that was declared by Congress in 1889.

After the war, Thomas J. Davis initially settled his family on a farm near La Crosse, Wisconsin, then moved to Little Sioux, Iowa, in 1872. Losing a sawmill operation to a flood, T. J. and Lucinda Davis moved their growing family of six children to a farmstead in the Red Water Creek area of the Black Hills, South Dakota, in 1877. Upon their retirement from farming in 1891, Davis and his wife moved by covered wagon to the Camas Valley, Oregon. They remained in that location until fire destroyed their home in 1899. The couple returned to South Dakota in 1900 and made their last move to a small house near Belle Fourche in 1907. T. J. Davis died 31 January 1915 in Belle Fourche and was buried in Pine Slope Cemetery.

Ransom J. Chase mustered out of the 42nd Wisconsin on 20 June 1865. Returning to Madison, he resumed his law practice and joined several partnerships over a nine year period. On 20 October 1868, Chase and Mary M. (Baker) Kurtz, a widow, were married at Muncie, Indiana. Bothered for years by the poor health that had forced him to leave the army in 1863, Chase moved with his wife and five children to Sibley, Iowa, in 1874 to recuperate. Within a year he moved to Sioux City, Iowa, built a new law practice, and retired a millionaire in 1883. Chase continued to act in a consulting capacity for corporate interests and became a civic leader in Sioux City. He was a member of the Grand Army of the Republic, the Military Order of the Loyal Legion of the United States, and the Society of the Army of the Tennessee.

Ransom J. Chase died of pneumonia on 13 March 1911 in Seattle, Washington. His remains were returned to Sioux City and were interred in Floyd Cemetery.

333

Bibliography

Adams, George Worthington. *Doctors in Blue*. Baton Rouge: Louisiana State University Press, 1962.

Ambrose, Stephen E. *Halleck: Lincoln's Chief of Staff*. Baton Rouge: Louisiana State University Press, 1962.

Ambrose, Stephen E. (ed.). *A Wisconsin Boy in Dixie: Civil War Letters of James K. Newton*. Madison: University of Wisconsin Press, 1961.

Andriot, John L. *Population Abstract of the United States*, vol. 1, tables. McLean, Va.: Andriot Associates, 1983.

Bailey, Ronald H. *Battles for Atlanta*. Alexandria, Va.: Time-Life Books, 1985.

Barefoot, Daniel W. *General Robert F. Hoke: Lee's Modest Warrior*. Winston-Salem, N.C.: John F. Blair, Publisher, 1996.

Barrett, John G. *Sherman's March through the Carolinas*. Chapel Hill: University of North Carolina Press, 1956.

Bastian, David F. *Grant's Canal*. Shippensburg, Pa.: Burd Street Press, 1995

Bearss, Edwin Cole. *Vicksburg Campaign*, vol. II: *Grant Strikes a Fatal Blow*. Dayton, Ohio: Morningside, 1986.

Boatner, Mark M., III. *The Civil War Dictionary*. New York: Vintage Books, 1991.

Bowers, Claude G. *The Tragic Era*. Cambridge, Mass.: Literary Guild of America, 1929.

Brown, Alonzo L. *History of the Fourth Regiment of Minnesota Volunteers during the Great Rebellion 1861–1865*. St. Paul, Minn.: Pioneer Press, 1892.

Cozzens, Peter. *The Shipwreck of Their Hopes*. Urbana: University of Illinois Press, 1994.

Cromie, Alice Hamilton. *A Tour Guide to the Civil War*. Nashville: Rutledge Hill Press, 1992

Cunningham, Edward. *The Port Hudson Campaign*. Baton Rouge: Louisiana State University Press, 1963.

Davis, William C. (ed.). *The Confederate General*, vols. 1, 3, and 6. Harrisburg, Pa.: National Historical Society, 1991.

Dickson, Paul. *War Slang*. New York: Pocket Books, 1994.

Dyer, John P. *From Shiloh to San Juan*. Baton Rouge: Louisiana State University Press, 1989.

Estabrook, Charles E. (ed.). *Wisconsin Losses in the Civil War*. Madison, Wis.: Democrate, 1915.

Faust, Patricia L. (ed.). *Historical Times Illustrated Encyclopedia of the Civil War*. New York: Harper & Row, 1986.

Grant, Ulysses S. *Personal Memoirs of U.S. Grant*, vol. 1. New York: Webster, 1885.

Hamilton, Virginia Van Der Veer. *Seeing Historic Alabama*. Tuscaloosa: University of Alabama Press, 1982.

Hickenlooper, Andrew. *"Our Volunteer Engineers," Sketches of War History, 1861–1865*. Cincinnati: Ohio Commandery of Mollus, 1890.

Jones, Jenkin Lloyd. *An Artilleryman's Diary*. Madison: Wisconsin History Commission, 1914.

Klement, Frank L. *Wisconsin and the Civil War*. Madison: Wisconsin Civil War Centennial Commission, 1963.

Lewis, Lloyd. *Sherman: Fighting Prophet*. New York: Harcourt, Brace, 1932.

Long, E. B. *The Civil War Day by Day, An Almanac, 1861–1865*. Garden City, N.Y.: Doubleday, 1971.

Lord, Francis A. *They Fought for the Union*. Westport, Conn.: Greenwood, 1981.

Love, William De Loss. *Wisconsin in the War of the Rebellion: A History of All Regiments and Batteries the State Has Sent to the Field*. New York: Sheldon, 1866.

Magdeburg, Capt. F. H (comp.). *Wisconsin at Shiloh*. Madison: Wisconsin Shiloh Monument Commission, 1909.

Marszalek, John F. *Sherman: A Soldier's Passion for Order*. New York: Free Press, 1993.

McPherson, James M. *Battle Cry of Freedom, The Civil War Era*. New York: Oxford University Press, 1988.

Minkler, Levi. *Diary, March 30–May 27, 1861*. Typescript. Shihoh National Military Part Archives.

National Archives and Records Service. Compiled Service Records of Company C, 18th Wisconsin Volunteer Infantry Regiment, 1861, 1865.

———. Summary of Pioneer Corps History, Correspondence from E. O. Parker, 1973.

National Cyclopaedia of American Biography, vol. II. New York: James T. White, 1895

Nevins, Allan. *The War for the Union*. vol. 2. New York: Scribner's, 1960.

The North Western Times. Viroqua, Wis.: 1861–1865.

The Oshkosh Northwestern. Oshkosh, Wis.: 1936.

Quiner, E. B. "Correspondence of Wisconsin Volunteers, 1861–1865," 8 vols. Madison: State Historical Society of Wisconsin.

———. *The Military History of Wisconsin: A Record of the Civil and Military Patriotism of the State in the War for the Union*. Chicago, 1866.

Rood, Hosea (comp.). *Wisconsin at Vicksburg: Report of the Wisconsin–Vicksburg Monument Commission: Including the Story of the Campaign and Siege of Vicksburg in 1863*. Madison, 1904.

Sanborn, John B. *The Crisis at Champion's Hill: The Decisive Battle of the Civil War*. [St. Paul, Minn., 1903.]

Scott, Robert N. (ed.). *The War of the Rebellion: A Compilation of the Official Records of the Union and Confederate Armies*. Washington, D.C.: General Printing Office, 1880–1902.

Urwin, Gregory J. W. *Custer Victorious*. Lincoln, Nebr.: Bison Books, 1990.

"The Viroqua Centennial, August 17–18: 100 Years of Progress, 1846–1946." Program.

The Viroqua Expositor. Viroqua, Wis.: 1861–1862.

Warner, Ezra J. *Generals in Blue*. Baton Rouge: Louisiana State University Press, 1977.

Welcher, Frank J. *The Union Army: 1861–1865, Organization and Operations*, vol. I: *The Eastern Theater*. Bloomington: Indiana University Press, 1989.

———. *The Union Army: 1861–1865, Organization and Operations*, vol. II: *The Western Theater*. Bloomington: Indiana University Press, 1993.

Wiley, Bell I. *The Life of Billy Yank*. Garden City, N.Y.: Doubleday, 1971.

Wisconsin, *Annual Report of the Adjutant General: 1861*. Madison: Atwood & Rublee, State Printer, 1912.

———. *Annual Report of the Adjutant General: 1862*. Madison: Atwood & Rublee, State Printer, 1912.

———. *Annual Report of the Adjutant General: 1863*. Madison: W. J. Park, State Printer, 1912.

———. *Annual Report of the Adjutant General: 1864*. Madison: Atwood & Rublee, State Printer, 1912.

———. *Annual Report of the Adjutant General: 1865*. Madison: W. J. Park, State Printer, 1912.

18th Wisconsin
Infantry Regimental Statistics

Original Strength:	962
New Recruits (1863)	61
New Recruits (1864)	103
New Recruits (1865)	34
By Substitutes	28
By Draft (1864)	200
By Draft (1865)	71
By Reenlistment	178
Total	1637
Killed in Action	41
Died of Wounds	21
Died of Disease	212
Died by Accident	2
Total	276
Deserted	208
Missing	22
Transferred	23
Discharged	843
Mustered Out	265
Total	1361

18th Wisconsin Volunteer Infantry Organizational Chart: 1862–1865

1862

April	Attached to Miller's Brigade, 6th (Prentiss') Division, Army of the Tennessee
May	2nd (Oliver's) Brigade, 6th (McKean's) Division, Army of the Tennessee
October	2nd (Oliver's) Brigade, 6th (McArthur's) Division, Army of the Tennessee
December	2nd (Ransom's) Brigade, 6th (McArthur's) Division, Army of the Tennessee

1863

January	2nd (Ransom's) Brigade, 6th (McArthur's) Division, 17th Corps
May	1st (Sanborn's) Brigade, 7th (Crocker's) Division, 17th Corps
June	1st (Sanborn's) Brigade, 7th (Quinby's-J.E.Smith's) Division, 17th Corps
November	1st (Alexander's) Brigade, 2nd (J.E. Smith's) Division, 17th Corps
December	1st (Alexander's) Brigade, 3rd (J.E. Smith's) Division, 15th Corps

1864

February	1st (Bouck's) Brigade, 3rd (Smith's) Division, 15th Army Corps
March	1st (McCown's) Brigade, 3rd (J.E. Smith's) Division, 15th Corps
April	1st (Alexander's) Brigade, 3rd (J.E. Smith's) Division, 15th Corps

| September | 1st (McCown's) Brigade, 3rd (J.E. Smith's) Division, 15th (Corps |
| November | (non-veterans on Sherman's March) Buswell's Brigade, 15th Corps |

1865

January	1st Brigade, 1st Provisional Division, Army of the Cumberland
March	2nd Provisional (S.P. Carter's) Division, New Berne, NC
April	2nd (W.T Clark's) Brigade, 4th (Corse's) Division,15th Corps
July	2nd (W.T. Clark's) Brigade, 4th (Corse's) Division, 15th Corps

Roster of Company C, 18th Wisconsin Volunteer Infantry

Rank	Home	Enlistment	Remarks
Captains			
Layne, Newton M.	Viroqua	12-9-61	22; Capt: 12-9-61 POW: Shiloh,4-6-62 Resigned: 1-8-64 Died: 2-29-64 New Brookville, WI
McMichael, Robt. S.	Newton	11-21-61	34; Sgt: 11-21-61 1st Lieut: 3-11-64 Capt: 5-64 Resigned: 6-3-65
Carter, Wm. N., Jr.	Readstown	11-22-61	18; Sgt.; 1st Sgt. 1st Lieut: 3-18-64 Capt: 7-1-65 M.O: 7-18-65
First Lieutenants			
Pitcher, Charles W.	Viroqua	12-9-61	36; Resigned:1-23-62
Graham, John H.	Lynxville	12-12-61	31; 1st Lieut:1-23-62 Resigned: 9-20-62
Carter, Wm. N., Sr	Readstown	11-18-61	44; Sgt: 11-18-61 2nd Lieut: 8-16-62 1st Lieut: 8-18-62 Resigned: 12-24-63
Decker, Thomas J.	Viroqua	11-26-61	24; Wagoner, Sgt., 1st Lieut: 7-1-65, M.O. 7-18-65
2nd Lieutenants			
Goode, John	Viroqua	12-9-61	34; Resigned: 1-20-62
Burnett, Allen A.	Springville	11-26-61	34; Sgt: 11-26-61 2nd Lieut: 1-23-62 Resigned: 6-16-62

343

			Reenlisted: 64: Capt. in 37th Wisc. Vol. Inf. Died: 8-16-64
Chase, Ransom J.	Viroqua	12-18-61	21; Corp: 12-18-61 1st. Sgt, 2nd Lieut: 8-18-62 Resigned:1-23-63 Reenlisted 64: Capt. in 42nd Wisc. Vol. Inf.
Hickok, Gould	Viroqua	12-2-61	26; Corp: 12-2-61, Sgt., POW: Shiloh, 4-6-62; 2nd Lieut.-not mustered; M.O. 7-18-65

Enlisted Men

Allen, Levi E.	Springville	12-28-61	26; POW:Shiloh 4-6-62 Died: 8-19-62 at Evansville,IN
Ames, Charles	Viroqua	12-2-61	22; Transf. to: Co. K
Arnott, David	Viroqua	11-29-61	44; Trans. To: Veteran Reserve Corps 3-15-64
Baker, Henry L.	Sterling	11-26-61	26; Sgt./Principal Musician:
Baltz, Sebastian	Viroqua	3-20-62	Disch:12-3-62, Disab. Disch. 8-5-63
Bankes, Leonard S.	Viroqua	12-29-64	M.O.: 7-18-65
Bankes, Nathan	Viroqua	12-9-61	37; M.O.: 7-18-65
Barney, James S.	Jamestown	10-6-64	Drafted; M.O.: 7-18-65
Bates, Daniel D.	Bloomingdale	12-26-61	26; Disch:6-17-62
Brayman, Melvin	Desoto	12-28-61	Transf. to: Co. K
Brightman, Jos. H.	Yankeetown	12-5-61	42; Corp: 12-5-61 POW:Shiloh, 4-6-62; prom:2nd Lieut., 3-7-64, 37th Wisc. Vol. Inf.
Broderick, Lawrence	Viroqua	12-9-61	34; M.O.: 7-18-65
Brown, Azariah	Viroqua	11-25-61	37; Disch: 6-6-62 Disab.
Brown, Charles	Sterling	9-3-64	M.O. 5-31-65 term exp.
Buckley, Joseph	Viroqua	12-10-61	36; Corp: 12-10-61 Disch: 8-8-62
Bugbee, Levi B.	Sierra	12-6-61	21; Disch:6-17-62
Campbell, Peter S.	Desoto	12-13-61	37; POW: Shiloh, 4-6-62; Corp., Sgt., M.O. 7-18-65
Campbell, Robert	Wheatland	9-3-64	M.O. 5-31-65
Carey, Edward	Jamestown	10-6-64	Drafted; M.O. 7-18-65
Carewell, Adam		11-19-62	Disch: 2-1-63 Disab.
Carpenter, John	Jefferson	2-27-64	Corp., M.O. 7-18-65
Caulkins, David	Sterling	12-30-63	M.O. 7-18-63
Chadeayne, Geo.	Readstown	11-29-61	27; Died: 2-27-64 Cairo, IL
Chaney, John L.	Bergen	12-22-63	M.O. 7-18-65
Clear, Jacob S.	Viroqua	11-23-61	21; Transf. to: Co. K
Cleary, Henry	Springville	1-2-62	26; Disch: 1-31-65 Disab.

Cleary, William	Springville	11-21-61	23; POW: Shiloh, 4-6-62 Corp., Sgt., M.O. 7-18-65
Cooley, Aaron	DeSoto	3-1-62	Musician, Disch.:5-29-62 Disab. Died after discharge
Corey, Roswell F.	Readstown	11-22-61	36; Corp.: 11-22-61 Deserted: 4-15-62
Cox, William	Viroqua	11-26-61	25; Corp.: 11-26-61 Sgt., M.O. 3-14-65
Crandall, Edwin E.	Newton	11-21-61	18; M.O. 7-18-65
Cummings, Ham	Springville	11-30-61	24; Transf. to: Co. K
Dailey, William	Readstown	11-22-61	41; Disch: Disab.
Davis, Leonard C.	Towerville	12-4-61	25; M.O. 3-14-65
Davis, Thomas J.	Springville	11-20-61	29; Deserted: 6-19-65
Day, Martin V.	Readstown	12-2-61	21; Deserted: 9-62
Day, Travis	Readstown	11-7-61	22; Died:6-28-62, Keokuk, IA
Delap, William M.	Romance	12-2-61	34; M.O. 3-14-65
Dennison, William F.	La Crosse	11-15-64	34; Drafted, M.O. 7-18-65
Dickson, John S.	Bloomingdale	11-26-61	30; Sgt: 11-26-61 POW: Shiloh, 4-6-61; 2nd Lieut.: 46th Wisc. Vol. Inf.
Dikeman, Wm. W.	Lynxville	12-5-61	25; M.O. 3-14-65
Downie, William	Hockley	12-3-61	24; Wounded: Corinth, 10-3-62 Died: St. Louis, 11-30-62
Evans, Benjamin	Ridgeway	9-28-64	Drafted; M.O. 5-31-65
Finley, Thomas J.	Lynxville	12-9-61	24; Transf. to: Co. K
Fish, Samuel	S. Bad Axe	12-9-61	29; Wounded: Shiloh, Died 4-21-62, Evansville, IN
Fletcher, Burdett	Springville	12-24-61	41; Died: Covington, KY
Forsyth, Elijah	Springville	11-25-61	Died: 6-21-62, Keokuk, IA
Frasier, Elijah	Jefferson	2-20-64	M.O. 7-5-65
Fretwell, Thomas	Viroqua	12-25-61	44; Sgt.: 12-25-61 POW: Shiloh, 4-6-62 Died: 7-21-62 Macon, GA
Gander, Joseph G.	Yankeetown	12-5-61	24; POW: Shiloh, 4-6-62 Died/Disease: 6-62 at Huntsville, AL
Garber, James	Harmony	12-29-63	M.O. 7-18-65
Garrett, Noah	Viroqua	12-6-61	39; Died: 7-27-63 Milliken's Bend, LA
Graham, Robert E.	Viroqua	11-18-61	27; Wounded: Corinth, 10-3-62 Disch:12-4-62
Gray, John S.	Warner's Landing	12-10-61	24; POW: Shiloh Died: 7-31-62,Macon, GA

Greenman, Benj.	Hockley	12-3-61	25; Disch: 12-1-62
Guist, Cleason B.	Viroqua	12-18-61	27; On detached duty: 1-63
Hall, William M.	Genoa	2-10-64	M.O. 7-18-65
Harris, Benj. F.	Viroqua	12-9-61	21; Prom. Corp. 6-65, M.O. 7-18-65
Hart, Theo. F.	Leon	2-29-64	M.O. 7-18-65
Herron, John M.	Jefferson	2-16-64	M.O. 7-18-65
Hickok, LeGrand	Sterling	12-25-63	M.O. 7-18-65
Hunter, Joseph	Springville	12-1-61	Trans. To: Co. D, 18th Wisc., POW: Shiloh, Died Huntsville, Ala.
Janes, John	Readstown	11-22-61	43; POW: Shiloh 4-6-62 Transf. to:Vet. Res. Corps 1 -15-64
Johnson, Byron W	Harmony	1-2-64	Died: 3-3-65 Newbern, NC
Johnson, Henry C.	Springville	12-2-61	33; Deserted: 1-65
Kingston, James	Harmony	12-22-63	Corp., M.O. 7-18-65
Kingston, John	Bergen	12-10-61	21; Corp., Sgt., M.O. 7-18-65
Kirkpatrick, John	Towerville	12-9-61	29; Wound: Shiloh 4-6-62 Disch:8-23-62 Disab.
Kittle, William	Lynxville	12-5-61	41; KIA: Shiloh 4-6-62
Koher, Christopher	Readstown	11-22-61	32; M.O. 7-18-65
Lindley, Harvey D.	Bloomingdale	11-23-61	19; POW; Disch 10-1-63 for disability
Loper, Alfred S.	LaCrosse	12-19-64	M.O. 7-18-65
Loper, Peter D.	LaCrosse	12-19-64	M.O. 7-18-65
Loucks, William	Bad Axe	12-10-61	21; POW: Shiloh 4-6-62 Corp., 6-65, M.O. 7-18-65
McClelland, James	Sierra	12-6-61	32; POW: Shiloh Died: 11-30-62
McMichael, Samuel	Viroqua	12-9-61	39; Corp., POW: Shiloh 4-6-62; Died: 6-27-62 Macon, GA
Masterson, Wm. A	Sierra	12-6-61	25; Corp., Disch:2-4-63 for disability
Merrill, John B.	Viroqua	11-28-61	23; Corp, POW: Shiloh 4-6-62 Died: 7-23-64 Nashville
Metcalf, John C.	Readstown	11-30-61	38; POW: Shiloh 4-6-62 Disch: 1-9-65 Disab.
Miers, Richard	Bergen	11-15-64	Drafted;M.O. 7-18-65
Miller, Charles W.	Ridgeway	9-28-64	Drafted; M.O. 5-31-65
Mills, Nelson	Retreat	12-8-61	28; Corp., POW: Shiloh 4-6-62, M.O. 7-18-65
Moody, Hiram	Viroqua	12-4-64	44; Disch:1-23-65 Disab.
Mooney, Patrick	Sierra	12-6-61	23; POW; M.O. 3-14-65

Moore, Samuel W.	Harmony	12-22-63	Corp., M.O. 7-18-65
Morley, Calvin	Viroqua	11-28-61	43; Sgt., Disch:10-31-62
Morley, Julius C.	Viroqua	12-23-61	18; Died:6-2-62 Evansville, IN
Morrison, Archibald J.	Springville	12-61	39
Mosholder, Daniel	Bloomingdale	12-6-61	40; Deserted: 8-18-62
Munyon, Bazzle	Viroqua	12-14-61	21; Disch: 6-17-62
Newell, Isaac C.	Retreat	12-3-61	23; Disch: 7-1-63 to accept prom. to 8th La. C.T.
O'Dell, Walter W.	Springville	12-22-61	Died: 5-4-62 Monterey, TN
Owens, Edward	Fountain	9-28-64	Drafted; M.O. 5-31-64
Page, Lawrence H.	New Brookville	11-21-61	23; Died: 5-4-62 on steamer "Imperial"
Pennell, John	Viroqua	3-25-62	M.O. 7-18-65
Pokeland, Samuel	Madison	11-10-62	Trans. To: Veteran Reserve Corps
Powell, Jasper N.	Sylvan	11-29-61	18; Corp.,POW: Shiloh 4-6-62; Wounded: Allatoona, GA, 10-5-64; M.O. 7-18-65
Powell, Simon	Harmony	9-22-64	Drafted; M.O. 5-31-65
Prince, Sanford C.	Lynxville	12-5-61	24; Disch: 6-17-62
Quinn, Laughlin	Viroqua	12-6-61	25; POW: Shiloh 4-6-62 Disch: 1-3-63 Disab.
Rantz, Benj. F.	Viroqua	12-2-61	Wounded: Shiloh 4-6-62 Disch: 8-8-62 Disab.
Rantz, Daniel	Viroqua	11-29-61	24; Disch: 8-8-62 Disab.
Raymer, Charles	Viroqua	11-18-61	Prom: 1-13-63 1st Lieut., 27 Wisc. Inf.
Rodgers, Edward	Harmony	12-23-63	M.O. 5-4-65
Rodgers, George M.	Harmony	12-31-63	M.O. 7-18-65
Rodgers, Merrick	Lafayette	2-25-64	M.O. 7-18-65
Ross, John Joseph	Lynxville	12-18-61	POW: Shiloh 4-6-62, Wounded: Allatoona, GA, 10-5-64 M.O. 7-18-65
Sager, Samuel	Retreat	11-20-61	Wounded: Shiloh 4-6-61 Died of wounds: 4-9-63 St. Louis, MO
Sayre, Harrison	Geneva	12-29-63	23; M.O. 7-18-65
Saxton, Norris W.	Bad Axe	11-25-61	40; KIA: Shiloh 4-6-61
Sharpe, Henry	Harmony	12-16-63	Corp., M.O. 7-18-65
Sharpe, Isaac	Vernon	9-24-64	Drafted; M.O. 5-31-65
Shepherd, Nathaniel	Viroqua	12-23-63	Died:6-13-65 Alexandria, VA
Singer, Augustus	Viroqua	1-2-62	Died.
Singer, Philip	Viroqua	12-29-61	21; POW; Deserted 5-4-63
Singles, John H.	Clayton	12-5-61	25; KIA: Allatoona, GA 10-5-64

Smith, Jesse	Greenfield	2-25-64	Deserted: 6-25-65
Spear, Danford J.	Retreat	12-3-61	23; Corp: 12-3-61 Disch: 6-17-62
Starbuck, WilliamP.	Kickapoo	12-9-61	29; Died/Disease: 4-27-62 Shiloh, TN
Stewart, Gilbert	Seneca	9-30-64	Drafted; M.O. 5-31-65
Stokes, John M.	Kickapoo	12-6-61	43; Musician; Disch: 9-28-62
Swain, Allen L.	Viroqua	11-29-61	23; Disch: 10-18-62 for disability
Swain, HenryV.	Viroqua	12-2-61	Disch: 6-17-62 for disability
Swain, John J.	Viroqua	11-29-61	30; Wounded: Shiloh, 4-6-62 Disch: 7-16-62 Disab.
Swan, Samuel	W. Prairie	11-26-61	38; Sgt., Died: 2-23-62, Milwaukee
Taylor, George W.	Retreat	12-3-61	24; POW: Shiloh 4-6-61 Died: 5-2-62 Macon, GA
Taylor, Isaac	Forest	11-15-64	Drafted; Died:6-26-65 Louisville, KY
Thomas, Evan	Ridgeway	9-28-64	Drafted; M.O. 5-31-65
Thompson, Wm. H.	Viroqua	12-4-61	Died: 7-6-62 Corinth, MS
Tippin, John	Newville	11-25-61	31; Trans. To: Co. K
Tooker, Orrin	Lynxville	12-9-61	25; POW: Shiloh 4-6-62 Died/Disease: 1862, Huntsville, AL
Welles, Benj. F.	Viroqua	3-25-62	Disch: 2-27-63 Disab.
Welsh, Albert D.	Whitestown	11-5-64	Drafted; M.O. 7-18-65
Whitney, Parley	DeSoto	12-19-61	42; POW; Trans.: 1-20-63 to Marine Brigade
Williams, George	Viroqua	12-9-61	49; Trans. to: Co. K
Williams, James	Warner's	12-2-61	32; Disch: 2-5-63 Disab. Landing
Young, James	Jamestown	9-24-64	Drafted; M.O. 5-31-65

Note: Information was gathered from several sources including the muster roll for Company C and Viroqua newspaper rosters, both compiled in January 1862, the Company C muster-out roll compiled in June 1865, and "Roster of Wisconsin Volunteers," published in 1886. The "Remarks" column is to be read as follows:

age at time of enlistment (if known)	M.O.: mustered out of service
Capt.: captain	POW: prisoner of war
Corp.: corporal	Prom.: promoted
Disab.: disabled by injury or diseasee	Sgt.: sergeant
Disch.: discharged from service	Trans.: transferred
Lieut.: lieutenant	

Badax Tigers Statistics

Original Strength:	107
New Recruits (1862)	2
New Recruits (1863)	12
New Recruits (1864)	28
Total	149

Killed in Action	3
Died of Wounds	3
Died of Disease	26
Total	32

Deserted	7
Missing	2
Transferred	16
Discharged	29
Resigned	8
Mustered Out	55
Total	117

INDEX

351

Pittsburgh, Pa., 303
Pokeland, Samuel, 148, 347
Pope, John, 32, 61, 66, 75
Port Gibson, Miss., battle of, 164
Port Hudson, La., 139, 181, 184
Port Royal, S.C., U.S. occupation of, 14
"Portage County Infantry" (Company E), 12
Porter, David D., 157
Powell, Dick, 83, 90, 97
Powell, Jasper N., 43, 183, 283, 285, 288, 296, 347
Powell, Lid, 228
Powell, Simon, 347
Prentiss, Benjamin M., 35–37, 59
Price, Sterling, 9, 53–54, 100, 104–105, 108, 113–14
Prince, Sanford C., 149, 347
prisoners-of-war/parolees: Allatoona Creek, Ga., 284, 287; Appomattox Court House, Va., 318; Arkansas, 133; Atlanta, Ga., Campaign, 266–67, 272, 275; Chattanooga, Tenn., 210–11; Evansville, Ind., 150; Holly Springs, Miss., 133, 150; Iuka, Miss., 101; North Carolina, 317; Kinston, N.C., 311; Sayler's Creek, Va., 315; Shiloh, Tenn., 46, 56, 58–59, 62, 68, 79–80, 83, 106, 150, 182; Vicksburg, Miss., Campaign of, 164, 179, 182
prisons: Bayfield–Superior, Wisc., parole camps, 183; Macon, Ga., 148; Memphis, Tenn., 58–59, 61, 68; Mobile, Ala., 68; Montgomery, Ala., 59; Selma, Ala., 59; Tuscaloosa, Ala., 59, 68
Providence, La., 141–45
Pulver, Ben, 208, 316
Pulver, George, 316

Purdy, William H., 18

"Queen of the West, U.S.S." (gunboat), 139
Quinn, Laughlin, 42, 347

Raleigh, N.C., 294, 310–11, 316, 318
Randall, Alexander, 18
Rantz, Benjamin F., 39, 42, 45, 224, 347
Rantz, Daniel, 149, 347
Raymer, Charles, 149, 347
Raymond, Miss., battle of, 159, 167
Redman, Henry, 51
Reserve Corps, 209
Richardson, Orla O., 50, 180
Richmond, La., 158
Richmond, Va., 246, 252, 260, 288, 315
Roberts, Joseph W., 12
Rogers, —— (Capt.), 180
Rodgers, Edward, 240, 249, 256, 272, 276, 278, 289–91, 347
Rodgers, Elias, 256, 267, 276, 278, 289, 310
Rodgers, George M., 227, 270, 310, 347
Rodgers, Jeremiah D., 12
Rodgers, Merrick, 241, 248, 253, 260, 300, 347
Rosecrans, William S., 53, 101, 105, 108, 128, 141, 200, 20
Ross, John Joseph, 43, 183, 283–84, 288, 296, 347
Ruggles, Daniel, 75
Rusk, Jeremiah, 91, 178

Sager, Samuel, 39, 42, 149–50, 347
Sallee, Green, 86, 91, 314
Salomon, Edward, 55
Sanborn, John B., 159–61, 167
Sanders, Horace F., 27–28
Sanitary Commission, United States, 4, 73
Saxton, David H., 312
Saxton, Norris W., 39, 42, 64, 78, 148
Savannah, Ga., 298–300, 305
Saxton, Norris W., 347
Sayre, Harrison, 287–88, 291, 347
Schofield, John M., 294, 309

THE PRIVATES DO ?

Our dailies teem with daring deeds,
And books are filled with fame,
Brass bands will play and cannons roar,
In honor of the name
Of men who held commissions, and
Were honest brave and true,
But still the question comes to me,
What did the privates do ?

Who were the men to guard the camp
When foes were hovering round ?
Who dug the graves of comrades dear ?
Who laid them in the ground ?
Who sent the dying message home
To those he never knew ?
If officers did all of this
What did the privates do ?

Who were the men to fill the place
Of comrades slain in strife ?
Who were the men to risk their own
To save a comrade's life ?
Who was it lived on salted pork,
And bread too hard to chew ?
If officers did this alone
What did the privates do ?

Who laid in pits on rainy nights
All eager for the fray ?
Who marched beneath a scorching sun
Through many a toilsome day ?
Who paid the sutler double price,
And scanty rations drew ?
If officers get all the praise,
Then what did the privates do ?

All honor to the brave old boys
Who rallied at the call—
Without regard to name or rank
We honor one and all.
They're passing over one by one,
and soon they'll all be gone
To where the books will surely show
Just what the privates done.

J. S. Ellis, "National Tribune"
(date unknown)